The
HAMPTONS
Book
A Complete Guide

The windmill at Bridgehampton

THE
HAMPTONS
BOOK
A Complete Guide

**With Special Sections On
The North Fork and Shelter Island**

THIRD EDITION

Suzi Forbes Chase

Berkshire House Publishers
Lee, Massachusetts

On the Cover and Frontispiece
Front Cover: *Quiet time at Main Beach, East Hampton,* photo © Ralph Pugliese, Jr.
Frontispiece: *Windmill in Bridgehampton,* photo © Morgan McGivern.
Back Cover: *Sag Harbor; Southampton: Parrish Art Museum; local pleasure craft,* all photos © Ralph Pugliese, Jr.

The Hamptons Book: A Complete Guide
Copyright © 1994, 1997, 1999 by Berkshire House Publishers
Cover and interior photographs © 1994, 1997, 1999 by credited sources

Library of Congress Cataloging-in-Publication Data
Chase, Suzi Forbes.
　　The Hamptons book: a complete guide: with special sections on the North Fork and Shelter Island / Suzi Forbes Chase. — 3rd ed.
　　　　p.　　cm — (Great destination series)
　　Includes bibliographical references (p.　　) and indexes.
　　ISBN 1-58157-002-3
　　1. Hamptons (N.Y.)—Guidebooks. 2. North Fork (N.Y. : Peninsula)—Guidebooks. 3. Shelter Island (N.Y. : Town)—Guidebooks. I. Title. II. Series.
　　F127.S9C48　　　　1998
　　917.47'25—dc21　　　　　　　　　　　　　　　　98-33695
　　　　　　　　　　　　　　　　　　　　　　　　　　CIP

ISBN 1-58157-002-3
ISSN 1056-7968 (series)

Editor: Marcia Stamell. Managing Editor: Philip Rich. Text design and typography: Dianne Pinkowitz. Cover design and typography: Jane McWhorter. Maps: Matt Paul/Yankee Doodles.

Berkshire House books are available at substantial discounts for bulk purchases by corporations and other organizations for promotions and premiums. Special personalized editions can also be produced in large quantities. For more information, contact:

Berkshire House Publishers
480 Pleasant St., Suite 5; Lee, Massachusetts 01238
800-321-8526
Website: www.berkshirehouse.com
E-mail: info@berkshirehouse.com

Manufactured in the United States of America

First printing 1999

10 9 8 7 6 5 4 3 2 1

No complimentary meals or lodgings were accepted by the author and reviewers in gathering information for this work.

The <u>GREAT DESTINATIONS</u> Series

The Berkshire Book: A Complete Guide
The Santa Fe & Taos Book: A Complete Guide
The Napa & Sonoma Book: A Complete Guide
The Chesapeake Bay Book: A Complete Guide
The Coast of Maine Book: A Complete Guide
The Adirondack Book: A Complete Guide
The Charleston, Savannah & Coastal Islands Book:
   A Complete Guide
The Newport & Narragansett Bay Book: A Complete Guide
The Hamptons Book: A Complete Guide
Wineries of the Eastern States
The Texas Hill Country Book: A Complete Guide
The Nantucket Book: A Complete Guide
The Sarasota, Sanibel Island & Naples Book: A Complete Guide
The Monterey Bay, Big Sur, & Gold Coast Wine Country Book:
   A Complete Guide

The Great Destinations™ series features regions in the United States rich in natural beauty and culture. Each Great Destinations™ guidebook reviews an extensive selection of lodgings, restaurants, cultural events, historic sites, shops, and recreational opportunities, and outlines the region's natural and social history. Written by resident authors, the guides are a resource for visitor and resident alike. They are updated with each reprinting. The books feature maps, photographs, directions to and around the region, lists of helpful phone numbers and addresses, and indexes.

*To my mother,
who first encouraged my sense of curiosity,
taught me the joy of discovery,
and who suggested my first trip to one of
"the last great places" — the Hamptons*

Contents

CHAPTER EIGHT
Practical Matters
INFORMATION
217

CHAPTER NINE
From Vines to Wines
NORTH FORK
241

CHAPTER TEN
A Charming Green-Clad Island
SHELTER ISLAND
285

Acknowledgments

Writing this book was a privilege and a joy, but I couldn't have done it without some expert help. First and foremost, I want to thank Lisa Beth Pulitzer, who diligently contacted hundreds of shops, transportation companies, and town halls to verify spelling, addresses, and telephone numbers.

In a guidebook, a photograph is worth a hundred words. If the photographs in this book allow people to visualize the Hamptons, it's because of the fine photographers who contributed their images. I especially want to thank Morgan McGivern, Tulla Booth, Laurin Copen, and Jason Green. Their excellent skills have given this book its spirit, style, and tone.

I also wish to thank several people who read portions of my manuscript for accuracy, especially the references to local history. Robert Keene, former town historian for the Town of Southampton, not only had an eagle eye for spelling, but also always had dependable answers when I frequently called him with questions.

Carleton Kelsey, the Director of the Amagansett Free Library, unselfishly shared his vast wealth of historical knowledge with me on numerous occasions. His expertise goes far beyond Amagansett. He has such a firm grasp of local history that each time I spoke with him, I came away richer.

Dorothy Ingersoll Zaykowski, former historian at the John Jermain Library in Sag Harbor, was kind enough to make several suggestions about Sag Harbor that improved my manuscript, but her help didn't end there. She continued to verify my facts and called several weeks after we had completed our discussion, saying, "I've been researching this issue and believe if you stated it this way, it would more clearly reflect what actually happened." Thank you.

Most of all, I wish to express my deep thanks to wonderful, marvelous Dorothy King, Librarian of the Long Island Collection at the East Hampton Library. I feel as though I lived at the library while I was conducting my research. As I got to the writing stage, I called her over and over again with obscure questions. She always knew exactly where to find the answers and often supplied me with additional information that helped fill out the book. Her wealth of knowledge was invaluable. Thank you, thank you, Dorothy. My thanks also to the rest of the staff of the East Hampton Library; Beth Gray, Director, and Ola, both Sheilas, Joyce, Jean, Jane, Elizabeth, and Debbie were always helpful. We are fortunate to have such a strong local resource.

Thanks also go to Marina Van, Director of the East Hampton Chamber of Commerce, and to Millie Fellingham, Director of the Southampton Chamber of Commerce, for their help. With their fingers on the pulse of the business community, they were quick to tell me about new businesses or changes in existing ones.

My profound thanks to the staff of Berkshire House Publishers: Jean Rousseau, publisher, who agreed to this rewrite (we all know how rapidly things change in the Hamptons) and for his constant support; Philip Rich, Managing Editor, who handled all of the details from photo selection and map designations to indexing and ushering the book through production — always with supreme diplomacy and humor; Marcia Stamell, who quickly and efficiently read my manuscript and expertly suggested editorial corrections; Carol Bosco Baumann, who is one of the most enthusiastic and professional promotion and marketing representatives I've encountered in publishing; and special thanks to unsung hero Mary Osak, who patiently answered my questions, relayed my messages, and listened to me.

Finally, thanks go to my husband Dustin, who accompanied me to restaurants, and who spent many nights on his own while I slaved over the manuscript for this book. His encouragement and patience sustained me. It takes courage to agree to the expenditures necessary to put together a book of this nature, and I appreciate his belief in me.

I hope I have done justice to this "last great place." Each of us has our own favorite shop, restaurant, beach, and memory. There was so much more I would have liked to include, but space simply didn't permit it. If your favorite spot isn't here, it was just a judgment call. In the Hamptons, where the scene changes so rapidly, I will certainly do another revision before long.

Introduction

I'll never forget my first visit to the Hamptons. It was in 1972, and I was living in Seattle. I was on my first trip alone to New York City, and as much as I loved the city, I wanted to see the Hamptons. So I called for the train schedule. If I caught an early morning train (around 7:00 a.m.), I could be in East Hampton by 10:00 a.m. That would give me time to see the village, spend time on the beach, and catch the afternoon train back.

Only it didn't work out that way. I fell in love with this idyllic place. It was one of those clear, blue-sky days, with the temperature hovering in the mid-70s. Luckily, I had packed a few essentials in my beach bag, so my first stop was The Maidstone Arms. What luck! One room had just been vacated. As the clerk took me up the back stairs, he explained that Joanne Woodward and her daughter Nell had checked out early that morning. The room was very modest (The Maidstone has since gone through two renovations), with camp-style, iron beds, and I believe the bath was down the hall. I couldn't have cared less.

I freely admit that I am a beach zealot. If the sun is shining, I can't resist. So, without further ado, I walked to the most spectacular beach that I had ever seen. I had lived in Hawaii, but nothing prepared me for the miles and miles of clean, broad, sparkling white sand, fringed by sea grass-covered dunes, that I found in the Hamptons. I was hooked.

From that day on, I have returned to the Hamptons at every possible opportunity. While living in Seattle, it was generally once a year, but when I moved to New York City in 1979, I started spending summers here. At first, I stayed in different inns, motels, or bed-and-breakfasts every weekend (they were pretty funky then). Then I started renting houses or cabins for the summer, although I also frequently came in the spring, fall, and winter.

With the first hint of warm weather in the spring, I'd drive my 1966 MGB from Manhattan to the Hamptons to feast my eyes on all of the budding trees. I came in the fall to take home pumpkins and gourds, and I came in the winter to sit at Main Beach to hear the waves crash and to assure myself that it was all still here. Even after marrying in 1987 and moving to the Berkshires, I dragged my husband to the Hamptons three or four times a year.

I love the Hamptons when there's snow on the ground, and the bluebird sky beams down. I love to see the first buds of spring burst into flower against the tapestry of the evergreen trees. I love to see the osprey return in the spring and to see their babies begin to fly, to observe the cranes on the marshy bays as they fish for dinner, and to watch the way anything planted in the garden blossoms forth. I love the kaleidoscope of autumn's oranges and reds, and I love the beach — that glorious, ever-changing, constant expanse of white sand. I love early morning walks when the ocean spray lifts to meet the fog.

The memories that I cherish most are here. There's a peace and a tranquility, but it's also rejuvenating, relaxing, inspirational, and exhilarating, all at the same time.

Frankly, writing a guidebook to the Hamptons has been a conflict for me. The public's opinion of the Hamptons is that it's the playground of the rich, so why would the rest of us want to come? Part of me says it's better to allow that belief to remain, because the roads and the beaches are too congested in the summer as it is. On the other hand, if more people learn the secret joys of a walk through Morton National Wildlife Refuge in the spring or a canoe trip on Georgica Pond, then perhaps more visitors will appreciate the precious resource that we have and will help with its preservation.

Using this book as an outline, I encourage you to make your own discoveries, to delve into and savor the Hamptons' rich history, to reflect on the paintings inspired by our scenery, to admire the picturesque windmills and the traditional and futuristic houses — to canoe on the ponds, fish in the ocean, trek across the nature trails, and soak up the sun on the beaches — with a spirit of new discovery. Stop to smell the fresh salt air, to watch the magnificent osprey in their nests, and to feel the sand sift through your toes. Then you'll reach beneath the surface and touch the spirit of the Hamptons.

Suzi Forbes Chase
Long Island

THE WAY THIS BOOK WORKS

The Hamptons Book is divided into ten chapters. Entries in each of these chapters, except those on the North Fork and Shelter Island, are divided into Southampton Town and East Hampton Town. Under each of the towns, entries are further broken down by individual village in alphabetical order.

Most entries include specific information about address, telephone number, hours of operation, and owners or managers to ease your quest for a reservation or information. Although we checked all of the information as close to publication as possible, it's best to verify hours and additional information, as changes inevitably occur.

PRICES

You will note that specific prices are not listed, since they are likely to fluctuate. Instead, we have coded them within various ranges. Lodging price codes are based on the average between the highest and lowest rate per room, double occupancy. If a continental or full breakfast is included, it will be noted under "Special Features." In general, these rates exclude local taxes and any service charges that may be added to your bill.

Dining price codes indicate the average cost of an individual meal, including appetizer, entrée, and dessert, but excluding cocktails, wine, tax, or tip. Similarly, rather than indicating the exact hours that each restaurant is open, we have specified which meals are served.

Price Codes

	Lodging	**Dining**
Inexpensive	Up to $90	Up to $25
Moderate	$90 to $125	$25 to $35
Expensive	$125 to $175	$35 to $50
Very Expensive	$175 or more	$50 or more

Credit Cards

The credit cards accepted at restaurants and lodging establishments are coded as follows:

AE	American Express	DC	Diner's Club
CB	Carte Blanche	MC	Master Card
D	Discover	V	Visa

AREA CODES

The area code for the East End of Long Island is 516. All telephone numbers are within that area code, unless otherwise noted. Although it's always best to make reservations in advance, The East End Chambers of Commerce are not only excellent sources of local information, but they also will assist with last-minute lodging. Please consult Chapter Eight, *Information,* for local Chamber telephone numbers in the Hamptons, or for the North Fork and Shelter Island, see Chapters Nine and Ten.

TOWNS IN THE HAMPTONS

On Eastern Long Island, town government is the predominant local lawmaker and enforcement agency, but within each town, individual, incorporated villages are also self-governing. The incorporated villages generally have legal and enforcement influence within their boundaries, including maintaining their own police force, but smaller hamlets depend on the town for these services. Most villages have a village hall where local business is conducted. Beach permits for village beaches, for example, are issued by the village, while permits for the town beaches are issued at the town office.

There are two towns in the Hamptons. Southampton Town takes in the villages of (traveling from west to east) Remsenburg, Speonk, West Hampton Dunes, Westhampton, Westhampton Beach, Quogue, East Quogue, Hampton Bays, Southampton, Water Mill, Sag Harbor (although a portion of Sag Harbor is also in the Town of East Hampton), Sagaponack, and Bridgehampton. East Hampton Town is composed of Wainscott, East Hampton, Amagansett, Springs, and Montauk.

The
HAMPTONS
Book
A Complete Guide

CHAPTER ONE
The Land & Its Peoples
HISTORY

The history of the Hamptons is laced with adventure, intrigue, and wisdom, a romantic tale of daring and enterprise and of evolution. It's a region shaped by New England principles of hard work and thrift, with a strong religious foundation. It possesses an unparalleled natural beauty — poets often rhapsodize about it, and artists spend lifetimes trying to capture it on canvas. The majestic Atlantic Ocean lies at its front door, while varied bays lie behind it. In between, the lakes and ponds are separated by hills and marshes — all interspersed with nature preserves, wildlife and bird sanctuaries, and hiking and nature trails.

Suzi Forbes Chase

The Montauk Point Lighthouse is one of New York State's most popular attractions, with over 100,000 visitors a year.

NATURAL HISTORY

The earliest English settlers, the Puritans, would have had difficulty taming the great movement of rock and debris that formed Long Island some 15,000 years ago. Even today, we find it difficult to tame the land movements that cause the erosion near the Montauk Lighthouse and the shifting of sand-bars and inlets, resulting from hurricanes and storms.

The terrain of present-day Eastern Long Island was shaped by the slow, relentless movement of ice during the last Ice Age — the forward thrust of massive boulders, soil, and accumulated debris as it rolled and grew and the deposits of rocks and ice as it receded. The resulting pile left on the South Fork of Suffolk County is known as the Ronkonkoma Moraine. It is submerged beyond Montauk Point, but surfaces again to form Block Island, Martha's Vineyard, and Nantucket. The moraine also disappears beneath the sandy surface of Napeague, indicating that Montauk itself may, at one time, have been an island. Even today, as the cliffs at Montauk Point continue their evolution through erosion, the residue is deposited at Napeague, creating an ever wider landmass. Probably about 4,000 years ago, after the ice receded, and the soil began to nurture plant and animal life, the first peoples arrived.

SOCIAL HISTORY

When the first English settlers landed on the shores of Long Island, they were greeted by tribes of peaceful inhabitants who were adept at farming and fishing. It is believed that these residents were descendants of peoples who had migrated to these shores after years of nomadic wandering, first across the Bering Strait, then east across North America, and eventually south to Long Island. The accounts of the earliest explorers indicate that the hills of Eastern Long Island were well populated. ". . . it was full of hilles, covered with trees, well peopled, for we sawe fires all along the coaste," recorded Giovanni da Verrazano as he sailed along the south shore of Long Island in 1524.

Unlike the native peoples, who were content to live within nature's protective cloak, the Puritans viewed the bounty of natural resources as a challenge, placed there for them to tame, control, and use. In the years to come, these settlers cut down trees for their homes and mills; created thriving fishing and whaling industries; and harnessed wind and water to grind corn and wheat and to saw wood.

EARLY TRADERS

In 1633, only 13 years after the landing at Plymouth Bay and only three years after the settlement of Boston, John Winthrop, governor of the Massachusetts Bay Colony, sent a ship to the Connecticut coast on an exploratory expedition. Much to his surprise, the captain returned and reported, "having made a further discovery of that called Long Island." This discovery was particularly interesting because he brought back "wampampeag, both white and blue, it being made by the Indians there."

Whereas the native inhabitants elsewhere made pottery, blankets, or beaded headdresses, the native residents of Long Island made wampum, which was highly prized. They searched through piles of clam, whelk, and other shells, selecting those of the right size and color, and then bore a hole through the small, highly polished beads for stringing; a pointed wooden stick was used for this painstaking, skilled work. Those who could bore the holes rapidly, without breaking the shell, were considered true artisans. When the English arrived, they introduced these artisans to the mux, or awl, a sharply pointed metal instrument that made the job much easier. Individual beads were strung on sinew and hung around the neck or woven into a belt for transporting.

Wampum was the chief means of trade among the early colonists. They exchanged furs, coats, tools, and other implements with the natives for wampum, which the settlers then used to barter and buy goods among themselves. The value of wampum was as closely regulated by the colonists as is United States currency today.

Christopher R. Vagts described the importance of wampum in *Suffolk, A Pictorial History* (1983).

> *The fur trade went something like this: A European trader brought cheap woven trade cloth (duffel) to coastal Indians on Long Island. The cheap cloth was traded for wampum at a good rate of exchange. The wampum was taken to inland Indians where it was highly valued. Lengths of beads were exchanged for beaver and other furs. The furs were shipped to Europe where they commanded high prices. Thus, at each step of this trade, enormous profits were possible. Long Island — the wampum "mine" — was of critical importance!*

EARLY ENGLISH SETTLERS & SETTLEMENTS

One can only imagine the excitement generated in Massachusetts by the news of the wampum trade on Long Island. In order to get there before the Dutch, who had established a settlement at New York in 1625, Governor Winthrop encouraged Massachusetts residents to move to Long Island; several families from Lynn accepted the invitation. When the intrepid band of colonists landed at Conscience Point on Peconic Bay in 1640, they established the first English settlement in New York State, a village named Southampton in honor of the Earl of Southampton. These early colonists had received a land grant from James Farrett, the representative of the Earl of Stirling. Respectful of the natives' claim to the land, the colonists also purchased the land from them.

The native residents were very helpful to the colonist newcomers, sharing their agricultural and cooking techniques; teaching them to fertilize corn by placing an oily fish, the *menhaden,* in each seed hole; showing them how to use the bone and oil of beached whales; pointing out where to harvest an abundance of shellfish; and demonstrating how to make *samp,* a porridge that became a staple of colonial tables. In exchange, the English provided them with protection against other marauding tribes, particularly the Pequots and Narragansetts of Connecticut.

Although there appear to have been few conflicts between the new English settlers and the native inhabitants, life apparently did hold a few aggravations. Edward Johnson, an early settler, wrote in 1640, "There are many Indians on the greatest part of this Island who at first settling of the English there did much

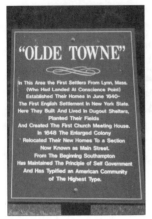

The East End's first settlers were New Englanders from Lynn, Massachusetts. They founded the village of Southampton in June, 1640.

Suzi Forbes Chase

to annoy their Cattel with the multitude of Doggs they kept, which ordinarily are young wolves brought up tame, continuing of a very ravening nature."

Of much more serious consequence was the scalping of Phebe Halsey, one of the earliest settlers of Southampton. It was proven that those who broke into her home were from one of the Connecticut tribes, intent on starting trouble between the Long Island tribes and the English. They were captured quickly and sent back to Connecticut, where they were executed.

The indigenous tribes that resided on the South Fork when the English arrived were the Montaukets who lived in Montauk, with an influence that extends to present-day East Hampton, and the Shinnecocks who lived in Southampton. With no immunity to English diseases, however, the Shinnecock population decreased rapidly until, in 1686, there were only 152 Shinnecocks in Southampton; today, the Shinnecocks count approximately 400 tribal members, residing on their reservation in Southampton.

Although early colonial life must have been difficult, settlers on Eastern Long Island were spared many of the tribulations encountered in other areas. The flat, treeless land and rich soil were easy to till and produced bountiful crops; the sea yielded an abundance of seafood; and the freedom from attack encouraged the growth of stable, prosperous communities within a relatively short time.

The settlers from Lynn were New Englanders through and through. They built their houses and villages to reflect the styles of their northern neighbors, and their religion was strict Calvinist. Rev. Abraham Pierson was ordained minister of the Southampton Colony in 1640.

In his book, *The Early History of Southampton, L.I. New York* (1887), George Rogers Howell gives the following account of East End life.

An interesting question is that of the food and appliances of the table of the colonists of the Puritan period. They raised on the farm Indian corn, wheat (both

winter and summer varieties), oats, barley, beans, and peas, but no potatoes . . . .
The waters abounded in fish, clams, and oysters, though the shellfish seem to have
been used but sparingly. Cows, oxen, goats, and sheep were raised in considerable
numbers, both for home consumption and for export. At a later period, many
horses were shipped to the West Indies. Tea and coffee were unknown.

Wine, cider, beer, homebrewed ale, milk and water were the only drinks used by
the settlers upon the table. (Tea arrived in England about 1657.)

Heavy farm work was done by oxen. The only vehicle in use for a long time was
the two-wheeled oxcart. Men and women traveled on horseback, and when the
horse was wanting, on one occasion at least, a bovine was pressed into service.

In Suffolk County, the Governor authorized in 1692 two fairs to be held, one at
Southampton. These fairs were as in old England — an occasion for everybody to
offer for sale whatever he wished to dispose of for money or by way of exchange.
These fairs were frequented by peddlers on whom the ladies depended for articles
of finery and light silk goods.

Although the settlers from Lynn are credited with establishing the first
English colony on Eastern Long Island, an English family was already in residence nearby when they arrived. In 1635, Lieutenant Lion Gardiner and his
wife Mary sailed from London to the mouth of the Connecticut River. Mr.
Gardiner was a military engineer who had been commissioned by Lords Say
and Brook to build a fort in Connecticut where the town of Saybrook is now
located. Upon completing his task in 1639, he received an entire 3,500-acre
island located between the North and South Forks of eastern Long Island as a
land grant. He prudently purchased it from the native residents and then
changed its name from The Isle of Wight to Gardiner's Island. His daughter,
Elizabeth, was the first English child born in New York State.

Lion Gardiner was both a diplomat and statesman, whose influence
extended throughout Eastern Long Island and into Connecticut. He learned
the Montauk language and befriended Chief Wyandanch, *sachem* (leader) of
the Montauks, whom he had met at Saybrook — a friendship that proved to be
mutually beneficial. At one point, Gardiner played an instrumental role in
securing the release of the Chief's daughter, Heather Flower, after she was kid-
napped by the Pequots on her wedding day. In appreciation, Wyandanch gave
Gardiner a large tract of land in what is now Smithtown.

Lion Gardiner and his descendants, the "lords of the manor," exercised total
manorial rights over Gardiner's Island from 1639 until 1788, when it was
annexed to East Hampton. A self-sufficient, agrarian economy was established, and the Gardiners grew and raised their own food, as well as that
needed for barter. Today, the island still is managed by the Gardiner family —
the only known English land grant in America to remain in the possession of
the original family.

At the suggestion of Governor Winthrop, Lion Gardiner sponsored a young
man in the new colony of East Hampton by the name of Thomas James.

Arriving in 1650, Mr. James became the first pastor in East Hampton, where he soon established himself as a highly influential cleric and businessman. It is noteworthy that the first settlers were so fiercely independent from the British crown that it would be 200 years before any Episcopal church, which was closely affiliated with the Church of England, was established. On the other hand, even though they strongly advocated total separation of church and state, the clergy were hired by the town fathers, paid out of the town coffers, and furnished with a house and pastureland at town expense.

In matters other than religious, the spread of ideas and commercial activity expanded rapidly throughout the East End. Word quickly reached Connecticut and Massachusetts that Long Island offered a mild growing climate, with temperate winters and cool summers, as well as rich soil that yielded abundant crops; that congenial settlers had formed agreeable communities; and, best of all, that the native people were accommodating. By 1649, the census lists 45 heads of households in Southampton. Other settlements were soon established: East Hampton was settled in 1648; Wainscott in 1652; Springs in 1652; Bridgehampton in 1656; the village of Sagaponack in 1656; and Amagansett in 1680.

The Gardiner Windmill was built in 1771 and was in operation until the hurricane of 1938. Restoration work on the mill is just about complete.

Morgan McGivern

By 1644, the first crude post windmills were constructed to grind corn and wheat, saw wood, and perform other tasks. These first windmills were constructed on a tall platform supported by a wooden frame. The structure was turned to catch the wind by means of a long pole reaching to the ground. There are no remaining windmills of this type today, but the Hamptons can still claim the largest collection of later-styled windmills in the United States.

By the late 1600s, technology had advanced beyond the early post windmills, and mills were built with the machinery housed in a stationary octagonal tower capped by a revolving hood that held the sails and turned to allow the sails to catch the wind. Several of these so-called smock windmills, built in the early eighteenth century, remain and are open for public viewing in Hamptons' villages.

The Dominy family of East Hampton built some of the finest windmills.

They also were renowned for their finely handcrafted furniture, especially their extraordinary tall-case ("grandfather") clocks. In all, Nathaniel Dominy IV built six wind-powered gristmills and three wind-powered sawmills. The Hook Windmill in East Hampton is the finest example of his workmanship. Among the laborsaving devices in the Hook Windmill are a sack hoist, a grain elevator, a screener to clean the grain, and bolters to sift the flour and cornmeal.

The first gristmill in Water Mill was built in 1644 to provide the town of Southampton with grain. The town supplied the millstone and built the required dam. Edward Howell built the mill, powered by a huge waterwheel that depended on the ponds that flowed into Mecox Bay. If there was an insufficient flow of water from the ponds to the bay, town law decreed that " . . . when the miller calleth, on three days warneing," the men of the village would gather to enlarge the water's passage into the bay.

This first gristmill in Water Mill's history has retained its usefulness and dignity over the years. As the needs of Southampton changed, however, so did the mill. It has been used to spin yarn, to weave cloth, and to manufacture paper; as a place for ice storage; a post office; an ice-cream factory; and a tearoom. Today, the fully restored and functioning mill is known as the Water Mill Museum.

As early as 1656, the English settlers worried about Dutch expansion into their territory. In addition, they had learned of Dutch attempts to turn the neighboring tribes against them. They were, therefore, granted protection by their nearby neighbors in Connecticut. Even when the Dutch surrendered New York to the English in 1664, the independent East Enders resisted association with the rest of Long Island. As far as they were concerned, they were New Englanders, and their loyalties remained with Connecticut.

This attitude created considerable anxiety in New York. Lord Cornbury wrote in 1703 that "the people of the East End of Long Island are not very willing to be persuaded to believe that they belong to this province. They are full of New England principles. They choose rather to trade with the people of Boston, Connecticut, and Rhode Island than with the people of New York."

Architecture, as well as politics in the early villages, followed New England examples. Wooden saltbox houses had steeply slanted roofs and were faced with shingles that were allowed to weather naturally. The houses were lined up on both sides of a grassy main road, with dirt wagon tracks in the center; cows, pigs, sheep, and geese were allowed to graze on the grass. Eventually, villages required residents, whose homes bordered the road, to build fences to contain their livestock. Most villages also set aside a common pasture for both cattle and sheep.

By 1661, settlers had adopted the practice of collecting their cattle into one large herd and driving them to the hills of Montauk for summer fattening, along with sheep and horses. It's said that cattle joined these great drives from as faraway as Patchogue. A description of the scene along the dusty Montauk route to pasture, traveling on what later became the Montauk Highway, is contained in Madeline Lee's book, *Miss Amelia's Amagansett* (1976).

The high point of village life came twice a year when Main Street became the scene of immense cattle drives. Cattle and sheep raising was an important industry on Long Island from the seventeenth century through the nineteenth century, and the principal grazing grounds were . . . Montauk. 1,200 to 1,500 head of cattle were driven "on" to the pastures at Montauk in the spring and "off" again in the fall. From miles around, they would be funneled through the Amagansett Street, which was at that time 150 feet wide (and still is) to accommodate these herds.

These great cattle drives continued until the 1920s. Second House, one of three houses where the cattle and sheep tenders lived during those languid summer months, now houses a fascinating museum; Third House serves as the headquarters of Suffolk County's Montauk County Park.

The sight of ships rounding Montauk Point would not have surprised the Montauk cattle tenders, but one ship that must have aroused suspicion was an unwelcome visitor to Gardiner's Island in 1699. Pirates often plied the waters off the Long Island shore and are known to have landed at Montauk several times. In 1699, Captain William Kidd, a respected New York captain who had been hired by the British to detain French vessels and confiscate their cargo during a French/British war, ran afoul of his sponsors. They declared him to be a pirate.

One of the ships that Kidd waylaid was a French pirate ship loaded with bounty. Kidd was on his way to deliver the spoils to his sponsors but, under the circumstances of having been declared a pirate, rightly feared for his life. He stopped at Gardiner's Island and persuaded John Lyon Gardiner, the third lord of the manor, to give him food and drink. Gardiner complied and also agreed to allow Kidd to bury his treasure on Gardiner's Island. Kidd then sailed on to Boston, where he had been assured of safety. Nevertheless, he was arrested. Gardiner was summoned to Boston to deliver the treasure and did so, but Kidd subsequently was taken to England and executed in spite of the treasure's return. Although the Gardiner family retains an ancient receipt for the bounty, a legend persists that a vast stash remains buried on Gardiner's Island, waiting to be unearthed by some future treasure seeker.

REVOLUTIONARIES

Fierce loyalty to New England principles of independence from the British prevailed in the area at the onset of the American Revolution. Citizens were outraged at the heavy taxes imposed by England and at the events in Boston. In 1775, every eligible citizen of East Hampton signed a document that read, in part:

. . . shocked by the bloody scene now going on in Massachusetts Bay, do in the most solemn manner, resolve never to become enslaved and do associate under all the ties of religion, honor, and love to our country, to adopt whatever may be recommended by the Continental Congress.

In 1775, Sag Harbor resident John Hulburt organized a company of minutemen. One of their first acts was to march to Montauk Point where they discovered three British men-of-war and nine transport ships, preparing to land. Determined to protect their land and grazing cattle, Hulburt ordered his men to march down a hill in sight of the British ships. At the bottom, where they were hidden from view, they turned their jackets inside out and then paraded back up the hill — thereby fooling the British into thinking that there were twice as many troops. The British decided not to land.

Later, Hulburt's men marched to Ticonderoga, taking with them a flag designed with thirteen stars on a blue field and thirteen alternating red and white stripes. It is believed that this flag was the model that Betsy Ross used to create her flag.

When General Washington was defeated in the Battle of Long Island in August 1776, all of Long Island fell under British rule, and signers of patriotic documents had reason to fear for their personal safety and possessions. Many families fled to Connecticut and lived there for the seven years of British occupation. Those who remained continued to live as they had, but the years held many hardships; those who remained were required to sign an oath of allegiance to England.

Henry P. Hedges addressed the Sag Harbor Historical Society in 1896 and described the suffering.

> *The history of that seven years' suffering will never be told. Philosophy has no adequate remedy for silent, unknown, unpitied suffering . . . . Left to the tender mercies of the foe; plundered by countryman and stranger of their property and ripened harvest; robbed of the stores which they reaped and garnered; slandered by suspicious brethren; taunted and scoffed at by the mercenary victors; they never wavered. Their hearts were in their country's cause; and in the memorable language of their great compatriot, "sink or swim, live or die, survive or perish," they were true to their country. Unterrified, unalterable, devoted Americans.*

The only military action that took place on the East End during the Revolutionary War occurred in Sag Harbor and made Colonel Return

Every year the East Hampton Historical Society holds a Militia Weekend to acquaint adults and children with the customs, crafts, and foods of East Hampton's early settlers.

Morgan McGivern

Jonathan Meigs a hero. The British had established a naval blockade and a garrison there to prevent supplies from leaving Sag Harbor to aid American troops, stationed across Long Island Sound in Connecticut. On the night of May 23, 1777, Meigs sailed with his men across the sound from Connecticut to a point on the North Fork. They carried their boats over a narrow neck of land to Orient Harbor, and then, hugging the coastline between Shelter Island and the North Fork, they eventually crossed Shelter Island Sound, arriving near Noyack about midnight. After hiding their boats, the men marched to Sag Harbor, killed six sailors, captured the British commander along with 90 of his troops, set fire to 12 British brigs and sloops, and confiscated the needed supplies. Returning with their prisoners and the goods, Colonel Meigs accomplished his mission in 25 hours, with no loss of American lives.

WHALERS, SHIPMEN, MANUFACTURERS

In 1783, at the end of the British occupation, most home owners returned to their villages. Reconstruction was a slow, difficult process, however. Ground that had not been plowed had grown hard and unyielding. Family homes and possessions had been destroyed. Nevertheless, residents were much more concerned with the future than with the past. In 1791, the first newspaper on Long Island was established in Sag Harbor.

Dr. Samuel Buell became the third pastor of the Presbyterian church in East Hampton in 1746 (his ordination was presided over by the renowned cleric Jonathan Edwards). He took an active but conciliatory role in the British occupation of the East End during the Revolution, but was more known for being instrumental in starting the first secondary school in New York. Although elementary schools had been organized shortly after East End villages were settled, Clinton Academy in East Hampton, which was established in 1784, was the first secondary school. One interesting facet of this academy is that, although colleges, such as Harvard and Yale, were open only to men, Clinton Academy was always coeducational. In addition to the classics, such practical subjects as accounting, navigation, and surveying were taught. For almost 100 years, students from faraway places and nearby homes received their education there. Many graduates went on to Harvard, Yale, and Princeton. Finally, in 1881, its school days came to an end. It subsequently became the site of town meetings, plays, and dances, and eventually it housed the newspaper *East Hampton Star* and the library. This impressive building still stands on Main Street, where it is now a museum devoted to local history.

Long before the arrival of the English, whaling was an important activity for the original inhabitants. When, during the winter months, the ocean tempests tossed a whale on the shore, they raced to the beach to carve up the giant mammal. The English were quick to learn the many uses for whale carcasses, and they joined forces on these great whaling expeditions. By agreement, the settlers reserved the fins and tail for the native residents, as these parts were cherished for religious ceremonies. The rest of the whale, however, was tryed-out (boiled) or boned and used for a variety of purposes.

By the 1660s, the colonists, not content to wait for whales to float onto their beaches, established four whaling companies with ships that sailed the ocean coast, searching for whales. By 1687, the fleet had grown to seven ships. Following these earliest whaling trips, the whales were brought to East End beaches where their blubber was boiled in giant black kettles called *try pots*, to render the oil that was so highly valued for lamp fuel. Later, self-contained *try works* were constructed on the ships themselves. From the beginning, the colonists recognized the expertise of the native whalers and hired them as hands on the whaling vessels.

Sag Harbor, established in 1730, soon became an influential whaling and shipping port. The first wharf was built in 1753, and construction on the grand Long Wharf began in 1771. Although the American Revolution interrupted the growth of Sag Harbor and the whaling industry for some ten years, in 1785, a Sag Harbor whaler returned from a voyage to Brazil with a load of 360 barrels of oil, and in 1789, Sag Harbor became the first port of entry in New York State.

Additions to Long Wharf in 1808 and 1821 increased its length to 1,000 feet, and Sag Harbor was poised on the brink of history. This bawdy, raucous seaport was the antithesis of the more elegant villages to the south. As the ports of call of Sag Harbor sailing ships became more diverse, so did the variety of men who returned to the home port.

James Fenimore Cooper came to Sag Harbor in 1818 and stayed on to purchase and outfit a whaling vessel. Later, he wrote the whaling adventure, *The Sea Lions* (1849), in which he describes Sag Harbor's attitude toward whalers.

> *There was scarcely an individual who followed this particular calling out of the port of Sag Harbor, whose general standing on board ship was not as well known to all the women and girls of the place, as it was to his shipmates . . . . His particular merit, whether with the oar, lance, or harpoon is bruited about, as well as the number of whales he may have succeeded in "making fast to."*

In Herman Melville's *Moby Dick* (1851), Queequeg comes to Sag Harbor to learn Christian ways.

> *But alas! the practices of whalemen soon convinced him that even Christians could be both miserable and wicked; infinitely more so than all his father's heathens. Arrived at last in old Sag Harbor; and seeing what the sailors did there; and then going on to Nantucket, and seeing how they spent their wages in that place also, poor Queequeg gave it up for lost. Thought he, it's a wicked world in all meridians. I'll die a pagan.*

A red-light district sprang up in Sag Harbor, and taverns thrived; an anchored ship served as a jail for drunken sailors. A variety of new occupations kept Sag Harbor men employed in shipbuilding and manufacturing supplies for the whaling ships. By 1839, the whaling fleet had grown to 31 ships, making Sag Harbor the third largest whaling port in the world. Eighty businesses flourished there, including coopers, who made the barrels to store the whale oil, masons, boatbuilders, blacksmiths, and tool and rope manufacturers. The fleet had increased to 63 vessels by 1845, and the population had grown to approximately 4,000 residents. Sag Harbor became known the world over when a local whaler made the first voyage to the waters surrounding Japan.

Sag Harbor's Oakland Cemetery contains many fascinating monuments, attesting to the town's colorful maritime history.

Suzi Forbes Chase

People in nearby villages were fascinated by Sag Harbor and a bit envious of it. Business opportunities flourished in nearby communities. Shelter Island, for example, due to its abundance of white oak, became an impressive shipbuilding center. There was some dismay, however, about Sag Harbor. From his pulpit in East Hampton, Reverend Lyman Beecher railed against the Infidels, a Sag Harbor society organized specifically to attack the Christians.

On lower Main Street, which was filled with taverns, shops, and warehouses, the selling of rum was widespread. The downtown atmosphere was that of an energetic, irrepressible seaport. On upper Main Street, however, the fashionable homes of the shipowners stood in stark contrast. Cosmopolitan society held sophisticated balls and social gatherings; worshippers were welcomed at the elegant Whaler's Church, which was completed in 1844 and boasted a spectacular 185-foot steeple; and amusing vaudeville shows entertained citizens in the fine music hall.

In 1845, a devastating fire raged through Sag Harbor's downtown, destroying 57 stores, shops, and warehouses, but merchants quickly rebuilt. The village's most productive year was 1847, with 32 vessels hauling in 3,919 barrels of sperm oil, 63,712 barrels of right whale oil, and 605,340 pounds of whalebone.

Then it was over. Petroleum products and gas lighting replaced whale oil. In 1849, only two whaling ships left the harbor. The discovery of gold in California in 1849 created a mass exodus. The last-recorded voyage of a Sag Harbor whaler was in 1871. By 1913, this village that once had been designated the first port of entry for New York was decommissioned.

BAYMEN, TRAWLERS, BOOTLEGGERS

Other industries replaced whaling on the East End. Fishing continued to yield a profit. *Menhaden,* the fish long used by the native inhabitants for fertilizer, was processed in large plants along Gardiner's Bay. At first, the catches were hauled in from the ocean, but by the 1890s, the shoreline of the bay was thick with ships using purse seines to gather the schools of fish. It was estimated that at one point over 230 sailing ships and 20 steam vessels were engaged in the trade. Eventually the last of these died out in the 1960s.

But the East Enders continued to gather other varieties of fish, as well. A local Water Mill resident recalls his youth with a fishing crew.

> *When I was a kid, every so far along there were fishing crews on the ocean, and they had wood shanties on the beach with tar paper roofs . . . . A load of fish was a lot of fun. Men hung onto the net, while others crawled in to get the fish out of the net and throw them on the beach. We would load the fish onto handbarrows and carry them to the road . . . . We'd bring the fish home to pack them in wood boxes and ice them down. The trucks would come right to the house to pick up the fish and cart it to Fulton Street in New York. We always put a fish box out as a sign for the truck driver to stop, while another crew member tied a rag to a telephone pole to signal the driver.*

Fishing and shellfishing remain important industries on the East End today, although local baymen are finding it more and more difficult to prosper. Delectable tiny bay scallops, cherrystone and littleneck clams, lobsters, mussels, and oysters are gathered seasonally for markets locally and in New York. Commercial and sportsfishing off Montauk Point yield striped bass, sturgeon, swordfish, white marlin, tuna, bluefish, and shark.

From 1920 to 1933, liquor was prohibited throughout the United States, and the East End found itself in the thick of the controversy. Sag Harbor, along with North Haven and Noyack, became part of the infamous "Rum Row" that attracted boats from Europe. By 1927, however, bootleg distilleries in the United States were producing such high quality products that illegal imports were no longer necessary, and the boat traffic dried up. During its heyday, however, the East End of Long Island was called the *wettest place in the country,* a bootlegger's paradise.

TRAVELERS & VISITORS

Passable roads barely predated Prohibition. Montauk Highway was paved to Amagansett in 1908, but not beyond to Montauk until 1921. The crude paths laid out in the area's early days were in regular use for many years, connecting the sparse settlements on the East End to the ports in the Northwest and North Sea and to Fireplace, where passengers and goods were ferried to

Gardiner's Island. Eventually, several of these paths were used by scheduled horseback riders delivering messages and mail to isolated villages.

In 1772, a stagecoach route was established from the Fulton Ferry in Brooklyn to Sag Harbor; from Sag Harbor, travelers could take a boat to Connecticut, or even to Boston. With the stagecoach, also came inns, which provided overnight accommodations for the travelers. The trip from Brooklyn to Sag Harbor took three days. Travelers stopped on the first night at Samuel Nichols' inn on the Hempstead Plains, at Benjamin Haven's inn at St. George's Manor on the second, and at Duke Fordham's in Sag Harbor on the final night. James Fenimore Cooper stayed at Mr. Fordham's hotel while writing his novel, *Precaution* (1820).

A classic stagecoach poem by an unknown author commemorates the end of the journey at Fordham's.

> *Long ago at the end of the route*
> *The stage pulled up, the folks stepped out.*
> *They all passed under the tavern door,*
> *The Youth and his bride and the gray three-score.*
> *Their eyes so weary with dust and gleam,*
> *Three days gone by like an empty dream,*
> *Soft may they slumber and trouble no more*
> *For their dusty journey, its jolt and roar*
> *Has come to an end at Fordham's door.*

Even with the stagecoach, distant Montauk had no official mail delivery. This oversight was remedied by the tall, colorful Native American, Stephen (Pharaoh) Talkhouse, who charged $.25 to carry a letter from Montauk to the stage in East Hampton, stepping forth in the giant stride that allowed him to complete the round-trip, 35-mile journey in one day.

With the advent of the railroad, branch lines fanned out across the United States, and eventually, the Long Island Rail Road was established. The main line along the North Fork to Greenport was completed in 1844. Then the South Fork was added, first to Westhampton Beach, Bridgehampton, and Sag Harbor in 1870, then to East Hampton, Amagansett, and Montauk in 1895. The Hamptons began to change, from a strictly rural, farming area to one that attracted leisure travelers.

All these new visitors needed places to stay, and village residents complied by opening their homes. By the 1850s, it was reported that all rooms in East Hampton were fully booked at $7.00 a night. Southampton soon built hotels to accommodate its many guests, notably the Canoe Place Inn and the grand Irving House, with its old Terry Tavern annex. Due to the more remote location of East Hampton, however, boarding houses remained the preferred accommodation there. To reach East Hampton and Amagansett, travelers took a stage from the train station at Bridgehampton (after 1870) or from the New York steamer that landed in Sag Harbor. By 1895, when the railroad came to East Hampton, over 800 summer visitors arrived with it.

Carriages and buckboards parade at Mulford Farm in East Hampton.

Morgan McGivern

Julia Gardiner Tyler added a touch of glamour to the Hamptons in the mid-1800s. In 1844, at the age of 24, this beautiful, impetuous Gardiner married the tenth president of the United States, 54-year-old John Tyler. She brought the same style and elegance to East Hampton, where they summered, as she did to the White House. The vivacious heiress, who shared Tyler's life for 18 years and bore him seven children, never forgot her heritage and ancestry, reveling in her jewels, fine clothes, and exquisite manners. The house that they occupied on Main Street is still standing, although privately owned.

ARTISTS, WRITERS, DESIGNERS

Lured by the rural quality of East Hampton, artists from New York began arriving in the 1870s. They were delighted with the bucolic charm, the seascape vistas, and the opportunity to congregate, paint, and live more economically than they could in New York City. Most of these artists were members of the Tile Club, an artist's organization founded to "preserve good fellowship and good talk." They gathered in Greenwich Village on long winter evenings to paint on eight-inch square, Spanish tiles. Among the members of this group were Augustus Saint-Gaudens, Stanford White, Winslow Homer, William Merritt Chase, Thomas Moran, and Childe Hassam.

The Tilers at first stayed in East Hampton at the old house called Rowdy Hall, across the street from the Clinton Academy, where they took their classes. Rowdy Hall was later moved and became the childhood summer home of Jacqueline Bouvier Kennedy, who was born at the Southampton Hospital.

William Oliver Stevens described the artists' visits in his book, *Discovering Long Island* (1939).

The Tile Club made East Hampton their headquarters lured by the Lombardy poplars lined up like a regiment on each side of the street . . . .

Naturally they sketched here with great zeal, not only along the street but also on the beach. The musicians (honorary members) loafed about and posed for their friends as quaint natives and old salts, whenever such figures were needed . . . .

It was probably through these members of the Tile Club and their articles in Scribner's Monthly *that word spread abroad regarding the artistic attractions of East Hampton, for within five years of their first visit, the village was being written up as the "American Barbizon." Thomas Moran (known for his paintings of the national parks) made his home here, and summer art classes flourished, especially large groups from the Art Student's League of New York. This all ended, however, when a Tile Club Member, William Merritt Chase began his art school in Southampton in 1891, and suddenly everyone flocked there . . . .*

FARMERS, HOTELIERS, SOCIALITES

The summer influx was firmly established, and industrialists, doctors, lawyers, and judges began to build the fine estates for which the Hamptons are renowned. Hotels and inns flourished as well, and some of the earliest continue to welcome guests today.

Not only did the railroad bring wealthy weekenders to the Hamptons to build grand mansions, but it also created new business enterprises. In the 1920s, small farms that grew a variety of crops gave way to large farms, concentrating on single crops. The Hamptons' temperate climate, with a growing season that begins in early April and lasts until mid-November, makes the area ideal for potato farming. Potatoes are now the predominant local crop. Each June, fields of white potato blossoms stretch down the neat rows, announcing the arrival of a new crop in the fall.

In the 1930s, another crop, still closely associated with Long Island, gained nationwide popularity. White Pekin (Peking) ducks, with more succulent meat than domestic ducks, were imported from China to Long Island in the 1870s. Gradually the famed Long Island Duckling became a necessary item on fancy menus across the United States. In 1939, there were 90 duck farms in Quogue alone, and by 1969, Suffolk County was raising fully 60 percent of the nation's ducks.

The ducks gained fame off the table as well, however. In *Discovering Long Island,* (1939), Stevens says, "Its plumage is such a pure white that at a distance one of these duck farms looks like a field where patches of March snow have not yet melted. But he is something of a whited sepulcher, for all his angelic plumage. Each little White Pekin is a most active fertilizer factory, and when the wind is right, not all the perfumes of Araby could sweeten this little land of duck farms." Since that time, due to increasing land values, environmental concerns, and objections to the smell, the numbers have been on the decline. Today about 15 percent of the nation's ducks are raised on Long Island.

Unlike the other Hampton villages, Montauk has both an older and yet a younger history. It boasts the oldest cattle ranch in the United States. Deep Hollow Ranch was built in 1658 and claims to be the birthplace of the American cowboy. A descendant of those early summer grazing pastures, it includes Third House, where the early cattle tenders lived.

In an article in *Scribner's Monthly* in 1879, titled "The Tile Club at Play," Montauk was described as follows:

> . . . *our tourists came out upon a scene of freshness and uncontaminated splendor, such as they had no idea existed a hundred miles from New York. The woods rolled gloriously over the hills, wild as those around the Scotch lakes; noble amphitheaters of tree-tufted mountains, raked by roaring winds, caught the changing light from a cloud-swept heaven; all was pure nature fresh from creation.*

Walt Whitman, who was raised on Long Island, cherished the Montauk's isolation. In celebration of its wild abandon, he wrote his acclaimed poem "Montauk Point."

Until 1879, Montauk languished peacefully, with fishing and cattle ranching being virtually its only occupations. In that year, however, land developer Arthur Benson purchased much of Montauk for $151,000. Shortly thereafter he formed the Montauk Association and engaged the renowned architectural firm of McKim, Mead, and White and the landscape architect Frederick Law Olmsted. Benson invited several of his friends to join him in building houses on a bluff, overlooking the ocean. McKim, Mead, and White built seven spectacular shingle-style houses with wraparound porches, gabled roofs, cupolas, and bay windows. Olmsted created roadways and gardens that enveloped the houses, as well as a clubhouse, laundry, and stables. The houses remain today and comprise a very private, exclusive compound.

In 1895, Austin Corbin, president of the Long Island Rail Road, extended the South Fork of his line to Montauk and laid plans to develop Fort Pond Bay as a transatlantic port of entry to New York City. It was a good idea, designed to shorten the journey from Europe by at least one day and to avoid the congestion of New York Harbor. Due to his untimely death in a carriage accident in 1896, however, his dream was never realized.

In 1898, Teddy Roosevelt and 30,000 of his Rough Riders, fresh from the Spanish-American War, spent several months recuperating at Third House. A general breakdown of medical and sanitary conditions had left some of the men with yellow fever, malaria, or typhoid. Numerous casualties were taken ashore on litters and were detained at Montauk until the danger of contagion was past.

Most recently, in 1926, another dreamer ventured to Montauk with a plan. Carl G. Fisher had developed Miami Beach and the Indianapolis Speedway. He reasoned that just as visitors flocked to Miami in the winter, they would flock to Montauk in the summer. He and his investors bought 10,000 acres, which included nine miles of waterfront. High on Fort Hill, he built Montauk

A Bonaker

The history of the tiny village of Springs is one of the most interesting in the Hamptons, although, to the uninitiated, the hamlet may appear to be no more than a cluster of nondescript buildings randomly placed at the junction of Springs Fireplace Road and Old Stone Highway. It's the heart of Bonakerland, an area that claims, among other things, a language all its own.

The Nature Conservancy, in the *South Fork Shelter Island Preserve Guide* (1990), defines a Bonaker as " . . . someone who descended from either the Bennett, King, Lester, or 'Green River' Miller families who lived in the area around the Springs and Three Mile Harbor. The Indian name Accabonac, however, means 'place where groundnuts are gathered.' This refers to a tuberous plant that once grew around the harbor, supplementing shellfish as the Indian's main source of protein."

Jason Epstein and Elizabeth Barlow in their excellent book, *East Hampton, A History & Guide* (1985), say, "'Bonaker,' the term often used to describe any East Hampton settler, originally meant a person who lived on Accabonac Harbor, particularly the baymen who made their living from the fish and shellfish in the harbor. When it first gained currency, 'Bonaker' was a derisive epithet akin to 'hick,' 'hayseed,' or more appropriately, 'lazy clamdigger.' Subsequently, it has become a chauvinistic badge."

It is unclear exactly how the long-time residents of the Springs obtained their distinctive language, but recent scholarly studies indicate that it may be due to their relative isolation. This rural area of farmers, baymen, and fishermen seems to retain vowel pronunciations that hark back to the time of Shakespeare. Perhaps such pronunciations as "git" for "get," "yit" for "yet," "turrble" for "terrible," and "awchit" for "orchard" are simply the result of having so little contact with the rest of the population, they seldom heard the subtle changes. Local historian Stephen Taylor wrote in the chapter "Playing Hide and Seek with History," which was included in the pamphlet, *Springs — A Celebration*: "For three centuries, the residents of the Springs . . . continue to speak the dialect that their forebears brought from post-Elizabethan England . . . . Above all else, history is change: freeze the world in place and there's no history. The Springs appears to want no part of it. It's as if the Springs engages history in a subtle game of hide-and-seek."

Change has occurred in Springs, however. Beginning in the 1950s, Springs was discovered by developers, and forested acres gave way to housing. Taylor concluded his paper by writing, "Where tradition was once the real architect of most of the structures in the Springs, the designers of these newer ones are 'creative' and 'imaginative.' Clusters of older Springs houses become de facto historic districts, enclaves of times past . . . . (but) what might seem like a desecration of history isn't anything of the sort; it *is* history — history catching up with the Springs at last."

The first of these new residents were artists (illustrators, writers, designers) who were looking for a peaceful, quiet hideaway. They were soon joined by painters, sculptors, and artists of considerable acclaim. Springs is now recognized as a secluded community of artists who live side by side with the descendants of the original Bonackers.

Today the term Bonacker is often used with pride, in recognition of a people who cling fast to old traditions. In fact, the East Hampton High School sports teams proudly call themselves the Bonakers, symbolizing a team that never gives up.

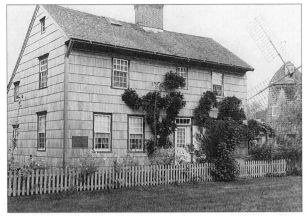

It is said that this boyhood home was the inspiration for John Howard Payne to write his famous poem and song "Home, Sweet Home."

Morgan McGivern

Manor, a luxury hotel. On Montauk's town square, he built a seven-story office building. A golf course, polo grounds, a yacht club, and a pier followed. He filled his office building with salesmen, poised to find buyers to fulfill his grand scheme, but it was not to be. The stock market crash of 1929, a decline in the Florida real estate market, a hurricane in Florida, and the Great Depression conspired to bring an end to the "Miami of the North."

The Great Hurricane of 1938 devastated the East End. The glorious steeple on the Whaler's Church in Sag Harbor came crashing to the ground, as did that of the Methodist Church. Trees were uprooted; roofs and porches blew away. The turbulent sea cut a new inlet into the barrier reef, separating the ocean from Moriches Bay at Westhampton Beach. Another more recent storm in 1992, destroyed parts of Dune Road and took away many houses, creating a new island. Yet, despite such devastation, the natural beauty of the Hamptons prevails.

To capture this spectacular landscape, another wave of artists arrived in 1945. When the abstract expressionist Jackson Pollock and his wife, Lee Krasner, established their home and studio on a site overlooking Accabonac Harbor in Springs in 1945, other contemporary artists soon followed. Robert Motherwell, Willem de Kooning, Fairfield Porter, Alfonso Ossorio, and others enlivened the artistic scene. In the 1950s, New York's Museum of Modern Art held summer classes at Ashawagh Hall in Springs that firmly established the area's arts-oriented reputation. The quiet rural charm of Springs continues to attract renowned artists, just as other Hampton areas do.

And so history moves on — never ending, always evolving. After all, tomorrow's history is today's news event. The history of the Hamptons is as entwined with the baymen's efforts to eke out a living and The Nature Conservancy's land preservation efforts, as it is with the glittering social scene and the sprawling estates. The latter lasts for two months, but the former is the true heart of the Hamptons.

CHAPTER TWO
The Journey & The Visit
TRANSPORTATION

Before the first settlers arrived, the native inhabitants of eastern Long Island frequently crossed the great body of water now known as Long Island Sound. The 16 miles of water between Long Island and the Connecticut/ Rhode Island shore offered a more hospitable mode of transportation than did the overland route. In canoes carved from the trees that covered the hillsides, they traveled back and forth to hunt, fish, trade, and barter with other tribes. By the time the English arrived, the native residents of Long Island were paying tribute (wampum) to the Pequots of Connecticut for their peaceful coexistence.

Morgan McGivern

When it snows, creative modes of transportation must be used.

It was natural, then, for the settlers to follow their example. The settlers arrived via Connecticut, and transportation and communication were, at first, developed solely with Connecticut rather than with the western part of Long Island, which was settled by the Dutch rather than the English.

This strong link to New England created East End towns that looked and felt like New England towns. They used a common green for grazing community cattle, built New England saltbox cottages, and constructed a planned, strictly regulated community where only those settlers who possessed skills needed by the town were invited to live there.

Eastern Long Island became more and more English because overland communication was infrequent and slow. Western Long Island developed strong loyalties and ties to the Dutch, who occupied New York City. As might be imagined, loyalty to New England caused East Enders considerable discomfort during the American Revolution.

Overland mail routes were established in the early 1700s, but more sophisticated communication links waited until the first stagecoach route was established in 1772. This route would serve as the only overland transportation link for almost 100 years from New York and points west to the South Fork. In 1844, the Long Island Rail Road built a rail line from New York to Greenport on the North Fork. But it wasn't until 1870 that they extended it along the South Fork to Bridgehampton and Sag Harbor and not until 1895 did it reach East Hampton and Montauk.

The access provided by the railroad forever changed the face of Eastern Long Island. At first, rail service provided a valuable transportation link for farmers, who could ship their produce by train to lucrative markets in New York, but as more and more people traveled to the East End, the permanent and summer populations mushroomed. Slowly, an economy that once had depended on the sea and the land evolved into one that supported a tourist and weekend population. Old main streets of dirt, sand, crushed shells, and rock were joined in a paved road of stone and tar called Montauk Highway, which reached Amagansett in 1908; it was extended to Montauk in 1921.

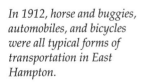

In 1912, horse and buggies, automobiles, and bicycles were all typical forms of transportation in East Hampton.

C. Frank Dayton Collection, East Hampton Library Historical Collection

Transportation continues to play an important role in the life of the Hamptons. As road space becomes more and more scarce, alternatives to traveling by car are devised. Several excellent bus companies now relieve the congestion on the highways and augment the mass transportation services provided by the Long Island Rail Road. In addition, a number of airports offer charter services and landing space for small aircraft.

Today there are several options for getting to and from the Hamptons and also for traveling around while here. Just remember, any travel difficulties will fade into dim memories once you arrive.

GETTING TO THE HAMPTONS

BY CAR

L et's go to the Hamptons! Get the kids, pack the car, and, inevitably, the question is, "What route do we take?" No matter how the conversation starts, if the destination is the Hamptons (a distance of about 100 miles from Manhattan), the quest for the illusive back roads that avoid the congested, bumper-to-bumper traffic on Montauk Highway becomes the hot topic.

A librarian in East Hampton claims that the easy way is to "just turn right." Can you figure it out? There are old favorites that, if you are a true believer in back roads, will get you around all of the Montauk crawl. Those in the know, however, say you won't save time, just aggravation; and, generally, these roads are considerably out of the way, unless your destination happens to be the villages along the north shore of the South Fork — Noyack, Sag Harbor, or Springs, for instance.

Personally, I think it's a shame to bypass the villages because they're all so charming. I want to see what new shops have opened and what they have to offer; how the restaurants are doing; and what has happened since last week. One way to avoid the traffic is to leave for the Hamptons by 12:00 noon on Friday and return at dawn on Monday, although at times I have started for the Hamptons at dawn on Saturday and returned at 4:00 p.m. on Sunday, with no significant traffic problems.

Turtles are cautioned to stay within the 35 mph speed limit in East Hampton.

Suzi Forbes Chase

With agreeable road conditions, the trip from New York City to Southampton should be an easy 2-hour drive. As Timothy McDarrah said, however, in *Dan's Papers,* "One thing about roads: If you build them, cars will come. One thing about roads to the Hamptons: There are no shortcuts."

From New York City, most people head straight out on the Long Island Expressway (Interstate 495). I must admit my preference, however, is the Northern State Parkway because generally it has fewer cars, and trucks are prohibited on all New York State parkways. Nevertheless, when the Northern State Parkway ends at the Sagtikos Parkway, the Long Island Expressway cannot be avoided. Most drivers leave the Expressway at Exit 70 in Manorville to take Route 111 on its straight diagonal course to Route 27, the Sunrise Highway. If your destination is Westhampton Beach, Hampton Bays, or another town west of these villages, you probably won't find many traffic problems at all.

If, however, you run into congestion as Route 27 narrows to two lanes on the outskirts of Southampton, you might find it easier to turn south on Tuckahoe Road, beside the Southampton Campus of Long Island University, and head for Route 27A, Montauk Highway. Turn left there and continue through the village of Southampton on that route, which is called Hill Street within the village.

One difficulty with traveling by car from Southampton to Montauk is that all of the roads are two-lane; a tractor or a truck can slow traffic to a crawl for miles. Many residents prefer it that way, hoping to discourage further development. After all, the farmers were here first. Others join in a frustrated howl.

An alternative, of course, is to let someone else do the driving. We'll get to the train, bus, plane, and boat options in the following pages, but it's not that unusual to see limousines and chauffeured town cars stuck in the same traffic jams as everyone else, while their passengers work diligently on a laptop computer or relax with a good book. If this is a driving option that appeals to you, here are several suggestions. Otherwise, pack a selection of cassette tapes or CDs and endure the inevitable snags.

Archer Town Car (town cars only) 800-273-1505

East Hampton Limousine 516-324-5466

Hampton Coach (limousines) 516-728-0063

Hampton Hills Limousine Ltd. 516-653-7820 or 800-795-6801

Hampton Jitney (limousines) 516-287-4000

Southampton Limousine, Ltd. 516-287-0001

For information about rental cars and taxis, see the following section that gives information about travel once you've arrived in the Hamptons.

BY BUS

Not long ago the only method of travel to the Hamptons was by car, train, or private plane. Now there are a variety of options.

HAMPTON JITNEY

516-283-4600 (Long Island); 800-936-0440 (New York metro area only); 800-327-0732 (outside New York metro and Long Island).
Mailing Address: The Omni, County Road 39A, Southampton, NY 11968.
Price: Southampton–Montauk $22 one-way, $40 round-trip; lower midweek rates to Westhampton Beach; pets $10 (in carriers only); bicycles $10.
Credit Cards: AE, MC, V.
Schedules: (summer hours) 7:00 a.m.–11:30 p.m. from New York City; 5:50 a.m.–11:15 p.m. from the Hamptons (varies by day of the week).
Reservations: Strongly recommended.

Hampton Jitney began service in 1974 and now has a large fleet of buses that ply the highways between New York City and the Hamptons many times a day. In addition to regular departure points, they have four pickup spots along Lexington Avenue in Manhattan, from 86th Street to 40th Street. Also, they will drop off passengers at points on the Upper East Side on Third Avenue, as well as on the Upper West Side on selected trips. They have two runs: one from Southampton to Montauk and the other from Westhampton Beach to Sag Harbor. In general, the trip takes 2 hours from Manhattan to Southampton. There's an airport connection also, with pickup and drop-off service to several metropolitan airports. Package service and limousines can also be arranged. Hampton Jitney buses are modern, comfortable touring buses, with air-conditioning, wide seats, plenty of legroom, large windows, and rest rooms. An attendant on each bus serves coffee, juice, or water with a muffin, peanuts, or chips, depending on the time of day; newspapers are provided as well. Since the schedule does change according to requirements, it is necessary to call. The buses are sometimes filled far in advance, especially on holiday weekends, so make reservations early.

Hampton Jitney offers an alternative to automobile travel to the Hamptons.

Courtesy Hampton Jitney

MILEAGE AND TRAVELING TIMES

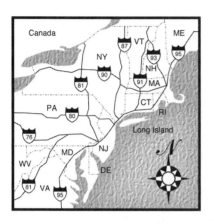

Location From Manhattan:	Mileage	Traveling Time
Westhampton Beach	83 mi	1 $^1/_2$ hrs
Southampton	96 mi	2 hrs
East Hampton	106 mi	2 $^1/_2$ hrs
Sag Harbor	105 mi	2 $^1/_2$ hrs
Montauk	123 mi	3 hrs
Greenport	102 mi	2 $^1/_2$ hrs

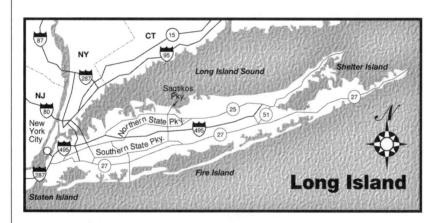

Location	Mileage	Traveling Time
Boston to Greenport (via Cross Sound Ferry from New London, CT to Orient Point)	141 mi to New London Ferry Crossing	3 hrs 1 hr 20 mins
Orient Point to Greenport (North Ferry)	10 mi	15 mins
North Ferry, Shelter Is., and South Ferry		1 hr

Suffolk County Transit (516-852-5200) is discussed in more detail under the section about travel within the Hamptons. When traveling to the South Fork from points within Suffolk County, however, this local bus company is certainly an option. It serves the county from Massapequa to Montauk, with regular service daily, except Sunday.

BY TRAIN

LONG ISLAND RAIL ROAD
718-217-5477 (New York); 516-822-5477 (Nassau County); 516-231-5477 (Suffolk County).
Price: Peak hours $15.25 one-way, $30 round-trip; off-peak hours $10.25 one-way, $20.50 round-trip; $17.50 additional for parlor car service; no charge for pets but must be in an approved AKC carrier; $5 pass required for bicycles, but pass takes about two weeks to obtain.

The Long Island Railroad has an excellent reputation for dependability, and for many, it's the only way to travel to the Hamptons. Now that Pennsylvania Station in Manhattan has been renovated, Manhattan departures and arrivals are much more pleasant than in the past. Clean, modern cars, equipped with rest rooms, are now augmented by "The Sunrise Fleet" of special parlor cars, available on selected weekend trips to the Hamptons. These are carpeted cars with comfortable seats, and an attendant serves light snacks and beverages, ranging from beer, wine, and mixed drinks to soda and bottled water; a special parlor car reservation is required. The trip takes about 2 hours from New York to Westhampton Beach and 3 $3/4$ hours to Montauk, with about eight trains a day on summer weekends. For those traveling to the North Shore, three or four trains leave and arrive daily at Riverhead during the week, but only two trains on the weekends. No reservations are taken on the Long Island Rail Road (except for the parlor cars). For fare and schedule information, consult local newspapers or call ahead.

Passengers line up at the East Hampton train station to purchase tickets for the return trip to New York City.

Morgan McGivern

Amtrak (800-523-8720) travels from Pennsylvania Station (NYC) to New London, Connecticut, where *Cross Sound Ferries* (860-443-5281) provide transportation to Orient Point on the North Fork. (See ferry information below.) Pets are not allowed on Amtrak. Bicycles are permitted, as long as the train has a baggage car or a bicycle rack. If the bicycle is to be transported in the baggage car, it must be in a box, which can be purchased at Pennsylvania Station for $5. The train station in New London is an easy walk from the ferry terminal.

Metro North (212-532-4900) trains make frequent trips from Grand Central Station (NYC) to Bridgeport, Connecticut, where the *Bridgeport & Port Jefferson Steamboat Company* (516-473-0286) takes passengers and cars to Port Jefferson. (See ferry information below.) Small pets that are able to sit on the owner's lap are allowed on Metro North; there is no charge for pets. For bicycles, Metro North requires a bicycle permit, which can be purchased at Grand Central Station for $5. It's an easy walk from the train station in Bridgeport to the ferry terminal.

BY FERRY

Ferry service to Long Island is a pleasant option, especially if traveling from New England.

BRIDGEPORT & PORT JEFFERSON STEAM-BOAT COMPANY
516-473-0286.
Price: $35.50 peak hours, $30.50 off-peak hours for car and driver; $9.75 peak hours, $8.75 off-peak hours for additional passengers; pets must be on a leash; bicycles $1.
Credit Cards: D, MC, V.
Schedule: 7:30 a.m.–9:00 p.m. in the summer from Bridgeport; 6:00 a.m.–7:30 p.m. in the summer from Port Jefferson; shorter hours the rest of the year.
Reservations: Required for cars.

This ferry operates about ten trips daily in the summer for passengers and cars between Bridgeport, Connecticut, and Port Jefferson on Long Island's North Fork, with fewer trips the rest of the year. The drive from Port Jefferson to Southampton takes about 1 hour. These are large ferries, with snack bar service, a lounge where drinks are served, rest rooms, and plenty of deck space to relax in the sun during the 90-minute trip. Pets are allowed on deck, and bicycles are welcomed. A reservation is necessary for cars, especially during the summer months; cars are taken on a standby basis, if you forget to call. It's advisable to go upstairs shortly after you get on the ferry to purchase the ticket from the purser, as standing in line can take awhile. Tickets are collected when you reach the other side.

CROSS SOUND FERRY
860-443-5281.
Price: $31 one-way for car and driver; $9 for additional adults; $4.50 children 2–11; no charge for children

Cross Sound Ferry travels between New London, Connecticut, and Orient Point on the North Shore. It is the most direct route from Boston, Cape Cod, Rhode Island, and points east. There are about 15 trips daily in the summer, but

under 2; no charge for pets but must be leashed; bicycles $2.
Credit Cards: D, MC, V.
Schedule: 7:00 a.m.–8:45 p.m. from New London; 7:00 a.m.–9:00 p.m. from Orient.
Reservations: Required for cars.

NORTH FERRY
516-749-0139.
Price: $7 one-way for car and driver, $8 for same day round-trip; $1 each additional passenger; $2 each way for bicycles.
Schedule: 5:40 a.m.–11:45 p.m. from Shelter Island; 6:00 a.m.–12:00 midnight from Greenport. If you miss that, you'll have to drive, via Riverhead, to the South Fork.
Credit Cards: None.
Reservations: None.

SOUTH FERRY
516-749-1200.
Price: $7 one-way for car and driver, $8 for same day round-trip; $1 each passenger; $2 one-way, $3 round-trip for bicycles.
Schedule: 6:05 a.m.–1:50 a.m. from North Haven; 6:00 a.m.–1:45 a.m. from Shelter Island.
Credit Cards: None.
Reservations: None.

the ferry does run year-round. These are large ferries, with the two largest able to accommodate up to 16 motor coaches. They take passengers as well as cars, but, again, reservations are absolutely necessary for cars to avoid a prolonged wait for space. Pets are allowed on deck. The trip takes about 90 minutes, and they have outdoor and indoor space for relaxing, as well as rest rooms and snack bars. On the largest boats, they also offer full-service lounges with drinks, televisions, and a jukebox, as well as a video game room.

Those traveling from New England to the Hamptons generally drive from Orient Point to Greenport and then travel across Shelter Island, taking North Ferry from Greenport and South Ferry from Shelter Island to North Haven, just north of Sag Harbor. These ferries that putt back and forth are efficient throwbacks to an earlier age. There are no amenities here, just a drive- or walk-on, open-decked ferry that shuttles back and forth between the island and the North and South Forks. Both ferries operate year-round, but the schedule is more frequent in the summer than the rest of the year.

Suzi Forbes Chase

The North Ferry carries passengers and cars from Shelter Island to the North Fork. Here, it is also the site of a wedding.

BY AIR

Sound Aircraft (800-443-0031, outside 516 area code only, or 516-537-2202) They offer charter flights between East Hampton, New York's La Guardia Airport, and New York's 23rd Street Seaport, as well as charter service throughout the east. They have some planes that can land either on land or water; they also operate planes on a charter basis. Should you and your friends want to fly directly to your hunting preserve on an isolated island with no airport, these folks can help.

Broadcast Helicopter (732-517-1826, a beeper) This helicopter service offers 35-minute flights from New York's West 30th Street Heliport, the Wall Street Heliport, the East 34th Street Heliport, and the East 60th Street Heliport to East Hampton, Westhampton, or Montauk Airports, as well as to the Southampton Heliport on Dune Road.

The nearest airport providing scheduled service by major airlines is **Long Island/Islip MacArthur Airport** in Ronkonkoma. For recorded information about all airlines, call 516-467-3210. The following airlines, with their direct reservation numbers, serve MacArthur.

Air-Tran Airways	800-247-8726
American Airlines	800-433-7300
Business Express (The Delta Connection)	800-345-3400
Delta Express	800-325-5205
Northwest Air-link Airlines	800-225-2525
U.S. Air Airlines	800-428-4322

Several other airlines offer charter services to Montauk Airport, East Hampton Airport, and Suffolk County Airport (Francis S. Gabreski Airport) in Westhampton Beach. For information about prices and availability, contact: *Action Airlines Charter* (800-243-8623); *Eastway* (516-737-9911); *Executive Airlines* (516-537-1010); *Executive Fliteways Inc.* (516-588-5454); *New England Airlines* (800-243-2460); *Shoreline Aviation* (800-468-8639); and *Summit Aviation* (800-255-4625 or 516-756-2545); or contact *Sound Aircraft Services* (516-537-2202) for information about the airlines that they represent.

If you own a plane and wish to wing it, the following airports offer landing and tie-down services, and all can accommodate small jets. Then, just like local luminaries, you can be a true jet-setter.

East Hampton Airport	516-537-1130
Montauk Airport	516-668-3738
Suffolk County Airport (in Westhampton Beach)	516-852-8095

GETTING TO AND FROM AIRPORTS

Classic Airport Share-Ride (516-567-5100 or 800-666-4949) Provides door-to-door transportation from Long Island airports to anywhere on Long Island. Their courtesy 24-hour telephones are located at LaGuardia, Kennedy, and Islip airports, and one of their vans will be there to pick you up within 15 minutes. They're friendly, courteous, and helpful.

Hampton Coach (516-728-0063) Operates Lincoln town cars for 1 to 6 passengers and passenger vans that accommodate 10 to 14, from all major New York City airports, including Islip and Newark.

Winston Transportation (516-924-1200 or 800-424-7767) Provides door-to-door transportation between your home and Islip, LaGuardia, Kennedy, and Newark airports. Rides are shared so they take longer than direct service, but the price is lower. The company is efficient and reliable.

GUIDED TOURS

A few guided tours to the Hamptons are offered from New York. Among the best are those sponsored by the Long Island Rail Road from Pennsylvania Station (NYC), but bus companies also offer convenient ways to see the area without the trauma of fighting traffic. Travel agents are the best source of information for these tours, with some including overnight accommodations along with the ride.

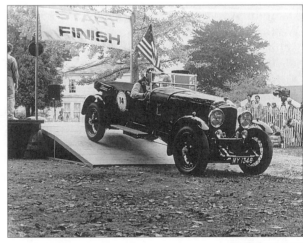

In Bridgehampton, a road race was first run in 1915 with new cars. Today, the race is recreated with antique cars.

Morgan McGivern

LONG ISLAND RAIL ROAD
718-558-7498.
Departure: Tours leave from Pennsylvania Station (NYC), Brooklyn, Jamaica, and Mineola.
Mailing Address: Sales & Promotions Department #1424, Jamaica, NY 11435.
Season: Mem. Day–early Nov.
Rates: Adults $48; children $36.
Credit Cards: None.

The Long Island Rail Road organizes a series of delightful tours each summer, including a Hamptons/Montauk trip, which is offered about six times from July to November. The trip is by train to Hampton Bays, where lunch is provided; then there's a museum tour and time for shopping in Southampton. The group then boards a bus for a scenic drive through the Hamptons villages to Montauk for a tour of the historic Montauk Lighthouse. Then it's back on the train in Montauk for the return trip to New York. Reservations are necessary, but the price is surprisingly low, considering lunch is included.

CAMELOT STAR
860-345-8591.
Departure: Tour leaves from Haddam, CT.
Mailing Address: 1 Marine Park, Haddam, CT 06438.
Season: Mid-Jun.–Labor Day operating daily, except Mon., Fri., Sat.; Labor Day–mid-Sept. operating Sun. only.
Rates: Adults $19.75; children under 12 half-price, under 5 free.
Credit Cards: AE, D, MC, V.

The Camelot Star is a 560-passenger cruise ship from Haddam, Connecticut, that operates excursion trips to Sag Harbor during the summer. The 3-hour cruise leaves Haddam at 9:00 a.m. and arrives in Sag Harbor at 12:00 noon; 3 hours of shopping, sight-seeing, or lunch in a restaurant are available prior to the 3:00 p.m. return to Haddam. The ship has an air-conditioned and heated deck as well as an outside observation deck. Bicycles are welcome at no charge.

Several specialty tours are also available to the Hamptons. For bicycling and hiking tours, see the section "Bicycling" in Chapter Seven, *Recreation,* or contact **Brooks Country Cycling Tours,** (212-874-5151). For sight-seeing tours by boat, see Chapter Seven, *Recreation.*

For organized tours from the Hamptons, the **Hampton Jitney** (516-283-4600) offers a variety of tours, including theater, museum, and shopping trips to New York City, as well as trips to Florida and to the Foxwoods Casino in Connecticut.

Also, **New England Tours** in conjunction with the **Port Jeff Ferry** (from Port Jefferson, about 1-hour drive west) (516-473-5138 or 516-473-6282) conducts tours to a variety of places in New England, including Boston, Newport, Rhode Island, Yale football games, and much more.

GETTING AROUND ONCE YOU'RE THERE

Getting here isn't nearly as much fun as getting around once you arrive. If you prefer to drive someone else's car instead of your own, here are several car rental options. Please be sure to call in advance to reserve.

CAR RENTALS

Avis Rent A Car National Reservation Number (800-331-1212); 59 Maple Avenue, Southampton (516-283-9111). Open May–mid–Sept. only.

Budget National Reservation Number (800-527-0700); 817 North Highway, Southampton (516-283-7042).

Enterprise Rent-A-Car (516-283-0055); Omni, 175 County Road 39A, Southampton, next door to the Hampton Jitney. Take the Jitney to Southampton. Open Mon.–Sat.

Hertz National Reservation Number (800-654-3131); Montauk Highway, Bridgehampton (516-537-8119).

All County Rent-A-Car (516-324-1018); Georgica Getty Station on the corner of Toilsome Lane and Montauk Highway just outside East Hampton. Rents used 1991–1995 cars that may be used for driving in the Hamptons only. Rentals are by the week.

Pam Rent-A-Car (516-727-7020); East Hampton on North Main Street.

TAXIS

For short-term transportation, the following taxis are reliable and often will deliver packages and make deliveries. Village location doesn't mean that a taxi is restricted to that village.

East Hampton

Hampton Coach (516-324-0077) Wainscott

Hampton Bays

Hampton Coach (516-728-0050)

Montauk

Pink Tuna Car Service (516-668-3838)

Sag Harbor

Sag Harbor Car Service (516-725-9000)

Southhampton

Bay Cab (516-283-0242)

Westhampton Beach

Westhampton Beach Taxi & Limo (516-288-3252)

PUBLIC BUSES

East End Hopping Tours (516-329-TOUR) Mae Bushman operates a local tour company that offers a variety of tour options. Perhaps you're interested in learning about Hamptons history from a third-generation native. She can take you down tiny back village roads that are otherwise inaccessible, and tell you things you'll never read in history books. Or perhaps you want to find the finest antiques shops specializing in 18th- and 19th-century English and American furniture. She'll save you time by taking you directly to them. Or in the summer, she will arrange a clambake on the beach at the most spectacular spot for watching the sun set.

Suffolk Transit (516-852-5200 or 516-360-5700) Mon.–Sat. $1.50, with an additional charge of $.25 for each transfer. Operates buses that crisscross the Hamptons, from Montauk to Westhampton and beyond, including the North Fork as far as the Orient Point Ferry. For some reason, the information numbers are always busy, and they're only in operation from 8:00 a.m.–4:30 p.m. Mon.–Fri. The best bet is to pick up the schedule and fare information from the local Chamber of Commerce offices. The schedules are well prepared, with maps that clearly show the routes, the transfer points, and just about anything you need to know. Suffolk Transit will stop anywhere along the route if you flag them down. In general, the buses travel each way about every 2 hours. You must tell the driver when you get on if you want a transfer. **Please note:** Exact fare is required, as the drivers do not carry change.

CHAPTER THREE
Hospitality Hamptons' Style
LODGING

Hampton residents have been taking in boarders for more than 200 years. In her book, *Up and Down Main Street, an Informal History of East Hampton and Its Old Houses* (1968), Jeannette Edwards Rattray states that the Huntting Inn (then the Huntting home) accommodated boarders as early as Revolutionary times. It is said that in the eighteenth century, the 1770 House was open on Saturday nights to God-fearing churchgoers who came from other villages

Morgan McGivern

The Hedges Inn originally was home to one of the founding families of East Hampton. It's now an inn and a restaurant.

to attend East Hampton's churches. Rowdy Hall was housing guests when the artists of The Tile Club first discovered the Hamptons in the late 1800s. W.L. Osborn and his wife ran a boardinghouse as early as 1858 in "their big house on the little hill overlooking Town Pond." The Sea Spray Inn in East Hampton was legendary, as was the Irving House in Southampton.

Duke Fordham's inn on Sag Harbor's main street was certainly in business before the stagecoach route from the Fulton Ferry in Brooklyn to Sag Harbor was established in 1772; it was chosen as the final stop on the three-day stage-coach trip. In 1877, Addison Youngs opened the American Hotel in Sag Harbor. This hotel was one of the most modern hotels on Long Island, with steam heat, electric lights, and indoor bathrooms. Sag Harbor's Sea View Hotel was built in 1891 and stood on a hill overlooking Noyack Bay; it was famous for attracting celebrities, such as Enrico Caruso. Later called Hill Top Acres, it burned to the ground in 1970.

Ye Olde Canoe Place Inn was built on the small isthmus where native inhabitants carried their canoes from the Great Peconic Bay to the Shinnecock Bay. First constructed in 1750 as a small house, it later became a stagecoach stop. Over the years, it was owned by the Buchmüller family, who had previously owned the Waldorf-Astoria Hotel, and by Julius Keller, owner of Maxim's restaurant in Manhattan. The inn was destroyed by fire on July 4, 1921, but was rebuilt to follow the lines of the original. The new structure included 34 bedrooms, four banquet rooms, 20 baths, and a gigantic kitchen. It became a favorite watering hole during the Roaring Twenties, and its Saturday night dances attracted hundreds. Among its famous guests were Governor Al Smith, who made it his summer headquarters for some 30 years, Franklin Roosevelt, John L. Sullivan, Helen Hayes, Albert Einstein, and Cary Grant. The inn is still in operation as a nightclub and restaurant.

Of the old-time inns, the American Hotel in Sag Harbor, The Huntting Inn, The Hedges Inn, and the Maidstone Arms in East Hampton are still welcoming guests, but most others have long since burned or been demolished. The Irving Hotel in Southampton, for example, survived until the 1970s, only to be demolished. The Irving Annex across the street, however, survives as the main house of the Village Latch Inn.

Innkeeping continues to be a Hampton tradition today, much as it was some 200 years ago, but with modern comforts. Today's inns often include cable television, air-conditioned rooms, fluffy down pillows and comforters, and chocolates on the pillow. Private baths may include a collection of amenities, from special soaps and shampoos to thick towels and warm robes.

In the block of information printed with each lodging description, you will see a price code rather than specific prices. This code is based on the average between the highest and lowest rates per room, double occupancy. If a continental or full breakfast is included, it will be noted in the information block under "Special Features." The rates indicated throughout this book are subject to change, so to be safe, confirm prices when you call for reservations. These rates generally exclude local taxes and any service charges that may be added to the bill. The price codes are as follows:

Price Codes

Inexpensive	Up to $90
Moderate	$90–$125
Expensive	$125–$175
Very Expensive	$175 and up

Accepted credit cards are indicated by the following abbreviations.

Credit Cards

AE	American Express
CB	Carte Blanche
D	Discover
DC	Diner's Club
MC	Master Card
V	Visa

High season in the Hamptons runs from the July 4th weekend through Labor Day. Almost all bed-and-breakfast establishments, inns, and motels, however, open earlier and close later in the season, and more and more are remaining open year-round. When possible, dates of operation are indicated, but since they may vary from year to year, it is best to call first. Also in high season, inns and motels often require two- and three-night minimum stays on weekends and four-night stays on holidays.

Bed-and-breakfast establishments are as varied as their owners. Some are elegant and classy, while others are whimsical and humorous, with all the variations in between. Some are decorated with such élan that they belong in *Architectural Digest;* others offer a homey combination of handmade quilts and pillows. Some pride themselves on the complete breakfasts that they serve; others lay out a buffet of fruits and breads. The one common thread, however, is that each owner of a bed-and-breakfast has invested a bit of himself or herself in their establishment; staying in one is often a very personal experience.

Hamptons' inns and bed-and-breakfasts have a limited number of rooms, and it is necessary to reserve the finest rooms well in advance. Therefore, it is advisable to make reservations as soon as you know your plans. A deposit generally will be required, and strict cancellation policies are followed. Be sure that you understand the policy and abide by it; otherwise, you may lose your deposit.

Children under the age of 12 and pets are often discouraged in bed-and-breakfasts in the Hamptons. Most have strictly enforced no-smoking policies within the house, but some do allow smoking on porches or on the grounds. In-room telephones often are not available in bed-and-breakfasts, but a surprising number of inns are now offering color televisions with cable hookups. Although more of the inns are now providing air-conditioning, it has been assumed for some time that the balmy ocean breezes make it unnecessary; generally, that is true.

Listings are divided into townships, East Hampton Town and Southampton Town, and are also listed by individual village or hamlet. If you are not sure which town a village is in, please refer to the list below. Places to stay on the North Fork and on Shelter Island are included in those specific chapters.

TOWNS, VILLAGES, HAMLETS

Town	*Villages, Hamlets*
East Hampton Town	Amagansett, East Hampton, Montauk.
Southampton Town	Bridgehampton, Quogue, Sag Harbor, Southampton, Westhampton Beach

The East Hampton and Southampton Chambers of Commerce operate an excellent accommodation referral service. Each publishes a free book that lists its members, including those who offer lodging. They also have information and telephone numbers of homes, inns, hotels, and motels that have current vacancies.

East Hampton Chamber of Commerce (516-324-0362) 37A Main Street, East Hampton.

Southampton Chamber of Commerce (516-283-0402) 76 Main Street, Southampton.

BED-AND-BREAKFASTS, INNS, RESORTS

EAST HAMPTON TOWN

Amagansett

The Gansett Grenn Manor is a lovely collection of cottages — each with its own kitchen and patio.

THE GANSETT GREEN MANOR
Innkeeper: Gary Kalfin.
516-267-3133.
Website: www.peconic.net/
  gansettgreenmanor/
273 Main Street, Amagansett.
Price: Moderate–Very
  Expensive.
Credit Cards: AE, MC, V.
Open: Year-round.
Mailing Address: P.O. Box
  799, Amagansett, NY
  11930.

The Gansett Green, a fixture of Amagansett life since 1915, is in tip-top shape. What was once a ramshackle collection of cottages was recently transformed into a delightful haven. Each weathered shingle cottage now has crisp white trim, an individual garden or patio, and wainscoted interior walls; the decor is inspired. The Hidden Garden suite is furnished with rare, blackwood Chinese pieces, imported from China by Gary, and has a walled garden with a fishpond. Several of the cottages, including the Hampton Classic Horse Room,

Special Features: Spacious
landscaped grounds;
kitchens; children
welcome; pets with prior
permission.
Directions: On Route 27, in
the village.

have furniture that is hand-painted by artist David
Tabor. All 14 units have kitchens, private baths,
new flagstone terraces, antiques, and so much
more. The two-acre parcel that once was over-
grown with weeds and brush held many surprises;
Gary found an old tandem wooden sled and beside
the big barn, a covered wagon. All such discoveries
remain, as well as the fountains and meandering
pathways.

THE HERMITAGE
Manager: Rita O'Neill,
Dune Resorts.
516-267-6151;
fax: 516-267-1071.
Montauk Highway,
Amagansett.
Price: Moderate–Very
Expensive.
Credit Cards: MC, V.
Open: Mid-Mar.–New Years.
Mailing Address: P.O. Box
1127, Amagansett, NY
11930.
Special Features: On the
ocean; kitchens; pool;
tennis courts; private
sundecks; 7 landscaped
acres; cable TV; air-
conditioning; telephones;
no pets.
Directions: On Montauk
Highway, 5 miles east of
Amagansett.

L ocated on the expansive sandy beach of
Napeague, midway between Amagansett village and Montauk, these ultramodern, bleached
wood, two-story buildings rise from the surrounding dunes. Each of the 56 units has two bedrooms,
two baths, a living room, a full kitchen, a dining
room, and a deck for private sunbathing. The decor
is the typical Hampton motif of pale woods and
pastel fabrics. Views from the oceanside rooms are
spectacular. The seven acres of landscaped
grounds include two tennis courts and a pool with
a lifeguard in attendance. This is a great place for
children.

**MILL-GARTH COUNTRY
INN**
Innkeeper: Tommie Alegre.
516-267-3757.
23 Windmill Lane,
Amagansett.
Price: Expensive–Very
Expensive.
Credit Cards: MC, V.
Open: Year-round.
Mailing Address: P.O. Box
700, Amagansett, NY
11930.

T he Mill-Garth has a certain lived-in comfort to it.
The collection of cottages on two acres (it
always seems larger than that) enfolds private little
bowers, as well as open spaces, which are popular
for weddings and receptions. The pretty tile-floored,
lattice-enclosed arbor is filled with white wicker and
is the preferred place for breakfast and afternoon
tea. Accommodations are widely varied and include
five cottages, four suites, and three studio apartments. The decor is eclectic, not elegant, but yet
spiced with some nice old pieces. You'll love the
tiny duplex windmill that has a desk and a tele-

Special Features:
Wheelchair accessible; 2 landscaped acres; some units with kitchens; continental breakfast; afternoon tea; children under 12 free; no pets.

Directions: From Montauk Highway turn onto Windmill Lane at Miss Amelia's Cottage. The inn is on the left in $^1/_4$ mile.

OCEAN COLONY BEACH AND TENNIS CLUB

Manager: Patricia Price, Dune Resorts.
516-267-3130; fax: 516-267-1032.
Montauk Highway, Amagansett.
Price: Moderate–Very Expensive.
Credit Cards: D, MC, V.
Open: Apr.–Oct.
Mailing Address: P.O. Box 7050, Amagansett, NY 11930.
Special Features: On the ocean; heated pool; tennis courts; kitchens; air-conditioning; cable TV; game room; children welcome; no pets.
Directions: Located on Montauk Highway, 4 miles east of Amagansett.

SEA CREST ON THE OCEAN

Manager: Elizabeth Miller, Dune Resorts.
516-267-3159 or 800-SEA DAYS; fax: 516-267-6840.
Montauk Highway at Navajo Lane, Amagansett.
Price: Inexpensive–Very Expensive.
Credit Cards: D, MC, V.

phone for guests to use. The Dairy Cottage is light and airy, with a black-and-white tile floor in the kitchen. The English Ivy Cottage has ivy stenciling across the door frames and the ceiling moldings. A private flagstone patio with wicker furniture makes this pretty cottage a particular favorite. The continental breakfast includes homemade muffins and coffee cake and afternoon tea is offered.

The Ocean Colony Beach and Tennis Club is a 69-unit, weathered gray, three-level resort built in 1983. It is located on an eight-acre site with 400 feet of private oceanfront. Units range in size from studios to three-bedroom units; all contain a living area, a sleeping area, a kitchenette, and a private deck or terrace. Some have ocean views and all have handsome furnishings. Unit 16-21 is a well-designed three-bedroom unit with a powder room on the first level, and a full bath upstairs, but no ocean view. The cottage (Room 511) has a very private site on the ocean with walls of windows and wraparound decks for direct views of the crashing waves. There are two bedrooms, a bath and a superb kitchen. The grounds include a pool, two tennis courts, and a clubhouse/game room with Ping Pong.

Sea Crest on the Ocean is a co-op, set on over nine acres, with 150 yards of unspoiled beach. The gray-shingled resort contains 74 units, ranging from studios to two-bedroom units. Facilities in Rapallo, Saint-Tropez, and San Remo have views of the ocean, while those in the other buildings have views of the pool or partial views of the ocean. All, however, have pleasing, well-designed living and sleeping areas, kitchenettes, and private decks or terraces; larger accommodations have

Open: Year-round.
Mailing Address: P.O. Box 7053, Amagansett, NY 11930.
Special Features: On the ocean; pool; tennis courts; kitchenettes; playground; basketball; racquetball; volleyball; handball; shuffleboard; cable TV; telephones; air-conditioning; outdoor grille; no pets.
Directions: Located on Montauk Highway, 5 miles east of Amagansett village.

two levels with two decks. The grounds are very well maintained and include abundant flower beds, a heated pool, two tennis courts, and an elevated, planked walkway over the dunes to the beach; a variety of activities are also held on the grounds.

East Hampton

BED AND BREAKFAST ON COVE HOLLOW

Innkeeper: Ann Colonomos.
516-324-7730.
145 Cove Hollow Road, East Hampton.
Price: Moderate–Very Expensive.
Credit Cards: AE.
Open: May–Oct.
Mailing Address: P.O. Box 2234, East Hampton, NY 11937.
Special Features: Nonsmoking inn; pool; lovely flower gardens; continental breakfast; bicycles; outdoor shower; hammock; small dogs acceptable.
Directions: Turn right off Montauk Highway onto Cove Hollow Road (Jerry and David's Red Horse Market will be across the street). The inn is on the right, behind Cafe Max.

This charming, shingled cottage offers a terrific bed-and-breakfast option. It's used exclusively by guests, and the owner lives in a separate cottage behind. There's an attractive living room with natural wood floors and a full kitchen. All four rooms are bright and cheerful and include painted white wood floors, covered by a rag or a sisal rug, with oak dressers and wicker beds, dressed in sun-washed fabrics. Two rooms have private baths and the other two rooms share a bath. In the back, a pool is surrounded by a brick terrace and enclosed by a fence, and there are brick pathways through the garden. Breakfast, which is laid out on the kitchen counter each morning, consists of fresh muffins, croissants, fruit, juice, granola, cereals, coffee or tea. I love to take my breakfast outside to the tables on the lawn behind the house and watch the bees flit from flower to flower in the abundant border flower beds. This is also the perfect spot to relax with a glass of wine after a hot day on the beach. She will also rent the whole house for a week.

Suzi Forbes Chase

Centennial House in East Hampton offers gracious accommodations, with antiques, Oriental rugs, and warm hospitality.

CENTENNIAL HOUSE
Innkeepers: David A. Oxford and Harry Chancey, Jr.
Manager: David A. Oxford.
516-324-9414;
   fax: 516-324-0493.
13 Woods Lane, East Hampton, NY 11937.
Price: Expensive–Very Expensive.
Credit Cards: MC, V.
Open: Year-round.
Special Features: Nonsmoking house; pool; lovely landscaped grounds and gardens; full breakfast; telephones; air-conditioning; not appropriate for children; pets with prior permission.
Directions: On Route 27, just before the traffic light and Town Pond.

When the innkeepers were restoring this gracious old East Hampton house in 1988, they found a board with the year "1876" carved into it, inspiring the inn's name. From the broad porch overlooking Woods Lane (Route 27) to the handsome gray-shingled exterior with its white trim, it is obvious that this was the residence of prosperous owners. Today the inn is reminiscent of an English country home. Oriental rugs decorate polished pine floors, and antique chairs are upholstered in English, floral-glazed chintz prints. There's a shelf of liqueurs in the living room, European oil paintings on the walls, a grand piano, and a fireplace. The stunning dining room has ceiling-to-floor bookshelves in a corner and an elegant, antique breakfront, holding heavy silver serving pieces. Breakfast is eaten on gilt-edged china on a magnificent mahogany table, lighted by a brass chandelier. The meal includes fruit, juice, bacon, eggs, pancakes, French toast, or some other special treat. The four rooms are elegantly appointed, and all have spectacular baths. The Rose Room has a canopy bed, a fireplace, Oriental rug, and a bath with a draped curtain over the footed tub. The Bay Room has an antique tobacco four-poster bed, wide-planked pine floors, Spy prints, a fireplace, and a large bath with a former pulpit that has been turned into a sink. My favorite room is the green and burgundy Lincoln Room, which has an ornate armoire and matching Victorian bed, similar to the one in which Abraham Lincoln died; its bath has a marble sink with brass legs. The grounds are as lovely as the house. There are spacious lawns, a profusion of flowers in season, and a pool tucked away in a secret spot in the back. A three-bedroom cottage offers an ideal accomodation for families; a barn is outfitted with fitness equipment.

EAST HAMPTON HOUSE
Manager: Jo Anne Koehler, Dune Resorts.
516-324-4300 or 800-698-9283; fax: 516-329-3743.
226 Pantigo Road, East Hampton, NY 11937.
Price: Inexpensive–Very Expensive.
Credit Cards: AE, D, MC, V.
Open: Year-round.
Special Features: Pool; tennis courts; telephones; cable TV; air-conditioning; children under 2 discouraged in the summer.
Direction: On Route 27, 1 mile east of the village.

From the street, this appears to be an attractive, well-maintained motel, but in reality, the white brick two-story buildings envelop five parklike acres of flower beds and manicured lawns that include a pool, tennis courts, and a children's play area. This is a co-op, so the decor of the units may vary, but each is superbly maintained and attractively furnished. There are two sizes of rooms: studios and two-room suites, and each of the 56 units has either a private sundeck or a patio. In the summer, a light continental breakfast is available, which may be taken to the room. Although the beach is about a mile away, the pool and the lovely landscaping make this one of the most popular motels in the Hamptons.

EAST HAMPTON POINT
Manager: Dominique Cummings.
516-324-9191;
fax: 516-324-3751.
295 Three Mile Harbor Road, East Hampton.
Price: Expensive–Very Expensive.
Credit Cards: AE, D, MC, V.
Open: Year-round.
Mailing Address: P.O. Box 847, East Hampton, NY 11937.

It's hard not to fall in love with these jewelbox cottages, now renovated into lovely accommodations. Each of the cottages has a modern kitchen with a refrigerator and a Jenn-Aire stove, Mexican tile floors, bleached pine cabinets, tile baths, and private brick patios or wooden decks. Some of the 13 cottages have duplex bedrooms and skylights. There are both one- and two-bedroom units, and all but one of the baths has a Jacuzzi. Cottage 3 has a bath with painted Mexican tile surrounding the Jacuzzi tub and the shower, but cottage 2 is absolutely stunning. The main floor has a terrific kitchen, a large

The cottages at East Hampton Point are joined by brick walkways and profuse flower beds.

Suzi Forbes Chase

Special Features: Pool; tennis court; fitness center; saunas; masseur on call; continental breakfast in the summer; 5 1/2 wooded acres; van service, including airport pickup; a fine restaurant and marina on the premises; children and pets welcome.
Directions: Bear left off Main Street at the windmill; when the road forks, bear left again onto Three Mile Harbor Road. East Hampton Point will be on the left in 4 miles.

THE HEDGES INN
Innkeeper: Linda Calder.
516-324-7100;
    fax: 516-324-5816.
74 James Lane, East
    Hampton, NY 11937.
Price: Moderate–Very
    Expensive.
Credit Cards: AE, DC, MC,
    V.
Open: Year-round.
Special Features: Smoking
    outside only; continental

deck, and a tiled powder room. Upstairs, there's a bedroom and a bathroom that boasts a glass ceiling, Mexican tile floor, large Jacuzzi, and a room-sized glass shower. As one might imagine, this cottage is especially popular with honeymooners. The cottages are connected by brick pathways and are bordered by abundant flower beds, all in a very private, wooded setting. In the midst, there's a small chapel that's been converted into a fitness center, complete with a TV. Although the popular East Hampton Point restaurant is on adjacent property, it's well removed from the cottages, as is the pool. There's a marina down on the harbor and a ship's store where guests can purchase breakfast in the morning and snacks all day.

The Hedges Inn is one of the oldest and most historic inns on the East End. The Hedges family, one of the founding families of East Hampton, began taking in boarders as early as 1870; it is believed that parts of the house date from the mid-1700s. The main house became an acclaimed inn in 1935, when Mrs. Harry Hamlin restored it and put her own cook and butler in charge. It achieved widespread acclaim in the 1950s, when it became home to a restaurant owned by famed chef and restaurateur, Henri Soulé. Legend has it that the

breakfast; air-conditioning; a restaurant on the premises; children welcome; no pets.
Directions: At the traffic light on Route 27, just before turning left toward the village, you will see the inn straight ahead.

famous underground wine cellar was once part of the Underground Railroad. Today The Hedges Inn has been fully restored and all 11 rooms have private baths. Room 1 has creamy beige walls with white wainscotting, turquoise carpeting, a taupe-colored sofa, and an iron canopy bed, while Room 14 has another turquoise carpet, a polished cherry bed, and floral paper on the walls. The baths are done in sparkling white tile, with black marble counters. A continental breakfast, consisting of fruit, juice, and muffins or croissants is served in the pretty, airy breakfast room. A side terrace serves as an auxiliary breakfast room in the summer, but it's also a refined place to sip a glass of wine in the afternoon. The James Lane Café is open seasonally.

THE HUNTTING INN

Innkeeper: Linda Calder.
516-324-0410;
     fax: 516-324-6122.
94 Main Street, East
     Hampton, NY 11937.
Price: Moderate–Very
     Expensive.
Credit Cards: AE, DC, MC,
     V.
Open: Year-round.
Special Features: Smoking
     outside only; continental
     breakfast; air-conditioning; telephones;
     a fine restaurant on the
     premises; children
     welcome; no pets.

This old inn, dating from the Revolutionary War, has been a prominent fixture on East Hampton's Main Street since 1699, when it was built as a home for Reverend Nathaniel Huntting, the second minister in East Hampton. Over the years, it has grown as it took in more and more boarders, which accounts for the narrow hallways with their quirky twists and turns. The Hampton Jitney stops directly in front of the inn, making it a most convenient place to stay. The tiny lobby of the Huntting bustles at night when it serves as the greeting place for diners at The Palm Restaurant, which is located on the main floor. Off the bar, however, there are several parlors where guests can spend quiet time in the afternoon, viewing the gardens. The 20 guest rooms vary in size and are often funky, although each has a smattering of antiques and a private bath. Room 203 has a king-sized bed, a fluffy daybed for lounging, and a wicker desk. Room 105 has an iron and brass bed, and Room 102 is a suite that is decorated in peach and white colors. The side flower garden is a riot of color from spring to fall.

LYSANDER HOUSE

Innkeepers: Larry and
     Leslie Tell Hillel.
516-329-9025.
132 Main Street, East
     Hampton, NY 11937.
Price: Expensive–Very
     Expensive.

Larry and Leslie Hillel traveled the globe before settling in East Hampton and opening their bed-and-breakfast. Their 1885 Victorian farmhouse inn, situated on two grassy acres, is charmingly filled with art that they collected along the way. In the parlor, there are masks from Mexico and Japan,

Lysander House, a Victorian farmhouse on Main Street, was built in 1885. It is decorated with interesting folk art pieces.

Morgan McGivern

Credit Cards: None.
Open: Year-round.
Special Features: Smoking outside only; wraparound porch; on 2 grassy acres; full breakfast; afternoon refreshments; air-conditioning; children over 14 welcome; no pets.

as well as an engaging New England village folk art scene, painted by Neil Connell, on a wooden plank that hangs over the fireplace. All of the floors are painted white, and there is wonderful, antique furniture, mixed with painted chests and tables. In the dining/living room, which is a cheery yellow with white trim and white shutters on the windows, there's a Japanese step tansu, a clever device that at one time served both as a stairway and as a storage space, with drawers under each of the stairs. The three guest rooms are light and bright and also cleverly decorated. Liza's Suite, which is the largest, has an iron headboard, and a pine bookcase and dresser. On the pale pink wall, there's a contemporary watercolor, while a folk art painting graces the sitting room. The bath has wainscotted walls, a pedestal sink, and a tiled shower. Alexander's Master Bedroom, which is painted a sunny yellow, includes an iron and brass bed, a pine wardrobe, and more of Neil Connell's folk art on the wall. All of the rooms have custom-made mattresses imported from Sweden, and private baths. Breakfast is a gourmet treat that includes freshly baked breads, muffins, or scones and a hot entrée, such as a frittata or oatmeal yogurt pancakes. You'll depart this delightful inn with a bag of freshly baked cookies.

THE MAIDSTONE ARMS
Owner: Coke Anne Saunders.
Managing Director: William S. Valentine.
516-324-5006;
fax: 516-324-5037.

There's been an inn on this site, looking much as the present Maidstone Arms does today, since 1750. In 1992, this grand dame of East Hampton inns was purchased by Coke Anne Saunders, an architect, and was fully restored. Located on a knoll across from Town Pond, the inn is a classic

Since 1750, a boardinghouse or inn has welcomed guests on the site of The Maidstone Arms.

Morgan McGivern

207 Main Street, East Hampton, NY 11937.
Price: Expensive–Very Expensive.
Credit Cards: AE, MC, V.
Open: Year-round.
Special Features: Limited wheelchair access; overlooks Town Pond; continental breakfast; maid service; telephones; fireplaces in the cottages; a fine restaurant on the premises.

beauty, with its white-shingled exterior with blue shutters and a Greek Revival doorway. The clubby Water Room, just off the lobby, has a woodstove, antique love seats, plaid-upholstered chairs, and walls decorated with hunting and fishing prints and antique fishing gear. This is the perfect place to sip a hot mulled wine in the winter, while watching children ice skate on Town Pond. It's also a pleasant place to begin the day while reading the complimentary copy of the *New York Times.* There are 16 guest rooms and three cottages, all with private baths; some have fancifully painted furniture and others have antiques. The duplex cottage suite has a beige carpet, white walls, a walnut sleigh bed, and a fireplace with a tile front. Room 14 has a verdigris iron bed and French doors leading to a private, glassed-in porch with wicker furniture.

MILL HOUSE INN
Innkeepers: Dan and Katherine Hartnett.
516-324-9766.
Website: www.millhouse inn.com.
33 North Main Street, East Hampton, NY 11937.
Price: Moderate–Very Expensive.
Credit Cards: MC, V.
Open: Year-round.

The charming Mill House Inn enjoys a convenient, in-town location and a lovely view of the historic Hook windmill. The inn changed hands in 1994, and the new owners have infused this historic inn with new vitality. Where "folksy" and "homey" aptly described the decor before, it now has an elegant, colonial charm. There are exposed beams and fireplaces in the living and the dining rooms. Each of the eight rooms has a private bath — four of them have wirlpool baths—and six of the rooms have working fireplaces. Hampton Breezes, for

Special Features:
Nonsmoking inn; full breakfast; telephones with voice mail; bicycles available; children welcome; no pets.

Directions: From Main Street, bear left at the fork just before the Hook Windmill. The inn is on the left, across from the windmill.

example, has plum carpeting, a pine sleigh bed, an antique armoire, a wicker love seat, and a fireplace; its large tiled bath has a whirlpool tub. Hampton Holiday has a fireplace, a mission-style sleigh bed, and a large bath with a whirlpool. Katherine was a chef at the Pierre Hotel in New York City, so the breakfasts here are very special. There might be frittatas, pancakes, or French toast, accompanied by fresh juice and a fruit plate. Even if you don't stay here, stop and buy a copy of her new cookbook, *Tasting the Hamptons: Food, Poetry, and Art from Long Island's East End.* We love to follow a day at the beach with some quiet time on the screened-in porch, sipping a refreshing lemonade, or before the fireplace in the winter, enjoying a hot cider.

THE PINK HOUSE

Innkeepers: Dan and Katherine Hartnett.
Manager: Mercedes Dekkers.
516-324-3400; fax: 516-324-5254.26 James Lane, East Hampton, NY 11937.
Price: Expensive–Very Expensive.
Credit Cards: AE, MC, V.
Open: Year-round.
Special Features:
Nonsmoking house; pool; full breakfast; air-conditioning; children over 5 welcome.
Directions: James Lane parallels Main Street on the opposite side of Town Pond.

This lovely, pink Victorian house, in a central in-town location, feels secluded and private. Perhaps it's the tall hedges that enclose it or that it's located next door to St. Luke's Rectory, but loud noises seldom seem to disturb the quiet. The broad porch, with its wicker furniture, is an inviting place to relax and admire the flower gardens. Inside, the living and dining rooms are low-key and traditional in decor and are spiced with interesting sculptures and paintings. Do take note of the lively watercolors painted by Walter Steinhilber, Ron's grandfather; the paintings are colorful images of his journeys around the world. Also, note the lamp in the living room that was made from a street lamp that Ron rescued from Brooklyn's old Myrtle Avenue El as it was being demolished. A bountiful breakfast of waffles, pancakes, French toast, or frittatas, along with homemade granola, yogurt, fresh fruit, and juice, is served on the back porch in the summer or in the formal dining room in the winter.

All four guest rooms have private baths and include canopy beds, window seats, and antique dressers. The pool in the back is a very private retreat, with comfortable lounges and tables for reading or sunning. You'll love the inn dogs: Ginger, Rosie, and Katie.

THE PLOVERS NEST

Innkeepers: Fred and Adele Filasky.

Sequestered behind a privet hedge, this delightful bed-and- breakfast is located in a weathered shingle house that dates to East Hamptons' earliest

516-329-1120.
199 Main Street, East
   Hampton, NY 11937.
Price: Expensive–Very
   Expensive.
Credit Cards: AE, MC, V.
Open: Year-round.
Special Features: Smoking
   outside only; continental
   breakfast; air-
   conditioning; cable TV;
   children over 12
   welcome; no pets.

days. The innkeepers have faithfully preserved the character of their 1774 home by exposing the hand-hewn beams and polishing the wide-planked pine floors to a soft luster. In the living room, where wine and hors d'oeuvres are served every afternoon, there's a lovely fireplace. The dining room, which is painted an antique blueberry wash, has another fireplace and an adjoining brick patio. Although there are no telephones in the guest rooms, Fred and Adele have thoughtfully provided an office area that is complete with a desk, telephone, and fax machine. There are four guest rooms, and although they each have a private bath, one of the baths is located off the hallway. Both the Blue Room and the beamed Green Room have wood-burning fireplaces; the Raspberry Room, located on the top floor, has sloping ceilings, an iron and brass bed, green wicker furniture, and a private bath. The inn has a secluded garden in the back. Breakfast includes such homemade treats as fruit scones, muffins, or breads, along with fresh fruit, juice, and homemade jams.

Morgan McGivern

There are private spots for relaxation in the formal gardens of The J. Harper Poor Cottage. Inside, the decor was inspired by William Morris.

THE J. HARPER POOR COTTAGE
Innkeepers: Gary and Rita
   Reiswig.
516-324-4081;
   fax: 516-329-5931.

For many years, this distinctive, buff-colored stucco mansion was the home of the owners of 1770 House and served as an adjunct to the rooms in their inn. In 1996, however, the handsome house was transformed by Gary and Rita Reiswig, for-

Website: www. jharper poor.com; E-mail: info@jharperpoor.com. 181 Main Street, East Hampton, NY 11937. Price: Very Expensive. Credit Cards: AE, DC, MC, V. Open: Year-round. Special Features: Smoking outside only; full breakfast; afternoon refreshments; air-conditioning; cable TV/VCR; video library; masseur available; room safe; children welcome; no pets.

merly the owners of The Maidstone Arms, into the Hampton's premier bed-and-breakfast. Every detail of the major restoration has been executed to perfection. The original structure dates to the 1650s, although the house has been expanded and embellished significantly over the years. In the 1900s, Mr. Poor created its current appearance, and the Reiswig's have restored it to that period. In the sunken living room, there are bay windows, a carved plaster ceiling, and a massive tile-fronted fireplace. An oak library table graces the library, which has a wall of books. In keeping with the style and age of the house, the elegant furnishings are all of William Morris design. The guest rooms, which have beamed ceilings, are very large, with spacious closets and equally spacious tiled baths; most have fireplaces. My favorite is Room 13, which has an iron bed, a wood-burning fireplace, hand-hewn beamed ceilings, paneled walls, and a private balcony, overlooking Main Street. All the rooms have William Morris-style fabrics and wallpapers imported from England, Ralph Lauren bed dressings, and fluffy Frette bathrobes. Breakfast is served in the informal lounge, which has wicker chairs, a plumped sofa in front of a woodstove, a bright blue rug on the wood floor, and a beamed ceiling. The full breakfast may include an omelette or pancakes, accompanied by freshly baked breads, fruit, and juice. In the afternoon, wines and cheeses are set out in the informal lounge.

Thu / Fri / Sat 3 nights

1770 HOUSE

Innkeepers: Wendy Van Deusen and Adam Perle. 516-324-1770. 143 Main Street, East Hampton, NY 11937. Price: Moderate–Expensive. Credit Cards: AE, MC, V. Open: Year-round. Special Features: Non-smoking inn; full breakfast; a fine restaurant on the premises; air-conditioning; telephones; working fireplaces; no children under 12; no pets.

Room #

Although 1770 House has been graciously welcoming guests for over 200 years, it doesn't look its age thanks to the loving care of its current owners. Located in the heart of the original village, over the years it's served as a general store, a dining hall for Clinton Academy, a private home, and a public inn. When Sid and Mim Perle purchased the inn in 1977, they began a restoration that transformed the tired house into a fine country inn. Now run by their daughter and son, you'll find lovely antiques, oil paintings, and polished furniture throughout the inn. All of the guest rooms have private baths. Room 2 is a large room with a paneled wall, canopied bed, and a fireplace; Room 10 is even larger, with a fireplace, a dressing room, and a private entrance. Room 3 has a bed with a fishnet canopy and a museum-quality, antique chest-on-chest. The library, with another paneled wall and a fireplace, is a cozy nook where one can contemplate dinner plans while sipping an aperitif. Breakfast may include fresh juice, French toast made with challah bread and served with raspberry-melba sauce or another of Wendy's creative dishes. Do go into the office before you leave to see the remnants of the East Hampton Post Office that Sid retrieved when it was moved to its present location. The old brass window cages, glass headers, carved walnut front panels, and even the old mailboxes are all here.

Montauk   *called*

GURNEY'S INN RESORT & SPA

General Manager: Paul Monte.
516-668-2345;
   fax: 516-668-3576.
290 Old Montauk Highway, Montauk, NY 11954.
Price: Moderate–Very Expensive.
Credit Cards: AE, D, DC, MC, V.
Open: Year-round.
Special Features: Spectacular ocean views; beach access; 10 landscaped acres; health and beauty spa; indoor-heated sea water pool; two restaurants on the premises; conference facilities; children welcome; no pets.
Directions: Located on Old Montauk Highway, approximately 10 miles east of Amagansett village and 2 1/2 miles west of Montauk Village.

Gurney's was the first spa on the East Coast, and it's been sitting on its bluff, overlooking the Atlantic Ocean, for more than 70 years. Taking advantage of its natural access to saltwater, this is the only spa on the North American continent to use marinotherapeutic treatments — the therapeutic use of sea water and seaweed. There's sea water in the Roman baths and in the tubs where thalasso therapy (underwater massage with jets of water) takes place and in the Swiss needle showers in the Vichy rooms. In addition to the spa treatments, there are numerous health and fitness activities, such as aerobic beach walks, tai chi, yoga, and a full range of exercise equipment, including a cardiovascular fitness circuit. The Sea Grill, an elegant dinner restaurant serving three meals a day (including a slimming spa menu), has panoramic views of the ocean below. Caffe Monte offers a more casual dining experience, and it's open for breakfast, lunch, and dinner. Nightly entertainment includes tarot card readings, bridge, bingo, and karaoke. Because of its range of activities and size, Gurney's is popular for conventions and tour groups. Gurney's 109 guest rooms are eclectic in style, reflecting the varied tastes of the individual time-share co-op owners. Rooms in the Foredeck and Forward Watch buildings have private decks and unobstructed ocean views. Several beachside cottages have fireplaces, and one has a Jacuzzi. The most private cottage, Skipper's Cottage, sits on a bluff overlooking the ocean.

MONTAUK MANOR

Manager: Janice Nessel.

Montauk Manor was built by Carl Fisher, the developer of Miami Beach, in 1927 as part of

Morgan McGivern

Montauk Manor was built in 1927 by Carl Fisher, the developer of Miami Beach, as part of his grand plan to turn Montauk into the Miami of the North.

516-668-4400;
   fax: 516-668-3535.
Website: www. peconic.
   net/tourism/mm/
236 Edgemere Street,
   Montauk.
Price: Inexpensive–Very
   Expensive.
Credit Cards: AE, D, MC, V.
Open: Year-round; daily
   May–Sept.; Fri–Sat. only
   Sept.–May.
Mailing Address: RD #2,
   Box 226C, Montauk, NY
   11954.
Special Features: Wheelchair
   accessible; indoor and
   outdoor pools; cable TV
   (some with VCRs); air-
   conditioning; telephones;
   kitchens; doorman; maid
   service; health club with
   Jacuzzi and saunas;
   conference facilities;
   seasonal van service; 3
   tennis courts; exercise
   room; indoor squash
   court; restaurant on the
   premises, serving B, L, D
   in the summer only.
Directions: From Main
   Street, travel north on
   Edgemere Street and
   follow the signs to the
   resort, which is up a hill
   on the right.

his grand plan to turn Montauk into the Miami of the North. It's an imposing building that resembles a feudal English Tudor castle, and it sits high on Montauk's highest hill. It boasts spectacular views of the harbor, where Fisher planned to build grand docks for the ocean liners that were to depart and arrive from Europe. None of that came to pass, however, and for years the hotel sat idle. In 1987, it was converted into 140 co-op apartments (70 are rented on a transient basis) that range in size from studios to three-bedroom units. Half of the units have balconies and most have views. Montauk Manor is on the National Register of Historic Places. The lobby, soaring three stories high, has multiple massive fireplaces along its tiled corridor. The rooms are well designed and tasteful, each with a modern kitchen and tile bath. If you are lucky enough to rent unit 135, you'll find the arched fireplace that once graced the dining room, a sofa bed in the living room, a loft bedroom, and an arched doorway framing French doors to a mammoth terrace; mirrored walls in the dining and living rooms expand the space.

MONTAUK YACHT CLUB RESORT & MARINA

Manager: Bob Scheiner.
516-668-3100;
fax: 516-668-3303.
32 Star Island Road,
Montauk.
Price: Moderate–Very
Expensive.
Credit Cards: AE, DC, MC,
V.
Open: Apr.–Oct.
Mailing Address: P.O. Box
5048, Montauk, NY 11954.
Special Features: Nonsmoking
designated rooms;
waterfront; wheelchair
accessible; outdoor and
inside pools; tennis courts;
resident pro; health club;
marina; 2 restaurants on
the premises; lounge; cable
TV; air-conditioning;
telephones; conference
facilities; children welcome;
no pets.
Directions: Travel east on
Montauk Highway and
continue through the
village of Montauk; turn
left on West Lake Drive.
Travel 1.8 miles and turn
right on Star Island Causeway. The Yacht Club is on
the right in about $^1/_4$ mile.

The Montauk Yacht Club Resort & Marina underwent a multi-million dollar renovation in 1998 that transformed it from a struggling bank-owned property to the luxury resort that it used to be. This one-stop retreat offers complete lodging, restaurant, and recreational facilities for the entire family. Each of the 107 guest rooms has been attractively upgraded with light colors against a background of beige and white. They are equipped with contemporary furniture. Some of the rooms have water views and all feature telephones with voice mail and dataports, hair dryers, and coffee makers. The rooms in the former Florenz Ziegfield estate, located a short drive away at the end of the street, have individual charm. Built in the 1920s, the 23 "villas" have interesting little alcoves with pretty patios, and some feature fireplaces. The Lighthouse Grill is a fine restaurant offering dining with views of the bay and entertainment on week-ends. Breezes Café. which is open for breakfast and lunch only, has a casual, comfortable ambience.

PERI'S BED & BREAKFAST

Owner: Peri Aronian.
516-668-1394; fax: 516-668-6096.
206 Essex Street, Montauk,
NY 11954.
Price: Inexpensive–Very
Expensive.
Credit cards: V, MC (3%
surcharge).
Open: Year-round.
Special features: Non-
smoking B&B; full
breakfast; afternoon wine
and hors d'oeuvres;
gardens; children

You understand that a creative talent with an artist's eye is at home at Peri's the minute you walk in the door. Peri Aronian used to be a New York fashion designer. Now she has transformed this beautiful Carl Fisher Tudor house of stucco and half-timbers into a fabulous B&B that's full of elegant furnishings laced with playful whimsy. The living room, for example, has a gorgeous carved wooden fireplace mantel and polished oak floors topped with a huge bearskin rug before a great leather sofa. In the summer, this may be replaced by an Oriental rug. The three bedrooms transport their occupants to Peri's favorite travel destinations. Fez, designed with the Moroccan city welcome during the week; children over the age of 12 only on weekends.

in mind, has azure blue walls and an iron canopy bed hung with an Oriental runner. Marais, which inspires dreams of Paris, has lime green walls, a beautiful French marble-topped dresser, and a French bed. A little private balcony admits the sounds of the birds and the scent of roses. Peri's home had at one time been owned by Henri Soulé, the famed proprietor of New York's Le Pavillion restaurant. One imagines gracious dinner parties in the huge billiard room, which has French doors leading to a flagstone patio. Peri recreates that same Hampton's weekend gustatorial experience with her gourmet breakfasts and afternoon get-togethers for wine and hors d'oeuvres. For utter relaxation, however, guests may partake of a soothing massage or facial al fresco, or in the privacy of the quiet treatment room.

THE SURF CLUB
Manager: Richard Edelstein, Dune Resorts.
516-668-3800 or 800-LAST WAVE; fax: 516-668-9296.
Surfside Avenue and South Essex Street, Montauk.
Price: Inexpensive–Very Expensive.
Credit Cards: None.
Open: Mid-Apr.–mid-Nov.
Mailing Address: P.O. Box 1174, Montauk, NY 11954.
Special Features: On the ocean; limited wheelchair access; tennis courts; pool; cable TV; kitchens; daily maid service; steam baths; workout room; children welcome; no pets.
Directions: From Montauk's Main Street, turn south onto Essex Street.

This luxurious, gray-shingled, oceanfront resort, with its 500 feet of private beach, is the classiest place to stay in Montauk. The resort has 92 one- and two-bedroom units, each with a modern kitchen, living and dining area, and a private terrace for sunbathing; the units in the oceanfront buildings have spectacular views. The resort is located on eight acres that include a pool with brick terraces and wraparound wooden decks, two tennis courts, and landscaped grounds. Most of the units feature a second-story bedroom with a color television in both the living room and the bedroom. The decor in the units is attractive and contemporary.

SOUTHAMPTON TOWN

Bridgehampton

BRIDGEHAMPTON INN
Owner/Innkeeper: Anna Pump.
Assistant Innkeeper: Maureen Brown
516-537-3660.

This venerable, old colonial home in Bridgehampton is one of the most handsome in town. Circled by a white picket fence, the white-shingled structure was totally restored in 1993. The decor has a restrained elegance that's punctuated by

2266 Montauk Highway, Bridgehampton.
Price: Expensive–Very Expensive.
Open: Year-round.
Mailing Address: P.O. Box 1342, Bridgehampton, NY 11932.
Special Features: Nonsmoking inn; full breakfast; gardens; cable TV; air-conditioning; children welcome; no pets.
Directions: On Main Street (Route 27), just west of the village.

clever artwork and extravagant floral displays in the common rooms. There's a welcoming fireplace in the living room, with French doors leading to several brick terraces and expansive gardens beyond. The decor in the four guest rooms and two suites is restrained and sophisticated, with beige carpeting, handcrafted four-poster beds, antique dressers and tables, and well-designed marble and tile baths that feature unique European fixtures, including mansion-sized showers with a shower head in the middle of the ceiling rather than on the wall. My favorite is Room 7, which has red-striped twill fabric on a Victorian settee and a polished antique chest with brass pulls; a Victorian table holds the TV. Room 6, a suite, is furnished with a spectacular eight-piece antique Biedermeier suite.

The owners also own the popular Loaves and Fishes catering company, so breakfasts are divine. A full breakfast that includes Swedish pancakes with fresh blueberry sauce, ham and eggs, and homemade pastries is included in the price of the room.

Quogue

THE INN AT QUOGUE
Manager: Theresa Fontana.
516-653-6560;
    fax: 516-653-8026
47 & 52 Quogue Street, Quogue.
Price: Moderate–Very Expensive.
Credit Cards: AE, MC, V.
Open: Year-round.
Mailing Address: P.O. Box 521, Quogue, NY 11959.
Special Features: Smoking permitted in guest rooms; 5 landscaped acres; limited wheelchair access; continental breakfast in the summer; pool; a restaurant on the premises; bicycles and beach passes available; children and pets welcome in the "cottages," but not in main houses.

Quogue is called the "quiet Hampton," and it's so quiet that many don't consider it a Hampton at all. It's a jewel of a village, composed mostly of gracious old homes on lovely, wide, tree-lined streets. Ideal for walks and bicycling excursions, the streets are wide and flat; there's a bicycle path along Dune Road to the beach. The main building of The Inn at Quogue dates from the late 1770s, and although the exterior is in need of a paint job, the 70 rooms have been restored to bring out their best qualities. There are many charming touches, with little nooks and crannies throughout. Room 14, for example, has wide-plank pine floors, a fireplace, and a bath with a blue-and-yellow tartan tile floor. Some rooms are lovely; others, especially those that are part of the former Weathervane Inn, are small and somewhat disappointing. The small motel rooms (the staff call these "cottages") are the least desirable. There is a nice pool, and guests may use the Quogue village beach and a nearby tennis club. The inn has an attractive restaurant and an

Directions: From Sunrise Highway (Route 27), travel south at Exit 63 (Route 31) to Montauk Highway (Route 27A), then east to Quogue Street. Turn right on Quogue Street. The inn is on the right in ¹/₂ mile.

inviting bar with a fireplace, where a pianist often performs on the weekends. This inn offers total relaxation in a very quiet, country atmosphere.

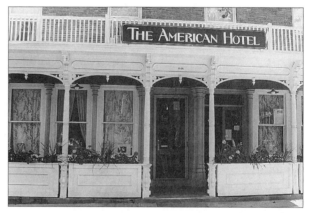

The American Hotel in Sag Harbor has been welcoming guests since 1877.

Morgan McGivern

Sag Harbor

AMERICAN HOTEL
Innkeeper: Ted Conklin.
Manager: Coleen Shannon.
516-725-3535;
   fax: 516-725-3573.
Main Street, Sag Harbor.
Price: Moderate–Expensive.
Credit Cards: AE, CB, D,
   DC, MC, V.
Open: Year-round.
Mailing Address: P.O. Box
   1349, Sag Harbor, NY
   11963.
Special Features: Smoking
   permitted; continental
   breakfast; whirlpools;
   telephones; a fine
   restaurant on the
   premises; no pets.

The American Hotel, that great, early-Victorian brick edifice on Sag Harbor's Main Street, dates back to 1845 when Nathan Tinker, a cabinetmaker, built it to house his cabinet shop. As an adjunct to the shops on the ground floor, he built apartments above. In 1877, the building was converted to a hotel by Addison Youngs and, with the addition of steam heat, baths, and electric lights, it became one of the most modern hotels on Long Island. Owned by Ted Conklin for almost 30 years, this gem of a hotel retains all of the charm of a fine Victorian inn. The tiny parlor has games of backgammon and checkers awaiting players, and the glass-topped reservation counter displays a selection of fine cigars. The restaurant, considered by many to be the best classical restaurant in the Hamptons is tucked among four, main floor rooms. There are eight spacious and highly distinctive guest rooms in the hotel — all have tall ceilings and are decorated with Victorian and art deco antiques that exude a faded men's club gentility. There are overstuffed chairs, massive dressers with ornate mirrors, worn antique Oriental rugs, mahogany sleigh beds, carved Victorian walnut headboards, and brass beds. There's also an antique Victorian table set with cordials, liquors, and crystal glasses, and accent pieces might include an old manual typewriter or radio. All of the baths are private, and each has a tile floor, a Jacuzzi for two, and an impressive array of soaps, shampoos, and lotions.

Called LIGHTHOUSE ON THE BAY

Innkeepers: Regina and
   Stephen Humanitzki.
516-725-7112;
   fax: 516-725-0906.
North Haven (address
   given when reservations
   made).
Website:
   www.southampton.com
   /chamber/lighthouse
   onthebay.
Price: Expensive–Very
   Expensive.
Credit Cards: None.
Open: Year-round.
Special features: Non-
   smoking inn; full
   breakfast; water and
   marsh views; private
   beach reached by
   boardwalk; spacious
   decks; air conditioning;
   robes in rooms;
   complimentary beach
   towels and chairs;
   children over the age of 8
   welcome; no pets.
Directions: Provided when
   reservations made.

If you are seeking a wonderfully romantic night in a magical setting, I can't imagine a better place than Lighthouse on the Bay. The panoramic views are positively breathtaking from the living room, the dining area, and the wraparound decks, as well as from the guest rooms. On one early summer afternoon, I was able to spy on three white herons sitting on their nests in their close-up marshy habitat. The house was built by Regina and Stephen Humanitski in 1997 to resemble a lighthouse (or, more accurately, two lighthouses joined together). "When we bought this property, we had fallen in love with the land and intended renovating a house on the property, but we decided instead to tear it down and start over." The result is a contemporary house sheathed in natural shingles and on a stone foundation, with flagstone floors, walls of floor-to-ceiling windows, and expansive decks. The Tower Suite, on the second floor, is the premier guest haven. This six-sided room has a fabulous view from the bedroom, but the clincher is the observation room reached via a spiral stairway that has a 360-degree water view. There are comfortable sofas up here as well as a TV. The Queen Room, on the first floor, has a pine sleigh bed. My favorite bedroom, however, is the Round Room, which is actually the Humanitskis' own room. It has a round tower of clerestory windows, an expansive view, a private deck (also with a view), and a wonderful tile bath with a Jacuzzi enclosed in a mahogany cabinet and a granite surround. An iron canopy bed is draped in gauzy fabric. Regina, who loves to cook, serves a full breakfast that might include fresh fruit, home-baked muffins or bread, and maybe a cheese soufflé or her special French toast.

SAG HARBOR INN
Manager: Diane Weber.
516-725-2949;
   fax: 516-725-5009.
West Water Street, Sag
   Harbor.
Price: Inexpensive–Very
   Expensive.
Credit Cards: AE, MC, V.
Open: Year-round.
Mailing Address: P.O. Box
   2661, Sag Harbor, NY
   11963.
Special Features:
   Nonsmoking rooms;
   continental breakfast;
   pool; telephones; air-
   conditioning; children
   welcome; no pets.
Directions: From Main
   Street, circle the flagpole
   and bear right onto Long
   Island Ave. Bear right
   onto West Water Street
   just beyond the Post
   Office and continue
   about ¹/₄ mile. The inn is
   on the left.

The Sag Harbor Inn is more like a hotel than an inn, but it's been built and decorated with style. There are 42 units in a two-story building. Most have balconies or patios overlooking the pool or the harbor; those with bay views are especially nice. Each of the rooms is furnished with eighteenth-century, reproduction pine furniture that includes two-poster headboards. A telephone is provided in each room. The continental breakfast of muffins, bagels, juice, cereal, and coffee or tea is served in a light, airy room that has a terrace for summer breakfasts. The hotel is within walking distance of the village, which has excellent restaurants and shops.

Southampton

EVERGREEN ON PINE
Innkeepers: JoAnn and
   Peter Rogoski.
516-283-0564.
89 Pine Street, Southampton,
   NY 11968.
Price: Expensive–Very
   Expensive.
Credit Cards: D, DC, MC, V.
Open: Year-round.
Special Features: Smoking
   outside only; continental
   breakfast; children over
   12 welcome; no pets.
Directions: From Main
   Street, travel east on
   Meeting House Lane.

Were I to come to the Hamptons on business, I would choose to stay at Evergreen On Pine. Not only would I have an attractive room with my own bath, but also I would have my own telephone, complete with a dataport and modem so I could connect my PC. Best of all, I could step right outside my door and walk to the fantastic shops on Main Street and Job's Lane or to a sophisticated restaurant. This glistening white house is entered from the sidewalk through an arched privet hedge. Flowers spill from borders along the walkway leading to the broad porch, which has wicker chairs and tables. Inside this center-hall colonial, there are oak floors and a fireplace in the dining/living area. The five bedrooms, each with its own private bath (two are in hallways), are nicely decorated. One has a brass bed, another has a canopy bed, and a third has a mahogany four-poster bed. In the sunny yellow room that's decorated with Laura Ashley fabric, the

Evergreen On Pine in Southampton is filled with lovely antiques. Breakfast is served in this elegant dining room.

Morgan McGivern

furniture is wicker. Elegant, white metal furniture with umbrellas are placed on a brick side terrace, a sought after spot for breakfast and for afternoon relaxation.

FIELDS OF DREAMS
Innkeeper: Monika
  Heitmeyer.
516-283-4691.
276 Majors Path,
  Southampton.
Price: Expensive.
Credit Cards: None.
Open: Mid-Apr.-Oct.
Mailing Address: P.O. Box
  2481, Southampton, NY
  11969.
Special Features: Full
  breakfast; pool; air-
  conditioning; portable
  telephones available;
  children 12 and older
  welcome; no pets.
Directions: From County
  Road 39, turn north onto
  North Sea Road, then
  immediately take the
  right fork onto Majors
  Path. In 1 ¹/₂ miles, see
  sign in a long private
  driveway on the right.

Although Fields of Dreams is a newly constructed house, there's nothing contemporary about it. This is a traditional, gray-shingled estate house with elegant finishes, polished wood floors, and exquisite French country furnishings. Set on four acres and surrounded by horse farms and orchards, the view across the fields to the gardens is spectacular. The gardens are enchanting: there's an all white garden and fields of wildflowers as far as you can see, and the pool is in such a natural setting as to give it the appearance of a pond. Monika Heitmeyer is a vivacious, gracious hostess, who will make you feel as if you're staying with a friend. As she says, she wants to create "a spirit of a small family atmosphere." Her lovely old dolls in their antique buggy will greet you as you climb the stairs. The five guest rooms are very large, with fine antiques. The largest room has an iron and brass bed, a fireplace, a painted leather screen, and an armoire. In another room, a collection of antique coffee pots is on display, and there's a private herbal garden for afternoon book reading. French doors in all of the guest rooms lead to broad decks; spectacular European baths have footed tubs, pedestal sinks, hardwood floors, and needlepoint rugs. You'll find antique linens on the beds and feast upon a gourmet breakfast that you'll not forget.

THE IVY
Innkeepers: Melody Kniley and Phil Tierney.
516-283-3233;
fax: 516-283-3793.
244 North Main Street, Southampton, NY 11968.
Price: Expensive–Very Expensive.
Credit Cards: AE, MC, V.
Open: Year-round.
Special Features: On almost an acre; pool; gardens; full breakfast; smoking outside only; children over 12 welcome; no pets.
Directions: From County Road 59, turn right at the traffic light onto North Main Street. The B&B is the seventh house on the left.

The Ivy has a wonderfully romantic story to tell. Thirty years ago Melody Kniley was dating Phil Tierney when he was sent to Vietnam, and his letters were still neatly bundled in a box when they were re-acquainted at their 30th high school reunion. Although he had just moved to Arizona and Melody lived in New York, neither of them wanted to be a GU (geographically undesirable) to one another. So, Melody gave up her career in the fashion industry, and Phil sold his home in Arizona. They bought a pretty shingled house on a street not far from Southampton's train station and wove their lives together. As Melody said, "We often sit out on the terrace [which is covered by a latticed arbor trailing wisteria and clematis] with a cup of coffee in the morning, admiring the flowers and trees in the garden, and laugh out loud at how lucky we are." But so are guests at this very special B&B. You will enter a spacious brick-floored living room with butter yellow barnwood walls and white trim. A pretty fireplace is flanked by sofas dressed with yellow floral Ralph Lauren fabric. There's a huge pine breakfront in the living room and another in the dining room, which has raspberry red walls. The five guest rooms, which all have private baths, are charming. Room 3 has yellow walls, a four-poster rice bed, and a terrific new tiled bath with a skylight. In Room 2, which has a cathedral ceiling, black and white toile fabric is combined with a dramatic striped fabric on the polished steel canopy bed, and the tiled bath has exposed beams. The gardens and lawn are spacious and very private, and in a raised secluded spot there's a pool with a brick apron hidden behind a lattice-work fence, reached by climbing several grass-clad stone stairs.

MAINSTAY INN
Innkeeper: Elizabeth Main.
516-283-4375 or 516-287-6230; fax: 516-287-6240.
579 Hill Street, Southampton, NY 11968.
Price: Moderate–Very Expensive.
Credit Cards: MC, V.
Open: Year-round.

Elizabeth Main is always doing something new and wonderful to her inn. This 1870s colonial had good "bones" to begin with, with a weathered shingle exterior and white trim. The building began life as a country store. On the front porch, white wicker chairs embellished with floral print cushions lend a hint of the antiques found inside. The whimsy of the decor is evident as you enter the

Special Features: Smoking outside only; continental breakfast; pool; gardens; behaved children welcome; no pets.
Directions: Located about 1 mile west of Southampton Village on Route 27A, which is the Old Montauk Highway, and then Hill Street.

foyer, which is sponge-painted in a spring green. The adjacent parlor has dried flowers over the door, a bead-board ceiling, and a fireplace. In the kitchen, which is open to guests, a marvelous mural of English climbing roses covers a wall, while in the country dining room, there are sponge-painted ochre walls fancifully painted with grapes, apples, and pears. This room also has wainscoted walls and a great, old woodstove. A country pine cupboard displays a collection of colorful pottery made by Elizabeth that is used for the breakfast meal. Each of the guest rooms is furnished with either an iron or a country pine bed, and all are for sale. Of the eight rooms, five have private baths and three share a bath. Room 5 has a fireplace and a wall of books, while Room 6 has painted hydrangeas climbing the walls in such profusion that the iron and brass bed seems to be in a garden. Room 8 is the newest room; it is a two-room suite and has a bath with wainscoted walls and a slanted ceiling. In the gardens, iron and wicker furniture provide additional retreats for private breakfasts or afternoon refreshments. There's a secluded pool in the back.

In the heart of Southampton, next door to Saks Fifth Avenue, parts of the 1708 House date to 1648.

Morgan McGivern

1708 HOUSE
Innkeepers: Skip and Lorraine Ralph.
Managers: Peter Rever and Bernadette Meade.
516-287-1708;
fax: 516-287-3583.
126 Main Street, Southampton, NY 11968.
Price: Very Expensive.
Credit Cards: AE, MC, V.

I love to see an old building brought back to life. Skeptics had advocated tearing the old house down, but fortunately, Skip and Lorraine Ralph had a better idea. They transformed it into Southampton's finest bed-and-breakfast. From top to bottom, this inn shines. The house dates to 1648, one of the oldest in Southampton, and remarkably, has only been in three families during that time. In the parlor, there are polished pine floors, exposed

Open: Year-round.
Special Features: Smoking outside only; wine cellar; on 1 acre; continental breakfast; children over 12 welcome in main house, those under 12 in cottages only; no pets.
Directions: On Main Street, just beyond Saks Fifth Avenue.

hand-hewn oak beams, and a wood-manteled fireplace. The elegant antique tables and chairs were supplied from the couple's antique shop around the corner and are for sale. An adjoining parlor, with tables that are used for card games in the evening and for breakfast in the morning, has a fireplace and the original paneled walls. Downstairs, there's a brick room where wine and cheese are served as classical music plays in the background. Each of the nine guest rooms and three cottages is spacious and luxurious. The South Wing is on two levels and has a huge private deck. Suite 2 has fabulous antique beds, an armoire, bead-board walls, and a pine floor. There are two two-bedroom cottages, each with an eat-in kitchen; and there's a cabana cottage in the back. Gracious flower gardens surround spacious lawns. For breakfast, guests enjoy fresh fruit, juice, croissants, bagels, and perhaps a quiche.

Westhampton Beach

WESTHAMPTON COUNTRY MANOR
Innkeeper: Susan and Bill Dalton.
516-288-9000;
    fax: 516-288-3292.
Website:
    www.hamptonsbb.com;
E-mail: innkeepers@ hamptonsbb.com.
28 Jagger Lane,
    Westhampton, NY 11977.
Price: Moderate–Very Expensive.
Credit Cards: AE, MC, V.
Open: Year-round.
Special Features: Smoking outside only; on 2 ¹/₂ acres; full breakfast; afternoon cordials; pool; business amenities; children over 14 welcome; no pets.
Directions: Located between Westhampton Beach and Remsenburg. From Montauk Highway (Route 27A), travel south

When Bill and Susan Dalton decided to "retire," they began their search for an ideal bed-and-breakfast. They found a beauty in this historic 1865 house. Originally a stagecoach stop, then a doctor's home and office, and eventually a boardinghouse, today the old house serves a much more sophisticated clientele. There are feather beds, individual telephone numbers, and answering machines. There's just about any amenity a business traveler might want, including a PC, a fax machine, a modem, on-line hookups, a printer, a copier, and a desk. The location is as quiet as country can get and well off the beaten track. This buff-colored colonial with front dormers sits on two and one-half acres that include a cottage near the road and a picturesque green barn. A swimming pool is surrounded by a picket fence, and a Har-tru tennis court is nearby. The house itself is spacious and welcoming; there is a generous living room with a handsome fireplace and a concert grand piano. Cordials and stemmed crystal glasses sit on a silver tray, waiting for guests to imbibe. To the side, a screened-in porch, filled with wicker furniture and on Tanners Neck Road to South Country Road. Turn right. The inn is on the corner of South Country Road and Jagger Lane. an abundance of plants, beckons guests in the summer. The dining room, with its stained glass lamp and huge round table, is where the gourmet breakfast is served. This meal starts with freshly baked scones, muffins, or cinnamon rolls and a fruit plate, followed by baked French toast or perhaps shirred eggs. Beside the dining room, a comfortable and homey room has been set aside for TV watching and games. There are five guest rooms, and all have private baths. My favorite is Room 4, which has an antique iron bed and a brand new tiled bath. Room 1 has a spool bed, while Room 2 has an antique iron and brass bed. All the baths have been renovated and have black and white tiles, white wall tiles, and pedestal sinks.

CABINS & MOTELS

There are so many cabins, motels, and resorts in the Hamptons that it was impossible to describe them all. The codes, following the accepted credit cards for each listing, indicate whether it is a bed-and-breakfast (B), a series of cabins (C), a motel (M), or a full-service resort (R).

EAST HAMPTON TOWN

Amagansett

White Sands Motel On The Ocean (516-267-3350) 28 Shore Road, Amagansett. Mailing Address: P.O. Box 747, Amagansett, NY 11930. Owners: Bernhard Kiembock and Sara Menboza. Price: Moderate–Very Expensive. Open: Mid-Apr.–mid-Oct. 20 units; on the ocean; private location; spotlessly maintained; outdoor grill area; family operated; children welcome; no pets; *highly recommended;* MC, V; (M).

Montauk

Lenhart Cottages (516-668-2356) 421 Old Montauk Highway, Montauk, NY 11954. Manager: Charles Pilch. Price: Moderate–Very Expensive. Open: Year-round. 12 individual cottages, ranging from studios to two-bedrooms; shingled exterior; ocean view; log-burning fireplaces; kitchens; pool; cable TV; air-conditioning; *highly recommended;* MC, V; (C).

Snug Harbor Motel and Marina (516-668-2860; fax: 516-668-9068) 156 West Lake Drive, Montauk, NY 11954. Manager: Cynthia Brauch. Price: Inexpensive– Expensive. Open: Mar.–Thanksgiving. 34 units, ranging from studios to one-bedroom apartments; on the lake; some kitchens; pool; marina; playground; bicycles; outdoor grill area; waterskiing; telephones; cable TV; air-conditioning; AE, MC, V; (M).

Wainscott

Cozy Cabins (516-537-1160) Montauk Highway, Wainscott, NY 11975. Mailing Address: P.O. Box 848, Wainscott, NY 11975. Owner: Dennis Lazicki. Price: Inexpensive–Moderate. Open: Mid-Apr.–mid-Nov. 22 cabins, ranging from studios to one-bedroom units; some fireplaces; kitchens; hot tub; shuffleboard; outdoor grill; *excellent value;* MC, V; (C).

SOUTHAMPTON TOWN

Hampton Bays

Bowen's By The Bays (516-728-1158) 177 West Montauk Highway, Hampton Bays, NY 11946. Owners/Managers: Kevin and Eileen Bowen. Price: Inexpensive–Moderate. Open: Apr.–Oct. 16 units (eight motel rooms; cottages with one or two bedrooms); on three and a half acres; pool; lighted tennis court; playground; kitchens; cable TV; air-conditioning; shuffleboard. AE, D, MC, V; (M) (C).

The Hampton Maid (516-728-4166) 295 Montauk Highway, Hampton Bays, NY 11946. Manager: Marion and John Poulakis. Price: Inexpensive–Moderate. Open: May–Oct. 30 units; pool; antique shop; cable TV; air-conditioning; telephones; restaurant (breakfast only); AE, MC, V; (M).

Westhampton Beach

The Bath & Tennis Hotel (516-288-2500; fax: 516-288-2558) 231 Dune Road, Westhampton Beach, NY 11978. Manager: Dan Rutan. Price: Expensive–Very Expensive. Open: May–October. 101 units; marina; salt-water swimming pool; four tennis courts; exercise room; ladies' and men's solariums; air conditioning; shopping arcade; restaurants; lounge. Credit cards AE, MC, V; (R).

CHAPTER FOUR
From the Bounty of the Land
RESTAURANTS & FOOD PURVEYORS

When the renowned Manhattan restaurateur, Henri Soulé, opened his summer restaurant in the village of East Hampton in 1954, he launched a trend. Lured by the abundance of farm fresh vegetables and fruit, fish from local waters, and duck from nearby duck farms, he created a respect and appreciation for local cuisine that has increased every year. Not only did he attract gourmet diners who couldn't abide a summer away from the elegant cuisine that he had made famous at Le Pavillion, but he also attracted other fine chefs to the Hamptons. Pierre Franey, his executive chef in New York, came to the Hamptons. Craig Claiborne, food editor for the *New York Times,* and chef and author Michael Field soon came as well. Soulé had struck a nerve. Where fish houses on the docks had once prevailed, appreciation for the finer nuances of food preparation was gaining ground.

Morgan McGivern

Fresh produce, freshly baked breads, entrées, desserts, and friendly service are among the specialties at the Barefoot Contessa in East Hampton.

Today, Henri Soulé would be proud of Hamptons' chefs and the food that they are serving. It's inventive, well presented, and, in general, prepared in healthful ways. Butter and cream-based sauces have been replaced by those made of vegetable reductions. Fresh local seafood and produce, the pride of the Hamptons, are used cleverly and well.

Henri Soulé's original restaurant is now The Hedges Inn. The James Lane Café, located on its main floor, as well as on a covered patio, is still noted for its cuisine. The Maidstone Arms, located down the street from the James Lane

Café is also still recognized for its outstanding cuisine. In addition, a remnant from the old East End whaling days, the venerable 1846 American Hotel in Sag Harbor is recognized nationally for its food and wine list.

In style, Italian restaurants seem to be the vogue of the day with French restaurants coming in a distant second. Naturally, fine seafood restaurants are also in abundance, and American cuisine, served in bistro settings, is also popular. Fish houses on the docks of Montauk allow diners to watch as the catch of the day is transferred from boat to dock to table, and the spectacular sunsets from East Hampton Point are renowned. The decor of choice, however, seems to be a blend of Santa Fe, California, and Italy, with spare furnishings, tile floors, and whitewashed walls that blend together to create a distinctive Hamptons' chic.

This chapter is not intended to be a critical review of all of the restaurants in the Hamptons. If a restaurant does not meet the criteria that would allow its recommendation, it has not been included. Furthermore, there are so many fine restaurants in the Hamptons today that space precludes including every single one. Instead, I have included those that I believe are the very best. For most of the restaurants listed here, I have highlighted their signature dishes.

In preparing these listings, the overall comfort level and inviting appeal of a restaurant were important factors; these include the service and attitude of the staff and the excellence of the food and the decor. Especially in the better restaurants, it is imperative that the staff know which ingredients are used in a dish and understand its preparation. Recognizing the importance of wine to the East End, it is also important to have staff who can make specific wine recommendations and who appreciate the pairing of wines with specific appetizers and entrées. On the other hand, a concerted effort has been made to include the best cafés and budget-priced restaurants, where this level of knowledge is not expected. It has been my intention to profile the restaurants that offer the best dining experiences in the Hamptons in a broad range of price categories.

As much information as possible about each restaurant has been included. Rather than indicating the exact hours that each restaurant is open, I have specified the meals that are served. In the block of information included with each description, abbreviations are used for any accepted credit cards. In addition, price codes, rather than specific prices, are indicated. These codes are based on the average cost of a meal for one person, including appetizer, entrée, and dessert, but not cocktails, wine, tax, or tip. Many Hamptons' restaurants offer prix fixe menus at exceptionally low prices off-season. This is a great way to eat out without breaking the bank. Be aware that days and hours of operation change with the season. It's always best to call ahead.

The listings have been divided into East Hampton Town and Southampton Town, then they are further broken down by individual village or hamlet. If you are not sure in which town a village or hamlet is located, a chart is provided below. Restaurants on the North Fork and on Shelter Island are included in those specific chapters.

Serving Codes

B	Breakfast	HT	High Tea
BR	Brunch	D	Dinner
L	Lunch	LN	Late Night

Credit Cards

AE	American Express	DC	Diner's Club
CB	Carte Blanche	MC	Master Card
D	Discover	V	Visa

Price Codes

Inexpensive	Up to $25	Expensive	$35 to $50
Moderate	$25 to $35	Very Expensive	$50 or more

Towns, Villages, and Hamlets

Town	**Villages and Hamlets**
East Hampton Town	Amagansett, East Hampton Village, Wainscott
Southampton Town	Bridgehampton, East Quogue, Hampton Bays, Sag Harbor, Sagaponack, Southampton Village, Water Mill, Westhampton Beach

RESTAURANTS

Strange to see how a good dinner and feasting reconciles everybody.

Samuel Pepys, *Diary, November 9,* 1660

EAST HAMPTON TOWN

Amagansett

ESTIA
516-267-6320.
177 Main Street,
   Amagansett.
Cuisine: American.
Serving: B, L, D.
Open: Daily year-round for

Alec Baldwin says this down-home, all-American place is his favorite restaurant. The rest of us also love its straightforward, honest food. For breakfast, there are lots of omelettes prepared as you like them and "tortilla starts," such as a breakfast burrito or a white vegetable quesadilla. Naturally, you can also

breakfast and lunch; dinner daily Jun.–Aug., Thurs.–Sun. from Sept.–May.
Owner/Chef: Colin Ambrose.
Price: Inexpensive–Moderate; prix fixe offered.
Credit Cards: None.

get bagels, muffins, or freshly made oatmeal. For lunch, sandwiches include burgers and clubs, grilled cheese, tuna melts, and Reubens, as well as great pastas and salads. Dinner features owner/chef Colin Ambrose's appetizers of Turtle Rolls (it's a secret) or shredded chicken quesadilla, as well as fresh, homemade pasta dishes that include a long-time favorite called Sophia's Choice (a Mediterranean-style dish with tomato sauce, olives, and feta). You can also get a terrific Estia Burger that comes with Yukon gold fries and a variety of cheese choices. The wine list includes about 30 selections. The ambiance is that of a 1950s American diner with booths upholstered in watermelon-colored vinyl, pine tables, knotty pine walls, paper place mats, and stools at the long counter. It's a favorite with families at lunchtime for the special children's menu that includes a peanut butter and jelly sandwich for $1.50, hot dog and fries for $2.00, and a grilled cheese and apple slices sandwich for $2.50.

Morgan McGivern

George Polychronopoulos has been creating some of the Hampton's finest cuisine for 25 years.

GORDON'S
516-267-3010.
Main Street, Amagansett.
Cuisine: Continental.

Gordon's is one of the most personal, hands-on restaurants in the Hamptons. Locals, who have been coming here for years, know it's one of the best, but it's not on the trendsetter's prowl. It's

Serving: L, D.
Open: Dinner daily, except
Mon., Mar.–Dec.;
Thurs.–Sat. only in Jan.;
closed Feb.; Lunch daily,
except Mon., Sept.–Dec.;
Thurs.–Sat. in Jan.; daily
Mar.–Jun. (closed for
lunch in Jul., Aug.).
Owner: George
Polychronopoulos .
Chef: George
Polychronopoulos.
Price: Expensive–Very
Expensive, prix fixe
offered.
Credit Cards: AE, DC, MC,
V.
Special Features:
Wheelchair accessible.

the creation and passion of owner/chef George Polychronopoulos who has been doing what he does so well for more than 20 years. Listen to the nightly specials and follow the advice of the knowledgeable waiters, who still wear tuxedos, just as they did in the 1960s. Fishermen, baymen, and farmers deliver their best to the kitchen door everyday. One night in the early fall, we had a dish of Peconic bay scallops that were absolutely ambrosial — fresh, tender, and lightly broiled with butter and lemon. That's the key to George's success. He understands and appreciates the ingredients that he uses and doesn't try to alter them with elaborate sauces or seasonings. George's wine list is one of the largest and most impressive in the Hamptons. He has more than 300 selections and an 4,000+ bottle cellar. It includes local wines, as well as rare imported vintages, and they're surprisingly well priced. As George said, "We're not trendy. I just want to prepare good food that people will enjoy."

THE LOBSTER ROLL RESTAURANT

516-267-3740.
1980 Montauk Highway,
Amagansett.
Cuisine: Seafood.
Serving: L, D.
Open: Daily Jun.–mid-
Sept.; weekends in May
and from mid-
Sept.–mid-Oct.; closed
the rest of the year.
Owners/Managers: Paul
DeAngelis, Andrea and
Fred Terry.
Price: Inexpensive–
Expensive.
Credit Cards: MC, V.
Special Features:
Wheelchair accessible;
outdoor dining.
Directions: Located on
Route 27, about 4 miles
east of Amagansett
village.

Everyone knows it as "Lunch" because of its huge, red neon sign on the roof. Don't be fooled, they also serve dinner. There are no pretensions here. It's a roadside fish shack, with paper place mats on picnic tables, butter in foil, and good, fresh fish at realistic prices; most of the fish is caught locally. Fish and chips and the tender, juicy puffers (blowfish) are prepared in a finger lickin' good tempura batter, and the creamy tartar sauce is so good, we wish it was served in larger cups. A specialty of the house is, of course, the lobster roll, but there's a lot more on the menu, too, including seafood platters, fresh flounder in season, and tuna burgers. The wine and beer list is limited. Desserts include carrot cake, studded with nuts and raisins and topped with a cream cheese frosting, and pies made by Briermere Farms in Riverhead. The raspberry pie in season, heated and served with cinnamon ice cream, is delicious, but all of the pies are recommended.

PACIFIC EAST
516-267-7770.
415 Main Street,
Amagansett.
Cuisine: Asian Seafood.
Serving: D.
Open: May–Sept. nightly.
Owners: Alexander Duff
and Michael Castino.
Chefs: Michael Castino and
Christian Plotczyk.
Manager: Eric Lemoniades.
Price: Expensive–Very
Expensive; prix fixe
offered.
Credit Cards: AE, MC, V.
Special Features: Brick court-
yard, wheelchair access.
Directions: From the center
of Amagansett, proceed
east on Montauk
Highway. The restaurant
will be on the left in
about ¹/₂ mile.

Michael Castino has been fascinated with Asian cuisine since he was a child, so it's not surprising that Pacific East, which opened in Amagansett in 1998, should fuse Asian and American cuisine in a new and trendy way. You might start a meal in the crisp white rooms with a lobster and shiitake pancake in champagne kim-chi cream or a cool shrimp spring roll with gingered cucumber, Thai basil, peppermint, and yamabuki miso. Fish is king here, so although you could order chicken, pork chops, or roast duck, you will be delighted with several of the seafood entrées. You might try a whole ginger-stuffed yellowtail snapper tempura with green curry, rice noodles, and sizzling Hong Kong dipping sauce, for example, or a Saigon grilled mahi mahi with butternut squash and Vietnamese red pepper sauce. There's a spacious bar at the entrance and a brick courtyard facing the street. Snowy white linen tablecloths are set with cobalt blue vases holding an orchid stem or a sprig of flowers. All in all, this is a terrific new addition to the Hamptons restaurant scene.

East Hampton

**BLUE PARROT BAR &
GRILL**
516-324-3609.
33A Main Street, East
Hampton.
Cuisine: Southern
California/Mexican.
Serving: L, D.
Open: Apr.–Dec. daily in
the summer; fewer days
the rest of the year.
Owners: Lee Bieler and
Roland Eisenberg.
Manager: Roland
Eisenberg.
Chef: Kevin Henry.
Price: Inexpensive–
Moderate.
Credit Cards: AE, MC, V.
Special Features: Smoking
on the patio only; limited
wheelchair access;
covered patio.

Tucked away in a little courtyard between Main Street and the Park Place parking lot, this little bar/restaurant serves up hefty margaritas that are so potent, you may begin talking to the stuffed parrot. The decor is funky and original and very casual — the perfect place to go before a movie. The floor is painted blue, and antlers and old movie posters hang on the walls. There are colorful serapes at the windows, and strings of lighted chili peppers hang from the tiled bar. They modestly claim, "This is the best Mexican food this side of Baja." The nachos grande are enormous with plenty of cheese, black beans, sour cream, guacamole, salsa, and jalapeño peppers. The grilled chicken fajitas are served with warm flour tortillas, and the enchiladas, quesadillas, and burritos are excellent, too. For those not in the mood for Mexican, there are burgers, swordfish, and chicken. There are two interesting dishes: a Mexican lasagna that uses tortillas in place of pasta and a paella served with warm flour tortillas. The low-fat swordfish has been rubbed with a fruity chili paste before it is grilled. Desserts include a homemade flan and a real key lime pie. There's also a late-night (after 11 p.m.) menu that features South of the Border Tortilla wrap sandwiches and Southwestern sushi (Honest!!).

Max Weintraub, owner and chef of Cafe Max stands outside his restaurant.

Laurin Copen

CAFE MAX
516-324-2004.
85 Montauk Highway,
  East Hampton.
Cuisine: American/
  Continental.
Serving: D year-round; BR
  Sun., off-season only.
Open: Dinner daily except
  Tues., Jul.–Nov; daily
  except Mon. & Tues.
  Apr.–Jun. and Dec.–Feb.;
  brunch served Sun.
  except Jun.–Sept.;
  restaurant closed Mar.
Owners/Managers: Max
  and Nancy Weintraub.
Chef: Max Weintraub.
Price: Moderate–Expensive,
  prix fixe offered.
Credit Cards: MC, V.
Special Features: Limited
  wheelchair access;
  award-winning wine list.
Directions: On Route 27, at
  Cove Hollow Road.

Max Weinbraub was the chef at The Maidstone Arms for a number of years, but when the inn changed hands in 1991, he opened his own restaurant. Outside, it's a rather nondescript, gray building. Inside, however, it's warm and inviting. There are rough-sawn cedar walls, a cathedral ceiling, natural oak floors, and paisley drapes that give the space a country feeling. Old photographs of Nancy's family line the walls of the bar. We love the food at Cafe Max. The crab cake appetizers are light and fluffy, and a selection of pastas is always available both as appetizers and as entrées. My favorite entrées are the salmon fillet, glazed with honey and roasted, then served on spinach with mushrooms and the tomato and perfectly roasted free-range chicken, seasoned with rosemary and herbs. The wine list contains 80 selections; the list won awards in both 1995 and 1997. Although most of the wines are from California, there are several Long Island choices. At least seven wines are available by the glass every night. For dessert, don't miss the angel food cake, which is sliced into layers that are soaked in Grand Marnier and then reassembled into a cake — the layers alternating with white chocolate mousse. What a finale!

DELLA FEMINA
516-329-6666;
fax: 516-329-3547.
99 North Main Street, East
  Hampton.
Cuisine: Local East
  Hampton.
Serving: D.
Open: Daily in the summer;
  Wed.(or Thurs.)–Sun. the
  rest of the year.
Manager: Carol Covell.
Chef: Kevin Penner.
Price: Expensive–Very
  Expensive, prix fixe
  offered.
Credit Cards: AE, MC, V.
Special Features:
  Wheelchair accessible;
  fireplace.
Directions: From Main
  Street, continue past the
  traffic light and turn left
  at the fork before the
  windmill. Drive past the
  windmill (it will be on
  the right) and under the
  railroad trestle. The

When Jerry Della Femina opened this restaurant in 1991, it was an immediate hit. Unlike East Hampton Point, which he also owns, Della Femina provides a private, but still celebratory atmosphere. This restaurant works well. A profusion of colorful flowers spill from the window boxes in the summer. The bar is light and airy, and it's fun to join the game of seeing how many of the caricatures of local luminaries that you can identify. There's abundant space between tables in the quiet, elegant dining room, which is decorated mostly in subdued, earthy beiges and whites. The food is first-class. Fresh hot rolls from Zabar's in Manhattan are crisp on the outside and chewy on the inside; they're served with a chickpea spread, white fava beans, and garlic. One night, for an appetizer, we had a grilled Hudson River Valley foie gras with a banana pancake, caramelized pineapple, and a pineapple-rum glaze. It was excellent. Pan-roasted salmon fillet comes on a bed of wilted spinach with caramelized onions on top — rare and creamy on the inside, and properly crisp on the outside. The pan-roasted Indiana Amish "natural" chicken is served with a wild mushroom, potato and leek "egg roll," haricots verts, pearl onions, and truffle sauce. The wine list is extensive. Definitely save room for the decadent, warm Valrhona chocolate cake, an unmolded ramekin of chocolate with a mound of chocolate-hazelnut ice cream and three chocolate sauces on the side. The desserts, just as the entrées, are not served, but presented. In this case, the cake is dusted with confectioners' sugar, and the plate is decorated with the sauces. It's worth every calorie. Bravo to Kevin Penner!

EAST HAMPTON POINT
516-329-2800.
295 Three Mile Harbor
  Road, East Hampton.
Cuisine: American.
Serving: BR (Sun. only), L,
  D.
Open: Apr.–Sept.; July–
  Labor Day daily lunch
  and dinner, brunch Sun.;
  fewer days the rest of the
  year.
Chef: Gerry Hayden.

Were someone unfortunate enough to have time for only one dinner out while in the Hamptons, I would recommend East Hampton Point. The food and service are excellent, and the sunset view is stunning. Brilliant pink, orange, and red streak across the sky and reflect in the calm waters of Three Mile Harbor, where the slap of sailboat rigging against masts provides soothing background music. Happy memories invariably result. The tiered dining room provides a watery view from every seat by the use of cleverly placed mir-

Suzi Forbes Chase

The outside deck at East Hampton Point is a popular spot for afternoon lunch.

Price: Expensive–Very
  Expensive, prix fixe
  offered.
Credit Cards: AE, MC, V.
Special Features: Smoking
  on the outside deck and
  in the bar only;
  wheelchair accessible;
  waterfront views; outside
  dining.
Directions: From Main
  Street, turn left just
  before the Hook
  Windmill onto North
  Main Street. After two
  street lights, the road will
  fork. Take the left fork
  onto Three Mile Harbor
  Road. The restaurant is
  on the left in about 4
  miles.

rors, and the crisp, marine blue-and-white decor is so subtle that it offers no distractions. For dinner, I love to start with the salmon and crabmeat cakes, which are served with Armagnac remoulade. They're rich, but so light that you don't feel guilty. The entrées are straightforward and expertly prepared. Juicy chicken is served with a Vidalia onion crust and served with roasted garlic mashed potatoes and a lemon-rosemary sauce. You can't go wrong with one of the fish dishes either. Desserts include banana ice-cream profiteroles with chocolate and caramel sauces and a chocolate brownie ice-cream sandwich with chocolate sauce and marinated dried cherries. Sailors arrive in their yachts from nearby estates with their weekend guests in tow for the generous buffet brunch on Sundays. Even the bar has a special attraction; a polished mahogany 5.5 liter sloop is suspended from the ceiling that divides the bar from the restaurant. A portion of the deck is dedicated to casual dining and cocktails; a lighter menu is available.

THE FARMHOUSE
516-324-8585.
341 Montauk Highway,
  East Hampton.
Cuisine: American bistro.
Serving: D.
Open: Daily year-round.
Owner: Fred and Susan
  Lieberman.

This is one of the most famous (or infamous) drinking and eating establishments on the East End. It boasts the oldest bar (c. 1926–après Prohibition) in the Hamptons, and at one time it was the place to be seen. On one sad night in 1956, this is where Jackson Pollock had been drinking just before he raced to his death on the road to his

Morgan McGivern

The farmhouse burst on the dining scene in 1996. There are six distinctive dining rooms and a pretty garden in back.

Chef: Raymond Higgins.
Manager: Michael
  Gluchman.
Price: Moderate–Very
  Expensive; prix fixe
  offered.
Credit Cards: AE, MC, V.
Special Features: Outdoor
  dining; fireplaces;
  wheelchair accessible.
Directions: From the center
  of East Hampton, travel
  east on Montauk
  Highway for one mile.
  The restaurant will be on
  the left.

home in Springs. (Beware of the Pollock-sized 8 oz. martinis served today.) Just like a cat with seven lives, this drinking hole has been through a number of deaths and rebirths of its own. We remember it fondly as Springs Close and less fondly as several others. Now, it appears there's a winning team in charge who have dedicated themselves to creating a fine restaurant. For one thing, the seven dining rooms have been decorated in a subdued Ralph Lauren style. They have wide-plank pine floors (original), beige burlap (Ralph Lauren fabric) cafe curtains on the windows and bunches of dried flowers hanging on the walls and from the hand-hewn exposed beams. There are fireplaces in several dining rooms and Mason jars hold fresh flowers in one. A pretty floral Ralph Lauren fabric covers the banquettes in another. Two flagstone-floored garden rooms are wonderful summer venues. The cuisine is first-rate. A summer seafood salad holds shrimp, scallops, conch, octopus, mussels, and calamari. Entrées include horseradish-crusted salmon with beet risotto and chive butter sauce and the grilled bistro steak comes with Farmhouse pommes frittes and bordelaise sauce. For dessert, try the flourless chocolate cake fondant with white chocolate bavarian cream and raspberry purée.

THE GRILL
516-324-6300.
29 Newtown Lane (off
    Main Street), East
    Hampton.
Cuisine: American.
Serving: L, D, LN (in the
    summer).
Open: Year-round.
Manager: Paul Campanella.
Price: Inexpensive–
    Expensive.
Credit Cards: AE, MC, V.
Special Features:
    Wheelchair accessible;
    patio dining.

Reliable and trustworthy, The Grill is East Hampton's upscale pub. Lots of dark wood, ceiling fans, and brass prevail. Although it can be noisy, I like the tables beside the sidewalk for people gazing (the French doors are wide open in the summer) and the high-backed booths in back for their intimacy and their collection of Americana art (wooden flags, etc.) on the walls. The typical pub fare of sandwiches and burgers (excellent!) is supplemented by salads and grilled tortilla pizzas. For a more serious dinner, the restaurant offers comfort food, such as chicken pot pie, ribeye steak with port wine sauce, and grilled tuna steak with lemon caper butter.

Morgan McGivern

The James Lane Cafe carries on a proud legacy. This was where famed chef and restaurateur Henri Soulé had his restaurant in the 1950s.

**JAMES LANE CAFE at
    THE HEDGES INN**
516-324-7100.
74 James Lane, East
    Hampton.
Cuisine: Continental/
    Mediterranean.
Serving: D.
Open: May–Sept.
Chef: Gregory Todd.
Price: Moderate–Very
    Expensive.

The James Lane Cafe at The Hedges Inn has one of the most attractive dining rooms in the Hamptons. There are polished pine floors, a fireplace, and French doors leading to an enclosed flagstone-floored garden room. This is definitely the preferred place to eat on balmy summer evenings when the perfume from the flowers, spilling from the planters and the sounds of chirping birds through the open windows heighten the

Credit Cards: AE, MC, V.
Special Features:
Wheelchair accessible;
patio dining.
Directions: At the traffic
light on Route 27, just
before turning left
toward the village, the
inn is straight ahead.

sense of romance. Although under the same management as The Palm restaurant at The Huntting Inn, the cuisine here is more delicate and refined than the heavy steaks for which its sister property is known. Chef Gregory Todd has revamped the kitchen and the menu. You might have plank-roasted salmon crusted with horseradish, or a grilled veal chop that's been marinated in garlic and fresh rosemary. There's a moderate-sized, reasonably priced wine list. The desserts are good, but not adventurous and include crème brûlée, tiramisu, and mascarpone cheesecake in a chocolate-walnut graham cracker crust.

THE LAUNDRY
516-324-3199.
31 Race Lane, East
Hampton.
Cuisine: American/
Mediterranean.
Serving: D.
Open: Daily year-round.
Manager: Robert
Fairbrother.
Chef: Rob Rawleigh.
Price: Moderate-Very
Expensive.
Credit Cards: AE, CB, DC,
MC, V.
Special Features:
Wheelchair accessible;
fireplace; award-winning
wine list; reservations
not accepted.
Directions: From Main
Street, turn onto
Newtown Lane and then
turn left onto Railroad
Avenue and left again at
the light onto Race Lane,
just past the train station.
The restaurant is on the
right in the middle of the
block.

This casual, comfortable, jeans-OK place just keeps on serving good food. As one waiter said, "Some places you put down the dish and run before they throw it at you. Here, you wait to hear the raves." The building was once the East Hampton Steam Laundry, and the extractor still sits in the courtyard next to the bocci court. A gorgeous bouquet of fresh flowers on the bar sets the mood. The walls are brick and rough-sawn cedar. There are vaulted ceilings and a free-standing brick fireplace in a sunken conversation pit with black vinyl banquettes. Red vinyl banquettes line the walls, and red-painted bentwood chairs provide the rest of the seating. A hip, older crowd has made this their own; celebrities gravitate to the raised portion behind the fireplace wall where they can dine without being noticed; and children congregate in the fireplace pit early in the evening to draw and talk among themselves. Later at night, the conversation pit is a relaxed place to sit while waiting for a table, which is generally necessary as no reservations are accepted. Appetizer bar food, while you are waiting, includes East Coast oysters on the half shell and a selection of tapas. The salad of mixed greens with warm goat cheese is excellent, and the Caesar salad is large enough for two. Fresh Parmesan and black pepper are grated at the table. For entrées, the sautéed Chilean sea bass with spinach, roasted tomato, and lobster chervil sauce is firm but juicy, and the chicken breast with rosemary has a crispy, delicate skin and flavorful, moist meat. Hamburgers arrive at the table with a side of crisp, herbed, shoestring potatoes, accompanied by a basket containing A-1

Sauce, Worcestershire sauce, catsup, and Dijon mustard. For dessert, a caramel and pear napoleon with hazelnut praline and chocolate sauce is fabulous, but the apple and strawberry crisp is outstanding (other fruits may be used, depending on the season). It is served hot, with vanilla ice cream.

THE MAIDSTONE ARMS
516-324-5006;
fax: 516-324-5037.
207 Main Street, East
  Hampton.
Cuisine: New American.
Serving: B, L, D, LN.
Open: Daily year-
  round.
Managing Director/Chef:
  William S. Valentine.
Price: Expensive–Very
  Expensive, prix fixe
  offered.
Credit Cards: AE, D, MC, V.
Special Features: Fireplace;
  outdoor patio in the
  summer; award-winning
  wine list.
Directions: Overlooks
  Town Pond on the south
  end of Main Street.

Although The Maidstone Arms is an inn as well as a restaurant, this is anything but a typical hotel dining room. The food is absolutely first-class. William S. Valentine is a fitting descendant of the Maidstone's culinary days of glory in the 1950s, when chef and cookbook author Michael Field presided here. For a trip to yesteryear, Hamptons' style, The Maidstone Arms can't be beat. The Water Room lounge is clubby and sophisticated; guests can enjoy a drink before the woodstove while waiting for their table. There are two distinctly different dining rooms. The Boat Room is informal and cozy with polished pine floors, a massive fireplace, and upholstered armchairs for seating. A multitude of boat paintings and prints line the walls. The main dining room has blue plaid carpet, pale gold wallpaper, a fireplace, and blue porcelain plates decorating the walls. The setting is elegant and comfortable, without being stuffy. Chef Valentine, who formerly brightened the restaurant scene in Los Angeles, has created a menu that reflects creativity and imagination. The appetizer of carpaccio of Long Island tuna, served with a vegetable salad and ginger-chili mayonnaise, is so good that you consider ordering several more. It would be a shame, however, to pass up the roasted free-range chicken, served with snap pea risotto and roasted wild mushrooms or the crispy, potato-wrapped striped bass on smothered red beans and crab butter. Desserts include an angel food layer cake with blackberries and a crème brûlée. The wine list is remarkable for its depth and breadth, as well as for its bargains. An excellent selection of white and red Long Island wines are particularly praiseworthy. Breakfast and lunch are popular here, too. The patio in the back is a refreshing summertime oasis.

**MICHAEL'S AT
  MAIDSTONE PARK**
516-324-0725.
28 Maidstone Park Road,
  East Hampton.
Cuisine: American.
Serving: D.

Because this is an out-of-the-way restaurant in a residential neighborhood, it's important to lure the customers beyond the village limits. Tim Myers does this by offering special prices year-round. For example, every night there's a $15.95 early bird special from 4:30 p.m. to 6:00 p.m. You can choose

Open: Daily year-round.
Manager: Tim Myers.
Chefs: Shawn Farrell and
   John Chuilo.
Price: Inexpensive–
   Moderate, prix fixe
   offered.
Credit Cards: AE, MC, V.
Special Features:
   Nonsmoking section;
   wheelchair accessible.
Directions: From Main
   Street, turn left just
   before the Hook
   Windmill onto North
   Main Street. Drive
   through two traffic lights
   and take the left fork
   onto Three Mile Harbor
   Road. Follow this road
   for 5 miles to Flaggy
   Hole Road. Turn left onto
   Flaggy Hole and left
   again onto Maidstone
   Park Road. The
   restaurant is on the left.

from 13 entrées, plus soup or salad and dessert for $15.95. The prices are equally reasonable the rest of the night. On Monday night, the entrées are $9.95; Tuesday is steak night for $13.95; Wednesday is lobster night for $13.95; Thursday features Southern specialties such as BBQ ribs or Southern fried chicken for $12.95; and on Friday and Saturday, prix fixe dinners, including soup or salad, entrée, and dessert are offered for $16.95 (or $18.95 for prime rib or lobster). Consequently, this is a very popular restaurant, especially with local, year-round residents. Few tourists even stumble across it. But now you know! Be forewarned. You **must** make reservations. The decor is old-fashioned and romantic, with soft candles glowing. There are several, small rose-colored rooms with knotty pine wainscoting. The tables are covered with flowered tablecloths and rose-colored paper place mats. Church pews are used as seats in one of the rooms. Seniors love this place, both for the value and for the food. It's a chalkboard menu, but most of the items do not change. The duck is crisp-skinned, and the steak is large.The prime rib and the lobster are outstanding. The wine list is OK. Desserts are limited, but good — a dense chocolate torte is served on a puddle of half-raspberry, half-chocolate sauce. Michael's serves good, substantial, all-American, home-style food.

NICK & TONI'S

516-324-3550.
136 North Main Street, East
   Hampton.
Cuisine:
   Italian/Mediterranean.
Serving: BR (Sun. only), D.
Open: Dinner daily in the
   summer; fewer days the
   rest of year. Brunch every
   Sun.
Owners: Jeff Salaway and
   Toni Ross.
Manager: Bonnie Munshin.
Chef: Joseph Realmuto.
Price: Moderate–Very
   Expensive; prix fixe
   offered at times.

There's something so comfortable about Nick & Toni's that one visit is never enough. Casual attire is fine; babies are welcome; seniors love it; this is family. What puts it at the top of the class? Everything just clicks: the food is often sensational; the help is knowledgeable, professional, and friendly; the setting is crisp and airy; the wine list is well chosen; and there are no pretensions, and no apologies are needed. It's the kind of place where celebrities eat frequently, because they know that they're among friends, and no one will bother them. Background music leans to progressive and vocal jazz. Hot, thickly sliced Tuscan bread comes to the table in a wooden trough to be dipped in zippy Monini olive oil; the combination is so terrific, it's devoured in a flash. No one should

One of the most popular restaurants in the Hamptons, Nick & Toni's offers a casual setting and a convivial atmosphere.

Morgan McGivern

Credit Cards: AE, MC, V.
Special Features:
Wheelchair accessible;
outdoor deck.
Directions: From Main
Street, turn left just
before the Hook
Windmill. The restaurant
is on the right, ¹/₈ mile
beyond the second traffic
light.

miss the zucchini chips; these little round morsels of paper-thin zucchini are dipped in a chickpea flour batter and deep-fried. A 620-degree wood-burning oven prepares meat with crackly crisp skin and tender, juicy meat. The delicious free-range chicken is rubbed with rosemary and roasted garlic, but the whole roasted fish, which is served with deep-fried radicchio and endive, is also outstanding. The wine list is well chosen and includes Italian, French, and American wines, with some North Fork selections. Desserts include a pecan shortbread sundae with malted milk ball sauce that is absolutely fabulous.

**THE PALM AT
HUNTTING INN**
516-324-0411.
94 Main Street, East
Hampton.
Cuisine: American.
Serving: D.
Open: Daily year-round
(may close one or two
nights midweek in the
winter).
Manager: Tomas Romano.
Chef: Anthony Tammaro.
Price: Expensive–Very
Expensive.
Credit Cards: AE, DC, MC,
V.

A visit to The Palm is like a trip to New York City, with none of the aggravation. This East End brother of the famous Manhattan steak house, which has been in the same family for three generations, has established itself as a Hamptons' fixture. It's the same formula as the original, but there are no sawdust floors here. The predominance of dark wood, booths, pressed tin ceiling, oak mirrors, and Victorian light fixtures is more reminiscent of a pub of yesteryear than of the original Palm. The enclosed porch, which is also used for dining, is bright and airy. The food is the same as you'll find at the original, however. Steaks are thick and cut from the finest meat. Portions are huge, but split plates are an alternative. The lobster is so large that it spills over

The Palm at Huntting Inn, a branch of The Palm in Manhattan, is noted for its thick, juicy steaks and enormous helpings.

Morgan McGivern

the edge of its platter. Take-home portions are so huge, they are returned to the table in shopping bags. No vegetables come with the entrées, but the Palm is noted for its creamed spinach. We generally order a combination plate of cottage fries and deep-fried onions; the fries are crisp, and the onions are sliver thin. Do try to save room for the typical New York cheesecake; it's an imported original. The high-priced wine list is well chosen and features California and Long Island wines, with a smattering of imported selections.

PECONIC COAST
512-324-6772.
103 Montauk Highway, East Hampton.
Cuisine: Mediterranean-influenced American.
Serving: D.
Open: Daily year-round.
Owners/managers: Dennis MacNeil and Dede McCann.
Chef: Dennis MacNeil.
Price: Inexpensive–Expensive.
Credit Cards: AE, MC, V.
Special Features: Patio dining in summer; reservations not accepted.
Directions: On Montauk Highway about two miles west of East Hampton village.

This bright newcomer on the Hamptons restaurant scene comes with excellent credentials. Both Dede and Dennis were at The Laundry for many years, so their own unique approach to Hamptons dining has evolved naturally. The restaurant is located in a building that was built to house Duke's, a less-than-successful venture in a building surrounded with windows and featuring soaring ceilings, giving the tiered dining room a bright and open feel. You might start the meal with oysters on the half shell from nearby Robins Island or with an oven-roasted portobello mushroom served with frisee, shallots, and Parmesan. Entrées include a fabulous just-caught striped bass that is served on a bed of zucchini gratin, and Atlantic salmon that's been glazed with balsamic vinegar and roasted with tomato salad. There are also pasta, chicken, and steak dishes, as well as an excellent burger. The wine list is broad and very well-priced. and there are some excellent selections

Price: Expensive–Very Expensive.
Credit Cards: AE, MC, V.
Special Features: Smoking in the bar only; fireplace.

ROWDY HALL
516-324-8555.
10 Main Street, East Hampton.
Cuisine: English Pub.
Serving: L, D.
Open: Daily year-round, except Mon.
Owners: Jeff Salaway and Toni Ross.
Manager: J. P. Gentry.
Chef: Gretchen Menser.
Price: Inexpensive–Moderate.
Credit Cards: None.
Special Features: Wheelchair accessible; fireplace, reservations not accepted.
Directions: In a mews, just off Main Street.

by the glass. Desserts are good too. One fall night we had a wonderful apple and blueberry crisp served with vanilla ice cream.

The name Rowdy Hall comes from a shingled boardinghouse that stood on Main Street. In the nineteenth century, it housed American impressionist painters from New York who came to East Hampton in the summer to paint. From the stories told, it appears they were quite rowdy at times. The building was eventually moved to Egypt Lane, and little Jacqueline Bouvier spent her summers there. Today its namesake is an English-style pub that those early painters would undoubt-edly call their own. Occupying the space at the end of a mews off Main Street where O'Mally's used to be, the interior has changed little. Although you now enter on the side, the bar and fireplace are just where they always were. There are oak tables on polished oak floors, mission-style chairs, and a banquette along one wall. You can always get a Rowdyburger, a worthy successor to O'Mally's big, juicy burgers, and load it up with all sorts of good-ies; it comes with railroad tie fries, which are gen-erous-sized steak fries. Local fresh fish and pro-duce are always used when available. The fish and chips are made with fresh local cod, deep-fried in a beer batter and wrapped in newspaper, just as in England. For a more substantial meal, the pan-roasted salmon with beurre blanc is served with a crispy potato cake. The wine and beer selections are excellent, as are the desserts. In the summer, there are English berry puddings and fresh fruit tarts. Year-round, you can order crème brûlée and mousse au chocolat, but you should not pass up the pear bread pudding with warm maple syrup.

SANTA FE JUNCTION
516-324-8700.
8 Fresno Place, East Hampton.
Cuisine: Southwestern.
Serving: D.
Open: Daily year-round.
Owners: Chris Eggert and Kevin Boles.
Manager: Lisa Narizzaro.
Chef: Moises Goodey.

Santa Fe Junction, located on an illusive side street running between Gingerbread Lane and Railroad Avenue, is definitely worth the effort to find. Opened in November 1994, it has been earning justifiable high praise for its food, decor, and ser-vice ever since. Santa Fe Junction features inventive, Southwestern cuisine. The setting is casual and comfortable with rough-sawn, cedar-planked walls, green vinyl banquettes, maroon tablecloths, and

Price: Moderate–Expensive.
Credit Cards: MC, V.
Special Features:
Wheelchair accessible;
reservations not accepted.
Directions: From Main
Street, turn onto
Newtown Lane. Turn left
onto Railroad Avenue.
Drive past the train
station and drive straight
ahead at the traffic light.
Turn left at the next
street, Fresno Place. The
restaurant is on the left.

cactus centerpieces. A geometric, Native American frieze circles the room, while Western paintings and a deer skull with antlers decorate the walls. Skylights in the raftered ceiling allow light to stream in during the day. The cuisine is inspired. The Blooming Onion appetizer, for example, is as pretty as it is delectable and is a marvelous shared dish: A whole onion is peeled and the top and bottom are cut off; it's then sliced from top to bottom into finger-sized wedges and then dipped into a tempura-style batter, seasoned with cilantro and red chili pepper, and deep-fried; in the deep-fry, it opens into a crisp flower, resembling a cactus blossom. Served with a refreshing avocado ranch dip, it's absolutely sensational. Other appetizers include quesadillas, tamales, and fried oysters that are coated with cornmeal. For entreés, there are chicken, beef, or seafood fajitas that arrive so hot, the onions are caramelized. All of the grilled items are cooked over mesquite, and they include smoked St. Louis ribs with a thick and tangy barbecue sauce; sea bass crusted with sweet potatoes and served on a bed of spinach; a chili-laced filet mignon served with roasted shallots and a chili-Madeira sauce; and paella. For dessert, the banana taco, a grilled banana rolled in a cinnamon crêpe and served with pecans and vanilla ice cream, topped with caramel sauce, is a house favorite. Traditional crisp Southwestern sopapillas, little, puffy fried breads served with honey, are also excellent. The popular front bar is a favorite local hangout. In the winter, it's a cozy and friendly spot where folks gather to watch a game on television. In the summer, it's packed with patrons eagerly anticipating their meal.

TURTLE CROSSING
516-324-7166;
fax: 516-324-7253.
221 Pantigo Road, East
Hampton.
Cuisine:
Southwestern/BBQ.
Serving: L, D.
Open: Year round.
Owner/Manager: Nancy
Singer.
Owner/Chef: Stanley
Singer.
Price: Inexpensive–
Moderate.
Credit Cards: AE, MC, V.
Special Features: Outside
dining; takeout.

The heady aroma wafting from the hardwood smoker in the kitchen will draw you in, but the juicy, smoky, tender ribs and chicken with their tasty barbecue sauces will keep you coming back for more. The *New York Times* has called this the best BBQ on Long Island. Stanley Singer grew up in Oklahoma City, where BBQ is king. After a stint in Paris at La Varenne, he and his wife Nancy opened this welcome addition to the Hamptons' dining scene. The front room of the restaurant is mostly for takeout, and there's a steady stream of people throughout the day. A small, adjacent dining room has a vinyl floor and Naugahyde booths along a wall that has been painted with a huge mural of rodeo riders. Typical Southwestern cow skulls gaze

Directions: On Route 27, 1 1/2 miles east of the village.

down on the room. You can choose from spit-roasted platters of chicken or smoked BBQ platters of ribs, chicken, brisket, pork, or duck, or a combination of several. With that order, you'll get corn bread and an order of "fixins," which change nightly and might include black beans, rice, or other side dishes. In addition, there are salads, sandwiches, such as BBQ shrimp, marinated grilled chicken breast, burgers, and "fancy wraps," which are flour tortillas with interesting stuffings, such as steak, chicken, or shrimp, grilled vegetables, or teriyaki tofu. There's a selection of Mexican beer and wine and a children's menu that includes peanut butter and jelly or grilled cheese sandwiches and burgers. There's always a selection of fresh fruit cobblers for dessert, but the best dessert is the fat square of bread pudding that's served warm with Jack Daniel's sauce.

Montauk

DAVE'S GRILL
516-668-9190.
Website: www.davesgrill.com.
468 Flamingo Road, Montauk.
Cuisine: American/Seafood.
Serving: D, L Sat.–Sun. (spring and fall).
Open: July–Labor Day daily; May, June, Sept., and Oct. open fewer days; closed Nov.–April.
Owners/Managers: David and Julie Marcley.
Chef: David Marcley.
Price: Moderate–Very Expensive, prix fixe offered.
Credit Cards: AE, D, DC, MC, V.
Special Features: Outdoor patio in the summer; live entertainment.
Directions: From the center of the village, take Edgemere Street north until it becomes Flamingo Avenue. Continue on Flamingo Avenue. The restaurant is on the right along the docks.

David Marcley, a chef, met Julie Goldstone, a singer, and eventually they fell in love, bought a dockside diner that served breakfast to fishermen all night, and got married in Barbados. As Dave's Grill gained popularity, they started serving dinner instead of breakfast. Now all remnants of the diner have vanished. The restaurant has an interior of dark wood and brass; a pretty patio overlooks the harbor for summer dining. Dave selects the fish right off the boats, and the nightly specials reflect his choices. There may be halibut with a horseradish crust, flash-fried Montauk flounder fillet with an onion and potato crust, or Dave's choppino, a combination of fish, lobster, scallops, clams, shrimp, mussels, and calamari. Desserts are a specialty here, too. The most popular is Dave's Chocolate Bag — Belgian chocolate shaped into a bag and filled with scoops of ice cream, resting in a poof of raspberry sauce and topped with whipped cream. There's an excellent wine list that includes Long Island whites and reds, as well as wines from California, France, Spain, and Italy. Some nights (generally Thursdays in the fall) guests gather to listen to jazz, with Julie at the microphone.

Morgan McGivern

Gosman's Dock serves fresh-from-the-boat fish, accompanied by a view of the fishing fleet.

GOSMAN'S DOCK
516-668-5330.
West Lake Drive, Montauk.
Cuisine: Seafood.
Serving: L, D.
Open: Mid-Apr.–mid-Oct.;
   daily, Mem. Day–Labor
   Day; fewer days the rest
   of the year.
Owner/Manager: Roberta
   Gosman.
Chef: Sam Joyce.
Price: Inexpensive–
   Moderate.
Credit Cards: AE, MC, V.
Special Features:
   Wheelchair accessible;
   outside dining in the
   summer.
Directions: From the center
   of the village, take
   Edgemere Street north
   until it becomes Flamingo
   Avenue. Continue on
   Flamingo Avenue to
   West Lake Drive and
   follow it to the end.

Gosman's is the ultimate fish house, definitely very casual and known for good fresh fish. There's a view from the dining room of the fishing fleet entering the harbor, but, because of Gosman's volume, this is not the sort of place that encourages dawdling over coffee. The decor is of the dark, lacquered table, Windsor chair, and paper place mat variety. Nevertheless, the seafood is fresh off the boat. The lobster is always a good choice, and the mahi mahi, in a delicate herb crust made of Oriental tempura flakes with ginger and cilantro, is crunchy but moist — a very nice dish. The yellowfin tuna with horseradish sauce is served with rice or baked or fried potatoes. For dessert, the peach and raspberry pie has a crumb crust and is served either hot or with a scoop of ice cream. Gosman's is a popular meal stop for families and bus tours. A clam bar next door offers a quick lunch, and the seafood market (also next door) is impressive for the variety and volume of seafood available.

Wainscott

SAPORE DI MARE
516-537-2764.
Montauk Highway,
   Wainscott.

This attractive restaurant on the banks of Georgica Pond, with its multilevel dining room and its peaceful view, is renowned for its lusty, Tuscan-style food. It attracts a classy, sophisticated

Cuisine: Italian.
Serving: D, L (Sat., Sun. only).
Open: Daily dinner in the summer, lunch Sat.–Sun.; closed Mon.–Wed. the rest of the year.
Owner: Pino Loungo.
Manager: Alysa Adler.
Chef: Roberrt Iaco.
Price: Expensive–Very Expensive.
Credit Cards: AE, DC, MC, V.
Special Features: Wheelchair accessible; glass-enclosed porch, overlooking Georgica Pond.
Directions: Located on Montauk Highway, between the hamlets of Wainscott and East Hampton.

crowd of celebrities who expect the best and are willing to pay for it. One of the most romantic restaurants in the Hamptons has a waterside, glassed-in porch, overlooking the pond, where trees reflect in the calm waters as swans glide by; the pond is illuminated by exterior lights at night. Inside, soft candlelight heightens the mood. A basket of warm Italian breads, including a wonderfully chewy focàccia, is delivered to the table with olive oil for drizzling. A grilled portobello mushroom on arugula salad is topped with freshly shaved Parmesan cheese for an appetizer. There's an array of excellent pastas and a nightly risotto; one night, it included fresh bay scallops with Parmesan. The fish dishes include a spicy seafood stew and a whole fish roasted in a brick oven. The wine list leans heavily toward fine Italian wines. Desserts are as outstanding as the main courses. The rich tiramisu, made with chocolate and mascarpone cheese, is encased in ladyfingers that have been soaked in espresso. It's so-o-o good.

SOUTHAMPTON TOWN

Bridgehampton

BOBBY VAN'S
516-537-0590.
Main Street, Bridgehampton.
Cuisine: American Steak House.
Serving: D daily; L Mon.–Fri.; BR Sat., Sun.
Open: Daily.
Manager: Jeffrey Streem.
Chef: Ralph R. Pagano.
Price: Moderate–Very Expensive; prix fixe offered Sept.–June.
Credit Cards: AE, MC, V.
Special Features: Smoking at bar only; wheelchair accessible.

Rising from the remnants of the old Bobby Van's, this shiny new version that opened in 1994 has captured the hearts and imaginations of Hamptons' residents and wanna-bes. Now under new ownership, the dark room with its quiet, seductive corners has been replaced with closely packed tables, divided occasionally by floor-to-ceiling potted palms. There are ceiling fans, bistro chairs, and absolutely first-rate steaks. Crowds pack the place, even in the winter. Understanding the Hamptons' mentality, however, the owners wisely left the original bar, along with the old celebrity photographs and the piano, which has been moved to the window and is played throughout dinner. It's a thoroughly 1990s place cloaked in 1960s nostalgia. In the summer, the French doors open directly onto the sidewalk. The menu includes a good selection of seafood. Unless you're a vegetarian, however, don't pass up one of Bobby Van's tender, succulent steaks, accompanied by a side of creamed spinach. Desserts include apple pie and cheesecake.

On the corner of Main Street and Ocean Road, the Bridgehampton Cafe burst on the scene in 1996.

Tulla Booth

BRIDGEHAMPTON CAFE
516-537-2929.
Main Street,
    Bridgehampton.Cuisine:
    Multicultural/ Healthy.
Serving: D, L/BR.
Open: Dinner daily Mem.
    Day–Labor Day,
    Lunch/Brunch Sat., Sun.;
    closed several days
    midweek the rest of the
    year.
Manager: Kevin Hallahan.
Chef: Steve Califano.
Price: Moderate–Very
    Expensive, prix fixe
    offered.
Credit Cards: AE, D, DC,
    MC, V.
Special Features:
    Wheelchair accessible.
Directions: On the corner of
    Ocean Avenue at the
    monument.

At last, this prime location has a restaurant worthy of it. Under new ownership in 1996 (the owners also have The Water Club in Manhattan) and with a new name, Bridgehampton Cafe also has a new look. The mullioned windows are now of uniform size and flood the room with light during the day. The spectacular 1902 pressed tin ceiling, with pressed tin boxed beams, and the walls are painted a creamy white, creating a neutral backdrop for the original paintings by local artists. The paintings change frequently and are for sale. There are mellow pine floors, marine blue banquettes along the walls, and light jazz playing in the background. A wooden basket arrives with French bread, sourdough, and healthy bread crisp; a creamy pot of hummus accompanies it. Vegetarian items are identified on the menu by a smiley face. A wonderful appetizer of aged goat cheese is served with a crispy potato gallette and caramelized shallots. An entrée of pan-roasted chicken comes in a huge, rimmed soup bowl and is perfectly cooked, tender, juicy and flavorful. It's accompanied by a tasty, grilled, marinated portobello mushroom and crisp tendrils of treviso, a leafy vegetable in the same family as radicchio and endive. The notable Yukon Gold mashed potatoes are rich with oil and are so addictive, you could make a meal of them. The wine list includes 16 whites and 16 reds, with several Long Island wines among them. In addition, there's a list of 23 beers and ales. For dessert, the Bridgehampton Cafe chocolate aphrodisia is a dense piece of pure chocolate. For a lighter finale, try the fruit tart, which is local, seasonal fruit in puff pastry, topped with ice cream. **Note: we were sorry to learn, just at press time, that the cafe has closed.**

KAREN LEE'S RESTAURANT AND WINE BAR
516-537-7878;
    fax: 516-537-2526.
Main Street,
    Bridgehampton.
Cuisine: French/Italian
    Provincial.
Serving: D.
Open: Mid-Mar.–Dec.; daily
    in the summer; fewer
    days the rest of the year.
Owner/Manager: Robert
    Durkin.
Chef: Natalie Byrnes.
Price: Expensive–Very
    Expensive, prix fixe
    offered.
Credit Cards: MC, V.
Special Features:
    Wheelchair accessible.

Karen Lee's, the original wine bar in the Hamptons, is my favorite restaurant. Consistently excellent food is prepared with a flair, and, summer or winter, the place inspires a very loyal (mostly local) following. We prefer the garden room for the light, airy feeling and for its quieter tone. But we love the great floral bouquets in both rooms. Fresh flowers in pitchers made by local potter Mary Flanagan are conversation starters. After a disastrous fire a few years ago, we thought we'd lost the place for good, but it's now back in stride and better than ever. The grilled and roasted vegetables, splashed with olive oil and topped with herbs, are excellent. The Petrossian smoked salmon on a lightly fried potato pancake is served with two caviars and a dollop of crème fraîche. The herb-crusted breast of chicken has a crackly, crisp skin, with moist and tender meat. It's been dusted with dried herbs, grilled, and then finished in a convection oven to give it a tender, moist, delicate flavor and is served with a tangle of crisp shoestring potatoes. A fillet of salmon is grilled and served with a grilled portobello mushroom over risotto, drizzled with truffle oil and is so tender that it flakes, to reveal a moist, pink center. Nevertheless, it's the Tuscan-style pot roast, comfort food at its very best, that customers won't allow to be replaced on the menu. As one would expect of a wine bar, there's a broad range of wines, with Long Island wines particularly well represented. The list is not extensive, but one that is wisely selected. Desserts should not be missed. The "fallen" chocolate soufflé cake and the almond cake with raspberry sauce were so luscious that we left not a crumb.

95 SCHOOL STREET

516-537-5555.
95 School Street,
Bridgehampton.
Cuisine: Long Island
Regional.
Serving: D, BR (Sun. only).
Open: Daily May–Sept.;
closed several days the
rest of the year.
Owners: Stuart Kriesler and
Riccardo Traslavina.
Chef: Riccardo Traslavina.
Price: Moderate–Very
Expensive, prix fixe
offered.
Credit Cards: AE, DC, MC,
V.
Special Features: Limited
wheelchair access.
Directions: From Main
Street, turn onto School
Street at the Community
Center.

The spare, white setting, the selection of newspapers and magazines to read while waiting, and the fact that it buys its chickens from the local Iacono Farm and its duck from Crescent Farm in Aquebogue have endeared this restaurant to local diners. In addition, it serves terrific food. The crisp, little disks of crab cakes have a cilantro-lime sauce that give them a kick and are served with a seaweed salad. The crispy duck has juicy, tender meat and is served with a variety of fruit sauces: a peach, plum, and sweet onion-sherry wine sauce or a spicy, black grape sauce. The chicken is pan-roasted and served with a side of garlic potatoes (mashed with their skins on), asparagus, and (in season) lovely little champagne grapes. The servers are eager and friendly, and the background music includes such old classics as "Frankie and Johnnie." The luscious dessert cobblers vary with the season. In early September, it was peach cobbler, served with a scoop of gelato and garnished with blueberries and raspberries. The wine list contains one of the best selections of Long Island wines in the Hamptons, although there are excellent California, Italian, and French selections as well. What's remarkable about the wine list are its prices; most of the white wines are under $30. This is a good place to try some delightful East End wines, served with excellent local cuisine.

East Quogue

STONE CREEK INN

516-653-6770.
405 Montauk Highway,
East Quogue.
Cuisine: French/
Mediterranean.
Serving: D.
Open: Mar.–Dec.; daily in
the summer, fewer days
the rest of the year.
Owner/Manager: Elaine
DiGiacomo.
Owner/Chef: Christian
Mir.
Price: Expensive–Very
Expensive, prix fixe
offered.
Credit Cards: AE, DC, MC,
V.

This welcome addition to the Hamptons' dining scene opened in 1996 in the white-shingled building that used to be the Ambassador Inn. Following a thorough face-lift, the space has now been voted the prettiest restaurant in the Hamptons by readers of *Dan's Paper*. In the bar, the 1930s carved mahogany back bar is enhanced by a new tile floor and a new mantel over the fireplace. The two dining rooms have oak floors and tall mullioned windows. Massive palm trees reach toward the tray ceilings, rustling gently in the breeze from the ceiling fans and giving the restaurant a romantic, tropical air. There's a fireplace in one room. Clever bark vases hold fresh flowers, and lovely Bernardaud china graces the tables. The young

Special Features:
  Wheelchair accessible;
  fireplaces in the dining
  room and bar.
Directions: On Route 27, $^1/_2$
  mile east of the village.

chef/manager, a husband and wife team, met while both were working at Tavern on the Green in New York City. Christian was raised in France, and his dishes bear a strong French influence. Christian uses local, seasonal ingredients, thus the menu changes frequently. In the fall, a lobster and pumpkin bisque was topped with corn and chervil. An entrée of crispy salmon was moist and pink inside and was served with whipped potatoes, baby carrots, and an oyster sauce. The excellent wine list leans heavily toward French wines. Do not miss the scrumptious desserts: an orange crème brûlée is glazed with Grand Marnier and a berry napoleon is served on a pool of vanilla sauce.

Sag Harbor

AMERICAN HOTEL
516-725-3535.
Main Street, Sag Harbor.
Cuisine: French/American.
Serving: L, D.
Open: Daily year-round for
  dinner; lunch weekends
  only off-season.
Owner: Ted Conklin.
Chef: Peter Dunlop.
Price: Moderate–Very
  Expensive, prix fixe
  offered.
Credit Cards: AE, CB, D,
  DC, MC, V.
Special Features:
  Exceptional wine list;
  fireplace; singer/pianist
  on the weekends.

It was almost 30 years ago when Ted Conklin purchased this 1846 hotel, one of the few remnants of Sag Harbor's glorious whaling days. The charming, Victorian rooms have such a European ambience that you feel as if you're eating in a French country inn. The rooms are formal and romantic and range from the dark, convivial bar with its fireplace to the skylighted atrium with its brick wall. Classical music plays gently in the background. An international crowd chatters away in a variety of languages, and the dress is partly New York chic and partly Hamptons' casual. The American Hotel has won twelve *Wine Spectator* Grand Awards for its legendary 46-page wine list, which includes a 1929 Château Margaux for $1,000 and a 1975 Château Latour for $450; it also offers a broad range of California and Long Island wines at lower prices. There are few half-bottles, but wines available by the glass are as well selected as those by the bottle. Over the years, the menu has slowly evolved away from strictly classical French dishes to some French, some American, and even some spa entrées. Dinner might start with a fresh sautéed foie gras, laced with sauterne or perhaps a Sevruga, Malosol, or Beluga caviar. Entrées include a pecan-crusted, baked chicken breast and a filet mignon with a sauce mignonette. Desserts generally include an excellent crème brûlée, a chocolate marquis, and a flourless chocolate cake, dusted with grated white chocolate and served on a pool of crème anglaise. There's a lovely selection of after-dinner sauternes and ports. Upstairs, there are eight remarkable guest rooms that are filled with antique furniture and Oriental rugs and have fantastic bathrooms with whirlpools.

B. SMITH'S
516-725-5858.
Long Wharf at Bay Street,
  Sag Harbor.
Cuisine: International/
  eclectic.
Serving: L, D.
Open: May–Oct.; from May
  to Sept. open daily; fewer
  hours rest of season.
Owners: Barbara Smith and
  Dan Gasby.
Manager: Christine
  Buechting.
Chefs: Henry Chung and
  John Poon.
Price: Moderate–Very
  Expensive.
Credit Cards: AE, MC, V.
Special Features:
  Waterfront dining on
  spacious decks; bar/
  lounge area; wheelchair
  access.

B. Smith's has been a popular Manhattan theater-area restaurant for some time. Now Ms. Smith has joined the Hamptons scene as well. The location has long been one of the premier sites in the Hamptons, as it overlooks the harbor and marina where huge sailboats and cruisers sit at anchor. B. Smith's strikes just the right note, as the owners have thoughtfully allowed the view and the food to take front seat. Creamy yellow walls are accented with white. Marine blue and white striped banquettes, and huge blue pots holding palm trees. Ceiling fans complete the decor. A multitude of French doors open the interior dining room to the outside. B. Smith is noted for its hickory ribs and you can get them here, served with corn, onion crisps, and "moppin'" sauce. You can also get fresh fish, roast chicken, and some lovely pastas. An excellent wine list that includes some local East End wines is available. Desserts may include a chocolate cake with local berries or a tangy Key lime pie.

CITRON
516-725-7575;
  fax: 516-725-7579.
62 Main Street, Sag Harbor.
Cuisine: Contemporary
  American/International.
Serving: D.
Open: Tues.–Sun.
Owners/Managers: Sue
  Calden and Lyn Leigh.
Chef: Frank Castellano.
Price: Moderate–Very
  Expensive, prix fixe
  offered.
Credit Cards: MC, V.
Special Features:
  Wheelchair accessible.

Citron has settled into its niche. The space, which is broken up into two dining rooms, is light and pretty, with one wall of brick, other walls of lemon yellow, a decorative tin ceiling, white tablecloths, and candles on the tables. You'll start with hot, seven-grain bread and perhaps continue with the best duck in the Hamptons. The crispy roast duck is served with a mixed berry reduction and wild rice pilaf. I also love the roasted free-range chicken, which is served with a rich brown provincial sauce. For dessert, the profiteroles are filled with vanilla ice cream and served with both chocolate and caramel sauces.

HARBOR ROSE
516-725-6060;
  fax: 516-725-6002.
16 Main Street, Sag Harbor.
Cuisine: Contemporary
  American.
Serving: L, D, LN, BR Sun.
Open: Daily year-round for
  dinner, lunch Fri.–Sat.,
  brunch Sun.

This handsome restaurant in the heart of Sag Harbor is a welcome addition. The grey stucco exterior with creamy white trim was originally the village's train station. The interior, which has burnished cherry floors and bentwood chairs with bright tapestry cushions, is inviting. One side of the spacious room, which has soaring ceilings, is devoted to a living room-style bar. There are sofas,

Harbor Rose is located in Sag Harbor's former train station.

Laurin Copen

Manager: Brian O'Leary.
Chef: John Marsh.
Price: Moderate–Very
  Expensive.
Credit Cards: AE, MC, V.
Special Features:
  Wheelchair accessible;
  outdoor dining; jazz
  Friday night.

tables, and chairs grouped to focus attention on the handsome black walnut bar. Two patios are used for summer outdoor dining. The menu features fresh seafood, chicken, and steak. A fillet of striped bass is sautéed and served with a lemon-chive sauce, while the salmon is pan-roasted and served with a citrus-oregano sauce, with grilled leeks and mashed potatoes on the side. The desserts are outstanding — far above average. Among the offerings are fresh berries with champagne zabaglione, a white chocolate and raspberry crème brûlée, and a chocolate truffle cake.

**IL CAPUCCINO
  RISTORANTE**
516-725-2747.
30 Madison Street, Sag
  Harbor.
Cuisine: Northern Italian.
Serving: D.
Open: Daily year-round,
  except major holidays.
Owner: Achille
  Tagliasacchi.
Manager/Chef: Jim Renner.
Price: Moderate–Expensive.
Credit Cards: AE, MC, V.
Directions: From Main
  Street, bear left at the
  monument onto Madison
  Street. The restaurant is
  on the right.

This rambling, old, wood building has three dining rooms, with tables and chairs tucked into various nooks and crannies. It's a restaurant of red-checked tablecloths, a brown-painted floor, and bentwood chairs. Decorations include original oil paintings by owner Achille Tagliasacchi, raffia-wrapped Chianti bottles hanging from the ceiling and walls, and lace curtains. A tumbling-down storefront next door was torn down and replaced with a new, similar building in 1995; this expanded the seating for summer dinners and for private parties. This is a homey Italian restaurant that could just as easily be located on a street in Naples. Everyone loves the hot, knotted, homemade dinner rolls, topped with garlic and parsley and dredged with melted butter. It is customary to sop up every drop of the potent garlicky butter from the bottom of the paper-lined basket. For entrées, there are chicken, fish, and pasta winners. Tortelloni al pistacchio is an excellent pasta stuffed with ricotta and served in an Alfredo sauce with Parmesan cheese. One of the desserts is an outstanding, rich, dark chocolate cake, layered with raspberry jam and surrounded with fudge frosting and chocolate shavings.

LA SUPER RICA
516-725-3388.
Corner of Main and Bay
Streets, Sag Harbor.
Cuisine: Mexican.
Serving: D.
Open: June–Oct.
Owner: Ken O'Donnell.
Price: Moderate.
Credit Cards: AE, MC, V.
Special Features:
Wheelchair accessible.

La Super Rica (sometimes spelled La Superica) serves inventive Mexican fare, all made with healthy, natural ingredients. There is no fryer in the restaurant, so you won't find crisp taco shells. What you will find is a dense salsa made daily from fresh tomatoes and onions that isn't overly incendiary, guacamole with chunks of fresh avocado, and excellent, inky, black beans. Everything is made on the premises, and the burritos, enchiladas, and quesadillas come in large portions. The margaritas are 17-ounce monsters, served in stemmed glasses; there's a good selection of Mexican beer, too. The decor is funky/diner with Formica tabletops and lighted chili peppers for decor. A young, trendy crowd appreciates the loud music.

O'MALLY'S SALOON
516-324-9010.
209 Montauk Highway,
Sag Harbor.
516-725-8012.
Noyac Rd., Sag Harbor.
Cuisine: American.
Serving: L, D.
Open: Daily year-round.
Owners/Managers: The
Mannino Family.
Price: Inexpensive–
Moderate.
Credit Cards: AE, MC, V.
Special Features: Smoking
at the bar only;
wheelchair accessible;
pub atmosphere; outdoor
patio.
From Sag Harbor, follow
Route 114 north across
bridge to North Haven.
In one mile, at traffic
light, turn left onto Long
Beach Road. At the end,
beyond the beach, turn

In 1998, the Mannino family opened the most exciting O'Mally's Saloon since they closed our favorite that was tucked away for years in the Mews in East Hampton. This new version of their tried-and-true formula is in a spectacular setting right on the water overlooking Noyac Bay and Long Beach. Spacious decks take full advantage of the view. In both restaurants, you can bring the kids — this is family dining at its best.There's a cozy, English pub feeling to the O'Mally restaurants. There are Tiffany-style lamps, old advertising signs, brass railings, and hanging plants. The tables are dressed with blue-and-white checked tablecloths that are topped with glass and then set with paper place mats and napkins. Booths are comfortable and roomy. The burgers here are fat and juicy, with a choice of 25–30 types that will satisfy most tastes; the bacon and blue cheese burger is scrumptious. There's an extensive list of grilled, chicken breast sandwiches: for example, one with eggplant and mozzarella, another with honey-mustard sauce, and more standard versions with right onto Noyac Road. The restaurant is on the immediate right. For the East Hampton restaurant, follow route 27 (Montauk Highway) about 2 miles east of the village. The restaurant is on the left.

cheese and bacon. There are also steaks, fish entrées, hot dogs, and other sandwiches.

SERAFINA
516-725-0101.
29 Main Street, Sag Harbor.
Cuisine: Italian.
Serving: L, D.
Open: Year-round; dinner nightly, lunch Thurs.–Mon.
Owner/Manager: Lynn Cardile.
Owner/Chef: Frank Caniglia.
Price: Moderate–Expensive.
Credit Cards: AE, D, MC, V.

Serafina (the restaurant is named for Lynn's great-grandmother) is one of the prettiest restaurants around. There are oak floors, tapestry draperies at the windows, fringed tapestry shades on the lamps, and elegant paintings on the walls. And although it may seem peculiar to rhapsodize about a restaurant ladies room, this one is pretty terrific. It's a two-level room decorated with teddy bears, dolls, plants and a Gothic-backed chair. Friendly, obviously happily employed staff are able to describe the ingredients and preparations of dishes with knowledge and enthusiasm. You might start with Fra Diavolo Prince Edward Island mussels in a Fra Diavolo sauce or fresh mozzarella with prosciutto bundles and sliced tomatoes served with basil oil drizzle. For entrées there are numerous pastas and veal dishes, such as veal Bettina, a dish of sautéed veal with wild mushroom saffron demi-glaze or the cotoletto Siciliano, crispy breaded Sicilian-style veal cutlet with tomato garlic sauce. The dessert list is long and varied. You might have a St. Honoré cake, or a rich chocolate fudge cake, or a toasted almond amaretto cream cake, or end the meal in a traditional Italian manner with biscotti and espresso.

Sagaponack

ALISON BY THE BEACH
516-537-7100.
3593 Montauk Highway, Sagaponack.
Cuisine: Country French.
Serving: D, L/BR (L/BR served Sun. only, Labor Day–Memorial Day).
Open: year-round; daily in the summer, fewer days the rest of the year.
Owner: Alison Becker Hurt.
Chef: Robert Gurvich.
Price: Expensive–Very Expensive.

Alison on Dominick Street in Manhattan is a favorite with New York City diners, and now Alison has brought her restaurant savvy to the Hamptons. The name may be a bit misleading, however. The restaurant is actually on Montauk Highway and is surrounded by potato fields; the nearest beach is about a mile away. Nevertheless, this lovely little French bistro is a welcome addition to the Hamptons' dining scene. Inside, the space looks little different than when it was Roger's (and before that Bruce's). There are three dining rooms, including the barroom. In the win-

Alison By The Beach is a little Hampton bistro located on Montauk Highway.

Morgan McGivern

Credit Cards: AE, D, DC, MC, V.
Special Features: Wheelchair accessible; outside dining; fireplace.
Directions: On Route 27 at Town Line Road, 2 miles east of Bridgehampton.

ter, the most romantic tables are by the fireplace near the bar. In the summer, tables are set up on the patio. The food is excellent. A goat cheese and potato terrine, served with a roasted beet salad and walnut oil, is one of the favorite appetizers. For an entrée, I had a perfectly cooked, country-style roast chicken that arrived with spinach, carrots, and potatoes in a rich broth. My companion had a fillet of sautéed striped bass that was served with a crispy potato roof. Desserts include such marvelous confections as a warm chocolate and hazelnut soufflé, served with burnt caramel ice cream and chocolate sauce and a warm apple napoleon with cinnamon ice cream and calvados crème anglaise.

OLD STOVE PUB
516-537-3300.
Montauk Highway, Sagaponack.
Cuisine: Steak House/ Greek Specialties.
Serving: D.
Open: Daily year-round in the summer; Fri., Sat. only in the winter; additional days in the spring and fall.
Owner/Chef: Stephen Johnides.
Manager: Coula Johnides.
Price: Expensive–Very Expensive.
Credit Cards: AE.
Special Features: Wheelchair accessible; gratuity added to the bill.

The sign on the highway reads, "When you're fed up with the Chic . . . Come to the Greek." And although it's true there's nothing chic about "the Greek," it does attract a very chic clientele. Throughout the summer, there's a steady stream of celebrities. The Old Stove Pub has been a Hamptons' landmark for some 30 years, and it's changed little during that time. The walls of the old-fashioned farmhouse are covered with autographed celebrity photos, Bugs Bunny cartoons, and a mish-mash of posters. There are red-checked tablecloths, paper napkins, and a casual attitude. A wrap-around porch provides supplemental seating in the summer. It's definitely the red meat that folks come for, although the Greek specialties are excellent. Huge steaks and lamb chops are served on huge

Directions: On Route 27, 2 miles east of Bridgehampton.

platters, and they still hang over the sides. The prices, however, can go as high as a hefty $37. The limited wine list includes mostly Greek wines, plus several local vintages. Although it has its detractors, "the Greek" has been doing what it does for years, and some folks wouldn't have it any other way.

Southampton

basilico
516-283-7987.
10 Windmill Lane,
  Southampton.
Cuisine: Italian.
Serving: L, D.
Open: Year-round dinner
  daily; lunch Sat., Sun. and
  occasionally additional
  days.
Owner: Philipp Manser.
Manager: Gayle Donahue.
Chef: Cliff Butler.
Price: Moderate-Very
  Expensive, prix fixe
  offered.
Credit Cards: AE, D, MC, V.
Special Features:
  Wheelchair accessible.

This restaurant has that fresh, airy feeling of Santa Fe, but the food is strictly Northern Italian. Stucco walls, tiled floors, high ceilings, and unusual, hanging, beaded lamp shades — create a casual, but upscale atmosphere. The menu offers a good selection of antipasti, pastas, and several interesting pizzas. But this is a much more serious restaurant than those dishes suggest. The basket of bread contains a lovely, dense, but light focàccia; rather than the tear-apart, thin versions often served, this focàccia has been baked in a round loaf and sliced. Freshly caught striped bass is braised and served with shrimp, arugula, and dry vermouth. All of the vegetables taste as if they have come directly from field to plate. A chicken breast has been marinated in lemon and fresh herb oil, then grilled and charred on the outside, but tender and juicy on the inside. The wine list is almost exclusively Italian, with only one Long Island Merlot and four California whites, but the Italian wines are well selected, if pricey. All desserts are made on the premises and include a tiramisu, chocolate-raspberry cheesecake, and crème brûlée.

THE COAST GRILL
516-283-2277;
  fax: 516-287-4496.
1109 Noyack Road,
  Southampton.
Cuisine: American
  Contemporary/Seafood.
Serving: D.
Open: Daily year-round,
  mid-Jun.–mid-Sept.; Fri.–
  Sun. the rest of the year.

The Coast Grill serves absolutely fresh fish prepared in a simple, straightforward manner. Before opening this restaurant, owner Joseph Luppi served as cooking assistant to the *New York Times* food editor, Craig Claiborne, and to the late chef and columnist Pierre Franey, so he learned from the best. The menu is not extensive, but diners can depend on expert attention to the preparation of each dish. For appetizers, the fish cakes with shrimp pieces, roasted sweet peppers, and green

Owner/Manager: Joseph
Luppi.
Chef: Tom Rutyna.
Price: Expensive.
Credit Cards: AE, MC, V.
Special Features:
Wheelchair accessible; on
the water.
Directions: From Montauk
Highway, drive north on
North Sea Road to the
intersection with Noyack
Road. The restaurant is 2
miles east on Noyack
Road in the Peconic
Marina.

onion tartar sauce are delicious, and the warm, wild mushroom salad is served with focàccia bread. An entrée of seared salmon is served with a horseradish and watercress vinaigrette. Every night the list of specials features the daily catch, which might include Peconic bay scallops, wild striped bass, or soft shell crabs. For nonfish lovers, there are double-rib lamb chops, steak, chicken, and pork. As one might expect, the wine list offers excellent accompaniments to the menu, with about 30 white wines and about 25 red wines. This tried-and-true restaurant offers dessert favorites that include apple or pear crisp, key lime pie, and the Coast Grill brownie, with ice cream and chocolate sauce.

THE DRIVER'S SEAT
516-283-6606.
62 Job's Lane,
Southampton.
Cuisine: Steak/Seafood/
Pasta.
Serving: L, D.
Open: Daily year-round.
Price: Inexpensive–
Moderate.
Credit Cards: AE, MC, V.
Special Features: Limited
wheelchair access;
outside bar and patio;
fireplace.

For consistently good hamburgers, The Driver's Seat is the ticket. Enter through the packed bar, shouldering through the narrow passageway (to avoid elbows in the ear, try not to eat at one of the tiny tables in this room) to the more expansive dining room beyond. There, you'll find tall ceilings and a large fireplace for winter dining or continue back to the patio that is open in the summer. In addition to hamburgers, the entrées include steak, ribs, Southern-fried chicken, and seafood dishes; the prime rib, available only on the weekends, is excellent. On Wednesdays, there's a two-for-the-price-of-one special. A small wine list is complemented by a larger selection of beers. Desserts are mostly from Kathleen's Bake Shop, so, of course, they're good.

LE CHEF
516-283-8581.
75 Job's Lane,
Southampton.
Cuisine: French.
Serving: L, D.
Open: Daily year-round;
closed Thanksgiving and
Christmas.
Manager: Cookie Lafitte.
Owner/Chef: Frank
Lenihan.

This pretty little restaurant with its tiny, up-front bar serves creative French fare, just as one would expect from a restaurant with a proud French tradition. The former chef, Bernard Miny, grew up in Lyon, France, and learned many of his techniques from such luminaries as Paul Bocuse. Now in the hands of his long-time restaurant partner (Mr. Miny has gone on to other culinary pursuits), the lovely restaurant continues to attract patrons who appreciate the fine cuisine in a conge-

Price: Inexpensive–
Moderate, prix fixe
offered.
Credit Cards: AE, MC, V.
Special Features:
Wheelchair accessible.

nial setting at reasonable prices. The $19.95 prix fixe dinner is the best buy in the Hamptons. You can choose from about 15 soups or salads. The mild, curried carrot soup is delicious, and the biscuit-sized crab cakes are creamy and filled with chunks of flaky crab. Next you can choose from about 15 entrées. The grilled fillet of salmon with a mustard-dill hollandaise is outstanding. Other entrées might include lobster, veal chop, or fresh sea bass. (Although there are supplemental charges for several, all entrées come with vegetables, potato or rice.) For dessert, the selection includes cappuccino mousse, cheesecake, crème caramel, and many more. Naturally, there's a fine wine list.

SANT AMBROEUS
516-283-1233.
30 Main Street,
Southampton.
Cuisine: Italian
Ristorante/Pasticceriâ.
Serving: L, D.
Open: Apr.–Dec. daily in
the summer; fewer days
other months.
Chef: Mario Daniele.
Price: Moderate–Very
Expensive.
Credit Cards: AE, MC, V.
Special Features:
Wheelchair accessible.

Similar to its sisters in Milan and New York, this authentic Italian confetterìa has glass cases in the front where the most remarkable cakes and other pastry confections are displayed. Sant Ambroeus has such a Milanese flavor that you feel as if you should speak Italian. The tempting selections in the front include gelati and Italian cakes, pastries, cookies, and chocolates. Midway into the restaurant, there's an espresso bar and behind the bar is a small, white linen tablecloth restaurant. Watermelon-colored Ultrasuede banquettes and bentwood chairs offer sophisticated backdrops for the wonderful risottos, pastas, and salads. For appetizers, the beef carpaccio with arugula and freshly shaved Parmesan cheese and the risotto with Parmesan and saffron are excellent. Veal Milanese and a thinly sliced veal paillard are among the entrée choices. There are about 15 selections of both red and white Italian wines to accompany the meal. For dessert, the choices are extensive. The chocolate mousse Sant Ambroeus, as one example, combines two different chocolates in a delectable cake confection.

SAVANNA'S
516-283-0202.
268 Elm Street,
Southampton.
Cuisine: Contemporary
American.
Serving: D, BR/L.
Open: year-round; daily
May–Sept.; Wed.–Sun.
from Oct.–April.

Slick and trim, Savanna's is also beautiful. In this transformation of Southampton's old village hall (and later a funky bar/restaurant), the formerly dark interior walls have been removed and three exterior walls contain windows, so a light-filled space now reigns. At night, votive candles line the windowsills, creating a magical effect. In the summer, an outdoor dining pavillion in the

Located in Southampton's former village hall, Savanna's is one of Southampton's most popular restaurants.

Tulla Booth

Manager: Roberto
Polesello.
Chef: Victor Vieira.
Price: Moderate–Very
Expensive; prix fix
offered.
Credit Cards: AE, D, DC,
MC, V.
Special Features:
Wheelchair accessible;
outdoor dining in the
pavillion; fireplace.

back is a marvelous place to dine; a tentlike structure is supported by Grecian columns. There are columns inside the restaurant, too, and a fireplace at one end. A large mesclun salad is dressed with a light, crisp vinaigrette and garnished with huge focàccia crisps. Focàccia bread and corn bread squares are served in a basket. The entrées are presented with flair: the wood oven-roasted half chicken is served with garlic, rosemary, homestyle potatoes, sautéed spinach, and tomato lemon bruschetta; the polenta-dusted Chilean sea bass is accompanied by grilled seasonal vegetables, smashed potatoes, saffron aioli, and sundried tomato and goat cheese crostino. There's an extensive selection of pastas and several pizzas as well. The wine list is excellent, both in the selections by the glass and the range of wines by the bottle. There are Long Island wines as well as California, Italian, and French, including a vintage Margeaux. After dinner, while you are contemplating the dessert selections, coffee is served with little teasers of peanut brittle and cookies. Savanna's desserts include a light and wonderful tiramisu, double cappuccino cheese cake, homemade profiteroles with vanilla bean ice cream and dark chocolate sauce, and deep dish Florida-style Key lime pie.

75 MAIN STREET
516-283-7575.
75 Main Street,
Southampton.
Cuisine: Long Island
Regional.
Serving: D, BR/L, LN.

Attracting a young, upscale crowd, 75 Main is trendy and casual. It has oak floors, daffodil-colored sponged walls and wainscoting, and French doors across the front that open to the sidewalk. The bar area in the front is as large as the restaurant in the back. It's a popular place to see

Open: Daily year-round.
Manager: Melissa Miller.
Chef: Rick Jakobson
Price: Moderate–Very
  Expensive.
Credit Cards: AE, MC, V.
Special Features: Smoking
  in the bar only;
  wheelchair accessible.

and to be seen. Furthermore, the food keeps getting better and better, and the wine list won a *Wine Spectator* award in 1996. The brick oven, behind a brightly tiled counter in the back, is responsible for several dishes, such as the roast organic chicken stuffed with spinach and arugula. The wild striped bass with provençal vegetables and the horseradish-crusted salmon with snow peas are equally popular, as are a variety of pastas. For dessert, my favorite is the warm chocolate soufflé cake with vanilla bean ice cream.

**SOUTHAMPTON
  PUBLICK HOUSE**
516-283-2800;
  fax: 516-283-2801; E-mail:
  mcsully@publick.com.
40 Bowden Square,
  Southampton.
Cuisine: Contemporary
  American/Microbrewery
Serving: L, D, BR.
Open: Daily year-round.
Manager: Kevin Sullivan.
Chef: Donald Sullivan.
Price: Inexpensive–
  Expensive.
Credit Cards:AE, D, MC, V.
Special Features:
  Wheelchair accessible;
  porch dining; fireplaces;
  valet parking.

The enormous stainless steel vats behind their glass viewing windows dominate one end of the dining room but that just adds to the charm of this casual, new restaurant. There are brick walls, oak floors, stenciling on boxed beams, a tin ceiling and tin walls, and fireplaces in the dining room and the taproom. Grilled Cornish hen with a cranberry Grand Marnier sauce is a trifling $14 and is served with a vegetable and garlic mashed potatoes or steak fries. A tossed mesclun salad is a mere $3. The most expensive item on the menu is the hefty, 20-ounce, Cajun-spiced rib eye steak at $20. There are eight microbrews on tap, and the wine list includes some local wines. On the weekends, there's live entertainment. There's a wonderful, broad front porch that serves as an outside dining room almost all year 'round.

Water Mill

MIRKO'S RESTAURANT
516-726-4444.
Water Mill Square,
  Montauk Highway,
  Water Mill.
Cuisine: Continental.
Serving: D.
Open: Please call for days
  and hours.
Manager: Eileen Zagar.
Chef: Mirko Zagar.
Price: Expensive–Very
  Expensive.

Mirko Zagar is Yugoslavian born, and his inventive cooking reflects both an Eastern European influence as well as that of France. The restaurant is tucked away in the back of Water Mill Square, definitely not a place you'd stumble onto by accident. Once there, however, you'll find a tranquil setting, far from the traffic noise of Montauk Highway. You'll also find a husband and wife team who are absolutely dedicated to making your dining experience so memorable that you'll return again and again. Eileen will greet you at the

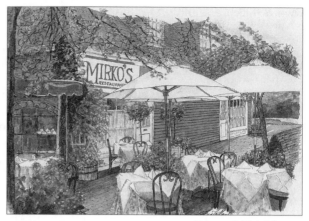

Mirko and Eileen Zagar have built a fine reputation for their hideaway retaurant and its esteemed French cuisine. The outdoor patio is a wonderful spot in warm weather.

Courtesy of Mirko's Restaurant

Credit Cards: AE, MC, V.
Special Features:
  Wheelchair accessible;
  outdoor patio; fireplace.
Directions: After turning
  into the Water Mill
  Square driveway, turn
  left. The restaurant is at
  the end.

door and see to your every dining need. Grilled shrimp and bacon is a wonderful appetizer; plump shrimp are wrapped in bacon, grilled, and served in a light lemon, pepper, and white wine sauce, laced with coarsely diced shallots. For entrées, the rack of lamb has an herb crust and is served with a mustard-mint vinaigrette, and the pan-roasted chicken breast is accompanied by oranges, rosemary, and almonds and served with an onion/raisin chutney. There's also a well chosen wine list. Among the desserts, I love the house specialty, "The Pear," which is as much a work of art as a sweet. A whole poached pear is balanced atop ice cream and drizzled with chocolate and raspberry sauces. Mirko and Eileen grow their own herbs and vegetables behind the restaurant. Inside the dining room, the fireplace is welcoming on chilly nights, and the small details — family photos on the mantel, botanical prints on the walls, country French accents that include golden-yellow sponged walls, Pierre Deux fabrics, exquisite sconces with pretty shades, lace curtains, and wainscotted walls — conspire to transport us to southern France.

THE STATION BISTRO
516-726-3016.
Station Road, Water Mill.
Cuisine: Country French.
Serving: D.
Open: Year-round; daily in
  the summer, Thurs.–Sun.
  the rest of the year.

This charming, small restaurant in the former 1903 Water Mill train station provides a delightful setting for a country French restaurant. The interior is a medley of dark green and white, with checked tablecloths topped by white overlays. Lace curtains cover the impressively tall windows. Soft, classical background music, fresh flowers, and candlelight make this a romantic retreat. There's a

Owners/Managers: Erica Van Acker and Gail Soltysik.
Chef: Tim Smith.
Price: Moderate–Very Expensive, prix fixe offered.
Credit Cards: MC, V.
Special Features: Wheelchair accessible; outdoor patio.
Directions: From Montauk Highway, turn onto Station Road just east of the hamlet of Water Mill.

pretty brick courtyard where drinks are served on hot summer days, and an adjacent, restored railroad club car that's open on Friday and Saturday nights. It has stunning glass windows and polished mahogany paneling. In the restaurant, hot bread straight from the oven is served at the tables on arrival. The wine list is small but well chosen, with affordable wines that include several local varieties. We started with a rich carrot soup, swirled with crème fraîche. Entrées included beef bourguignon and a roasted duck with caramelized apples, as well as filet mignon. For dessert, a chocolate cake, infused with apricots and studded with walnuts, served on crème anglaise was wonderful.

Westhampton Beach

ATLANTICA
516-288-6577.
Website: www.atlantica inc.com.
231 Dune Road, Westhampton Beach.
Cuisine: Upscale American with an emphasis on local seafood.
Serving: B, L, D, BR.
Open: Daily May–Oct.
Owner/Exec. Chef: Todd Jacobs.
Chef: Jeffrey B. Trujillo.
Price: Moderate–Expensive.
Credit Cards: AE, MC, V.
Directions: From Main Street, Westhampton Beach, drive south on Jessup Lane across the bridge to Dune Road. Restaurant is in the Westhampton Bath and Tennis Club straight ahead to the left.

The ocean-side setting is spectacular. This vast second-floor room with three walls of tall windows offers a panoramic view of the beach and the ocean beyond. Somehow Zina Glazebrook took a boxy room that resembled an airplane hanger and gave it intimacy and a romantic atmosphere. The room is divided by fat floor-to-ceiling columns that are draped in blue and white striped fabric, and the ceiling is tented in the same fabric. Numerous little lanterns hang from the ceiling, providing the illusion of lower ceilings. A marine-blue carpet and crisp white chairs upholstered in more blue and white stripes make this one of the prettiest dining rooms in the Hamptons. The restaurant is Todd Jacobs' (Tierra Mar) latest venture, and it hit the 1998 summer season with a splash. As one might expect, seafood figures prominently on the menu. You can start with a wonderful raw bar of local oysters, clams, and lobster, or perhaps with a steaming bowl of fresh mussels. For dinner one night I had a lovely charbroiled wild Alaskan (from the Copper River) salmon fillet that was creamy rare on the inside. It was served with a light vermouth butter sauce, basmati rice, and grilled, thinly-sliced zucchini. There's a diverse wine list with some nice Long Island wines. For dessert, I love the ethereal white and dark chocolate mousse served with hazelnut crème anglaise.

LE BISTRO
516-288-4610.
23 Sunset Avenue,
  Westhampton Beach.
Cuisine: French.
Serving: D.
Open: Year-round; daily
  May–Sept., Thurs.–Sat.
  Oct.–Apr.
Manager: Françoise Gendi.
Chef: Ali Fatalla.
Price: Expensive–Very
  Expensive, prix fixe
  offered.
Credit Cards: AE, D, MC,
  V.

In 1996, Ali Fatalla transformed Saffron, his Mediterranean restaurant, into a French bistro. The tiny room is carpeted, and there's a gauzy white fabric that creates a tent effect on the ceiling. White linen and lots of stemmed crystal reflect light from the candles, making it a romantic scene. Pair that with an outstanding wine list and a fine menu, and it's a winner. Fatalla was raised in Lyon, so his menu reflects his classical training, although he has added some typically Italian dishes to his repertoire. The petite seafood bouillabaisse is an original, rich, and robust starter, while the freshly shucked Long Island oysters or little neck clams in two sauces feature the best of the local waters. His crispy Long Island duck breast and leg confit is served in the traditional à l'orange style. The house specialty is a rack of lamb provençal with rosemary, but these French dishes are supplemented by entrées of risotto and homemade pasta. Desserts include a classic crème brûlée, a tart tatin, and a flourless bittersweet chocolate terrine, served with crème anglaise.

SAM HAMPTON'S
  SQUARE
516-288-1877.
10 Beach Road,
  Westhampton Beach.
Cuisine: American Eclectic.
Serving: D.
Open: Nightly year-round.
Owners: Tom Scionti and
  James Varasano.
Chef: Maurice Preciado.
Price: Moderate–Expensive;
  prix fixe and early bird
  prices available some
  nights.
Credit Cards: AE, CB, D,
  MC, V.
Special Features: Fireplace;
  live music and dancing
  some nights.

This charming building looks like an 1850s stagecoach stop, but it was once the game room of the Howell House, a hotel that was located on Main Street. The charm of the exterior is carried through to the inside, with beamed ceilings, paneled walls, and a cheery fireplace in the winter. The meal may begin with with filet mignon carpaccio or with an endive and Roquefort pear salad dressed with walnut cherry vinaigrette. For the main course, pan-seared salmon is served with corn relish, Dijon sour cream, and fresh flour tortillas. The breast of duck is julienned and served with red cabbage and shiitake mushrooms in a sweet and sour sauce, and then placed on a helping of fettuccine. Dessert lovers will want to try the warm pear crisp with vanilla ice cream. The wine list offers a well-chosen selection of East End wines, along with imported and California varieties.

STARR BOGGS
516-288-5250;
  fax: 516-288-5050.

Starr Boggs' setting in the Dune Deck Hotel is dramatic in its simplicity, highlighted by a mirrored wall that reflects the spectacular dunes and

379 Dune Road,
    Westhampton Beach.
Cuisine: Continental.
Serving: D, (L in the
    summer).
Open: Mid-May–Nov.; daily
    in the summer, Thurs.–
    Sun. after Labor Day;
    closed Dec.–mid-May.
Owner/Chef: Starr Boggs.
Manager: Adam Lovett.
Price: Expensive-Very
    Expensive, prix fixe
    offered.
Credit Cards: AE, CB, DC,
    MC, V.
Special Features: Oceanside
    dining with view; live
    entertainment some
    nights.
Directions: From Main
    Street, Westhampton
    Beach, drive south on
    Jessup Lane across the
    bridge to Dune Road.
    The restaurant is in the
    Dune Deck Hotel, on the
    left in 1.2 miles.

ocean outside. The story here is the food, however, not the setting. Chef Boggs is very particular about all of his raw ingredients. He does his own purchasing, often taking early morning trips to farm stands and fish markets to see what's best. He has his own label of wines and carries an excellent selection of Long Island, California, and French wines, including several exceptional ones, such as Opus One and a 1970 Château Margaux. For an appetizer, his Virginia crab cakes with southern pea salad and remoulade come straight from his Virginia roots. The almond-crusted flounder has a light citrus beurre blanc and is accompanied by a sweet potato puree, while the roast loin of pork is served with applesauce, braised red cabbage, and mashed potatoes; they're both accompanied by an abundance of fresh vegetables and a flower decorating the plate. All presentations are colorful and attractive. Even the little cookies that accompany the super rich crème brûlée are made here. On Monday nights things really swing — a distinct departure from the more sedate dining the rest of the week. Starr sets up a buffet lobster bake on the beach that includes a raw bar, plenty of salad and vegetables, and strawberry shortcake for dessert. A hot reggae band swings into action, and everyone heads for the dance floor. Experimenting with an American version of Cuisine Minceur, Chef Boggs has teamed up with nutritionist Layne Lieberman Anapol to create more nutritious and healthful food. Any item on the menu can be altered to a low-fat preparation.

TIERRA MAR
516-288-2700.
62 Montauk Highway,
    Westhampton.
Cuisine: New American.
Serving: L, D, BR (Sun.
    only).
Open: Daily year-round.
Owner/Chef: Todd Jacobs.
Manager: Ginny Jacobs.
Price: Moderate–Very
    Expensive.
Credit Cards: AE, D, MC,
    V.

Take a seasoned, inventive chef, stir well with experience, and you've got a recipe for success. Todd Jacobs worked for many years at the award-winning American Hotel in Sag Harbor, but in 1994, he struck out on his own. Tierra Mar, a sophisticated and stylish restaurant with a Mediterranean-in-the-Hamptons look, has food that has turned this restaurant into one of the most sought-after reservations on the East End. There are three dining rooms, each with its own distinctive style: the bright garden room is casual and summery; the barroom is a convivial gathering place, with bleached oak floors, a

Special Features:
  Wheelchair accessible.
Directions: Located on the
  Montauk Highway, 1
  mile west of Old
  Riverhead Road.

mahogany bar, ceilings punctuated by skylights, lots of tall greenery, and live entertainment on the weekends; and the third dining room is formal and refined, perfect for dressy occasions. Fresh ingredients inspire the menu offerings, with seafood a sure winner. Try the pan-seared Hudson Valley foie gras with oven-roasted pears, or the endive, radicchio, and arugula salad with toasted walnuts and Gorgonzola cheese. For entreés, the charbroiled, balsamic-glazed, Shinnecock striped bass (in season) is outstanding and is served with saffron fettuccine, sautéed spinach, and tomato fondue. The juicy chicken with a crispy crust is accompanied by fresh rosemary and roasted garlic whipped potatoes, while the roast Long Island duckling is served with a tart cherry sauce. All entrées are accompanied by a medley of perfectly grilled, roasted, sautéed, or blanched vegetables. The wine list includes more than 600 selections. Desserts include a white chocolate napoleon with fresh strawberries, a satiny rich crème brûlée, and a marvelous tray of cheese with sliced fruits, berries, champagne grapes, and crackers.

FOOD PURVEYORS

Social events, dinner parties, art gallery openings, fund-raising benefits, and al fresco picnics consistently give business to Hamptons' caterers, bakers, restaurant chefs, confectioners, delis, gourmet shops, and wineshops. Fish markets stock fish fresh from the morning catch, and farmers' markets sell produce straight from the field. Specialty food shops are filled with homemade jams, jellies, chutneys, and breads, as well as with the pungent smells of aging cheeses and freshly brewed coffee. Juice bars offer thick mixtures of fresh strawberries, bananas, lemons, and other fruits in season that are cool refreshers after a hot day at the beach. Recently popular coffee bars serve cappuccino, espresso, lattés, and American coffees.

BAKERIES

Beach Bakery Cafe (516-288-6552) 112 Main Street, Westhampton Beach. Open daily 7:00 a.m.–6:00 p.m., except in summer when it stays open until midnight. The wonderful aroma wafting from this little bakery is like a magnet, but so are the delicious goodies. Great breads, cookies, cakes, pies, and much more are made by Simon, the owner, and they are baked on the premises. In the summer, he also makes a terrific pizza that he will deliver. Simon tripled the size of his bakery in 1998 to make room for little cafe tables and chairs, where you can munch a goodie or savor some ice cream.

Holey Moses Cheesecake (516-288-8088) Building 115, Frances S. Gabreski Airport, Westhampton Beach. Open 8:30 a.m.–5:00 p.m. Mon.–Sat; closed Sun. Chris Weber's cheesecakes are sold in 300 restaurant and food outlets in an eight-state region. At his office, he'll take orders for a single cheesecake, or 1,000. His cheesecakes are so popular that restaurants proudly proclaim "cheesecakes from Holey Moses." His most popular flavors are pumpkin, Oreo cookie, lime, and the original recipe.

Kathleen's Bake Shop (516-283-7153) 43 North Sea Road, Southampton. Open daily 8:00 a.m.–6:00 p.m.; 8:00 a.m.–7:00 p.m. on the weekends in the summer. Kathleen King started baking cookies almost 20 years ago. Now she supplies 300 upscale gourmet shops and restaurants with her fabulous chocolate chip cookies, apple crumb pies, breads, scones, and so much more. Best of all, her baked goods are good for you. She uses all natural products with no preservatives and makes everything herself from scratch, just as our grandmothers used to do.

CAFES & COFFEEHOUSES

A restaurant is listed here as a café if, in general, dinner is not served. In several of the following, dinner is served as well as breakfast and lunch, but if it is best known and loved as a breakfast and lunch spot, it has been placed in the café category.

Candy Kitchen (516-537-9885) Main Street, Bridgehampton. Open daily in the summer 7:00 a.m.–10:00 p.m.; in the fall 7:00 a.m.–8:00 p.m.; in the winter 7:00 a.m.–7:00 p.m. The spot for breakfast or an afternoon ice-cream treat! This old- fashioned coffee shop and soda fountain has been in business since 1925. It's a legendary star hangout that looks much as it did when it opened. The food hasn't changed much either. Breakfast is of the bacon and eggs variety. In the afternoon and evening, there are hamburgers, clubs, and grilled cheese sandwiches. Milk shakes, ice-cream sodas, and egg creams are just as they should be. Sundaes have sauce dripping down the sides, with a mound of whipped cream, chocolate sprinkles, and a cherry. You can also get cherry and lemon cokes. The ice cream is made on the premises in a wide variety of flavors. There's nothing fancy here, just old-fashioned, good food.

The Golden Pear Café (516-537-1100) Main Street, Bridgehampton; (516-329-1600) 34 Newtown Lane, East Hampton; (516-283-8900) 99 Main Street, Southampton. Open daily 7:30 a.m.–5:45 p.m. The Golden Pear cafés, now in three locations, offer both eat-in and takeout. Newspapers are on hand, and these bright, welcoming, convivial spots are great for breakfast, for lunch, or just relaxing with a friend over a cup of coffee. There's nothing fast-food about these restaurants that owner Keith Davis has developed. Each has its own chef who prepares the menu items. There are fresh muffins and cookies hot from the oven, excellent salads, and a variety of hot dishes, such as pastas, chilis, chicken pot pies, and pies and cakes available whole or by the slice.

Grand Café (516-324-9207) 66 Newtown Lane, East Hampton. Open daily year-round. Ellen and Stephen Gottlieb used to own a four-star gourmet restaurant in Hopewell Junction, New York. When they established this casual, very popular East Hampton café, it was our gain. Crowds line the sidewalk, waiting for inside and outside tables in the summer, and it's equally popular in the winter. The prevailing design is art deco in silver and plum with etched mirrors. Essentially a breakfast and lunch spot, enormous muffins with crunchy tops and feathery centers arrive hot at the table; try the banana muffin with miniature chocolate chips. Other breakfast items include thick challah French toast, a frittata, or an omelette. At lunch, the restaurant emerges as "a lower East Side deli," serving overstuffed pastramis, juicy Reubens and Ruths (with turkey), as well as frankfurters, burgers, and focàccia sandwiches. Dinner is served in the summer only.

Superseeds (516-288-FOOD) 279 Montauk Highway, Westhampton Beach. Open year-round; daily in the summer 6:00 a.m.–9:00 p.m.; shorter hours the rest of the year. A new shingled building is now the home of Superseeds, a terrific, natural food gourmet café and deli owned by Chris O'Rourke. You still can get fresh, soft bagels, but now with a full-sized dining room, there are many more items. This is a good place to bring children for kosher and natural food items. There are soups, oven-baked sandwiches, pita sandwiches, salads, fresh turkey, an all-day juice and vegetable bar, and desserts. At night, the place becomes a coffee and dessert bar.

EGGS & POULTRY

Iacono Farms (516-324-1107) 106 Long Lane, East Hampton. Open Jun.–Sept. 8:30 a.m.–5:00 p.m. Mon.–Sat.; 10:00 a.m.–12:30 p.m. Sun.; Oct.–May closed Mon., Tues. The plump, juicy chickens that Salvadore and Eileen Iacono have been raising since 1948 are deservedly popular, as are their super fresh eggs. It's often advisable to order in advance on summer weekends, because they sell out early. And you'll also want to take home some of the breads and cookies made by their daughter. The Iaconos are some of the busiest and nicest folks around. No matter how many grouchy, impatient customers are lined up, there's always a pleasant word for each.

FARMS & FARM STANDS

The Amagansett Farmers Market is the place to go for breakfast and conversation.

Morgan McGivern

Amagansett Farmers Market (516-267-3894) Main Street, Amagansett. Open daily 7:00 a.m.–8:00 p.m. Jul.–Aug.; 8:00 a.m.–6:00 p.m. (8:00 a.m.–7:00 p.m. on the weekends) Mar.–Jul. and Sept.–Thanksgiving; closed Dec.–Mar. The steady expansion of this market over the years makes it popular on a variety of levels. It's the place to go, for example, on a sunny day for the newspaper, coffee, and sticky buns from the bakery. Patrons are encouraged to relax on the lawn or on benches down by the fishpond. The variety of fresh produce and fruit is staggering. In addition, the market includes a deli section with salads, pâtés, cheeses, and roast or fried chicken; a gourmet packaged goods grocery; and a cold section with sodas, egg creams, milk, eggs, and ice cream. Outside, there's a selection of plants for the garden. Let's not forget the prepared foods made right at the market: jellies, jams, preserves, pickles, barbecue sauce, chutneys, fresh peanut butter, catsup, syrups, sauces, and dried fruit — all carrying the Amagansett Farmers Market label.

Doug's Vegetable Patch (516-537-3224) Montauk Highway, Bridgehampton. Open daily 9:00 a.m.–6:00 p.m. Apr.–Oct.; closed Nov.–Apr. Doug Feinberg is the second generation to farm and sell produce from his family's 161 acres. He maintains about 30 acres in vegetables. In the spring and summer, lovely flowers are grown in the greenhouse and include brilliantly colored geraniums and fuchsias. This is the place to restock your home and garden.

The Green Thumb (516-726-1900) Montauk Highway, Water Mill. Open daily 8:00 a.m.–6:00 p.m. May–Dec.; later in midsummer. The 77-acre Halsey Farm has been in the family since 1644 and is now now in the capable hands of the eleventh generation. It's an award-winning, certified, fully organic farm. For dependable, high-quality produce, this farm stand can't be beat. The Halsey family grows over 15 varieties of lettuce, 12 kinds of salad greens, 19 different herbs, a colorful variety of sweet peppers, red and gold raspberries, beans, tomatoes, squash, pumpkins, flowers, and much, much more. At The Green Thumb, you can buy the tiny French green beans *(haricots verts)* and succulent, little yellow pear tomatoes, as well as other, more unusual varieties. The groaning farm wagon, laden with samples of the farm's bounty, is a welcome sight at the eastern edge of Water Mill.

Hayground Market (516-537-1676) Montauk Highway, Bridgehampton. Open daily Apr.–Nov.; 7:00 a.m.–9:00 p.m. in the summer; 7:00 a.m.–8:00 p.m. in the fall; closed Nov.–Mar. You'll recognize the Hayground Market by the tall ear of corn at the edge of Montauk Highway or the big cauliflower on a farm wagon. You'll also notice piles of pumpkins attractively displayed in the fall and washtubs full of brilliantly hued zinnias earlier in the season, as well as bountiful displays of produce, fruits, and berries. The 200-acre home farm that supports this large market has been in the Reeve family for many generations, and the farm stand has been operating since the early 1950s.

Round Swamp Farm Country Market (516-324-4438) 184 Three Mile Harbor Road, East Hampton. Open daily May–Nov. 8:00 a.m.–6:00 p.m. Mon.–Sat.; 8:00 a.m.–5:00 p.m. Sun.; closed the rest of the year. Round Swamp Farm, "Farmers of Land and Sea," is supported by the 20-acre Lester Farm that has been in the family for 250 years. Carolyn Lester Snyder started selling the family bounty when she was a child from a tiny, roadside stand built for her by her father. Now 16 family members contribute goods to the market. Piles of tender, white corn are heaped on a farm wagon; tomatoes, potatoes, and onions fill the bins; and the chilled produce room is stocked with a variety of lettuces, peppers, herbs, fruit, and berries. Baked goods are a family specialty.

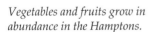

Vegetables and fruits grow in abundance in the Hamptons.

Tulla Booth

Cookies, breads, muffins, chutneys, relishes, and cakes are snapped up by loyal customers. Homemade soups and a small selection of salads are also popular. An adjacent fish market supplies fresh fish daily and also has a refrigerated milk, egg, and cheese section. Freshly cut flowers are also available.

FISH MARKETS

Gosman's Fish Market (516-668-5645) 484 West Lake Drive, Montauk. Open daily 10:00 a.m.–5:00 p.m. Apr.–Nov.; closed the rest of the year. Gosman's Fish Market is located on the Montauk docks near their restaurant. The range of fish and shellfish is one of the largest on the East End. You'll find tanks of clams, oysters, and lobsters, and cases of shrimp, salmon, bass, flounder, tuna, shark, and just about anything else — fresh from the fishing boats. Many locals consider this their favorite fish market.

The Seafood Shop (516-537-0633) Montauk Highway, Wainscott. Open daily year-round 8:00 a.m.–6:00 p.m. The Seafood Shop carries a wide array of fresh fish and shellfish. In addition, it has a crew of fishmongers who will fillet a whole fish, cut custom-ordered fish steaks, or prepare just about any other special order that you may want. This fish market has been around a long time and has a loyal following of summer and year-round residents.

Stuart's Fish Market (516-267-6700) Oak Lane, Amagansett. Open daily year-round 9:30 a.m.–6:00 p.m.; longer summer hours. Stuart's Fish Market is definitely not on the beaten track. It's on a narrow, residential side street between East Hampton and Amagansett, not even close to any water. Nevertheless, the owners are fishermen who catch what they sell. They're in Montauk waters in the summer, and off the Florida coast in the winter. There's a good seafood selection, with fresh shellfish still in their watery tank. Several local specialties also are made by Stuart's — the clam chowder (both New England and Manhattan varieties) is thick with chunks of potatoes, carrots, celery, onions, bacon, and clams, and the New England clam chowder is made with real cream. On request, they'll order the best homemade clam pies that you'll ever have.

GOURMET FOOD SHOPS & MARKETS

In general, the following shops operate busy catering businesses as well as storefront shops, and they have many more recipes in their culinary repertoire than meet the eye. If planning a party or a catered dinner, be sure to discuss the event with the catering manager, who can plan a menu specifically for you.

EAST HAMPTON TOWN

Barefoot Contessa (516-324-0240) 46 Newtown Lane, East Hampton. Open daily Jul. 4–Labor Day 9:00 a.m.–5:30 p.m., 9:00 a.m.–6:00 p.m. Fri., Sat.; fewer days the rest of the year. This is the Dean & Deluca of the Hamptons (actually Dean & Deluca occupied this building previously), and owner Ina Garten is one of the Hamptons' most popular caterers. The prepared foods available in her store, which used to be the East Hampton Post Office, are staggering. Near the entrance, there's a mouthwatering display of pies, cakes, and other desserts, including a delicious bread pudding. Straight ahead are piles of fresh breads. Glass counters enclose salads, cheeses, and prepared foods. Along the walls, floor-to-ceiling wire racks hold gourmet bottled and packaged items, and refrigerated cases display ice creams and soft drinks. In the middle, there are many prepared dishes: chicken salad with grapes and walnuts; sugar snap peas with black poppy seeds; honey-mustard chicken breasts; and polenta. There's a large selection of breads, including chocolate, rosemary, French, and others. The big event every year, held on Martin Luther King's birthday (January 15), is the annual sale when everything is reduced by one-third!

Morgan McGivern

Most of us flock to Dreeson's Excelsior Market in the mornings for fresh-from-the-deepfry donuts. Here owner Rudy DeSanti and Martha Stewart sample the fare.

Dreesen's Excelsior Market (516-324-0465) 33 Newtown Lane, East Hampton. Open year-round 7:00 a.m.–5:00 p.m. Mon.–Thurs.; 7:00 a.m.–5:30 p.m. Fri., Sat.; closed Sun. In business since 1920, Dreesen's is the local breakfast and lunch stop for East Hampton merchants and clerks. It's noted for its deli sandwiches and salads, its gourmet grocery, and its high-quality meat counter where everything is cut to order. Delivery service is available. The doughnuts, which you can watch being made in the window, are legendary. This is how doughnuts are supposed to taste — crispy on the outside and soft and airy inside. Owner Rudy DeSanti claims that they put all of the calories in the hole, so that you can eat as many as you like.

Jerry and David's Red Horse Market (516-329-6655) Montauk Highway at Cove Hollow Road, East Hampton. Open daily year-round 6:30 a.m.–7:00 p.m. From the time Jerry Della Femina and his partners opened the Red Horse Market in the summer of 1993, it's attracted a devoted clientele who know they can purchase all of their cooking needs in this large, well-stocked market. There are sections of fresh produce that stretch the length of the building, a fresh meat market, and a separate fish and shellfish section. Breads and cookies come in a variety of sizes and flavors; the chocolate chip cookies are so popular that they sell out quickly. There are sections of fresh flowers, prepared salads, entrées, and cheeses. You can even buy the daily newspapers here.

Plain and Fancy (516-324-7853) 85 Springs Fireplace Road, East Hampton. Open daily year-round 8:00 a.m.–5:00 p.m. in the summer; 8:00 a.m.–4:00 p.m. the rest of the year. Lines form around this shop on Saturday and Sunday mornings for Maria Bernier's fresh bagels, crullers, sticky buns, and scones. David Bernier's rosemary bread and entrées are equally popular. For example, the moist, tender chicken Francaise and the soft-shell crabs, dipped in milk and seasoned flour, grilled, and served on a French roll with fresh, homemade pesto sauce are marvelous. Quiches are thick and peasant-style and might include ham and Brie or asparagus with goat cheese. Individual fruit tarts feature in-season berries or fruit and have crumb toppings. Brownies range from a black, white, and raspberry (sensational) to lemon or coconut with raisins and pecans, as well as the traditional chocolate.

Villa Italian Specialties (516-324-5110) 7 Railroad Avenue, East Hampton. Open year-round 8:30 a.m.–6:30 p.m. Mon.–Sat.; 9:00 a.m.–2:30 p.m. Sun. This wonderful Italian deli, owned by Saverio and Carmela Naclerio, has been in business for almost 20 years, so you know that it's doing something right. For fresh Parmesan reggiano or pecorino Romano, real prosciutto, fresh puttanesca sauce, fresh ravioli or tortellini, or entrées, such as eggplant Parmesan or chicken cacciatore, this is definitely the place to come.

SOUTHAMPTON TOWN

The Curious Cook (516-283-1701) 24 Jagger Lane, Southampton. Open year-round daily 6:00 a.m.–8:00 p.m. Chef/Owner Larry Butler has built a solid reputation for his catering business and tiny café. In the morning, residents come here for the newspaper, a cup of coffee, and fresh, hot muffins. Among the items that he will happily cater are a variety of cakes and pies, beef Wellington, grilled rack of lamb, roast Long Island duck with fresh cranberry sauce, and poached salmon with dill-cucumber sauce. For $19.95 per person, he'll prepare a clambake for the beach.

Espresso (516-725-4433) 84 Division Street, Sag Harbor. Open daily 8:00 a.m.–9:00 p.m.; longer hours in the summer. Located off the beaten track in the village of Sag Harbor, Espresso is a great Italian deli/grocery that just keeps getting better. Luigi Tagliasacchi's hot focàccia bread, sprinkled with rosemary and garlic and splashed with olive oil, is heavenly. The market is run by Mr. Tagliasacchi and his wife Robin. The packaged Italian specialties include items that you often don't find at the finest Italian groceries in Manhattan. Prepared foods include salads, pastas (one special was spinach fettuccine with creamy Gorgonzola sauce), and a variety of entrées. Inventive breakfasts are served in the morning, and sandwiches are made-to-order at lunch.

Loaves and Fishes (516-537-0555) 50 Main Street, Sagaponack. Open daily 9:00 a.m.–5:30 p.m. Mem. Day–Labor Day; 9:00 a.m.–5:30 p.m. Fri.–Sun. Easter–Mem. Day and Labor Day–Christmas; closed Christmas–Easter. Anna Pump and her daughter Sybille Pump-Fengler have been partners for 11 years in this respected catering and gourmet food shop. They've earned a deserved reputation for excellence. From their fork-tender beef fillet to the chicken curry salad, from condiments, such as curried apricot mayonnaise or lemon curd, to freshly baked breads and exotic soups, some of the best dinner parties are catered by Loaves and Fishes.

Quogue Country Market (516-653-4191; fax: 516-653-6226) Jessup Avenue, Quogue. Open daily year-round 7:00 a.m.–8:00 p.m. weekdays in the summer; 7:00 a.m.–10:00 p.m. on the weekends; 7:00 a.m.–6:00 p.m. in the winter. This is a large, well-stocked market and deli that dates from the 1920s. In the fresh produce section, you can purchase farm fresh produce. There are over 20 kinds of prepared salads, a meat market (no packaged meats), a fresh fish counter, a large selection of gourmet canned and bottled food products, a fresh bakery with tiny little muffins (very popular), an extensive cheese counter, and fresh coffee and cappuccino. An extensive catering menu ranges from baked lasagna to stuffed fresh flounder with herbed cream cheese. It also sells newspapers, greeting cards, small gift items, and more. Bob and Gary Curran, the owners, are friendly, helpful, and knowledgeable.

Razzano's (516-537-7288) Bridgehampton Commons, Bridgehampton. Open daily 9:30 a.m.–7:30 p.m.; restaurant open 11:30 a.m.–8:30 p.m. (later in the summer). Vincent Razzano opened this terrific Italian market and café in 1994, and its popularity just keeps growing. Fresh pastas, homemade sauces, a full bakery with hearty Italian breads, crisp cookies, and a variety of cakes, plus a full line of takeout from lasagnas, meatballs, and rotisserie-baked chicken to olives, salads, and freshly made sausage are available. Imported bulk and grated cheeses, olive oils, vinegars, and freshly roasted coffee beans, as well as cappuccino, espresso, and latté are here as well. The adjoining restaurant serves pizza, pasta, and a variety of main-course dishes that include fish, veal, and chicken.

Sagaponack Main Store (516-537-6036; fax: 516-537-3696) 542 Sagg Main Street, Sagaponack. Open year-round daily in summer 7:00 a.m.–6:00 p.m.; shorter hours the rest of the year. The Sagaponack Main Store is the heart and soul of the hamlet of Sagaponack. The store takes up one-half of an old, white clapboard building, with the local post office occupying the other half. Customers arrive for the mail, morning paper, and a cup of coffee in their own Sagaponack Main Store mug, and sit on the steps to chat. Tom Wolfe, Kurt Vonnegut, George Plimpton, and other notables are as at home here as you and I. When Don and Mary Spellman left this little country store in 1995, we thought that we had lost an institution. Now, after a renovation, the post office is where the store was and vice versa. Best of all, a new team is preparing outstanding takeout that may even surpass earlier offerings. Bob and Rick Terando are the owners. You can get baked country hams with a honey-mustard glaze, roasted turkeys, pies, cakes, sandwiches, and lots more.

Sydney's "Taylor" Made Cuisine (516-288-4722) 194 Mill Road, Westhampton Beach. Open daily year-round 7:00 a.m.–6:00 p.m. After catering for four years, Erin Finley and David Blydenburgh have built a brand new building and opened a classy, new gourmet food store and deli. You will find a large selection of cheeses, salads, desserts, pâtés, and rotisserie-baked chickens and ducks. There are smoked fish, a full bakery selection, and bottled and packaged gourmet foods. This shop definitely fills a need in Westhampton Beach.

Village Cheese & Gourmet Shop (516-283-6949) 11 Main Street, Southampton. Open year-round 7:30 a.m.–6:00 p.m. Mon.–Thurs.; 7:30 a.m.–6:30 p.m. Fri., Sat.; 7:30 a.m.–5:00 p.m. Sun. The first thing that you do upon entering Rosemary and Adam Batcheller's cheese shop is to take a number; you can't place your order without a number in hand. Much more than a cheese shop, this is the place to come for a newspaper, coffee, and a bagel first thing in the morning or for a terrific deli sandwich before heading for the beach. You will find prepared hot dishes, salads, cold drinks, pâtés, charcuterie items, and a good selection of cheeses.

Crowds line up for the hot and cold deli treats at the Village
Cheese & Gourmet Shop in Southampton.

Morgan McGivern

ICE-CREAM PARLORS

Bridgehampton Ice Cream and Yogurt Company (516-537-0233) Main Street, Bridgehampton. Open daily Mem. Day–Labor Day; weekends only May, Sept., and Oct.; closed the rest of the year. Bridgehampton Ice Cream and Yogurt Company carries Steve's Ice Cream, Columbo Frozen Yogurt, and American Glacé.

The Fudge Co. (516-283-8108) 67 Main Street and 66 Job's Lane, Southampton. Open daily in the summer 11:00 a.m.–12:00 midnight; 12:00 noon—5:00 p.m. on the weekends the rest of the year. From these two respected shops, Hugo and John Fudge sell Columbo Soft Yogurt, Cream-of-the-Hamptons' ice cream, and their luscious homemade candies.

Scoop du Jour (516-329-4883) 37 Main Street, East Hampton. Open daily in the summer. Great ice cream, an old-fashioned soda fountain, and a location across the street from the East Hampton Cinema make this a very popular spot. They carry Steve's Ice Cream, T & W ice cream, and Columbo and American Glacé yogurt. This is also a coffee bar with espresso and cappuccino, ice-cream sundaes, sodas, and a comfortable atmosphere.

RESTAURANT DELIVERY SERVICE

A La Car (516-287-3663) 46 Main Street, Southampton. Open daily 5:00 p.m.–9:30 p.m. Mem. Day–Labor Day; 5:00 p.m.–9:30 p.m. on the weekends only the rest of the year. A La Car offers a unique service: Order a meal from your favorite restaurant and A La Car will deliver it hot to your home. First, select your order from the magazine that contains all of the restaurant menus (available at A La Car), then call A La Car and they will call the restaurant for you, pick up your order, and deliver it to your home. There's a minimum order of $30, plus a 20-percent delivery charge. You can pay with a variety of credit cards. They'll also deliver wine, mineral water, ice cream, and flowers.

WINESHOPS

Amagansett Wine & Spirits (516-267-3939) 203 Main Street, Amagansett. Open 10:00 a.m.–8:00 p.m. on weekdays; 10:00 a.m.–10:00 p.m. Fri., Sat. Amagansett Wine & Spirits can rival the finest shops in Manhattan, both for the depth of its wine collection and for its prices. Owner Michael Cinque buys directly from France and has assembled one of the finest wine cellars on the East End. If you walk the cool basement recesses with him, you will see rare old Latours and Margaux. He sponsors sophisticated wine tastings in the Hamptons and New York City, as well as wine appreciation classes. He also carries one of the most complete selections of Long Island wines and a wide variety of affordable, drinkable, light wines. His prices are so popular that he makes two to three delivery trips to Manhattan each week to supply his regular customers.

DePetris Liquor Store (516-537-0287) 2489 Main Street, Bridgehampton. Open 9:00 a.m.–8:00 p.m. weekdays; 9:00 a.m.–9:00 p.m. Fri., Sat. A good selection of Long Island, California, and European wines is available at this well-stocked Bridgehampton store. The Long Island wines, in particular, are well represented, with selections from every East End winery.

Herbert and Rist (516-283-2030) 63 Job's Lane, Southampton. Open 9:00 a.m.–8:00 p.m. Mon.–Thurs.; 9:00 a.m.–9:00 p.m. Fri., Sat. This excellent wineshop carries a good selection of Long Island wines, as well as those from California and Europe. Whether you're looking for a cold bottle to go with a sandwich, while sitting on the banks of Agawam Pond or a case for a party, this is the place to find it.

Long Wharf Wines & Spirits (516-725-2400) 12 Bay Street, Sag Harbor. Open 10:30 a.m.–8:30 p.m. Mon.–Sat. This well-stocked wineshop is strong on Long Island and Californian wines. The owner, David Mangusso, will help with selections for a casual, drinking wine or to match courses for a dinner party. The shop holds frequent wine tastings.

Wines by Morrell (516-324-1230) 74 Montauk Highway (in the Red Horse Market), East Hampton. Open year-round in the summer 9:00 a.m.–8:00 p.m. Mon.–Thurs.; 9:00 a.m.–10:00 p.m. Fri., Sat.; shorter hours the rest of the year. This branch of the great Manhattan store offers an excellent selection of wines, especially those from Long Island wineries. Throughout the shop, you will find unusual and interesting wines that are not available elsewhere.

A jug of wine, a loaf of bread, and a puppy.

Morgan McGivern

WINERIES ON THE SOUTH FORK

Viticulture and wine production have become big business on Long Island's East End. One day it may rival some California areas in quality, if not in production levels. Because most wineries are located on the North Fork, Chapter Ten, *The North Fork* contains extensive information about winemaking on the East End, wineries to tour, wine activities, and much more.

Wine production on the South Fork is more recent. **Bridgehampton Winery,** which is now defunct, began production in 1983; but they bought their grapes from other growers. **Sagpond Vineyards** planted the first vineyards intended for wine production on the South Fork in 1988. Their first bottling took place in 1993.

It's always interesting to visit wineries during the harvest, when the overflowing trucks bring the tiny grapes to the winery for processing. The following wineries offer tours, samples, and a sales room.

Channing Daughters Winery (516-537-7224) 1927 Scuttle Hole Road, Bridgehampton. Mailing address: P.O. Box 2202, Bridgehampton, NY 11932. Open: 11:00 a.m.–5:00 p.m. daily. The phenomenal success of Long Island wines has given encouragement to new ventures. Channing Daughters is one of the newest. Walter and Molly Channing, who have four daughters, planted 25 acres of their rather remote property north of Bridgehampton in 1988 in a mixture of Chardonnay and Merlot. They produced their first commercial wine, a 1993 Merlot, in 1995 and a Chardonnay in 1996. Larry Perrine is the winemaker. In August of 1998, they opened a pretty tasting room and winery where we can sample the results of this new winery.

Duck Walk Vineyards (516-726-7555) 162 Montauk Highway, Water Mill. Tasting and sales room open in the summer 11:00 a.m.–6:00 p.m. Mon.-Thurs.; 10:00 a.m.–6:00 p.m. Fri., Sat.; 12:00 noon–6:00 p.m. Sun.; closed Tues., Wed. the rest of the year. The former Southampton Winery was purchased in 1994 by Dr. Herodotos Damianos, who also owns Pindar Vineyards on the North Fork. The magnificent brick château, with its lush lawns and large terrace, was built in 1986, reputedly for $17 million. With the capability of producing 50,000 cases a year, the production had reached 25,000 by 1996. This stunning building is located on a slight hill overlooking the vineyards. It would be worth the trip to visit the vineyards and sample their steadily improving wines.

Sagpond Vineyards (516-537-5106) Sagg Road, Sagaponack. Tasting and sales room open daily 11:00 a.m.–6:00 p.m. Sagpond Vineyards was the first South Fork winery to produce estate-bottled wines. The first of its 50 acres of grapes was planted in 1988, with two-thirds in Chardonnay and one-third in Merlot. The first Chardonnays were produced in 1991. About 7,000 cases of wines were processed in 1996. (The Domaine Wolffer Chardonnay Reserve is a lovely accompaniment to fish; it is light and smooth, but also complex.) The land and winery are owned by Christian Wolffer, who also owns the horse farm Sagpond Farms, adjacent to the winery. Roman Roth is the winemaker. A lovely new winery building and tasting room were completed in 1997. It has soaring ceilings and a spacious deck overlooking the vineyard.

CHAPTER FIVE
Shop 'Til You Drop
SHOPPING

Shopping in the Hamptons can be as rewarding as shopping in Manhattan — and every bit as much fun. Many creative people have decided to live here, including a number of designers whose own workrooms are in the Hamptons, although they sell through larger retail outlets in New York City. As a result, you probably will pay less if you buy locally. And, in addition, some designers and entrepreneurs choose to offer

Morgan McGivern

During the summer, antique shows and sales take place frequently in the Hamptons. This one is at Mulford Farm in East Hampton.

their particular brand of artistry only in the Hamptons, priding themselves on bringing a unique flair and personality to their shops that can't be reproduced elsewhere. Manhattan shops have branches here, too. Whether choosing clothing or art, the Hamptons are a treasure trove.

The Hamptons offer another boon to treasure seekers. Yard sales abound, and they're unlike those that you'll find anywhere else. Many people bring items from their New York City apartments to the Hamptons for the annual yard sales. You'll find everything from priceless antiques to lawn mowers; from china to tools; from artwork to games; and from designer clothes to books. Artists hold home-based sales, book dealers weed out extra stock, and home owners do their spring cleaning in the summer. People review local newspapers each Friday night, hit the sales on Saturday from 8:00 a.m. to 12:00 noon, and then head for the beach.

In addition, the transfer stations have an unofficial recycling center for furniture, rugs, and other large pieces. Especially at the end of the summer, you can find some real treasures discarded here.

There is only one true mall in the Hamptons, although there are numerous shopping plazas. **Bridgehampton Commons,** because of its variety of shops, deserves special mention here. In addition to Caldor, King Kullen, and Rite Aid Pharmacy, the Commons also contains the following shops: The Gap, The Gap Kids, Williams-Sonoma, The Body Shop, Companie Internationale Express, Hallmark Shop, Speedo Authentic Fitness, Sunglass Hut, Banana Republic, Eddie Bauer, Athlete's Foot, Kay-Bee Toys, Lechter's, Encore Books, Record World, T.J. Maxx, Radio Shack, Razzanos, and Hampton Photo Arts, among others.

In this chapter, we have not tried to list every gallery, shop, and store. Instead, we have featured those that offer articles unique to the Hamptons. Although every attempt has been made to list the correct hours, they do change frequently. If in doubt, call.

ANTIQUES DEALERS & SHOPS

EAST HAMPTON TOWN

Amagansett

Balassas House Antiques (516-267-3032) 208 Main Street, Amagansett. Open daily in the summer 10:30 a.m.–5:00 p.m.; closed Tues., Wed. the rest of the year. Owners: George and Teda Balassas. From quirky pincushions to elegant, marble fireplace mantels, you'll find hundreds of antiques at Balassas. The rambling old house has room after cluttered room of both old and new, ranging from English tables to old tools, dishes, and mirrors, plus American and French furniture. When you've finished looking in the house, be sure to see the barn and the basement for even more finds.

East Hampton

Architrove (516-329-2229) 74 Montauk Highway (in the Red Horse Market), East Hampton. Open weekdays in the summer 10:00 a.m.–6 p.m.; 9:00 a.m.–6:00 p.m. Sat.; 10:00 a.m.–5:00 p.m. Sun.; closed Tues. and Wed. rest of year. Architrove carries a marvelous selection of elegant, antique marble- and wood-carved fireplace mantels, columns, top-quality furniture, crystal chandeliers, sinks, and even doorknobs and hinges. Everything is neatly arranged and very clean.

Circle Antiques (516-324-0771) 46 Main Street, East Hampton. Open year-round 10:30 a.m.–5:30 p.m. Thurs.–Mon. Owners: M.J. and Pete Miller. The owners have assembled a choice collection of fine antique English, French, and American furniture and decorative pieces.

The Grand Acquisitor (516-324-7272) 110 North Main Street, East Hampton. Open daily in the summer 11:00 a.m.–5:00 p.m.; closed Mon.–Thurs. the rest of the year. Owner: Maria O. Brennan. For elegant linen and lace tablecloths, sheets, coverlets, napkins, lacy pillowcases, and charming children's dresses, this marvelous store can't be beat. (This should be your first stop for an antique christening dress.) All the merchandise is neatly boxed and labeled, so items are easy to find even though the store inventories over 200,000 items. There are a few pieces of furniture, china, and silver, but Ms. Brennan is most noted for her fabric conservation.

Great Finds! (516-329-4448) 69 North Main Street, East Hampton. Open 10:00 a.m.–4:00 p.m. Thurs.–Mon. Great Finds! is no exaggeration. This shop truly is a Great Find! Partners Richard Cottrell and Bonny Reiff have cleverly filled their pretty shop—with its ornate tin ceilings and maple floors—with a wonderful assemblage of items. These range from blue and white porcelain dishes, to upholstered sofas and chairs, to interesting chandeliers, but the best items are the old pieces of furniture that have been cleverly painted by Richard. Chests, dressers, tables, and an iron baby bed are embellished with flowers or leaves or scenes. Don't miss this shop.

Victory Garden (516-324-7800) 63 Main Street, East Hampton. Open daily in the summer 10:00 a.m.–6:00 p.m.; Thurs.–Mon. the rest of the year. Owner: Paula Schulhof. If you have a secret garden that you've been wanting to embellish with cast-iron French furniture, the Victory Garden is just the place to look. This very elegant, French store also has French *faïence,* chandeliers, long baguette baskets, dining room furniture, needlepoint pillows, and so much more. The lovely aroma when you enter the shop is from the potpourri and rose balls.

Wainscott

Georgica Creek Antiques (516-537-0333) Montauk Highway, Wainscott. Open 11:00 a.m.–5:00 p.m. Mon.–Sat.; 11:00 a.m.–4:00 p.m. Sun. Jean Sinenberg has collected a marvelous array of unusual and interesting antiques in her spacious white building. On a recent visit I spotted a wonderful, carved French dresser, a cache of beautiful antique quilts in perfect condition, lamps, ornate silver candlesticks, a great crystal chandelier, and a set of beautiful gold-rimmed Limoges dishes. In back, there's a garden full of architectural elements such as columns and pillars, as well as wicker and Victorian wire planters and garden furniture.

SOUTHAMPTON TOWN

Bridgehampton

Devonshire specializes in fine garden and interior furniture and accessories.

Devonshire (516-537-2661) Main Street, Bridgehampton and (516-329-5392) 52 Newtown Lane, East Hampton. Open daily 10:00 a.m.–5:30 p.m. Mem. Day–Labor Day; 11:00 a.m.–5:00 p.m. Sun.; closed Tues., Wed. Apr.–Mem. Day and Labor Day–Thanksgiving; closed Thanksgiving–Apr. Devonshire carries an elegant selection of interesting, antique garden furniture and accessories. From pretty garden benches and tables to painted watering cans and birdhouses, a unique selection of antiques can be found. In addition, you'll find hand-painted lamp shades, pillows made of vintage fabrics, books, china, iron gates, and other original items.

English Country Antiques (516-537-0606, fax: 516-537-2657) Snake Hollow Road, Bridgehampton and (516-329-5773) 21 Newtown Lane, East Hampton. Open 9:00 a.m.–5:30 p.m. Mon.–Sat.; 10:30 a.m.–5:30 p.m. Sun. Chris Mead has assembled an extensive collection in his warehouse-sized showroom that specializes in English (and some French) antiques. Most of the armoires, china cabinets, beds, breakfronts, and tables are in pine. You'll also find birdcages, mirrors, lamps, chandeliers, candlesticks, weather vanes, whirligigs, and much more.

John Salibello Antiques (516-537-1484) Montauk Highway, Bridgehampton. Open in the summer 11:00 a.m.–5:00 p.m. Sat.; 11:00 a.m.–6:00 p.m. Fri.–Mon. the rest of the year or by appointment. John Salibello is noted for his opulent and elegant furnishings. In this shop, he carries a vast array of antiques, from jewelry and cast-iron doorstops to gilt French side chairs.

Legendary Collections (516-537-2211) Montauk Highway at the monument, Bridgehampton. Open daily 10:00 a.m.–5:00 p.m. Mem. Day–Labor Day; Wed. or Thurs.–Sun. the rest of the year. Owner: Justine Marko. Legendary Collections has fine eighteenth- and nineteenth-century, antique European furniture and decorative objects. The furniture includes both formal and country pieces and accessories, from lighting fixtures to paintings that are all showcased in the elegant rooms of a Late Federal building that once was the Bulls Head Inn.

Mill Antiques (516-537-5577) 2287 Montauk Highway, Bridgehampton and (516-288-0206) 164 Montauk Highway, Remsenburg. (These two stores are the retail outlets.) Open weekdays 10:00 a.m.–5:00 p.m.; weekends 10:00 a.m.–6:00 p.m. Mill Antiques sells antiques and manufactures finely carved French country furnishings (antique replicas), such as armoires, tables, chairs, and sofas; some pieces are upholstered in elegant French tapestries. They also import intricate architectural ironwork gates, fences, and other pieces.

Ruby Beets (516-537-2802) 1703 Montauk Highway, Bridgehampton. Open most days in the summer 11:00 a.m.–5:00 p.m.; 11:00 a.m.–5:00 p.m. Fri.–Sun. only the rest of the year. As though from a page of a Mary Emmerling book, this little house is crammed to the rafters with old painted furniture, baskets, pottery, enameled pitchers, weather vanes, and other funky country pieces. Outside, the lawn is cluttered with wood and iron chairs and garden urns and even has a garden bench with a back made from a picket fence.

Urban Archeology (516-537-0124) Montauk Highway, Bridgehampton. Open daily in the summer 10:00 a.m.–5:00 p.m.; closed Tues. the rest of the year. Owner: Gil Shapiro; Manager: Michael Scutellaro. Urban Archeology was born because the owners wanted to salvage great architectural elements from buildings about to be demolished. For antique columns, plumbing fixtures, fireplace mantels, letter boxes, lighting fixtures, and carousel horses, this is the place to come. The demand for the great old pieces has been so steady that the company now has its own line of reproductions: artisans in Spain make alabaster lamps; in Italy, they create iron pieces; and in Manhattan, they make a variety of objects in the lower recesses of the main store.

Sag Harbor

Fisher's Antiques (516-725-0006) Main Street, Sag Harbor. Open daily year-round 10:00 a.m.–5:00 p.m. Owners: Susan and Bob Fisher. This large shop features country pine antiques and reproductions, plus a vast selection of interesting and unusual home furnishings. You'll find 1940s flowered table-cloths and napkins, botanical prints, Soleido tablecloths and napkins, decorative pillows, and china. Pine furniture can be custom-ordered, and there's a restoration studio for repairs and custom finishes.

Main Street Antiques (516-725-8656) Main Street, Sag Harbor. Open 9:30 a.m.–6:00 p.m. Thurs.–Sun., Mar.–mid-Dec. or by appointment; closed the rest of the year. Owners: Claire and Herb Siegel. If you're looking for a painted, wooden Indian woman or a great old flag, a model ship, old costume jewelry, or brass telescopes, this shop has an interesting selection.

Southampton

Ann Madonia (516-283-1878 or 516-741-1882) 35 Job's Lane, Southampton. Open daily in the summer 10:00 a.m.–6:00 p.m.; 10:00 a.m.–6:00 p.m. Fri.–Sun. the rest of the year or by appointment. Owner: Ann Madonia. This store sells some of the most elegant antiques in town, from fine English and French furniture to silver and other accessories — all on two floors in a spacious, refined setting. The enclosed garden in back displays select garden furniture.

Another Time Antiques (516-283-6542) 765 Hill Street, Southampton. Open in the summer 11:00 a.m.–5:00 p.m. Thurs.–Mon.; shorter hours the rest of the year. Owners: Meredith and Thomas Joyce. The owners have filled their shop, as well as two adjacent buildings, to the rafters with dolls and toys, wicker chairs and desks, oak and mahogany tables, costume jewelry, collectible figurines and dishes, and much more. There are treasures to be found here.

Old Town Crossing (516-283-7740) 46 Main Street, Southampton. Open year-round 10:00 a.m.–5:00 p.m. Mon.–Fri.; 10:00 a.m.–5:30 p.m. Sat.; 12:00 noon–5:00 p.m. Sun. Owner: Judith Hadlock. Don't let this diminutive shop on Main Street fool you. Although Judith Hadlock displays an impressive array of mirrors, lamps, silver, silk tassels, and elegant, small furniture pieces, the bulk of the inventory is located nearby in a 5,000-square-foot warehouse. Customers are welcome to poke around the collection of eighteenth-century English beds, tables, dressers, and more.

Second Chance (516-283-2988) 45 Main Street, Southampton. Open 10:00 a.m.–5:00 p.m. Mon.–Sat.; 12:00 noon–5:00 p.m. Sun. Sheila Guidera is a fussy buyer. She'll only purchase antiques that are in the very best condition for her shop, thereby assuring her customers of top-notch quality. Among her finds are such treasure as Mme. Alexander and Nancy Ann dolls, antique cutwork linens, vintage floral drapes, Fiesta Ware, chenille bedspreads, jewelry, and a large collection of exquisite silver pieces: flatware, bowls, trays, napkin rings, and much more.

The Things I Love (516-287-2756) 51 Job's Lane (in Day's Court), Southampton. Open daily in the summer 11:00 a.m.–5:30 p.m.; closed Tues., Wed. the rest of the year. Tucked away in a brick courtyard, this little shop has some lovely antique clothing, needlepoint pillows, antique furniture, and much more. At one time, a hand-appliquéd, felt circle skirt with an entire village sewn along the bottom was for sale.

25 Hampton Road (516-287-3859) 25 Hampton Road, Southampton. Open daily 11:00 a.m.–5:00 p.m. Owners: Skip and Lorraine Ralph. With a collector's eye for fine antiques, Skip and Lorraine Ralph, who are also owners of 1708 House, an inn just around the corner, have filled this shop with the very highest quality English and American antiques. There are mahogany dining room tables and chairs, elegant walnut armoires, and beds with elaborately carved headboards and footboards. You can also see and purchase their antique pieces, which are on display in the guest rooms and common areas of the inn.

Water Mill

Donna Parker Habitat (516-726-9311) 710 Montauk Highway, Water Mill. Open in the summer 10:00 a.m.–5:00 p.m. Mon.–Fri.; 10:00 a.m.–6:00 p.m. Sat.; 11:00 a.m.–5:30 p.m. Sun. Donna Parker sells an array of important French and Italian furniture, and decorative objects such as a leafy iron table, or a crystal chandelier, or marble pedestals holding bronze busts or gilt mirrors, crystal lamps, and much more.

Water Mill Antiques (516-726-4647) 700 Montauk Highway, Water Mill. Open daily year-round 11:00 a.m.–5:00 p.m. Owner: Richard DiPierro. This interesting farmhouse is stuffed with antique furniture, chandeliers, mirrors, rugs, and decorative objects, and the front yard is so full of antique planters, garden benches, birdcages, weather vanes, statuary, and garden furniture that you can hardly thread your way to the door. But along the way you'll stumble across some wonderful bargains. I especially love the leafy white or black iron planter baskets that come in a pair. They're not antique but they're charming and very unusual.

Westhampton Beach

La De Da (516-288-5988) 8B Moniebogue Lane, Westhampton Beach. Open daily in the summer 11:00 a.m.–6:00 p.m.; shorter hours the rest of the year. Located in a charming building with a garden in front, this shop offers such treasures as antique building pediments, picture frames, mirrors, unique birdhouses, objets d'art, and salt-and-pepper shakers from the 1950s.

Mill Antiques International The Mill at Westhampton (516-288-0206) 164 Montauk Highway, Remsenburg and The Mill at Bridgehampton (516-537-5577) 2287 Montauk Highway, Bridgehampton. Open daily 9:30 a.m.–5:30 p.m. Mon., Wed.–Fri.; 10:00 a.m.–6:30 p.m. Sat., Sun. Owner: Claudette Romano. The Westhampton shop is in a picturesque old mill, but the Bridgehampton shop is located in a brand new building. Both carry a large selection of Country French antiques that range from carved wooden beds and armoires to tables and chairs. In addition, there are hoards of wrought iron pieces: gates, fences, and more.

BOOKS, MAGAZINES, TAPES

EAST HAMPTON TOWN

Book Hampton (516-324-4939) 20 Main Street, East Hampton. Open summer weekends 9:00 a.m.–11:30 p.m.; weekdays 9:00 a.m.–11:00 p.m.; closes 9:00 p.m.–10:00 p.m. the rest of the year. Manager: Jane Cochran. This is the Hamptons' all-purpose, everything-you-want bookstore. It has a wide selection in every category: best-sellers, paperbacks, local history, children's books, travel, cookbooks, videos, and tapes. Before the movies, after the movies — this is the place to shop.

Glenn Horowitz-Bookseller (516-324-5511) 87 Newtown Lane, East Hampton. Open daily 11:00 a.m.–6:00 p.m. Apr.–Dec.; shorter hours the rest of the year. For a selection of fine old books and prints, this shop has an excellent selection. There are a number of books and photographs that relate to local history, as well as some rare, old, leather-bound and first-edition books. If what you're looking for isn't here, it may be at their New York branch, or they'll do a search for you.

Long Island Sound (516-324-2660) 34 Main Street, East Hampton. Open daily in the summer 10:00 a.m.–11:00 p.m.; 10:00 a.m.–7:00 p.m. the rest of the year; and (516-283-6683) 76 Job's Lane, Southampton. Open daily in the summer 10:00 a.m.–9:00 p.m.; shorter hours the rest of the year. Not only do these stores carry a full selection of tapes, CDs, and accessories, but they also sell tickets for local events.

SOUTHAMPTON TOWN

Book Hampton (516-283-0270) 93 Main Street, Southampton. Open daily 9:00 a.m.–7:00 p.m. Manager: Tom Leo. This branch of Book Hampton has the same wide, all-encompassing selection as the East Hampton store.

The Book Mark (516-288-2120) 130 Main Street, Westhampton Beach. Open Mem. Day–Labor Day 10:00 a.m.–6:00 p.m. Mon.–Thurs.; 10:00 a.m.–10:00 p.m. Fri.–Sun.; daily 10:00 a.m.–5:00 p.m. the rest of the year. Owner: Mimi Calkin. The Book Mark has a good selection of hardbound and softcover books and greeting cards and is especially strong in children's literature, including the classics.

Canio's Books (516-725-4926) 490 Main Street, Sag Harbor and (516-725-4462) on Long Wharf, Sag Harbor. Open daily Mar.-Dec. 12:00 noon–6:00 p.m.; 12:00 noon–6:00 p.m. Fri.–Sun. only, Jan.–Feb. Owner: Canio Pavone. Canio is the literary community's friend. Not only is his shop a great place to find out-of-print books and new ones, but on many Saturdays at 6:00 p.m., there are book-signings or poetry or book readings.

Encore Books (516-537-2665) Bridgehampton Commons, Bridgehampton. Open 9:00 a.m.–9:00 p.m. Mon.–Sat.; 11:00 a.m.–6:00 p.m. Sun.; in the summer, open weekends 9:00 a.m.–10:30 p.m. Manager: Debbie Schall. Encore is a massive store, with hardbound books in every category, paperbacks (they claim to have 10,000), and magazines.

Sam Goody (516-287-7119) 14 Main Street, Southampton. Open 11:00 a.m.–5:00 p.m. Mon.–Wed.; 10:00 a.m.–9:00 p.m. Thurs.–Sat.; 11:00 a.m.–5:00 p.m. Sun. Music fans will find a prodigious selection of CDs, records, tapes, cassettes, videos, and other music-related items in this branch of this worldwide store. It's the place to pick up a Walkman and a few tapes before heading to the beach, as well as blank tapes or new headphones.

CIGAR & TOBACCO SHOPS

Even as restaurants are banning smoke in their dining rooms, the popularity of cigars are on the increase. In the Hamptons, as in Manhattan, exclusive clubs where one may smoke cigars are rising from the smoke. Often these include special rooms, open to members only, that offer locked, individual humidors and comfortable lounges where cigar smoking is welcomed. There also may be a Scotch and cordial bar and live entertainment.

EAST HAMPTON TOWN

The Cigar Box (516-324-8844) 10 Main Street (Parrish Mews), East Hampton. Open in the summer 10:00 a.m.–10:00 p.m. Mon.–Thurs.; 10:00 a.m.–1:00 a.m. Fri., Sat.; shorter hours the rest of the year. Tucked away off Main Street, the Cigar Box has a main floor shop where 30 brands of cigars and all sorts of accessories are sold. Humidors range from simple at $40 to elaborate at $4,000. In the upstairs lounge, there are upholstered sofas and chairs and a bar where single malt Scotches, cognacs, coffees, and wines are served; backgammon, chess, newspapers, and magazines are provided. (Kathleen Turner and Steven Spielberg sometimes smoke their stogies here.) A floor-to-ceiling bank of individual, locked humidors provides a place where members can stash their personal collection.

SOUTHAMPTON TOWN

Sag Harbor

The Cigar Bar (516-725-2575) 2 Main Street, Sag Harbor. Call for hours. This elegant shop has a fine selection of 30–40 imported cigars; pick your choice from those in a 12 x 10-foot walk-in humidor. You can also buy cigar accessories, including an elegant Spanish cedar humidor. There are overstuffed chairs, Oriental rugs on the floors, and a lounge with original art on the walls. At the little bar, you can select cognac, single malt Scotch, wine, espresso, or cappuccino for sipping. A pianist entertains on the weekends.

CLOTHING

FOR CHILDREN

EAST HAMPTON TOWN

East Hampton

Bonne Nuit (516-324-7273) 55 Main Street, East Hampton. Open daily 10:00 a.m.–6:00 p.m.; may close Tues., Wed. from Jan.–Mar. Owners/Managers: Ashlyn and Lorna Maloney. These fine lingerie shops carry the most beautiful, European children's clothing. Delicate, smocked dresses in Liberty of London fabrics and French sundresses, made of a Swiss cotton so fine that it feels like silk, are only a few of the offerings.

Punch (516-329-3897) 55 Newtown Lane, East Hampton and (516-725-2741) Main Street, Sag Harbor. Open daily in the summer 9:00 a.m.–10:00 p.m.; 9:00 a.m.–6:00 p.m. the rest of the year; closed in Mar. These fine children's clothing shops have outfits for all ages from newborn to older. There are coats, bathing suits, knit sweaters, felt-appliquéd jackets, corduroy overalls, and lots more.

The Red Pony (516-329-6685) 74 Montauk Highway (in the Red Horse Market), East Hampton. Open daily in the summer 10:00 a.m.–5:00 p.m.;

closed Tues., Wed. the rest of the year. Hampton moms need not traipse to Manhattan to elegantly outfit their children any longer. Children's clothing made of the finest fabrics and in the latest designs can be purchased right here at home.

SOUTHAMPTON TOWN

Southampton

Hopscotch (516-287-5385) 46 Job's Lane, Southampton. Open 10:00 a.m.–6:00 p.m. Mon.–Sat.; 11:00 a.m.–5:00 p.m. Sun. Owner: Pamela Botsford. This shop in a little courtyard off Job's Lane has adorable children's clothing that includes smocked dresses with matching leggings, coordinated mother-and-daughter outfits, pretty straw hats, designer-name clothing by Giesswin, Isabel Garreton, and Katy & Co., and fabulous fancy party dresses. The shop also carries preteen clothing and a full wardrobe of boys' polo clothing including blazers, coats, slacks, sweaters, T-shirts, etc.

Little Charlotte's Place (516-283-3333) 89 Job's Lane, Southampton. Open in the summer 10:00 a.m.–7:00 p.m. Mon.–Sat.; 12:00 noon–5:00 p.m. Sun.; shorter hours the rest of the year. Owner: Elena A. Ford (daughter of Charlotte). This tiny, little shop is filled with glorious things for the fortunate child. There are chests painted with flowers, pretty lacy bassinets, toys, and exquisite clothing in lovely fabrics, often with elaborate smocking.

FOR ADULTS

EAST HAMPTON TOWN

Ann Crabtree (516-329-6653) 20 Newtown Lane, East Hampton. Open daily in the summer 11:00 a.m.–5:30 p.m.; closed Tues., Wed. from Nov.–Jan.; closed Feb.–Mar. Owner/Manager: Ann Crabtree. For stylish, classy sports clothes, Ann offers a great look — perky Moschino shorts, cropped tops in lime green and orange, and classic slacks and sweaters.

Bonne Nuit (516-324-7273) 55 Main Street, East Hampton. Open daily, 10:00 a.m.–6:00 p.m.; may close Tues.–Wed. in Jan.–Mar.. Owners/Managers: Lorna and Ashlyn Maloney. Bonne Nuit, owned and operated by sisters, is also located in Manhattan. The stores carry fine lingerie, such as Pluto, chenille bed jackets, hair accessories, and pretty, painted ballet slippers.

Cashmere Hampton (516-324-5000) 85 Main Street, East Hampton. Open daily in the summer 10:00 a.m.–6:00 p.m.; closed Tues., Wed. the rest of the year. This upscale store sells chic merchandise that includes a wide variety of sweaters in various styles and colors, dresses, jackets, and skirts, all made of the softest and finest cashmere.

Eileen Fisher (516-324-4111) 26 Newtown Lane, East Hampton. Open in the summer 10:00 a.m.–6:00 p.m. daily; closed Tues., Wed. from Nov.–Apr. Located in the quirky, old shingled building that was formerly the Odd Fellows Hall, Nancy Goell has assembled a fine collection of svelte women's clothing, mostly in basic black, white, or brown.

Entre Nous (516-324-8636) 37 Newtown Lane, East Hampton. Open daily in the summer 10:00 a.m.–6:00 p.m.; closed Tues., Wed. the rest of the year. Owners: Phyllis Baden and Priscilla Helman. This shop has very elegant European clothing — silk knit sweaters, wool gabardine slacks, exclusive suits, and cocktail dresses. All clothing is imported from France or Italy and much of it is specially ordered.

J. Roaman (516-329-0555) 48 Newtown Lane, East Hampton. Open daily 10:00 a.m.–5:00 p.m. Owner: Judy Roaman. Ms. Roaman sells both men's and women's DKNY clothing in her bright shop. You'll find classic jackets, skirts, and slacks for women and slacks, sweaters, and jackets for men.

Kenar (516-324-1650) 53 Main Street, East Hampton. Open in the summer 10:00 a.m.–7:00 p.m. Mon.–Thurs.; 11:00 a.m.–10:00 p.m. Fri. & Sat.; 11:00 a.m.–7:00 p.m. Sun.; shorter hours the rest of the year. This classy, high-tech and high-profile shop has the latest selections for hip, young women from short Ultrasuede and knit skirts to knit tops and jackets.

Enter the world of Ralph Lauren's Polo Country Store in East Hampton.

Polo Country Store

Polo Country Store (516-324-1222) 33 Main Street, East Hampton. Open in the summer 10:00 a.m.–10:00 p.m. Mon.–Sat.; 11:00 a.m.–5:00 p.m. Sun.; 10:00 a.m.–6:00 p.m. the rest of the year. In the trademark setting of wooden floors, old resort signs, and leather, Ralph Lauren has done it again. If you've been invited to a garden party and you want something smashing to wear, this is the place to come. Men buy white linen slacks and "the blazer," as well as jeans, sweaters, and all of the classically correct Ralph Lauren gear. Women love the long, white linen dusters and swingy flowered skirts. This is a full-service Lauren shop, so in addition to clothing, you can find bedding, furniture, and even little herb garden identification stakes.

Shoe-Inn (516-329-4500) 36 Main Street, East Hampton. Open in summer 10:00 a.m.–10:00 p.m. Only in the Hamptons would you find a store devoted only to shoes designed by fashion designers. There are Anne Klein, Calvin Klein, and Ralph Lauren. The designers themselves often make announced visits to the store to promote their shoes, which creates a bit of a ho-hum in the Hamptons, where celebrity-sightings are commonplace.

Waves (516-329-0033) 25 Newtown Lane, East Hampton and (516-537-7767) Main Street, Bridgehampton. Open daily 10:00 a.m.–7:00 p.m.; shorter hours in the winter. Owner: Linda Li. In the summer, Waves has floral chintz shorts, French ballet slippers, and canvas espadrilles, along with Lucy Isaacs and Native American turquoise jewelry. In the winter, there are chic chenille sweaters and scarves in gem tones, panne velvet dresses, and floral oilcloth umbrellas.

Whitewash (516-324-6666) 38 Main Street, East Hampton. Open daily in the summer 10:00 a.m.–11:00 p.m.; shorter hours in the winter. In the summer, Whitewash specializes in all white clothing, much of it in gossamer, gauzy fabrics. In the winter, they switch to black.

SOUTHAMPTON TOWN

Bridgehampton

Brennan's Bit and Bridle, Inc. (516-537-0635) Bridgehampton Common, Plaza East, Bridgehampton. Open in the summer 10:00 a.m.–5:00 p.m. Mon.–Sat.; 10:00 a.m.–3:00 p.m. Sun.; 10:00 a.m.–5:00 p.m. Thurs.–Sun. the rest of the year. This is the place to come for elegant riding apparel, including crops, boots, custom-ordered saddles, tack, blankets, and bridles. They also carry a good selection of gift items.

Sag Harbor

The Hat Box (516-725-0898) Main Street at Long Island Avenue, Sag Harbor. Open in the summer 10:00 a.m.–6:00 p.m. Mon.–Fri.; 10:00 a.m.–10:00 p.m.; 12:00 noon–6:00 p.m. Sun.; shorter hours and closed Tues. the rest of the year. Wonderful, whimsical hats are custom-made here by designer Paula Del Percio. In the summer, she has strawhats and felt bowlers, decorated with picket fences and butterflies. She also has velvet cloches, crocheted hats, bridal veils, feather and flower confections, fabric-covered hatboxes, hat pins, and marvelous antique wicker.

Southampton

Cose Belle (516-283-7564) 79 Job's Lane, Southampton. Open daily in the summer 10:00 a.m.–6:00 p.m.; 10:00 a.m.–6:00 p.m. Fri.–Sun. only the rest of the year. Owner: Shannon McLean. This very classy branch of an upper East Side Manhattan shop has all Italian clothing in the classic lines and natural fibers for which the Italians are so well known. The wool crepe slacks and linen tunics are simple and very elegant.

Laura Ashley (516-287-2104) 87 Main Street, Southampton. Open 10:00 a.m.–5:30 p.m. Mon.–Thurs.; 10:00 a.m.–6:00 p.m. Fri. & Sat.; 12:00 noon–5:00 p.m. Sun. This combined clothing and decorator shop has pretty sundresses for women and children, as well as pleated lamp shades, sheets, and wallpaper.

Saks Fifth Avenue (516-283-3500) 1 Hampton Road (Main Store) & 50 Main Street (the Men's Store), Southampton. Open 10:00 a.m.–6:00 p.m. Mon.–Thurs.; 10:00 a.m.–7:00 p.m. Fri.; 10:00 a.m.–9:00 p.m. Sat.; 11:00 a.m.–6:00 p.m. Sun. A mini version of its big sister in Manhattan, you can nevertheless find enough clothing to outfit an entire family, from jewelry to shoes and from handbags to evening gowns.

Tracy Tooker Hats (516-287-3956) 81 Job's Lane, Southampton. Open daily Mem.–Labor Day and weekends May, Sept.–Dec. Tracy Tooker is a hat designer who truly knows her discriminating Hamptons' customers. Celebrities looking for the ideal chapeau for an elegant event and those who want knock-'em-dead bonnets for the Hamptons' Classic Horse Show, all go to Tracy Tooker. (She even has a booth at the Horse Show.) Tracy also maintains shops in Manhattan and Palm Beach.

Water Mill

De Bracieux (516-726-2605) Water Mill Square, Water Mill. Open in season 10:00 a.m.–4:00 p.m. Thurs.–Sat., Mon.; fewer days the rest of the year. Owner: Wayne Young. After 25 years on Newtown Lane in East Hampton, designer Wayne Young has moved to Water Mill. He still designs the simple but classic suits, blouses, and skirts for which he's noted. All fabrics are of natural fibers in subtle, earthy colors and are generally imported from Italy or England. Find him now in a little courtyard, opposite Mirko's Restaurant.

Westhampton Beach

Lon Sabella et Daniel (516-288-5988) 8B Moniebogue Lane, Westhampton Beach. Open daily 11:00 a.m.–5:30 p.m. This very stylish women's wear shop specializes in made-to-order and ready-to-wear fashions. There are beaded dresses, slinky black sheaths, filmy ball gowns, plus slacks outfits and jewelry.

Village Safari Clothiers, Ltd. (516-288-4541) 8D Moniebogue Lane, Westhampton Beach. Open daily 11:00 a.m.–5:30 p.m. Handsome men's clothing is displayed amidst dark wood antique furniture. You'll find sweaters, blazers, silk ties, linen shorts, and all of the necessary items for an elegant, summer garden party.

DECORATIVE ARTS, INTERIOR DESIGN, FURNITURE

EAST HAMPTON TOWN

Lars Bolander (516-329-3400) 5 Toilsome Lane, East Hampton. Open daily 10:00 a.m.–5:00 p.m. May–Sept.; closed Tues., Wed. the rest of the year. Beautiful, very high-quality European and painted furniture is imported by Lars Bolander for his shop. He also sells decorative objects, old prints, oil paintings, and does interior design.

SOUTHAMPTON TOWN

Bridgehampton

Cabbage Rose Interiors (516-537-9225) Main Street, Bridgehampton (above Country Gear). Open 9:00 a.m.–5:00 p.m. Mon.–Sat. This fine boutique is a one-stop shop for all interior design needs. There are fine fabrics for upholstery, draperies, and bed coverings.

Country Gear (516-537-1032) Main Street, Bridgehampton. Open daily year-round 10:00 a.m.–6:00 p.m. Designer Charles DiSapio's unique niche is appreciated by the most discriminating home owners. His shop is filled with fascinating, English and Irish country-style antiques that include harvest tables, fireplace mantels, and armoires. Although all of these are for sale, they are also used as models for his custom-designed work. Adapting a molding here or a finish there and using aged pine (generally 150–200 years old), he custom-designs libraries, entertainment centers, hutches, and armoires that won't be found anywhere else. Scattered throughout the shop are smaller, English antique accessories, such as metal bottle caddies, enamel kitchen boxes, mirrors, and birdcages.

Juan Garcia Habitat (516-537-2121) Main Street, Bridgehampton. Open daily, except Wed. and Sun., year-round 10:00 a.m.–5:00 p.m. This interior design studio has museum-quality antiques and a wide array of interesting fabrics. At the annual sale, fabrics are offered at terrific prices. Among the antiques, you might find a hand-carved, mahogany four-poster bed or a round, mahogany tilt-top table (dining room-sized) with a carved pedestal base.

Sag Harbor

Headley Studio (516-725-1194; Website: www.bestselections.com) 97 Madison Street, Sag Harbor. Open daily in the spring and summer 11:00 a.m.–6:00 p.m.; in the fall and winter 11:00 a.m.–5:00 p.m.; closed Wed. Owners: Barry Head and Stephen Hadley. The owners of this very special shop create decorative finishes, such as faux wood and trompe l'oeil, floorcloths and custom-made, decoratively painted furniture for private clients. Most of their work is done on commission, but in 1992, they opened this shop in their studio, and it's proven so successful that they keep expanding. In 1998, for example, Stephen started designing wonderful, comfortable, but creative clothing. In addition to their own work, they have unusual and very high-quality gifts and housewares for sale, including pillows, pottery, unusual covers for director's chairs, painted furniture, wastebaskets made of printed wallpaper (treated so that they can be rinsed out), and so much more. During the winter months, the owners hold classes for adults and children that are fun and very creative. This is one shop that *Guide Michelin* would say is "worth the trip."

Southampton

C.B. Summerhouse, Ltd. (516-287-1800) 70 Main Street Southampton. Open daily in the summer 10:00 a.m.–6:00 p.m.; fewer days the rest of the year. Owner: Cathleen B. Stewart. Ms. Stewart forsook a career in the stock market to open this Ralph Lauren shop, which includes beds, bedding, pillows, and delightful accessories.

Chez Morgan Home (516-287-3595) 53 Job's Lane, Southampton. Open 10:00 a.m.–5:00 p.m. Mon.–Fri.; 10:00 a.m.–8:00 p.m. Sat.; 11:00 a.m.–4:00 p.m. Sun. This design shop in a premier designer town has terrific furniture and decorator services. You might find a massive four-poster plantation bed, an ornate iron bed, a pine armoire, or a leather and wood daybed. Lush fabrics are used for upholstery and draperies.

Papago (516-287-7272) 53 North Sea Road, Southampton. Open in the summer 10:00 a.m.–5:00 p.m. Mon.–Thurs.; 10:00 a.m.–6:00 p.m. Fri. & Sat.; shorter hours the rest of the year. Located in a charming brick building, painted lemon yellow and trimmed in indigo blue, Donna Vita has assembled a collection of furnishings that are perfect for a beach home. There are pine tables and chairs, painted chests, and even a coffee table made from a painted door.

Westhampton Beach

Jeanne Leonard Interiors (516-288-7964) 10 Beach Road, Westhampton Beach. Open daily, except Tues., Sun., 9:30 a.m.–5:30 p.m. This impressive design store has a wide range of fabrics, antique and painted furniture, paintings and prints, rugs, lamps, and furniture, such as a pine breakfront, a double-doored armoire, and a shell-designed corner cupboard. There are even wrought iron gates and fireplace screens. Jeanne Leonard Going offers both residential and commercial interior design services.

FACTORY OUTLETS

EAST HAMPTON TOWN

Amagansett Square is composed of a very tasteful collection of cottages that house a variety of outlet stores, including Van Heusen, Le Sportsac, Bass, Sunglass Hut, Geoffrey Beene, Izod, and Joan and David. The prices are much better than retail, especially during sales.

Coach Store (The Factory Store) (516-267-3340) Main Street, Amagansett and (516-329-1777) 69 Main Street. Open daily year-round 10:00 a.m.–6:00 p.m. For leather handbags, briefcases, and wallets, plus T-shirts, sweats, and shorts, this shop has very reasonable prices.

SOUTHAMPTON TOWN

American Pacific (516-287-5156) 58 Job's Lane, Southampton. Open 10:00 a.m.–6:00 p.m. Mon.–Thurs.; 10:00 a.m.–9:00 p.m. Fri. & Sat.; 12:00 noon–5:00 p.m. Sun. This quilt shop has a broad selection of traditional American patchwork quilts that range from pretty pastel florals to bold geometrics — all made with American 100 percent cotton fabrics. Also available are pillows, crib quilts, duvet covers, and other accessories. The prices in this, the company's first outlet store, are phenomenally low, beginning at $59.99.

In Southampton, the Dansk Factory Store on Main Street sells all the great Dansk items at 40–50 percent below retail.

Morgan McGivern

Dansk Factory Outlet (516-287-2093) 5 Main Street, Southampton. Open daily 10:00 a.m.–6:00 p.m. Mon.–Sat.; 11:00 a.m.–5:00 p.m. Sun. This large store features Dansk baking dishes, serving pieces, china, silver, glassware, wooden bowls, trays and gift items. Prices are often 40–50 percent below retail.

John Rogers Collection Outlet (516-287-5567) 48 Main Street, Southampton. Open 10:00 a.m.–5:30 p.m. Mon.–Sat.; 12:00 noon–5:00 p.m. Sun. When John Rogers started importing and selling the unusual furniture, made in Indonesia to resemble antique, English colonial pieces, he had immediate success. Now he sells to major department stores and upscale catalog companies. Some of the factory seconds, however, are sold through his outlet store here.

Villeroy and Boch Factory Outlet (516-283-7172) 35 Main Street, Southampton. Open 10:00 a.m.–5:30 p.m. Mon.–Thurs.; 10:00 a.m.–8:00 p.m. (6:00 p.m. in the winter) Fri. & Sat.; 12:00 noon–5:00 p.m. Sun. This factory outlet store of the well-known German tabletop designer offers porcelain, silver, glassware, and gifts at discounts of 40–70 percent off retail.

GALLERIES

A rt galleries abound in the Hamptons and are the site of many art shows. Opening receptions for the shows attract glittering crowds of artists, writers, and actors. The gallery scene is such an established institution in the Hamptons, that the avid gallery hopper may attend as many as five openings in one night. The following listings represent only a few of the better-known galleries.

EAST HAMPTON TOWN

Galerie Select, Ltd. (516-329-5550) 6 Main Street in the Parish Mews, East Hampton. Open year-round 12:00 noon–7:00 p.m. Wed.–Mon. Owner: Manfred Huffman. This fine gallery has an elegant selection of original oil, watercolor, and acrylic paintings, as well as etchings, lithographs, and sculpture. It specializes in the early surrealists.

Giraffics Gallery (516-329-0803) 79A Newtown Lane, East Hampton. Open daily in the summer 10:00 a.m.–6:00 p.m; rest of year 10:30 a.m.–12:30 p.m. Mon.–Wed.; 10:30 a.m.–1:00 p.m. Thurs.; 10:30 a.m.–5:30 p.m. Fri.–Sun. Owners: Mary and Kevin Harty. This interesting gallery specializes in graphics, prints, and lithographs. It provides representation for such artists as James McMullan, Lynn Curlee, and Michael Paraskevas. An exhibit might include stage set sketches by well-known theater designers, such as Tony Walton.

Lizan/Tops Associates (516-324-3424) 66 Newtown Lane, East Hampton. Open in the summer 11:00 a.m.–6:00 p.m. Thurs.–Mon., 10:00 a.m.–9 p.m. Sat.; 10:00 a.m.–6:00 p.m. Fri.–Sun. the rest of the year. Owners: Arnie Lizan and Elizabeth Tops. Located in the back of 66 Newtown Lane, this shop is a bit difficult to find, but the search is worth the effort. These two esteemed Manhattan art dealers are especially well versed in nineteenth- and twentieth-century art, as well as contemporary American work. You'll find Long Island landscapes, Old Masters' prints, drawings, watercolors, architectural engravings, botanical prints, photography, and more.

Morgan Rank Gallery (516-324-7615) 4 Newtown Lane, East Hampton. Open daily in the summer 10:00 a.m.–5:30 p.m.; shorter hours the rest of the year; closed Feb. Owner: Morgan Rank. This gallery specializes in American primitive art, showing only the work of self-taught artists. You can depend on finding highly original, unusual artwork here.

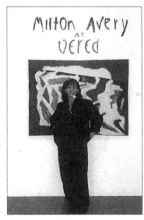

Vered Gallery

Ruth Vered in front of a painting by Milton Avery, one of the many artists represented by the Vered Art Gallery in East Hampton.

Vered Art Gallery (516-324-3303) 68 Park Place, East Hampton. Open daily in the summer 11:00 a.m.–6:00 p.m.; closed Tues., Wed. the rest of the year (and Thurs. in Jan.). Owner: Ruth Vered. The Vered Gallery represents some of the most prestigious artists in America — Willem de Kooning, Wolf Kahn, Milton Avery, Pablo Picasso, Henri Matisse, Marc Chagall, Alfonso A. Ossorio, Thomas Moran, Childe Hassam, Larry Rivers, Alfred Stieglitz, and Andy Warhol, among others.

Wallace Gallery (516-329-4516) 37A Main Street, East Hampton (on a mews off Main Street). Open 10:00 a.m.–7:00 p.m. Mon.–Thurs.; 10:00 a.m.–11:00 p.m. Fri. & Sat. from Jul.–Aug.; closed Tues., Wed. and shorter hours the rest of the year, except closed Jan.–mid-Mar. Terry Wallace is an expert in museum-quality nineteenth- and twentieth-century American art and specializes in art from that period, created by Eastern Long Island artists. In his shop, you'll find fine oil paintings and watercolors and at one time, a tile painted by William Moran, who was one of the members of the Tile Club, a group of painters who made East Hampton their home in the summer.

SOUTHAMPTON TOWN

Interesting art shows are held throughout the summer at the Elaine Benson Gallery.

Tulla Booth

Elaine Benson Gallery (516-537-3233) Montauk Highway, Bridgehampton. Open daily 12:00 noon–6:00 p.m., except Wed., mid-May–mid-Sept.; closed the rest of the year. This gallery was owned by perhaps the most influential art dealer in the Hamptons. Not only did Elaine Benson devote 30 years to promoting Hampton artists (many undiscovered until she championed them), but she also raised many dollars for various charities through her art previews and events. Her gallery always contains a range of interesting, unusual art. Sadly, Ms. Benson passed away just as we went to press.

Sundance Gallery (516-537-5513) Main Street, Bridgehampton. Open in the summer 11:00 a.m.–6:00 p.m. Sun.–Wed.; 11:00 a.m.–6:00 p.m. Thurs.–Sat.; fewer days and shorter hours the rest of the year. This unusual gallery sells local art and interesting and unusual craft art from around the world. There are oil paintings, pottery, and rare, beaded wood carvings in brilliant colors made by the Huichol Indians. These exquisite carvings are first carved into animal forms (a lizard is popular), and then colorful beads are painstakingly glued on with beeswax.

GIFTS

EAST HAMPTON TOWN

Claudia's Carriage House (516-668-5409) Main Street, Montauk. Open daily 10:00 a.m.–6:00 p.m.; later hours in the summer. Owners: Claudia and Brad Dickinson. If you don't find the gift you're looking for here, it probably isn't made. Choose from a selection of jewelry, dolls, children's clothing, stuffed animals, china, crystal, and lots of Christmas items, displayed on an old sleigh, a carriage, and a buckboard. The salespeople are very helpful.

Rumrunner (516-324-3444) 14 Main Street, East Hampton. Open daily in the summer 9:00 a.m.–11:00 p.m.; shorter hours in the winter; and (516-287-0583) 22 Main Street, Southampton. Open daily year-round 10:00 a.m.–6:00 p.m.; and (516-668-3174) West Lake Drive at Gosman's Dock, Montauk. Open in the summer 10:00 a.m.–11:00 p.m.; call for hours the rest of the year. With great style, Rumrunner offers a selection of cleverly selected furniture, bright Italian and Portuguese dishes, replicas of old signs, and mechanical banks. There are also painted tiles, pillows, and cards.

Zona (516-324-4100) 2 Newtown Lane, East Hampton. Open in the summer 9:00 a.m.–9:00 p.m. Mon.–Thurs.; 9:00 a.m.–10:00 p.m. Fri., Sat.; 9:00 a.m.–5:00 p.m. Sun.; shorter hours and closed Wed. the rest of the year. Owner: Lou Sagar. This upscale transplant of the Soho store is sort of a home furnishings' shop, sort of a garden shop, and sort of a clothing and card shop. Slick tile floors and brightly colored pottery are reminiscent of southern Italy. In the summer, they sell bunches of lovely miniature roses at reasonable prices.

SOUTHAMPTON TOWN

B. Glorioso's (516-537-3090) 43 Main Street, Bridgehampton. Open daily 11:00 a.m.–5:00 p.m. The Americana Collection at this shop is the best. If you're into flags, you'll love this shop. There are flags on pillows, weathered birdhouses, and blankets; flags are painted on wood for hanging on a wall, on wooden hearts for hanging around the neck, on benches, on baskets, and on many more items. You'll also find table linens (both with and without flags) and women's and children's cotton clothing.

O'Suzanna (516-288-2202) 108 Main Street, Westhampton Beach. Open daily 10:30 a.m.–6:00 p.m.; on the weekends in the summer 10:30 a.m.–10:00 p.m. Owner Suzanne Marchisello travels the back roads of Italy every year, finding new ceramic designers whose work she features in her store. Many of the designs are her own, and most of her pieces won't be seen elsewhere.

O'Suzanna's shop in Westhampton Beach is filled with colorful European pottery.

Tulla Booth

Come here to find bright, hand-painted Italian pottery in platters, vases, dishes, and plaques.

Pine Cone (516-288-8316) 1 Glovers Lane, Westhampton Beach. Open daily Mem. Day–Labor Day 10:00 a.m.–8:00 p.m.; 10:00 a.m.–12:00 midnight Fri., Sat.; 12:00 noon–6:00 p.m. Thurs.–Mon. the rest of the year. Owner: Judy Garry. This tiny shop has some very interesting pieces tucked into its small space. There are large collections of antique lead soldiers and ceramic teapots (some hand painted). All of the Limoges, Kosta Boda/Orrefors, Wedgewood, and Battersea dishes and figurines, as well as other porcelain lines, are discounted. There are also unusual dolls, a monocled, British serving gent (two feet high), picture frames, teddys, teddys, and more teddys, jewelry, brass candlesticks, cobalt glass vases, and more.

HANDCRAFTS

EAST HAMPTON TOWN

Local Color (516-329-2700) 32 Park Place, East Hampton. Open daily in the summer 10:00 a.m.–8:00 p.m.; shorter hours the rest of the year. Located just off the parking lot behind Main Street and Newtown Lane, this ceramics studio provides "greenware" plates, mugs, boxes, toothbrush holders, and a variety of other objects for hand painting by artists and wanna-bes. All of their pieces are lead-free and dishwasher-safe. They will give you instructions on painting and glazing your piece, and then they will fire it for you. It's lots of fun for children and a great way to personalize your gifts.

Thimbelina (516-324-0729) 32 Newtown Lane, East Hampton. Open daily in the summer 10:00 a.m.–5:00 p.m.; 10:00 a.m.–5:00 p.m. Tues.-Sat. the rest of the year. Owner: Lucy Sprunger. This marvelous shop is a needlepointer's dream. After selling hand-painted needlepoint kits to shops and through mail order for a number of years, Lucy opened her own shop. She's a very creative designer who specializes in personalized needlepoint canvases of homes, dogs, horses, and other treasured memories; her floral pillows, rugs, and needlepoint signs are very popular. She also sells Mario Buatta designs, beribboned scissors, pretty thimbles, a wide range of yarns, and other sewing accessories.

SOUTHAMPTON TOWN

Gayle Willson Gallery (516-283-7430) 43 Job's Lane, Southampton. Open in the summer 11:00 a.m.–5:00 p.m. Mon.–Sat.; 12:00 noon–5:00 p.m. Sun.; closed Tues. and sometimes Wed. the rest of the year. Owner: Gayle Willson. This store features art fabrics, wearable art, and contemporary, high-quality arts and crafts, including beautiful, handmade jewelry and clothing.

HOUSEWARES & KITCHEN SHOPS

Curly Willow (516-324-1122) 55 Main Street, East Hampton. Open daily in the summer 9:00 a.m.–6:00 p.m.; closed Tues., Wed. the rest of the year. Owner: Denise Rebaudo. There are pots and pans, kitchen utensils, pottery, placemats and napkins, and even birdhouses here.

Fishs Eddy (516-287-2993) 50 Job's Lane, Southampton. Open in the summer 10:00 a.m.–10:00 p.m. Sun.–Thurs.; 10:00 a.m.–11:00 p.m. Fri. & Sat.; shorter hours the rest of the year. This is a terrific place to purchase dishes for a party. Just as in the Manhattan stores, this great shop is stacked from floor to ceiling with dishes that are factory overruns or surplus orders. There are dishes with nautical motifs that were ordered for yacht clubs and bistro plates that were ordered for restaurants. One day, there were stacks of white plates with elaborate gold rims that had been ordered for the Helmsley Palace Hotel.

Kitchen Classics (516-537-1111) Main Street, Bridgehampton. Open daily 9:30 a.m.–6:00 p.m.; closed one day a week Jan.–Apr. Owner: Jane Rivkin. From cookbooks to gadgets, from tablecloths to pots and pans, this is a full-service kitchen shop. One fun and whimsical item is the hand-painted, Italian luncheon set that is brightly painted in such a variety of patterns that nothing matches.

The Sea Shell (516-288-2285) 128 Main Street, Westhampton Beach. Open in the summer 10:00 a.m.–5:00 p.m. Mon.–Sat.; shorter hours in the winter. Owner: Mrs. A. J. Farrell. There's a fine selection of elegant china here that features a wide range of Herend china, including the delicate figurines, and also table-ware, created by talented artist Lynn Chase who uses a palette of brilliant colors to create her dramatic porcelains.

Sylvester & Co. (516-725-5012) Main Street, Sag Harbor. Open daily in the summer 8:00 a.m.–9:00 p.m.; closed Wed. and shorter hours the rest of the year. Owner: Linda Sylvester. This is a kitchenware shop with all of the items that you'd expect, but it also sells gourmet items, pottery, china, place mats, gardening baskets, cookbooks and gardening books, fresh coffee, muffins, cookies, and pastries. The coffee pot is on all day, and it's a town gathering spot.

Tabletop Designs (516-283-1313) 39 Job's Lane, Southampton. Open 10:00 a.m.–6:00 p.m. Mon.–Sat.; 11:00 a.m.–5:00 p.m. Sun. Owner: Stephanie Queller. Ms. Queller carries a marvelous combination of antique and decorator china — all beautifully displayed as you might at your own dinner party. On one recent visit, I found some beautiful blue and white antique flo-blue plates with scalloped edges, and some handpainted dishes with gold rims. There are also silver flatware and serving pieces, napkins and place mats, and much, much more.

Williams-Sonoma (516-537-3040) Bridgehampton Commons, Bridgehampton. Open in the summer 10:00 a.m.–8:00 p.m. Mon.–Sat.; 11:00 a.m.–6:00 p.m. Sun.; same hours the rest of the year, except open 10:00 a.m.–7:00 p.m. Mon.–Sat. The addition of a new building at Bridgehampton Commons in 1994 brought this well-known kitchen store to town. Here you'll find terrific pots and pans, dishes, linen, silverware, glassware, knives, and such food staples as garlic oil, passion fruit vinegar, and coffee beans.

JEWELRY

EAST HAMPTON TOWN

Jewels by Virtu (516-324-1480) 60 The Circle, East Hampton. Open 10:00 a.m.–6:00 p.m. Mon.–Sat.; shorter hours the rest of the year. This fine jewelry store handles several designers who create elegant rings, necklaces, bracelets, and earrings. You can also buy watches and other pieces of jewelry.

London Jewelers (516-329-3939) 2 Main Street, East Hampton. Open in the summer 10:00 a.m.–5:30 p.m. Mon.–Thurs.; 10:00 a.m.–10:00 p.m. Fri. & Sat.; 11:00 a.m.–5 p.m. Sun.; shorter hours the rest of the year. After transforming a great old building that was in need of considerable repair, the owners opened this very elegant shop in 1996. This shop offers a selection of fine jewelry, plus one of the largest collections of MacKenzie-Childs handpainted furniture and dishes outside the couple's own shop in Manhattan. In addition, there's a Tiffany jewelry department and an Alfred Dunhill humidor room, where you can select fine cigars.

McCarver & Moser (516-324-7300) 27 Main Street, East Hampton. Open in the summer 10:00 a.m.–8:00 p.m. Mon.–Sat.; 12:00 noon–8:00 p.m. Sun.; shorter hours the rest of the year. In this fine and very elegant jewelry and gift store, you will find a selection of art glass by Daum, Baccarat, Steuben, and others, of watches by Cartier, of jewelry by Van Cleef & Arpels, and much more.

SOUTHAMPTON TOWN

Joan Boyce (516-288-1263) 116 Main Street, Westhampton Beach. Open in the summer only 11:00 a.m.–6:00 p.m. on weekdays; 11:00 a.m.–10:00 p.m. on the weekends. Joan Boyce, who also has shops in Manhattan and Aspen, Colorado, is a jewelry designer of international fame. She fashions elegant bracelets, earrings, necklaces, and rings from precious and semiprecious gems in her unmistakably graceful style.

Lee Gallery (516-283-9666) 49 Main Street, Southampton. Open daily in the summer 11:00 a.m.–6:00 p.m.; closed Tues. & Wed. the rest of the year. Owner: Lee Elliot. This store displays and sells very elegant, handmade, nontraditional gold jewelry designed by Lee Elliot, as well as the work of Ray Tracey. You'll find handcrafted designs in fiber, wood, ceramics, and glass.

Rose Jewelry (516-283-5757) 57 Main Street, Southampton. Open 9:30 a.m.–5:30 p.m. Mon.–Sat.; 12:00 noon–5:00 p.m. Sun.; closed Sun. only, Jan.–Mem. Day. Owner: Jan Rose. This very elegant jewelry shop carries unusual, handcrafted rings, bracelets, and other jewelry, and an excellent selection of gifts.

OLD-FASHIONED EMPORIUM

Hildreth's (516-283-2300) 51-55 Main Street, Southampton. Open 9:00 a.m.–5:30 p.m. Mon.–Fri.; 9:00 a.m.–6:00 p.m. Sat.; 11:00 a.m.–5:00 p.m. Sun. Also, **Hildreth House & Garden** (516-537-1616) 2099 Montauk Highway, Bridgehampton. Open 10:00 a.m.–6:00 p.m. Mon.–Sat.; 9:30 a.m.–5:00 p.m. Sun. Owner: Henry Hildreth. This is the granddaddy of Hamptons' department stores. Established in 1842, it's billed as "America's Oldest Department Store." This is still a general store, but one that sells all of the items necessary for today's home: thread, needles, fabric, furniture, bedding, towels, china, glassware, pots and pans, etc. Don't miss the end-of-summer sale, when items are sold at a 40–80 percent discount.

Sag Harbor Variety Store (516-725-9706) 45 Main Street, Sag Harbor. Open Jul.–Aug. 9:00 a.m.–9:00 p.m. Mon.–Sat.; 9:00 a.m.–5:00 p.m. Sun.; the rest of the year 9:00 a.m.–5:30 p.m. Mon.–Sat.; 9:00 a.m.–1:00 p.m. Sun. Remember the old five-and-dime stores — the ones with soda fountains and lunch counters, photo booths where you could have silly pictures taken, and shelves stacked from floor to ceiling with every delight imaginable? That tradition lives on in Sag Harbor. The photo booth and soda fountain may be missing, but how many of the old stores had two cigar-store Indians, guarding the entrance and an old Texaco pump, converted to a floor clock? The Sag Harbor Variety Store has been doing exactly the same thing for almost 75 years and that means selling pots and pans, fabric by-the-yard, sewing notions, candy, hats, cosmetics, jewelry, toys, and much more.

PHOTO SHOPS

Many pharmacies, groceries, and shops sell film and handle photo processing. The following listing gives you the names of the camera stores in the Hamptons that specialize in meeting the needs of photographers. These stores not only help with your film and film-developing needs, but they also sell cameras and accessories.

Hampton Photo Arts, Inc. (516-537-7373) Montauk Highway, Bridgehampton (in the Bridgehampton Common, behind Caldor). Open 10:00 a.m.–6:00 p.m. Mon.–Sat.; 10:00 a.m.–2:00 p.m. Sun. Owner: Dave McHugh. Not only does this store carry a full line of cameras and photographic supplies, but they also sell art supplies and offer custom-framing.

The Morris Studio (516-283-0085) 72 Main Street, Southampton. Open year-round 9:00 a.m.–5:00 p.m. Mon.–Sat.; 11:00 a.m.–4:00 p.m. Sun. Morris Studio has been around for over 100 years, so you know that they know what they're doing. A full-service photo shop, it processes film, sells cameras, film, and accessories, and also carries artists' supplies.

Reed's Photo Shop & Studio (516-324-1067) 54 Newtown Lane, East Hampton. Open daily in the summer 9:00 a.m.–5:00 p.m.; closed Sun. Oct.–Dec., and Thurs. and Sun. Jan.–May. Owner: Jon Reed. This excellent photo shop processess film and sells cameras, accessories, and a variety of film. It is the place to bring print film for quick developing. The salespeople are accommodating and friendly.

CHAPTER SIX
Developing Artistry
CULTURE

The Memorial Day observance in Southampton is accompanied by a cannon salute.

Over the last 100 years, cultural pursuits have played an increasingly important role in the lives of Hamptons' residents and visitors. And even as new artistic expression has flourished, appreciation for traditional art has not diminished. Instead, there is renewed and heightened interest in the history and heritage of the Hamptons.

Today, because of an active historic preservation movement in the Hamptons, there are 19 historic districts on the South Fork — 65 houses, buildings, windmills, sites, and even a wrecked ship are listed on the National Register of Historic Places. This appreciation for the old, combined with the daring thrust of new expression, gives the Hamptons a unique place in history.

We often read about the artistic skill of painters and sculptors from the Hamptons, but we hear less about the skilled craftspeople and artisans, past and present. For instance, the Dominy family lived and worked in East Hampton from around 1750–1850. These skilled furniture makers, who were far more than local carpenters, obtained ideas and tools from Europe and Boston and are known for their tall-case clocks, chests, chairs, and the solid windmills scattered across the East End. Their artistry is appreciated as much today as it was in the 1800s, and examples of their work appear in several local museums. Furthermore, the value of their work is nationally recognized — their workshop and the tools that they used were purchased by The Winterthur Museum in Delaware and are now part of its permanent collection.

This dual interest in old and new also exists in the fine arts. Although the works of Thomas Moran, Childe Hassam, and William Merritt Chase continue to be respected, collected, and admired, the Hamptons embraced and nurtured the art of the abstract expressionists in the 1940s and 1950s. New forms of art continue to be embraced and encouraged today.

Artists of all genres are attracted to the Hamptons, as much by this spirit of welcome and encouragement as by the area's natural beauty. Prominent writers and playwrights who have chosen to live in the Hamptons include P.G. Wodehouse, Truman Capote, John Steinbeck, E.L. Doctorow, Ken Auletta, Peter Matthiessen, Linda Bird Francke, Kurt Vonnegut, Tom Wolfe, Wendy Wasserstein, and many more.

Recording artists, entertainers, singers, composers, newscasters, magazine editors, directors, and producers — all artists of a different nature — are also attracted to the Hamptons. A few include Steven Spielberg, Billy Joel, Donna Karan, Barbra Streisand, Paul Simon, Kathleen Battle, Chevy Chase, Peter Jennings, Paul McCartney, Lauren Bacall, Chuck Scarborough, Martha Stewart, George Plimpton, and Dick Cavett.

CALENDAR OF EVENTS

The following events take place on Long Island's South Fork every year. For an excellent calendar with specific dates, times, and places for each event, contact the **South Fork Promotion Committee** of the local Chamber of Commerce, P.O. Box 64, Hampton Bays, or call the **Long Island Convention and Visitors Bureau** (516-951-3440). The telephone numbers for Chambers of Commerce on the South Fork are as follows:

East Hampton	516-324-0362
Hampton Bays	516-728-2211
Montauk	516-668-2428
Southampton	516-283-0402
Westhampton Beach	516-288-3337

January/February

Hikes and walks are sponsored on the South Shore during January and February by several organizations. These include the **Long Island Greenbelt**

Trail Conference (516-360-0753); the *Group for the South Fork* (516-537-1400); *The Nature Conservancy for the South Fork* (516-329-7689) or *The Nature Conservancy's Mashomack Preserve on Shelter Island* (516-749-1001).

Community Theatre Company (516-324-0806) Guild Hall, East Hampton. A series of theatrical productions.

March

East End Music Festival (516-324-0806) Guild Hall, East Hampton.
Members Exhibition (516-324-0806) Guild Hall, East Hampton.
Purim Carnival (516-324-9858) Jewish Center of the Hamptons in East Hampton. Also at Temple Adas Israel in Sag Harbor (516-725-0904).
St. Patrick's Day Parade (516-668-2428) Main Street, Montauk.
St. Patrick's Day Parade (516-288-3337) Mill Road and Main Street, Westhampton Beach, 12:00 noon.
Seal Watching (516-369-9840) sponsored by Riverhead Foundation for Marine Research and Preservation.

April

Easter Egg Hunts Amagansett Firehouse; Hampton Library, Bridgehampton; Maidstone Gun Club, East Hampton; Parrish Art Museum, Southampton.
Popular Artists Concert Series (516-324-0806) Guild Hall, East Hampton.

May

Dan's Papers Annual Potatohampton Minithon 10K (516-537-0500) Mem. Day weekend, Bridgehampton.
Meet the Writers Book Fair (516-537-3233) Elaine Benson Gallery, Bridgehampton. An annual event at which local writers sign and sell copies of their books to benefit the John Steinbeck writing program at Long Island University's Southampton Campus.

June

Blessing of the Fleet (516-537-0500) Takes place on a Sunday afternoon in Montauk. Fishing craft and private boats parade past a reviewing stand to receive a prayer for safety and a successful season.
The Mighty Montauk Triathlon (516-668-2428) Consists of a 1-mile swim, a 20-mile bike race, and a 10K run.
Pianofest (516-283-2044) Piano Recitals and concerts sponsored by Pianofest, Long Island University in Southampton.
Sag Harbor Cup Sailing Regatta (516-725-3886) Sponsored by Breakwater Yacht Club, Sag Harbor.
Southampton Rotary 8K Run (516-283-0402) Agawam Park, Southampton.

*President Clinton visits East
Hampton, August 1998.*

Morgan McGivern

Summer Pleasures (516-283-2118) Southampton. Sponsored by the Parrish Art Museum. Offers a tour of South Fork gardens and a series of seminars.

July

All for the Sea (516-725-0894) Southampton College. Annual rock concert. Performers in the past have included Tina Turner, Crosby, Stills and Nash, and The Allman Brothers Band.

Boy's Harbor Fireworks Display (516-324-0362) Duke Drive off Springy Banks Road, East Hampton.

Decorator Showcase (516-283-0774) To benefit Rogers Memorial Library, Southampton.

Fireworks Display (516-324-6868) Main Beach, East Hampton. Sponsored by the East Hampton Volunteer Fire Department, at dusk.

Fourth of July Village Parade (516-283-2530) Southampton. Sponsored by the combined veterans organizations.

Greater Westhampton Chamber of Commerce 5K Race (516-288-3337) Main Street, Westhampton Beach.

Hamptons Summerfest (516-725-0894) Old Whaler's Church, Sag Harbor. Classical concerts.

Ladies Village Improvement Society Fair (516-324-1220) 95 Main Street, East Hampton. Begins at 10:00 a.m. Great for kids — games, contests, rides, home-baked goodies, an evening barbecue, and square dancing.

Mary Fritchie Outdoor Art Show (516-288-3337) Sponsored by the Greater Westhampton Chamber of Commerce.

Morgan McGivern

Parades are plentiful in the Hamptons.

The Mercedes-Benz Polo Challenge (516-653-5252) Some of the world's most celebrated polo teams compete annually in the Hamptons. Sponsored by the Bridgehampton Polo Club.

Music Festival of the Hamptons (800-644-4418) Ten days of classical music, ranging from the Baroque to the Romantic periods, including chamber orchestras, a harp concert, children's and senior citizen's concerts, and much more.

Sag Harbor Historic House Tour (516-725-0401) Benefits the John Jermain Memorial Library.

Sir Thomas Crapper 5-Mile Run (516-324-4572) Springs.

August

Artists and Writers Softball Game (516-324-9292) Held in East Hampton. Well-known writers and artists compete in a very serious softball game.

Back at the Ranch (516-668-2744) This concert, benefitting many local organi-

The annual artists vs. writers softball game in East Hampton draws huge crowds to see the celebrity players.

Morgan McGivern

zations, is held annually on a Monday early in August at Deep Hollow Ranch in Montauk. Artists have included Paul Simon, Mary Chapin-Carpenter, The Allman Brothers Band, and Ray Charles.

Dan's Papers Annual Kite Fly (516-537-0500) Held at Sagg Main Beach, Sagaponack. Kites are judged in 24 categories.

Fisherman's Fair (516-324-9686) Held at Ashawagh Hall in Springs, traditionally on the second Saturday in August. Delectable food, annual art show, booths with crafts, children's games, and much more.

Guild Hall Clothesline Art Sale (516-324-0806) East Hampton, 158 Main Street.

Hampton Classic Horse Show (516-537-3177) Held in Bridgehampton at the end of August and beginning of September. Sponsored by the Hampton Classic Horse Show.

House and Garden Tour (516-537-1527) St. Ann's Episcopal Church, Main Street, Bridgehampton. Tour of homes in the Hamptons sponsored by St. Ann's.

King of the Bays Regatta (516-298-9755) Sailing race in Noyack and Gardiner's Bays, sponsored by Irland Boatyard of Shelter Island.

Lighthouse Weekend at Montauk Point (516-668-5340) Sponsored by the Montauk Historical Society.

Long Island Barrel-Tasting Barbecue (516-475-5492) The annual wine tasting and barbecue, sponsored by the Long Island Wine Council and *Wine Spectator* magazine, showcases East End wines and the cooking of local chefs.

Sand Castle Contest (516-324-6250) Atlantic Avenue Beach, Amagansett.

September

Cartier Grand-Slam Tennis Tournament (516-537-0189) Sponsored by the American Cancer Society.

Fit Hampton Triathlon (516-726-8700) 1-mile swim, 25-mile bike race, and a 6.2-mile run. Sponsored by Southampton Hospital.

Historic Sag Harbor Weekend (516-725-0011) Includes tours, a parade, whaleboat races, and a concert. Sponsored by the Sag Harbor Chamber of Commerce.

Historic Seaport Regatta and Breakwater International Regatta (516-725-3886) Sponsored by the Breakwater Yacht Club, Sag Harbor.

Shinnecock Powwow (516-283-6143) Held on the Indian reservation in Southampton, this event includes three days of traditional dances, songs, and lots to do, see, buy, and eat.

October

Architectural House Tour (516-283-3013 or 516-537-3361) In several villages, sponsored by the League of Women Voters.

East Hampton Chamber of Commerce Annual Georgica Jog 5K Run (516-324-0362) Part of the Fall Festival sponsored by the East Hampton Chamber of Commerce.

Jason Green

The Shinnecock Powwow is an annual Labor Day weekend event on the Shinnecock Indian Reservation in Southampton.

Fall Festival on the Village Green (516-668-2428) Montauk. Includes a Clam Chowder Contest and Tasting Competition, hayrides, bike race, and pumpkin decorating. Sponsored by the Montauk Chamber of Commerce.

Halloween Party (516-325-0200) For children and pets. Sponsored by Bide-A-Wee in Westhampton.

Hamptons International Film Festival (516-324-4600) Showings include new and art films. Stars and directors attend.

Montauk Annual Full Moon Bass Tournament (516-668-2428) Bluefish surf casting contest; striped bass derby.

November

Country Christmas (516-283-0402) Southampton. Celebration with Santa coming to town. Sponsored by the Southampton Chamber of Commerce.

Diver's Flea Market (516-283-4000) Southampton College. Sale of new and used diving equipment.

SweetPotatohampton (516-537-0500) Bridgehampton. Annual A.T. (after turkey) 8K run. Sponsored by *Dan's Papers.*

Turkey Day Run for Fun (516-324-4143) Montauk. Sponsored by East Hampton Town Recreation Department.

December

Gallery of Trees (516-324-0362) East Hampton. Trees decorated by businesses and celebrities. Sponsored by East Hampton Chamber of Commerce.

Holiday Historic House and Inn Tour (516-324-0362) Sponsored by the East Hampton Chamber of Commerce.

Santa Parade (516-324-0362) East Hampton. Sponsored by the East Hampton Chamber of Commerce. Also, tree lighting (516-324-0362). Sponsored by Southampton Village Decorating Committee.

Santa Visits the Montauk Point Lighthouse (516-668-3781).

ARCHITECTURE

What a wealth of architectural attractions we have! Architectural styles for residential dwellings range from New England saltbox cottages to elegant 1700s manor houses, Federal-style buildings, high Greek Revival mansions, ornamented Victorians, and modern contemporaries.

Today, the Hamptons are noted for the distinctive modern houses that seem to rise in geometric curves and angles from the dunes and potato fields, as if from another world. Just as famed artists have left their mark on the East End, so have famed architects. The Hamptons have become a laboratory for innovative new ideas in architecture. George Nelson, Richard Meier, Andrew Geller, Jacquelin Robertson, Gwathmey/Siegel, Norman Jaffe, and Robert A.M. Stern are only a few of the contributors.

As Robert B. MacKay said in his introduction to the *AIA Architectural Guide to Nassau and Suffolk Counties, Long Island* (1992):

> . . . *few parts of the country can boast the range and depth of domestic architecture that can be found on Long Island. Perhaps because the Industrial Revolution bypassed the region for lack of falling water to power mill turbines, Long Island's built environment was not seriously affected by subsequent development from the seventeenth century until the post-World War II period, when the G.I. Bill and the growth of the aircraft industry sent thousands eastward on Robert Moses' parkways toward new suburban communities, such as Levittown. As a result, Long Island possesses close to 100 First Period buildings, the greatest concentration of surviving windmills . . . most of its eighteenth-century manorial seats and dozens of relatively intact nineteenth-century villages. . . . Long Island is also significant for its Modern and Post-Modern architecture, the South Fork in particular having served as an incubator for progressive domestic design for over a century.*

CINEMA

Movie producers, directors, and actors make their homes (or at least their summer homes) in the Hamptons. Over the years, many films have been shot on location here, so it's natural for local residents to have an avid interest in movies. As early as 1915, The Sheik was filmed as Rudolph Valentino galloped across the dunes of Montauk. In 1932, No Man of Her Own, starring Clark Gable and Carole Lombard, was shot in Sag Harbor, as was Sweet Liberty, with Alan Alda in 1985. The 1988 movie, Masquerade, with Meg Tilly and Rob Lowe, was also filmed here. Since 1988, HBO has taken over the East Hampton Cinema in the summer for the screening of a major television film, attended by the cast of stars.

In 1993, The Hamptons International Film Festival was inaugurated, premiering 150 popular and art films over a period of five days in October. Films are shown at the East Hampton Cinema, with stars and directors on hand for the screenings and for lectures and symposia held at East Hampton's Guild Hall.

Hamptons' residents thus come by their appreciation of movies quite naturally. We have as much interest in seeing new movies the week that they come out as do New Yorkers, and our movie theaters don't disappoint us. Movies generally open here the same week that they do in New York City. Beware, however, we have often gone to the theater in East Hampton 30 minutes before show time, only to find that the film is sold out. It is advisable to buy the tickets early and then come back.

United Artists East Hampton Cinema (516-324-0448) 30 Main Street, East Hampton. A six-plex movie theater.

Loews Cineplex Hampton Arts (516-288-2600) Brook Road, Westhampton Beach. A twin movie theater.

The Movie (516-668-2393) 3 Edgemere Street, Montauk. A single-movie theater.

Sag Harbor Cinema (516-725-0010) Main Street, Sag Harbor. A single-movie theater that specializes in art and foreign films.

United Artists Southampton Theatre (516-287-2749) 43 Hill Street, Southampton. A four-plex movie theater.

Celebrities often come to the Hamptons for movie and TV film screenings.

Morgan McGivern

CULTURE COURSES

The Hamptons attract some of the finest art teachers, writers, photographers, and craftspeople who conduct summer and winter workshops, classes, courses, and seminars. Since many of these are arranged on short notice, it is important to watch the local newspapers every week for the listing of events scheduled for the next week. In addition, posters announcing special courses will often appear in local stores and offices. The courses listed here are taught annually.

The Victor D'Amico Institute of Art (516-267-3172) Mem. Day–Labor Day. The Art Barge in Napeague is a great East End resource. It offers innovative, refreshing courses, as envisioned by its founder, Victor D'Amico, who was Director of Education at the Museum of Modern Art before beaching his unique barge in Napeague Bay. A wide range of classes are offered, especially in painting and drawing, but also in photography, ceramics, sculpting, jazz, acting, and writing. There are also frequent play readings.

Guild Hall (516-324-0806) East Hampton. A variety of workshops are offered throughout the year, including courses in watercolor, figure drawing, French wheat bundling, collage, and much more. Call for a complete schedule.

Long Island University, Southampton Campus (516-283-4000 ext. 349) A diverse and outstanding selection of courses are offered year-round. The following list represents several of the special workshops offered each summer and does not begin to scratch the surface. Call for a catalog.

> **Master Workshop in Art** (516-283-4000 ext. 349) A renowned group of artists teach a creative course every summer for artists who have mastered the basic techniques. Studio space is provided for this four-week living and working experience, and enrollment is limited. Interaction among the artists is a valuable component. Call for information.

> **Photography Workshop** (516-283-4000 ext. 316) This is an annual workshop held by some of the nation's leading photographers who teach courses as varied as quality black-and-white printing, landscape and architecture in large-format photography, and electronic imagery and scanning photography. Call for a schedule.

> **Writer's Workshop** (516-283-4000 ext. 423) Every year an esteemed group of authors, poets, and playwrights conduct workshops that include fiction writing, poetry, children's literature, screenwriting, and more. Call for a schedule.

Silvia Lehrer's Cookhampton, (516-537-7831) Oliver's Cove Lane, Water Mill. Sylvia Lehrer has been writing the cooking column for *Dan's Papers* for some time; now she's also conducting great cooking classes in her home. Often Mrs. Lehrer will teach a cooking series herself on such subjects as the nuances of regional Italian cooking or the flavors of Provence. In these cases, the classes are hands-on and fully participatory in nature. Other times, she'll invite a well-known Hamptons chef to teach a demonstration class. In either case, the classes are instructional and lots of fun.

ART MUSEUMS

Some artists claim the light is better in the Hamptons than anywhere else — clearer, with a bluer sky and less haze. An account in *Scribner's Monthly* in 1879 of the first visit of the Tile Club to East Hampton claimed the light of the area was ideal, "The afternoon sky was filling with color, and the cumulus clouds that toppled from the horizon were turning to vast chryselephantine statue-galleries, ivory and gold." The area has also been praised for its peace and tranquility — the absence of noise, except for the occasional caw of a crow or the honk of geese flying overhead. Whatever the reason, for more than a century, artists have been attracted to Long Island's South Fork.

The rich tapestry of art now enjoyed in the Hamptons can be traced to those first artists who came here in the 1800s and spread the word. When Thomas Moran, Winslow Homer, Childe Hassam, and their friends from the Tile Club made East Hampton their summer home, they set up their easels at the beach, on the village streets, and on the dunes at Montauk. Their paintings not only captured romantic fancy, but also brought more artists and residents to the area every summer. When one of their members penned an article in 1879 for *Scribner's Monthly* titled "The Tile Club at Play," complete with charming sketches, the summer migration to the Hamptons began in earnest.

William Merritt Chase arrived several years after the Tilers and made Southampton his home, setting up his acclaimed school on the dunes and the Shinnecock Hills surrounding his home. The art of Moran and Chase was similar to the Barbizon or the Hudson River School — romantic landscapes and sunsets, fields of flowers, and pretty women and children — and the Hamptons were christened "The American Barbizon."

The work of Jackson Pollock, who came to the village of Springs in 1945, was art of a different sort. Full of bold color and raw energy, it looked to some like little more than wild abandon put to canvas, but to others it represented a brilliant new technique — and abstract expressionism assumed new importance. Pollock, as did Moran before him, attracted other artists who appreciated the tranquility of the region, as well as its proximity to New York City. Robert Motherwell, Larry Rivers, Willem de Kooning, and Alfonso Ossorio were only a few of those who followed Pollock to the Hamptons. The Museum of Modern Art held summer art classes at Ashawagh Hall in the mid-1950s. Fairfield Porter, who gained increasing stature with a more realistic style, came to Southampton in 1949 and stayed until his death in 1975.

The following list is a representative sampling of exhibition art galleries in the Hamptons. For information about commercial art galleries, see Chapter Five, *Shopping*.

Guild Hall in East Hampton is the site of concerts, theatrical productions, art shows, and numerous classes for both adults and children. Here, the annual Clothesline Art Sale is in progress.

Morgan McGivern

East Hampton

GUILD HALL
516-324-0806.
158 Main Street, East Hampton.
Open: Mid-Jun.–Labor Day daily 11:00 a.m.–5:00 p.m.; Labor Day–mid-Jun. 11:00 a.m.–5:00 p.m. Wed.–Sat., 12:00 noon–5:00 p.m. Sun.
Admission: $2 suggested contribution.

Guild Hall has three large galleries where artwork is exhibited throughout the year. This marvelous institution has been encouraging artists in a variety of genres for over 60 years. It also sponsors the H.R. Hays poetry series, in which readings by internationally acclaimed poets are conducted three times each year. Literary readings by young and emerging fiction writers also take place. Their Clothesline Art Sale, held in August, offers a place for both amateur and professional artists to exhibit and sell their work and is eagerly anticipated each year.

Southhampton

FINE ARTS GALLERY
516-283-4000.
239 Montauk Highway, Southampton.
Open: 1:00 p.m.–5:00 p.m. Mon.–Fri.
Admission: None.

The Fine Arts Gallery on Long Island University's Southampton Campus hosts a variety of art exhibits year-round, ranging from paintings and photography by students and faculty to work by a variety of local painters and sculptors.

THE PARRISH ART MUSEUM
516-283-2118.
25 Job's Lane, Southampton.
Open: Jun. 15–Sept. 15, 11:00 a.m.–5:00 p.m. Mon.–Sat.,

The Parrish Art Museum in Southampton was established in 1897 when its founder, Samuel Longstreth Parrish, hired architect Grosvenor Atterbury to build an addition to the existing Art Museum. The building, located in the heart of the

The Parrish Art Museum was established in 1897. It contains a fine collection of American art, especially from the nineteenth and twentieth centuries.

Morgan McGivern

except Wed.; 1:00 p.m.– 5:00 p.m. Sun.; Sept. 15– Jun. 15, closed Tues., Wed.
Admission: $2 donation.

village beside Rogers Memorial Library, contains exhibition space and a concert hall. The Parrish collection of American art of the nineteenth and twentieth centuries is especially strong in paintings by William Merritt Chase and Fairfield Porter who spent much of their working life in the area. This fine museum also has a sculpture garden and an arboretum and offers lectures, concerts, changing exhibits, and children's programs in art and theater. Adult programs are provided, including films, tours, musical performances, and more.

THE SOUTHAMPTON CULTURAL CENTER
516-287-4300.
2 Pond Lane, Southampton.
Open: Depends on exhibit or event.
Admission: Depends on exhibit or event.

The Southampton Cultural Center, on Pond Lane in the heart of the village, across from Agawam Lake, exhibits artwork by members of the Southampton Artist's Association (a group of 270 artists) about four times yearly. It also sponsors workshops, seminars, and courses. This is a Village of Southampton facility.

Springs

ASHAWAGH HALL
516-324-9802.
Springs-Fireplace Road and Old Stone Highway, East Hampton.
Open: Open for special art exhibits only.

Ashawagh Hall, in the center of the tiny community of Springs, serves as the cultural and community center for the hamlet. Art exhibits, featuring the work of local artists, are held here throughout the summer, as befits the area noted for the number of contemporary painters, sculptures, writers, and others who are inspired by the area.

HISTORIC HOUSES, SITES, MUSEUMS

One of the most progressive and active historic preservation movements in New York State exists in the Hamptons; therefore, many historic houses, museums, and sites have been identified and are open to the public. Southampton and East Hampton Towns currently have 19 historic districts and 65 historic sites. In 1993, in recognition of it's "effective efforts to sustain the beauty of the historic village," the Village of East Hampton was awarded the Pillar of New York Award by the Preservation League of New York State.

The historic houses, sites, museums, and landmarks below are listed here because their primary function is as a site or landmark. For an excellent history of East Hampton, with walking tours of Sag Harbor, East Hampton, Springs, Wainscott, Amagansett, and Montauk, a nature walk through Napeague, and three suggested bicycle tours, read *East Hampton, A History & Guide* (1985) by Jason Epstein and Elizabeth Barlow. Also, the book, *Hampton Style: Houses, Gardens, Artists* (1993) by John Esten and Rose Bennett Gilbert with photographs by Susan Wood, provides an inside look through photographs and text of Hamptons' homes. In addition, there are excellent house and garden tours in East Hampton, Sag Harbor, and Southampton every year.

EAST HAMPTON TOWN

Amagansett

EAST HAMPTON TOWN MARINE MUSEUM
516-267-6544.
Bluff Road, Amagansett.
Open: Jul. 4–Labor Day daily 10:00 a.m.–5:00 p.m.; Jun. and Sept. 10:00 a.m.–5:00 p.m. Sat., Sun.; closed the rest of the year.
Admission: Adults $2; children $1; seniors $1.50.
Mailing Address: 101 Main Street, East Hampton, NY 11937.

The East Hampton Town Marine Museum, overlooking the double dunes and Atlantic Avenue beach beyond, contains a fascinating collection of exhibits that describe and illustrate the history of whaling and fishing on the East End. There are dioramas, boats, tools, equipment, and explanations of the baymen's ongoing struggle with nature. An exhibit of haul seining illustrates the difficulty of this type of fishing; other exhibits describe shellfishing, harpooning, and the evolution of whaling. Outside, a series of displays are devoted to hunting in the Hamptons. Operated by the Hampton Historical Society, it can be reached from the center of Amagansett by traveling east on Montauk Highway and turning right onto Atlantic Avenue. At the end of Atlantic Avenue before the beach parking lot, turn right again onto Bluff Road. The museum is on the left.

MISS AMELIA'S COTTAGE
516-267-3020.
Montauk Highway and Windmill Lane, Amagansett.
Open: Summer and fall only, 1:00 p.m.–4:00 p.m. Thurs.–Sun.
Admission: Adults $2; children $1.
Mailing Address: P.O. Box 7077, Amagansett, NY 11930.

This delightful cottage provides a view into the life of Miss Mary Amelia Schellinger, who occupied the cottage from 1841-1930. The house was built in 1725 by one of Miss Amelia's ancestors and was moved to its present site in 1794. It contains a collection of furniture made by the Dominy family, as well as other examples of furniture and objects typical of the area. For insight into life in the Hamptons during a very interesting period of time, *Miss Amelia's Amagansett* (1976) by Madeline Lee and a tour of Miss Amelia's house, are highly recommended. The **Roy K. Lester Carriage Museum,** also located on the property, contains a fascinating collection of 30 carriages (several impeccably restored), including racing sulkies and sleighs and even a surrey with a fringe on top. The site is operated by the Amagansett Historical Association.

East Hampton

This one-room schoolhouse in East Hampton was built in 1731 and is now a museum.

Suzi Forbes Chase

The East Hampton Historical Society conducts an award-winning walking tour of East Hampton's historic downtown year-round. Tours are led by an actor dressed in colonial costume. This knowledgeable guide delivers a spicy historical narrative about East Hampton's colorful past. For information, call 516-324-6850.

CLINTON ACADEMY
516-324-6850.
151 Main Street, East Hampton.

Clinton Academy is a stately, three-story, brick and clapboard building that once housed the first secondary school, established in 1784, in New York State. Students came from as far away as the

Open: Jun. 1:00 p.m.–2:00
p.m. Sat., Sun.; Jul.
4–Labor Day daily 1:00
p.m.–2:00 p.m.
Admission: Adults $2;
children $1; seniors
$1.50.
Mailing Address: 101 Main
Street, East Hampton,
NY 11937.

West Indies to attend this esteemed school, one of the first to offer a coeducational program; its graduates attended Harvard, Yale, and Princeton. The Academy is one of East Hampton's primary historical museums, housing 12,000 articles that include furniture, clothing, textiles, ceramics, porcelains, tools, books, and photographs. It is operated by The East Hampton Historical Society.

HOME SWEET HOME
516-324-0713.
14 James Lane, East
Hampton.
Open: Jul.–Aug. 10:00
a.m.–4:00 p.m.
Mon.–Sat., 2:00 p.m.–4:00
p.m. Sun; shorter hours
Sept.–Dec. and
Apr.–Jun.; closed
Jan.–Mar.
Admission: Adults $2;
children $1.

Home Sweet Home, a 1650 saltbox house, was the boyhood home of John Howard Payne, author of the famous poem and song, "Home, Sweet Home," which presumably referred to this house. The house and all the furnishings have been impeccably restored. There is a very fine collection of English ceramics, including lustreware and blue Staffordshire china, American furniture, and textiles. The grounds include the 1804 Pantigo Windmill and a lovely garden. Home Sweet Home is operated by the Village of East Hampton.

HOOK WINDMILL
516-324-0713.
Montauk Highway, East
Hampton.
Open: Jul.–Aug. 2:00
p.m.–4:00 p.m. Fri.–Sun.
Admission: Adults $1.50;
children $1.
Mailing Address: 14 James
Lane, East Hampton, NY
11937.

This is one of the best surviving examples of the windmills that dotted the landscape of the East End for many years, grinding grain and sawing lumber, helping the area prosper. Although 11 windmills still remain — more than in any other part of the United States — many are not open to the public. The Hook Windmill was built in 1806 by Nathaniel Dominy IV and is one of the finest examples of Dominy workmanship. Among the laborsaving devices constructed here are a sack hoist, a grain elevator, a screener to clean the grain, and bolters to sift the flour and cornmeal. The Hook Windmill is operated by the Village of East Hampton.

**LADIES VILLAGE
IMPROVEMENT
SOCIETY**
516-324-1220.
95 Main Street, East
Hampton.
Open: Apr.-Dec. 10:00
a.m.–5:00 p.m. Tues.-Sat.;
Jan.-Apr. 10:00 a.m.–5:00
p.m. Fri., Sat. only.

Affectionately known as LVIS, this venerable organization is dedicated to the beautification and preservation of the parks, gardens, trees, and shrubs of East Hampton. It was founded in 1895, and every year its members supervise the planting of annual flowers at the entrances to the village; remind home owners to check their elm trees for Dutch elm disease; and maintain the village greens

This exquisitely furnished dollhouse was the raffle prize in 1995 at the Ladies Village Improvement Society's annual fair in East Hampton.

Morgan McGivern

Admission: None.
Special Features: Thrift shop and bargain books for sale.

and the trees on village streets. To raise funds for its work, the Society holds a perpetual flea market, which includes an enormous selection of used books, and holds an annual fair that families consider one of the highlights of the summer season. The headquarters are located in the Gardiner Brown House, built in 1740.

LONGHOUSE
516-329-3568.
Hands Creek Road, East Hampton.
Open: Open only for lectures, tours, and special events.
Admission: Varies with events.
Mailing Address: P.O. Box 2386, East Hampton, NY 11937.

This is the laboratory and home of renowned designer, Jack Lenor Larson. Events include a series of tours, seminars, and workshops, as well as visual arts, dance, and musical performances. Mr. Larson, a textile designer, art collector, gardener, and philanthropist, said, "This is a dimensional, evolving study in lifestyle, built with the firm belief that we all learn best when experiencing visual arts in the 'full round'. . . as opposed to the media." Operated by the LongHouse Foundation.

MULFORD FARM

516-324-6850.
10 James Lane, East Hampton.
Open: Jul. 4–Labor Day daily 10:00 a.m.–5:00 p.m.; Jun. and Sept. 2:00 p.m.–5:00 p.m. Sat., Sun. only.
Admission: Adults $2; children $1; seniors $1.50.
Mailing Address: 101 Main Street, East Hampton, NY 11937.

Mulford Farm was first settled in 1680 and was owned by the same family from 1712 to 1944. The farm, located in the heart of East Hampton, has been restored to its 1790s roots and provides an exceptional view of life on a prosperous, working eighteenth-century farm. This four-acre site includes the farmhouse with its original kitchen and implements, the original furniture, barn, and farm tools. Costumed guides give a narrated tour that includes an architectural history of East Hampton, as well as a look at early decorative arts and interior design. The tour also includes a living history exhibition where guides will demonstrate family activities, such as weaving and churning butter. Mulford Farm is operated by the East Hampton Historical Society.

TOWN HOUSE

516-324-6850.
149 Main Street, East Hampton.
Open: Weekends only Jun.–Sept.; Jul. 4–Labor Day daily 1:00 p.m.–2:00 p.m.
Admission: Adults $2; children $1; seniors $1.50.
Mailing Address: 101 Main Street, East Hampton, NY 11037.

The Town House, a small structure built in 1731, is an excellent example of a one-room schoolhouse. The potbellied stove at the front, old school desks that contain children's scribbled notes, and early books and slates reveal how children were educated. The building, which also served as the town's original meeting hall, was moved several times. It now stands next to Clinton Academy, on Main Street in the heart of the village, and is operated by the East Hampton Historical Society.

Montauk

MONTAUK POINT LIGHTHOUSE

516-668-2544.
Montauk Highway, Montauk.
Open: Mar.–Mem. Day weekends only 10:30 a.m.–4:30 p.m.; Mem. Day–Labor Day 10:30 a.m.–6:00 p.m. Sun.–Fri., 10:30 a.m.–8:45 p.m. Sat.; Labor Day–Columbus Day weekdays 10:30 a.m.–4:30 p.m., weekends 10:30 a.m.–6:00 p.m.; Nov. weekends only

The Montauk Point Lighthouse is one of the most recognizable landmarks in New York State. Located at the state's easternmost tip, more than 100,000 people visit each year. Its construction was authorized by President George Washington in 1792 to warn ships of the large land mass they were approaching. Although originally built 297 feet from the steep cliffs, erosion during its 200-year history has eaten away all but the remaining 50 feet. Efforts are underway to stabilize the cliffs, although the lighthouse remains open. A museum at the base of the lighthouse contains exhibits and an interesting videotape, which is narrated by Dick Cavett and

10:30 a.m.–4:30 p.m.;
Dec.–Feb. open for
holiday or open house
weekends only.
Admission: Adults $2.50;
children $1; parking $3.
Mailing Address: RFD #2,
Box 112, Montauk, NY
11954.
Special Features: Gift shop;
snack bar.

**SECOND HOUSE
MUSEUM**
516-668-5340.
Second House Road,
Montauk.
Open: Jul.–Columbus Day
10:00 a.m.–4:00 p.m.,
except Wed.; Mem.
Day–Jun. weekends only
10:00 am.–4:00 p.m.
Admission: Adults $2;
children $1.
Mailing Address: P.O. Box
81, Montauk, NY 11954.

THIRD HOUSE MUSEUM
516-852-7878 or
516-854-4949.
Montauk Highway,
Montauk.
Open: Mem. Day–Labor
Day 8:00 a.m.–4:00 p.m.
Fri.–Mon.
Admission: None.

describes the importance and function of light-houses. Children (at least 41 inches tall) and adults can walk to the top of the tower for a spectacular view of the ocean. A snack bar, a large picnic area beside the parking lot, and many trails lead to the beach and across the bluffs. This landmark is operated by the Montauk Historical Society.

Second House Museum was the second house built to shelter the cattle and sheep tenders who spent their summers on the Montauk pasturelands. From 1661 until the 1920s, tenders herded settlers' cattle each summer to the verdant pastures in Montauk. It is said that cattle joined these great cattle drives from as faraway as Patchogue. Second House was built in 1746 and is now the oldest building in Montauk. It's furnished with artifacts and beautiful period furniture, including lovely wicker and pine pieces. The original construction of handmade nails and pegged beams is still visible. It is operated by the Montauk Historical Society.

Third House Museum was built in 1749, the third and final house constructed for the "cowboys" who watched over the cattle, sheep, and horses on the summer pastureland in Montauk. It is a large, rambling, wooden house, where Teddy Roosevelt stayed in 1898 when he and his Rough Riders returned sick and injured from the Spanish-American War in Cuba. The house is used as the office for Theodore Roosevelt County Park. The **Pharaoh Museum,** containing Indian artifacts once belonging to the last family of the Montauk tribe to occupy the area, is in a wooden building on a hill behind Third House. Also on display are archeological tools and exhibits describing digging and dating techniques. Third House is on the left on the Montauk Highway, between the village of Montauk and the lighthouse. It is operated by the Suffolk County Parks Department.

Springs

It's been said of the ***Green River Cemetery*** that artists are "dying to get in." Ever since Jackson Pollock was buried here in 1956, other artists have been purchasing plots. Pollock's grave, in the back of the oldest section, is marked by a massive boulder called an *erratic,* deposited as the glaciers receded some 15,000 years ago. His wife, Lee Krasner, who was also an artist is buried in front of him. The cemetery is located on Accabonac Road, almost to Old Stone Highway.

Pollock-Krasner House and Study Center

Jackson Pollock's studio in Springs is open to visitors.

**POLLOCK-KRASNER
HOUSE AND STUDY
CENTER**
516-324-4929.
830 Fireplace Road, East
Hampton.
Open: May–Oct. 11:00
a.m.– 4:00 p.m. Thurs.–
Sat. Site tours by
appointment only.
Admission: $5.

Jackson Pollock's painting techniques were unique. Instead of using typical artists' paint, he preferred ordinary house paint. Instead of using artists' brushes, he devised several methods of splashing his canvas with color. He placed the canvas on the floor instead of on the wall; he sometimes poured directly from the can, sometimes spattered, dripped, or dribbled with a large brush, a stick, a filled basting syringe, or even applied the paint directly with his bare hands. Although his methods may have been considered primitive, the results that he achieved changed the face of American art; the critics called it abstract expressionism. This first, uniquely American, art technique gained acclaim and respect for American artists and put them on a par with their European contemporaries. Pollock's barn studio was so drafty that he filled the wide cracks with rags in the winter, but it was here, between 1946–1956, that he created his greatest masterpieces. After

Pollock's death in 1956, his wife Lee Krasner took over his studio and continued to paint well into the 1980s. The farm on which they lived, overlooking the peaceful marshes and bay of Accabonac Creek, the barn studio, and grounds are open to the public by appointment. The study center, containing the artists' personal papers and a valuable oral history library, is open year-round. Operated by The Stony Brook Foundation.

SOUTHAMPTON TOWN

Bridgehampton

CORWITH HOUSE
516-537-1088.
Montauk Highway,
  Bridgehampton.
Open: Mid-Jun.–mid-Sept.
  12:00 noon–4:00 p.m.
  Thurs.–Sat.
Admission: Voluntary
  donation.
Mailing Address: P.O. Box
  977, Bridgehampton, NY
  11932.

The Corwith House, an historic 1820s home in Bridgehampton, contains interesting colonial, Empire, and Victorian furniture and decor, displayed in room settings. A kitchen set up as a washroom reveals the difficulties of keeping all those white lace dresses clean and ironed. Upstairs rooms are devoted to lovely Victorian children's clothing, toys, and dolls. The Tractor Barn displays tractors and farm machinery, including a tall and unwieldy 1921 steam tractor. The Hildreth-Simons Machine Shop, on the same property, includes antique engines — all kept in working order. The George W. Strong Wheelwright Shop contains the tools used to make wagons and sleds. The machine shop and the wheelwright shop are generally open only on special occasions. Operated by the Bridgehampton Historical Society.

Flanders

THE BIG DUCK
516-852-8292.
Route 24, Riverhead.
Open: In the summer 10:00
  a.m.–5:00 p.m. Sun.–
  Thurs., 10:00 a.m.–7:00
  p.m. Fri., Sat.; fall and
  spring 10:00 a.m.–5:00
  p.m. weekends only.
Admission: None.
Mailing Address: P.O. Box
  144, West Sayville, NY
  11796.

Recognized as one of the most famous examples of roadside art, this gigantic white duck measures 30 feet long and 20 feet high. It was built in 1931 to attract customers to the Big Duck Ranch. The inside was a salesroom where clients could purchase Peking duck, otherwise known as Long Island Duckling. Today, it's a tourist information center and a shop selling Long Island gifts and "duck-a-bilia." Operated by the Friends for Long Island's Heritage.

Quogue

OLD SCHOOLHOUSE MUSEUM
516-653-4224.
Quogue Street East, Quogue.
Open: Jul. 4–Labor Day 2:00 p.m.–5:00 p.m. Mon., Weds., Fri.; 10:00 a.m.–12:00 noon Sat.
Admission: None.
Mailing Address: P.O. Box 1207, Quogue, NY 11959.

The Old Schoolhouse Museum provides a look at a much larger schoolhouse than the one in East Hampton. When built in 1822, it was acclaimed as the "largest and best in Suffolk County." It is in pristine condition, with polished wood floors, a large fireplace, and a weathered shingle exterior. Used as a school and community meeting house until 1893, it now contains artifacts from Quogue's history, including photographs, dolls, toys, furniture, and more. Workshops, lectures, and exhibits are held in the museum in the summer. It is operated by the Quogue Historical Society.

Sag Harbor

Sag Harbor has many interesting old houses and buildings. The Society for the Preservation of Long Island Antiquities has developed a handy walking map to help you find and identify them. The map is on the inside of the brochure for the Old Custom House. Also, the Information Center, located in the old windmill at the entrance to Long Wharf, is a good resource.

THE OLD CUSTOM HOUSE
516-725-0250 or 516-692-4664.
Garden Street, Sag Harbor.
Open: Mem. Day–Jun. 10:00 a.m.–5:00 p.m. Sat., Sun.; Jul.–Aug. daily 10:00 a.m.–5:00 p.m.; Labor Day–Columbus Day 10:00 a.m.–5:00 p.m. Sat., Sun.; closed the rest of the year.
Admission: Adults $3.00; seniors & children $1.50.
Mailing Address: 93 North Country Road, Setauket, NY 11733-1350.

The Old Custom House, on the corner of Main and Garden Streets across from the Sag Harbor Whaling Museum, was originally the home of Henry Packer Dering who became the second customs collector of Sag Harbor in 1789. He later became the first postmaster as well, handling both duties from this home. The room that he used as his office is especially interesting. It has interior wooden shields that Mr. Dering could slide across the windows to prevent people from seeing inside when he was counting money. The building contains many pieces of furniture and decorative details that help us understand how a sophisticated family lived in the eighteenth century. It is operated by the Society for the Preservation of Long Island Antiquities.

Oaklands Cemetery was established in 1840 and is the resting place of many of the old families that made Sag Harbor famous; George Balanchine is among its more recent occupants. The most arresting and photographed monument, however, is one dedicated to John Howell who died at 28 years of age while on a whaling expedition. The monument is a marble mast broken midway, with a coiled rope and a whaling frieze at its base. The epitaph provides lasting evidence of the perils of whaling. This is a lovely, well-kept cemetery, located on Jermain Street.

The first cemetery in Sag Harbor, the *Old Burial Grounds,* was opened in 1767. The oldest graves in Sag Harbor, dating to the American Revolution, are located here (Union Street at Church Street). A monument to Lt. Colonel Jonathan Meigs is near the entrance. In a single night during the Revolution, he captured 90 British soldiers, burned 12 British ships, and returned to his headquarters in Connecticut with a hoard of much needed supplies. The magnificent Whaler's Church was built next door in 1844.

SAG HARBOR WHALING MUSEUM
516-725-0770.
Main Street, Sag Harbor.
Open: May–Oct. 10:00 a.m.–5:00 p.m. Mon.–Sat.; 1:00 p.m.–5:00 p.m. Sun.
Admission: Adults $3; children $1; seniors $2.
Mailing Address: Box 1327, Sag Harbor, NY 11963.

The noble, Greek Revival mansion that is now the Sag Harbor Whaling Museum was designed by Minard Lefever in 1845 for Benjamin Huntting, one of the earliest of Sag Harbor's whaling scions. The museum is entered through the jaws of a right whale and features china, dolls, toys, a boat collection, ship models, whaling tools and artifacts, period furnishings, oil paintings, scrimshaw, and documents about Sag Harbor's glorious whaling days. This is also the Sag Harbor Historical Museum. Operated by the Sag Harbor Whaling and Historical Museum, it is located at the corner of Main and Garden Streets.

TEMPLE ADAS ISRAEL
516-725-0904.
Atlantic Avenue, Sag Harbor.

In 1881, Joseph Fahys established a watchcase factory in Sag Harbor (it later became a Bulova watch factory). As his business grew, he expanded his workforce to include some 40 Jewish families that he had brought directly from Ellis Island. Finding no place to worship, they built this first synagogue on Long Island in 1900.

THE WHALER'S CHURCH
516-725-0894.
Union Street at the end of Church Street, Sag Harbor.

This is the most magnificent church on the South Fork. Designed in 1844 by the well-known architect, Minard Lafever, it is set back from the street, with a broad platform of stairs reaching to the front door. It's impressive size, dignity, and stature command respect. This is a church that was meant to be noticed! It is sad, though, that the magnificent, 185-foot steeple tumbled off in the 1938 hurricane — what is left appears boxy and wanting. The interior holds up to 1,000 people, and its soar-

The magnificent Whaler's Church in Sag Harbor was built in 1844 and can hold up to 1,000 people.

Morgan McGivern

ing, three-story height is truly inspirational. Concerts are held here, and Presbyterian church services are conducted every Sunday.

Southampton

Conscience Point is the spot where in 1640, the first settlers from Lynn, Massachusetts, stepped from their boat onto the land that became part of the first English settlement in New York State. A huge boulder set with a brass plaque marks the spot, located off North Sea Road in North Sea.

ELIAS PELLETREAU SILVERSMITH SHOP
516-283-2494.
Main Street, Southampton.
Open: Call for information.
Admission: Voluntary donation.
Mailing Address: P.O. Box 303, Southampton, NY 11969.

The Elias Pelletreau Silversmith Shop is one of the few historic buildings still located on its original site, although the building now faces in a different direction. Built in 1686, the shop of this famous colonial silversmith is fully restored, exhibiting a workshop complete with tools. It is operated by the Southampton Colonial Society.

OLD HALSEY HOUSE
516-283-2494.
South Main Street, Southampton.
Open: Jun.–Sept. 11:00 a.m.–4:30 p.m. Tues.–Sun.
Admission: Adults $2; children under 12, $.50.
Mailing Address: P.O. Box 303, Southampton, NY 11969.

The Old Halsey House (known as Hollyhocks for many years) is the oldest wood-framed saltbox house in New York State, with two rooms dating from 1648 and the remaining rooms from 1653. This is a large home for its day and is in excellent condition, with wide plank floors, many fireplaces, and authentic seventeenth- and eighteenth-century furnishings. The acquisition of the furnishings was supervised by Henry Francis Du Pont, founder of the Winterthur Museum in Delaware, and many of the fine pieces are by renowned craftsmen. The grounds of the homestead contain colorful flower borders, an apple orchard, and an herb garden enclosed by privet hedges, reflecting how it must have looked when the Halseys were in residence. It is operated by the Southampton Colonial Society.

SOUTHAMPTON HISTORICAL MUSEUM
516-283-2494 or 516-283-1612.
17 Meeting House Lane, Southampton.
Open: Jun.–Sept. daily, except Mon. 11:00 a.m.–5:00 p.m.
Admission: Adults $2; children under 12, $.50.
Mailing Address: P.O. Box 303, Southampton, NY 11969.

The Southampton Historical Museum is a collection of 12 buildings and 35 separate exhibits. The main house, a large, white, whaling captain's home, was built by Captain Albert Rogers in 1843; it contains many interesting exhibits, including china, glassware, and tole collections, a Shinnecock Indian exhibit, Revolutionary War artifacts, dolls, toys, and period clothing and furniture. Another building, an old New York schoolhouse (1850), contains the school's original desks, books, and maps. The Red Barn houses the Charles Foster collection of whaling instruments. It is set on a village street with a carriage shed, carpenter shop, blacksmith shop, the Corwith Drugstore, and a cobbler and harness shop. The Country Store is located in the pre-Revolutionary War barn where the British stabled their horses during the occupation of Long Island; it includes an old post office and general store. The complex is operated by the Southampton Colonial Society.

Water Mill

WATER MILL MUSEUM
516-726-4625.
Old Mill Road, Water Mill.
Open: Mem. Day–Labor Day 11:00 a.m.–5:00 p.m.
Mon., Thurs.–Sat.; 1:00 p.m.–5:00 p.m. Sun.
Admission: Adults $2; seniors $1.50; children free.

The Water Mill Museum is located in the original mill constructed in 1727 for Southampton. This is a waterwheel mill rather than the wind-powered mills that dot the countryside. The museum exhibits the fully functional wooden gears, shafts, and restored wheel of this, the oldest operational mill on Long Island, and contains the tools of various local trades, such as farmers, blacksmiths, carpenters, spinners, weavers, and millers. Cornmeal ground at the mill is available for purchase. The museum is only open in the summer, but arts and crafts exhibits by local artists are also held during that time. It is operated by the Ladies Auxiliary of Water Mill.

LIBRARIES

L ibraries in the Hamptons are especially rich in local history; the *Morton Pennypacker Collection* in the *East Hampton Library* encompasses one of the finest resources on Long Island for local research. Although the libraries allow unlimited use of the material on the premises, several only permit residents to check out books; a nonresident library card can be purchased in some cases.

EAST HAMPTON TOWN

AMAGANSETT FREE LIBRARY
516-267-3810.
Main Street, Amagansett.
Open: 1:00 p.m.–5:00 p.m. Mon., Fri.; 1:00 p.m.– 5:00 p.m. and 7:00 p.m.–9:00 p.m. Tues., Thurs.; 10:00 a.m.–5:00 p.m. Sat.; closed Wed., Sun.
Fee: Free to year-round residents and taxpayers; $25 for nonresidents.
Mailing Address: P.O. Box 726, Amagansett, NY 11930.

The Amagansett Free Library was established in 1916 and is located in a building that dates from 1922. The Director, Carleton Kelsey, is noted for his keen sense of local history. His book, *Amagansett, A Pictorial History 1680-1940* (1986), contains valuable photographs and historical material not found elsewhere.

EAST HAMPTON LIBRARY
516-324-0222.
159 Main Street, East Hampton.
Open: 10:00 a.m.–7:00 p.m. Mon., Wed., Fri.; 10:00 a.m.–5:00 p.m. Tues., Thurs., Sat.; **Pennypacker Collection:** 1:00 p.m.–4:30 p.m. Mon., Wed., Fri., Sat.
Fee: Free to year-around residents and taxpayers of the East Hampton school district; $50 for nonresidents.

The East Hampton Library, established in 1897, just keeps growing and getting better. The main building was designed in an Elizabethan style by Aymar Embury II in 1911. It has been expanded several times in aesthetic and sympathetic architectural styles (once in 1946 by Embury), and another new addition was completed in 1997. The building is located on a parcel of land that once contained the home of Samuel Buell, East Hampton's third minister. It includes a local history and periodical room; a children's library where storytelling takes place; a video, record, tape, and CD lending library; a music-listening room; and a large lending library. This is the repository of the **Pennypacker Long Island Collection,** most of which was donated by Morton Pennypacker, at one time Historian of Suffolk County. The bequest has been bolstered by additional historic collections over the years, including the **Thomas Moran Biographical Art Collection,** and contains an outstanding assemblage of books, prints, newspapers, genealogies, and much more. Dorothy King, the library historian, is extremely helpful and knows exactly where to find even the most obscure materials.

MONTAUK LIBRARY
516-668-3377.

The Montauk Library, in a building completed in 1991, has bright spaces for reading and an

Montauk Highway,
Montauk.
Open: 11:00 a.m.–6:00 p.m.
Mon., Tues., and Fri.;
11:00 a.m.–8:00 p.m.
Wed.; 10:00 a.m.–5:00
p.m. Sat.; 2:00 p.m.–5:00
p.m. Sun.; closed Thurs.
Fee: Free to year-round
residents and taxpayers
of the Montauk school
district; $30 for
nonresidents.
Mailing Address: P.O. Box
700, Montauk, NY 11954.

SPRINGS LIBRARY
No telephone.
Old Stone Highway, East
Hampton.
Open: 10:00 a.m.–12:00
noon Mon., Tues., Fri.;
10:00 a.m.–12:00 noon
and 3:00 p.m.–5:00 p.m.
Wed.; 9:00 a.m.–12:00
noon Sat.; evening hours
6:00 p.m.–8:00 p.m. Fri.
Fee: $10.

interesting collection that is especially strong on fishing and early Montauk history.

The Springs Library is located in a 1700-era, small, white clapboard house, which was the former home of the Parsons family, one of the oldest Springs' families. The library is not open full-time and does not have a telephone, but it is an excellent resource for local Springs' history.

SOUTHAMPTON TOWN

**HAMPTON BAYS
PUBLIC LIBRARY**
516-728-6241.
Ponquogue Avenue,
Hampton Bays.
Open: 10:00 a.m.–5:00
p.m. Mon.–Sat.; evening
hours 7:00 p.m.–9:00
p.m. Mon., Tues.,
Thurs.; Columbus
Day–Victoria Day 1:00
p.m.–5:00 p.m. Sun.
Fee: Free to year-round
residents and taxpayers;
$25 for nonresidents
($20 refunded at the end
of the summer).
Mailing Address: P.O. Box
AU, Hampton Bays, NY
11946.

The Hampton Bays Public Library was established in the 1960s. It has a children's room with story hours; it lends videos, CDs, books on tape, and music tapes; and has an excellent collection of art books.

HAMPTON LIBRARY IN BRIDGEHAMPTON

516-537-0015.
Main Street,
  Bridgehampton.
Open: Jul.–Aug. 10:00
  a.m.–5:00 p.m. Mon.-Fri.,
  9:00 a.m.–5:00 p.m. Sat.,
  closed Sun.; the rest of the
  year 1:00 p.m.–5:00 p.m.
  Mon.-Fri., 9:00 a.m.–5:00
  p.m. Sat., closed Sun.
Fee: Free to residents in
  Bridgehampton and
  Sagaponack school
  districts; $35 for
  nonresidents for books,
  with an additional fee of
  $25 for videos.
Mailing Address: P.O. Box
  3025, Bridgehampton, NY
  11032.

The Hampton Library is housed in a white-shingled building built in 1876 and expanded in 1982. During the summer, the courtyard is the site of the library's popular "Fridays at Five," a discussion series with local authors. In addition to lending books, the library has a music room, a children's room, a video library, and a periodical selection. Children's story hours are held on Saturdays throughout the year.

Morgan McGivern

The imposing John Jermain Memorial Library was built in 1907.

JOHN JERMAIN MEMORIAL LIBRARY IN SAG HARBOR

516-725-0049.
Main Street, Sag Harbor.

The John Jermain Memorial Library was built with funds donated by Mrs. Russell Sage in 1907. This imposing, brick two-story building houses a fine collection of books. The former

Open: 10:00 a.m.–5:00 p.m.
Mon.-Sat.; evening hours
7:00 p.m.–9:00 p.m. Thurs.
Fee: Free to year-round
residents of Sag Harbor
(accepts library cards
from other local libraries);
$55 for nonresidents.
Mailing Address: P.O. Box
569, Sag Harbor, NY
11963.

library historian, Dorothy Zaykowski, wrote an excellent book, *Sag Harbor, The Story of an American Beauty* (1991), that chronicles the history of Sag Harbor.

QUOGUE LIBRARY
516-653-4224.
Quogue Street East,
Quogue.
Open: 2:00 p.m.–5:00 p.m.
Sun.–Tues. & Thurs.;
10:00 a.m.–5:00 p.m.
Wed. & Sat.; 2:00
p.m.–7:00 p.m. Fri.
Fee: Free to year-round
residents of Quogue and
for those with a library
card within Suffolk
County.
Mailing Address: Drawer
LL, Quogue, NY 11959.

The Quogue Library is located in a charming 1897 building of weathered shingles on the same property as the Old Schoolhouse Museum. The library also sponsors art events and summer programs for children and adults.

ROGERS MEMORIAL LIBRARY IN SOUTHAMPTON
516-283-0774.
9 Job's Lane, Southampton.
Open: Oct.–May 10:00
a.m.–9:00 p.m.
Mon.–Thurs., 10:00
a.m.–5:00 p.m. Fri., Sat.,
1:00 p.m.–5:00 p.m. Sun.;
Jun.–Sept. closed Sun.
Fee: Free to year-round
residents or taxpayers of
the Southampton or
Tuckahoe school
districts; $50 for
nonresidents.

The Rogers Memorial Library was established in 1896 through a gift of Harriet Jones Rogers. Designed by R.H. Robertson, the impressive brick Victorian with its arched entrance contains an extensive collection of books and also lends videos, tapes, and CDs. A Children's Program Reading Club sponsors popular storytelling activities.

WESTHAMPTON FREE LIBRARY
516-288-3335.
7 Library Avenue,
Westhampton.

The Westhampton Free Library has much more than books. There's a lending library of CDs, audio books, tapes, and videos, and activities, such as a Sunday bridge game, storytelling for children,

Open: 9:00 a.m.–9:00 p.m.
Mon.–Thurs.; 9:00 a.m.–
5:00 p.m. Fri., Sat.; 1:00
p.m.–5:00 p.m. Sun.
Fee: Free to year-round
residents and taxpayers
of the Westhampton
school district.

a French club, and a book discussion group. The library contains an extensive village history collection and is handicapped accessible. It is located on Library Avenue, just off Main Street in the village of Westhampton Beach.

MUSIC

Many musical events take place in the Hamptons, especially in the summer. The annual *All for the Sea* concert on Long Island University's Southampton Campus features popular artists, such as Tina Turner and The Allman Brothers Band. The *Back at the Ranch* concerts at Dune Hollow Ranch in Montauk have for several summers drawn large crowds for artists like Paul Simon, Mary Chapin-Carpenter, The Allman Brothers Band, Ray Charles, and others.

In addition, a *Fourth of July Music Festival,* sponsored by the East End Arts Council in Riverhead, features well-known artists, such as the Benny Goodman Alumni Orchestra and Richie Havens.

The Art Barge (516-267-3172) Napeague. Musical events, including blues, jazz, dance, and music performances, and more.

Bridgehampton Chamber Music Festival (516-537-3507) Main Street, Bridgehampton. Aug. Established in 1983, this concert series includes classical works by Mozart or Brahms and works by contemporary composers, such as Lucas Foss. Celebrated artists, such as Jean-Pierre Rampal and Lucas Foss join the core group.

The Choral Society of the Hamptons (516-324-1925) This 100-voice choir conducts several concerts during the year with orchestral accompaniment. Their performances are always eagerly anticipated for their mix of classical music, opera, and show tunes.

Hamptons Summerfest (516-725-0894) Old Whaler's Church, Church Street, Sag Harbor. Jul.–Aug. A series of classical concerts that might include a violin solo, a vocal concert, or an orchestra.

Hamptons Summer Music (516-329-7405) An esteemed roster of musicians, including Itzhak Perlman, Pinchas Zukerman, Lucas Foss, and Emanuel Ax, are directors of the Hamptons Summer Music. Classical concerts take place in August.

Music Festival of the Hamptons (800-644-4418) This Hamptons-only outgrowth of the Newport Music Festival has grown since its inception in 1995 to include chamber music, piano recitals, and vocal concerts that stretch over a ten-day period. The venue may take place in a private home or in a public building.

Opera of the Hamptons (516-728-8804 or 718-836-3653) Various locations in Southampton. Year-round. Light opera, performed at such places as dinner theaters, wineries, and Agawam Park.

Pianofest (516-283-2044) Fine Arts Theatre, Long Island University, Southampton Campus. Jun.–Jul. This weekly series provides Hamptons residents and visitors with a rare treat. Accomplished piano artists are selected by nomination and audition to attend a summer residential study program in the Hamptons. Often these students have already won prestigious competitions and are on the verge of launching concert careers.

Sag Harbor Chamber of Commerce (516-725-0011) Marine Park, Bay Street, Sag Harbor. Jul.–Aug. These free concerts might feature blues, jazz, or pop. Bring a blanket or a lawn chair.

Sag Harbor Community Band (516-725-9759) American Legion Post 388, Bay Street, Sag Harbor. Jul.–Aug. Free band concerts, followed by dancing with music by *Big Band East.*

Village of Southampton (516-287-4300) Agawam Park, Southampton. Jul.–Aug. Sponsored by the Village of Southampton and managed by the Southampton Cultural Center.

Westhampton Cultural Consortium (516-288-0780) Village Green Gazebo, Westhampton Beach. Jul.–Aug. Free concerts every summer include vocal, jazz, and classical music.

NIGHTLIFE

Nightlife in the Hamptons is frenetic in the summer. With bikini contests and free ladies' drinks, giveaways and theme parties, the clubs compete for business. The following are only a few of the many clubs that are popular. Most clubs stay open until 2:00 a.m. or even 4:00 a.m. on the weekends, allowing employees of restaurants, sports shops, and visitors from New York City to participate. The clubs listed here are noted for their entertainment, and many serve food as well. Although not listed here, many restaurants also offer live music on weekend nights. It's best to check the papers.

Amagansett

Stephen Talkhouse (516-267-3117) Main Street. This is the place to go for music, music, music. The rather small room is intimate, but has been around

The Stephen Talkhouse continues to pack in the crowds to listen to top name bands and entertainers.

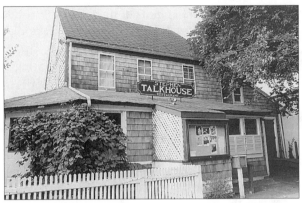

Morgan McGivern

since 1832, so it has the formula down pat. For name entertainers, such as Richie Havens or Kris Kristofferson, the cover charge can reach $35–$40, but on most nights it's $5. Stephen Talkhouse is also well known for the stars that just drop by to jam with their friends, such as Paul McCartney, Paul Simon, Billy Joel, Jimmy Buffet, G.E. Smith, etc. There's often a waiting line on weekends.

Bridgehampton

Wild Rose Café (516-537-5050) Sag Harbor-Bridgehampton Turnpike. This popular place is definitely "in" summer and winter. It's billed as the "Speakeasy for the '90s" and is a great favorite with year-round residents. The Lone Sharks play danceable rock and roll on Thursdays; live music that ranges from rock and blues to jazz is played on Friday and Saturday; and Sunday is open-mike night. There's food, but the scene and the setting, with shelves of books, overstuffed sofas, stained glass lamps, and a tin ceiling, as well as the entertainment, are the primary reasons to go.

Hampton Bays

CPI (the Canoe Place Inn) (516-728-4121) Montauk Highway at the Shinnecock Canal. CPI has an old history and a young crowd. It served as the summer home of New York's Governor Al Smith and as host, at various times, to Franklin Roosevelt, Helen Hayes, Albert Einstein, Cary Grant, and many others. CPI begins swinging by 10:00 p.m. and just keeps going. It's so large that it can hold 1,000 people in its four distinct lounges. The music ranges from 1950s music to rock and roll. Live bands, $1 drinks, cash prizes for bikini contests — it just goes on and on. The VIP lounge features comedy and karaoke.

Sag Harbor

Chili Peppers (516-725-5777) West Water Street at Long Island Avenue, at Baron's Cove Inn. Part restaurant and part nightclub, Chili Peppers specializes in Mexican and South American food, and music with a Latin beat. There's a waterfront bar, live music, and a Latin dance club.

Southampton

Jet East Lounge (516-283-0808) 1181 North Sea Road begins jumping on weekends at 11:00 p.m.

Westhampton Beach

Magics Pub (516-288-6105) Main Street. Open daily year-round. This longtime favorite (a tiny bar that increases its space in the summer by putting tables in the adjacent courtyard) still features big juicy hamburgers with a variety of toppings. You can also feast on steaks, fish, and huge salad platters. The Taproom is open until the early morning hours in the summer. Sports events are shown on the three TVs, and there are live bands on the weekends.

THEATER AND DANCE

The Bay Street Theatre Festival is noted for its marvelous productions. Here Dianne Wiest and Mercedes Ruehl perform in the 1994 world premiere of Blue Light.

Gary Mamay

**BAY STREET THEATRE
FESTIVAL**
516-725-9500 (box office),

The Bay Street Theatre Festival in Sag Harbor opened with a bang in 1992, and it gets better

516-725-0818 (office). Bay Street, Sag Harbor. Open: Year-round. Admission: $12–$24. Mailing Address: P.O. Box 810, Sag Harbor, NY 11963-0022.

every year. One the principles is Emma Walton, daughter of Julie Andrews and Tony Walton. On occasion her dad designs the sets and sometimes her mom stars or helps with fundraising benefits. Theatrical performances, play readings, pre-New York City openings, cabaret productions and much more are presented in an intimate 330-seat professional theater throughout the year. The company also sponsors courses in drama, directing, and playwriting, and it has established playwriting and performance curriculum in the local schools that culminates in a student production in the spring.

JOHN DREW THEATRE OF GUILD HALL
516-324-4051. Main Street, East Hampton. Open: Year-round. Admission: Changes, depending upon performance.

The John Drew Theatre of Guild Hall in East Hampton is the oldest playhouse on Long Island and sponsors theatrical productions, cabaret singers, poetry readings, and children's theater. During the summer, it teams up with several New York City theater companies, including the Circle Rep Theatre, to hold readings and premier performances of productions before the productions head for the city.

THE HAMPTON THEATRE COMPANY
516-653-8955. Quogue Community Theatre, Jessup Lane, Quogue. Open: Spring and fall.

The Hampton Theatre Company produces several plays during the spring and fall seasons, while the Quogue Junior Theatre Troupe produces several plays each summer. All are performed at the Quogue Village Hall on Jessup Avenue in Quogue.

THE PLAYWRIGHTS' THEATRE OF EAST HAMPTON
516-324-5373 or 212-759-4446. Open: Four weeks in late summer. Admission: $10 for play readings; $25 for benefits. Mailing Address: Summer: Talmadge Farm Lane, East Hampton, NY 11937; Winter: 200 E. 66th St., Apt. C1403, New York, NY 10021.

The Playwrights' Theatre of East Hampton conducts readings of new plays, but these are a far cry from ordinary play readings. Here, well-known dramatic artists, such as Tammy Grimes, Ben Gazzara, or Phyllis Newman might be heard reading a play by Joyce Carol Oates or Lucy Wang and directed by respected Broadway directors. These events take place at the LTV Studios, 75 Industial Road, Wainscott.

WESTHAMPTON BEACH PERFORMING ARTS CENTER
516-288-2350 (office), 516-288-8519 (fax).
Main Street, Westhampton Beach.
Open: July and August.
Admission: $15–$50, depending on performer.
Mailing Address: P.O. Box 630, Westhampton Beach, NY 11978.

Just as the decorative old Art Deco Westhampton Beach Cinema was sliding into a steep decline, a group of public-spirited citizens came to the rescue. With Herculean efforts that included fundraising events and an immense amount of volunteer effort, the ornamented interior now shines, and a full schedule of live performances inaugurated the refurbished theater in 1998. Beginning with a Hamptons version of *Forbidden Broadway* on July 4th weekend, the first season included performances by Claire Bloom, Ben Vereen, Marvin Hamlisch, Leslie Uggams, and Alan King, among others. There were theatrical productions such as *Killing Real Estate Women*, musical reviews such as the *Irving Berlin Songbook*, *Jazz All-stars*, and *Rhythm on the Rainbow*, as well as a performance by the New York Theatre Ballet. Special musical productions for kids included *Cinderella*, *Pinocchio, Peter Pan, The Wizard of Oz*, and *Sleeping Beauty*.

CHAPTER SEVEN
One of the Last Great Places
RECREATION

C. Frank Dayton Collection, East Hampton Library Historical Collection.

East Hampton's Main Beach is as popular today as it was when this scene was painted by Edward Lamson Henry in the 1880s.

The early Hampton settlers believed each day was placed before them in order to accomplish a goal — building a barn, tilling the soil, baking bread, tending a flock. Days were filled with hard work and the concept of recreation was foreign. Nevertheless, recreation is the Hampton's chief attraction today. An early morning walk along the beach, with the spray from the crashing waves rising to meet the mist; a jog along the bay at dusk, as the fiery setting sun leaves brilliant streaks of pink, orange, and red; a sail to Block Island, whisked along on bundling breezes; a quiet kayak trip through tall reeds, surprising a crane at its meal — these are only a few of the many joys to be experienced in the Hamptons.

The abundance and bounty of the waters surrounding the Hamptons attracts people who swear that right here are the best fishing, the best boating, and the best swimming in the United States. Hikers, bicyclists, horseback riders, and bird-watchers also have found their favorite haunts here, as have canoeists, golfers, tennis enthusiasts, scuba divers, and hunters.

Through the enlightened perseverance of The Nature Conservancy, The Peconic Land Trust, and Group for the South Fork, more land is in the public domain in the townships of East Hampton, Shelter Island, and Southampton than in many other places. The Nature Conservancy alone either owns or manages 25,000 acres, preserving them for us and our children to enjoy, appreciate, and gently use.

*Everybody needs beauty as well as bread, places to play in and pray in, where
Nature may heal and cheer and give strength to body and soul alike.*

John Muir, *Yosemite,* 1942

AUTO RACING

Racing in Bridgehampton began in 1915 with European-style road races along the streets. These races continued in one form or another until 1953 when the state banned races along village streets for safety reasons. Now an asphalt competition racecourse, 2.85 miles in length, is the site of an active season that runs from April-October with sports car, race car, formula Ford, motorcycle racing, and performance exhibitions. The track is located on *Millstone Road,* between Sag Harbor and Bridgehampton (516-725-0888).

BASEBALL, BASKETBALL, HANDBALL

Baseball fields are located at several town parks and schools, but reservations should be made for the fields since league games may be scheduled. There are basketball courts at schools and recreation fields throughout the Hamptons, and pickup games are often organized on the spur of the moment. Membership organizations offering the use of basketball and handball courts are listed in the section "Fitness Facilities & Spas" in this chapter.

BEACHES

The beaches are the glory of the Hamptons. They are clean, broad stretches of white sand that, in this writer's opinion, are the finest in the world. Unlike the beaches of France or Italy, for example, pesky flies and other bugs stay away. Unlike those in Hawaii and other Pacific beaches — often mere slips of sand hidden between rock cliffs or promontories — Long Island beaches seem never ending.

Don't be fooled into thinking that the best beaches are all on the ocean. When the fog hovers near the ocean well into midday, head for the secret bay beaches, where you might bask in brilliant sunshine from early morning on. In general, they are less populated than those on the ocean, so if you seek solitude or prefer a lazy swim in calm waters to the crash of the ocean waves, the bay will be your choice. Everyone has their favorite beach, and there are enough to go around, so start your quest for your own personal choice.

*East Hampton's Main Beach
attracts a crowd on sunny
summer days.*

Morgan McGivern

Beach rules are very strict in the Hamptons. Driving on beaches is permitted with a sticker, but generally in the summer, it is allowed only when swimmers and sunbathers are not using them. Signs posted at each beach give details about driving and also about when dogs are allowed on the beach (a controversial, ever-evolving issue). Check with town or village officials for the current rules.

Now for the tricky part — getting there. If you live within walking distance, walk! The next best mode of transportation is a bicycle — the ocean beaches provide an abundance of bicycle racks. If you must drive, be certain that you have the proper parking permit sticker from Memorial Day to Labor Day. A parking permit sticker from East Hampton Town, for example, will not allow you to park at an East Hampton Village beach or a Southampton Village beach. Qualifications for resident and nonresident status vary from village to village, so check with the town hall before you go. Parking is available at several beaches for a daily use-fee, but generally a sticker is required. A resident sticker is free (in Southampton Town, $10); nonresident stickers may be purchased for the following fees.

Nonresident Parking Permit Sticker Fees

East Hampton Town	$125	516-324-4142
East Hampton Village	$150	516-324-4150
Southampton Town	$100	516-283-6011
Southampton Village	$130	516-283-0247
Quogue Village	$125	516-653-4498
Sag Harbor Village	$100	516-725-0222
Westhampton Beach Village	$225	516-288-1654

The following beaches are by no means a complete list, but they are the most popular choices.

EAST HAMPTON TOWN

Amagansett

A sand castle contest is held annually at Atlantic Beach in Amagansett.

Suzi Forbes Chase

Atlantic Avenue Rest rooms; telephones; parking with East Hampton Town resident or nonresident permit, or $10 per day. A broad ocean beach, Atlantic Avenue has a number of additional amenities. The concession stand in the former coast guard station is terrific. Susan Bennett sells hamburgers, hot dogs, and great marinated chicken breast sandwiches, as well as old-fashioned comfort food desserts, such as ice-cream bars and Popsicles; they also rent beach chairs and umbrellas. Known for years as *asparagus beach* (because so many singles stood in packs, surveying everyone else), this is now a very popular family beach, where you might find numerous volley-ball games underway.

Fresh Pond Rest rooms; telephone; picnic tables; grills; nature trails; parking with East Hampton Town permit. Fresh Pond is a delightful spot at the end of Fresh Pond Road on Napeague Bay. Breakwaters create a sandy beach and from a park bench, you can contemplate the tranquility of the scene and watch the gulls wheel over the fishing nets in the water. The preferred sun site is the sandy beach surrounding Fresh Pond; small, shallow pools of placid, clean water at the entrance to the larger pond are ideal for families with children.

Indian Wells Rest rooms; telephones; mobile concession stand; parking with East Hampton Town resident permit. Indian Wells is near the spot where the Montauk Indians once came for freshwater. At the end of Indian Wells Highway in the middle of the Atlantic Double Dunes Preserve, the gleam-ing, white sand beach stretches as far as the eye can see. Unspoiled by development of any kind, this beach remains a favorite with sun lovers who want to pretend that they are on their own beach, on their own private island.

Lazy Point Boat launch; parking with East Hampton Town permit. Lazy Point, a protected point of land jutting into Napeague Harbor, is accessed through Napeague State Park. Surrounded by the tiny fishing cottages of the village of Napeague (no shops, just cottages), this beach is generally deserted, except for windsurfers who have found the bay breezes ideal for skittering across the water. **Main Beach** (516-537-2716), a surfing shop in Wainscott, rents windsurfing equipment from a truck on nice summer days.

East Hampton Village

Georgica Beach Rest rooms; showers; lifeguard; parking with East Hampton Village permit only; bicycle racks. Located at the end of Apaquogue Road and Lily Pond Lanes in the heart of the estate section of East Hampton, Georgica Beach is one of the preferred ocean spots. With a backdrop of estates and mansions just beyond the dunes, this sparkling clean beach is underutilized.

Main Beach Rest rooms; telephones; lockers and showers; lifeguards; tidal report; concession stand; beach chair and umbrella rental; parking with East Hampton Village permit, or $15 per day, weekdays only. No daily parking permits available weekends and holidays. Main Beach, at the end of Ocean Avenue, is consistently rated the number one beach in Hampton surveys. This broad expanse of pristine beach has it all, but it's also one of the most crowded. To bask in the glorious sun, to roll over and see the elegant mansions, to sit on the spacious, covered deck and gaze out to sea — this truly is summer heaven. Walk up to the pavilion and select a freshly sliced fruit cup, a tall glass of lemonade, a grilled hamburger, or an ice-cream cone from the Chowder Bowl concession, owned by Dave Driscoll for more than 30 years. If you find that you've forgotten something, there's a shop that sells everything from aspirin and suntan lotion to beach chairs.

Two Mile Hollow Parking with East Hampton Village permit. This beach is located at the end of Two Mile Hollow Road, almost on the village/town line. In the midst of a nature sanctuary, it is preferred by many village residents for its serene and peaceful surroundings. There's none of the mob scene of Main Beach here, but neither are there any facilities.

Montauk

Ditch Plains Rest rooms; showers; lifeguard; mobile concession stand; parking with East Hampton Town permit. Noted for its great surfing, Ditch Plains is an ocean beach off Ditch Plains and DeForest Roads. The usual snacks and ice cream can be purchased from the Beach Dog, the mobile concession stand.

Montauk's Ditch Plains beach is noted for its great surfing.

Morgan McGivern

Gin Beach Rest rooms; lifeguard; mobile concession stand; parking with East Hampton Town permit. Broad and sandy, Gin Beach is at the end of East Lake Drive, near the jetty where boats enter Lake Montauk. It's great for fishing and for watching the boats coming and going in the harbor.

Hither Hills State Park (516-668-2554) Camping (reservations required); parking $4 per day. This park has one of the finest beaches on the ocean — a broad, 2-mile expanse of clean, white sand. You can camp beside the beach and take a swim as soon as you awaken in the morning and the last thing at night. See additional information in the section "Parks & Nature Preserves" in this chapter.

Northwest

Sammy's Beach Parking with East Hampton Town permit. Sammy's is a broad crescent of protected bay beach that overlooks Gardiner's Bay. It's a wonderful place for waterskiing and boating (the boats can come directly to shore), but because of the quick drop-off, it is not a great place for children to swim.

Springs

Louse Point Boat launch; parking with East Hampton Town permit. At the end of Louse Point Road, you will find a two-sided beach separating Napeague Bay from Accabonac Harbor. Most locals say, "Please don't tell anyone about Louse Point. The tourists will come." The harborside is picturesque, dotted with marshy islands filled with birds — a favorite place for egrets, cranes, and osprey. At one time, the area fostered a rich oyster bed.

Maidstone Park Beach Rest rooms; lifeguard; baseball field; picnic area; pavilion; parking with East Hampton Town permit. Maidstone Park Beach is one of the all-time great places to watch a sunset. The long, broad, sandy beach hugs the jetty into Three Mile Harbor; it is an excellent spot for watching the yachts go by. Local anglers find the fish are plentiful off the jetty.

SOUTHAMPTON TOWN

Pretty girls are a common sight on Hampton beaches.

Morgan McGivern

Bridgehampton

Mecox Beach Parking with Southampton Town resident or nonresident permit, or $10 per day. Mecox Beach is on the ocean at the end of Job's Lane in Bridgehampton. A wooden walkway leads to the beach from the large parking lot. There are no rest rooms or food facilities.

W. Scott Cameron Beach Rest rooms; showers; lifeguard; concession stand; parking with Southampton Town resident permit. This beach is on the ocean in Bridgehampton at the end of Dune Road.

Hampton Bays

Meschutt Beach Parking with Southampton Town resident or nonresident permit, a $5 fee for Suffolk County residents with a "Green Key Card," or $10 per day. Meschutt Beach is a Suffolk County park, operated by the Town of Southampton. It is on North Highway where the Shinnecock Canal joins the Great Peconic Bay in Meschutt Park.

Ponquogue Beach Rest rooms; lifeguard; parking with Southampton Town resident or nonresident permit, or $10 per day. Ponquogue Beach is on the ocean, on Dune Road in Hampton Bays at the end of the Ponquogue Bridge, bordered by Shinnecock County Park East and West.

Road H Parking with Southampton Town parking permit. Road H, in the Shinnecock Inlet County Park East, is a favorite place for surfers and scuba divers. It's right beside the jetty from the ocean into Shinnecock Bay, where a rich supply of saltwater fish journey into the quiet bays to spawn.

Tiana Beach Rest rooms; lifeguard; parking with Southampton Town permit or $10 per day. Located on Dune Road, Tiana is on that great expanse of ocean beach sandwiched between Shinnecock Bay and the ocean. The Town of Southampton Parks and Recreation Department conducts a series of classes (swimming, sailing, windsurfing) at Tiana Beach.

Noyack

Foster Memorial Rest rooms; lifeguard; snack bar/restaurant; parking with Southampton Town permit, or $10 per day. Foster Memorial is on Long Beach, the stretch of land separating the inner harbors of Sag Harbor from Noyack Bay. The small snack bar/restaurant (open in the summer only) serves pizza and is a welcome change from the food that you get at most mobile beach concessions. On the Noyack end of the beach, a special section has been reserved for powerboats, and it's a popular spot to water-ski.

Quogue Village

Quogue Village Beach Rest rooms; bicycle path; parking with Quoque Village permit only. Located on Dune Road, this beach is accessed by the Post Lane Bridge from the Village of Quogue. Due to erosion, the beach is considerably narrower here than in many other places, and drive-on beach access is no longer permitted.

Sag Harbor Village

Havens Beach Rest rooms; lifeguard; picnic tables and grills; children's play area; parking with Sag Harbor Village permit only. Located on Bay Street in Sag Harbor Village, Havens Beach is part of the former Frank C. Havens estate. There are benches where you can watch the children playing on the sandy beach and the pleasure boats bobbing in the water beyond.

Sagaponack

Sagg Main Beach Rest rooms; showers; mobile concession stand; parking with Southampton Town resident or nonresident permit, or $10 per day (limited). Sagg Main Beach, on the ocean at the end of Sagaponack Main Road, is reached by passing through the sleepy village of Sagaponack. There are no designer boutiques here, just the local general store; the store may look old fashioned, but the food is homemade and excellent. Have the proprietors prepare a picnic lunch and head for the beach for a delightful al fresco outing.

Southampton Village

Southampton Village beaches stretch from Mecox Bay to the Shinnecock Inlet, an unbroken line of broad, white, splendid sand. The village does not require permits for all of its beaches, but pay close attention to the signs as the authorities are very strict about where you park. In general, parking lots where permits are not required are short street ends (an exception is Main Beach South); specific parking spots are clearly marked. The village police patrol the beach parking lots regularly and will definitely give you a ticket or have you towed away if you are parked illegally. The advice is to go early. There are many more street ends than identified here.

Cooper Neck Beach Rest rooms; concession stand; parking with Southampton Village permit, or $20 per day weekdays, $25 per day weekends and holidays. Located at the end of Cooper Neck Lane, this is the main public beach for Southampton Village. It's a favorite with the high school crowd.

Dune Beach Rest rooms; handicapped access; parking with Southampton Village permit. Located in Southampton Village, this beach is toward the end of Dune Road, almost to the Shinnecock Inlet. There is a wooden deck for picnics and a boardwalk over dunes that are covered with sea grass to the ocean.

Old Town Beach About 30 parking spaces, no permit required. Old Town Beach is uncrowded, perfect for relaxed reading or quiet contemplation. This is not a young person's beach; there are no rest room or food facilities.

Morgan McGiveern

An empty, moody evening beach is perfect for a romantic walk.

South Main Beach Parking lot at beach and in front of the Southampton Beach
Club and St. Andrew's Dune Church, no permit required; parking lot next to
Agawam Lake, Southampton Village resident parking only with permit
($55). This beach is located at the south end of Agawam Lake, next to the
Southampton Beach Club.

Water Mill

Flying Point Beach Rest rooms; lifeguard; mobile concession stand; parking
with Southampton Town resident or nonresident permit only. One of the
most popular beaches in the Hamptons is located on the ocean on Flying
Point Road. On the way there, alongside Mecox Bay, you'll see baymen with
handheld nets, plucking the fish from the rich waters.

Westhampton Beach Village

Westhampton Beach Village maintains some of the finest beaches along the
Atlantic Ocean, but village parking permits are required. They're free to residents
and taxpayers and can be purchased by residents of nearby Remsenburg, Quogue,
and Speonk. Even those who walk or bicycle to the beach must have a walk-on
pass (obtained from the village offices), or a photo ID with a local address. For
information about obtaining a permit, contact the village office at 516-288-1654.

Lashley Pavilion Rest rooms; showers; mobile concession; parking with
Westhampton Beach Village permit only. Lashley Pavilion is located at the
western end of Dune Road. This beach generally handles the overflow from
Rogers, although some people prefer it for its quieter crowd.
Rogers Pavilion Rest rooms; lifeguard; concession stand; handicapped access;
parking with Westhampton Beach Village permit. Rogers Pavilion is located
at the end of the Beach Lane Bridge on Village Beach. At the excellent concession stand, they have fresh fruit, and the sandwiches are made with fresh,
local produce.

BICYCLING

With miles of flat, paved roads, this is a cyclist's paradise. Although
Montauk Highway has a broad, paved shoulder that is frequently used
by bicyclists, in-line skaters, and joggers, the back roads offer the least traveled
byways for leisurely cycling, and the bayside roads tend to be hillier than
those near the beach. This writer's favorite short cycling trip is along Dune
Road in Southampton, with outrageous mansions on the ocean side and the
rich, marshy bird habitat on the bay side. Another favorite trip is to start in

Bridgehampton and ride past the potato fields and horse farms of Sagaponack, continuing through the village of Wainscott and then on to East Hampton. Other local, favorite excursions are cycling trips along Long Beach between North Haven and Noyack and on Shelter Island.

Two excellent guides include bicycle trips in the Hamptons and are highly recommended: *East Hampton, A History & Guide* (1985) by Jason Epstein and Elizabeth Barlow suggests three bicycle trips, described by Marvin Kuhn; *Short Bike Rides on Long Island* (1989) by Phil Angelillo mentions about eight trips.

Cycling in the Hamptons.

Morgan McGivern

Both guides have excellent maps and directions. The Chamber of Commerce offices of the villages of East Hampton and Southampton have maps and information that include several suggested bicycle rides.

If bicycling through a village, be sure to observe the signs. In East Hampton Village, for example, bicycling is not permitted on the sidewalks in the main business district, but it is permitted on the street. In Southampton Village, bicycling is not permitted in the main business district, either on the streets or the sidewalks. If you plan to rent a bicycle, please remember to call ahead. Shops often run out of rental bicycles early in the day.

Bicycle touring in the Hamptons is increasing in popularity. **Brooks Country Cycling Tours** (212-874-5151) conducts several bicycles tours in the Hamptons, including a trip along the South Fork to Montauk, with two nights at a local resort; a trip along the North Fork; and a four-day trip to Shelter Island that includes a stay at a country inn and visits to Southampton and the North Fork.

Rotations Bicycle Center (516-283-2890) in Southampton sponsors diverse and interesting, weekend group bicycle rides for beginners, intermediate cyclists, and racing enthusiasts. The following shops have bicycles to rent, generally fairly basic 12-speeds or less, unless otherwise noted.

Amagansett

Amagansett Beach & Bicycle (516-267-6325) Montauk Highway at Cross Highway, Amagansett. $6/hour, $25/day for English, hybrid, mountain, and children's bicycles.

East Hampton

Bermuda Bikes (516-324-6688) 36 Gingerbread Lane, East Hampton. $10/hour, $18–$28/day, $112/week.
Espo's Surf & Sport (516-329-9100) The Old Barn, Main Street, East Hampton. $8/hour, $25/day.
Village Hardware (516-324-2456) 32 Newtown Lane, East Hampton. $6/hour, $18/day, $60/week, $100/month.

Montauk

Plaza Sporting Goods, (516-668-9300) Main Street, Montauk $8/hour, $22/day for English or mountain bicycles; $25/hour and $60/day for mopeds.

Sag Harbor

Bike Hampton (516-725-7329) 36 Main Street, Sag Harbor. $6/hour, $25/day for mountain bicycles, hybrids, or cruisers. Tandem bicycles and in-line skates are also available.

Southhampton

Flying Point Surf & Sport (516-287-0075) 28 Main Street, Southampton. $25/day. In-line skates are also available.
Rotations (516-283-2890) 32 Windmill Lane, Southampton. $5/hour, $25/day.

Wainscott

Cycle Path Bikes (516-537-1144) 330 Montauk Highway, Wainscott. $25/day, $55/week for mountain bicycles or hybrids. They'll even deliver the bikes to you if you're renting for more than several days.

Westhampton Beach

Bike 'n Kite Ltd. (516-288-1210) 112 Potunk Lane, Westhampton Beach. $25/day, $60/week, $95/month. Rental includes a helmet, lock, and rack.

BOATING & SAILING

Over 80,000 boats use Long Island's network of waterways. The quiet, tranquil bays between the North and South Forks or between the sandy barrier bar and the South Fork along the ocean provide many opportunities to fish, sail, swim, or water-ski, or to just bob quietly while soaking up the sun. Many marinas provide daily, weekly, and monthly moorage. In addition, boats can be rented, either for group charter or on daily, scheduled sails. For fishing charters and excursions, please see the section in this chapter, "Fishing & Shellfishing" and for windsurfing, see "Surfing, Windsurfing, Waterskiing, Jetskiing."

PUBLIC MARINAS & LAUNCHING RAMPS

The towns provide many launching ramps in this boat-oriented area, but they also require permits to use the ramps and to park. Contact town offices for requirements and maps showing locations of launching ramps. In addition, several of the towns provide marinas for transient use, sometimes for a fee and, in other cases, on a complimentary basis.

The *Town of East Hampton* has about 100 marina spaces available every season, but seldom on an overnight basis. Applications for space must be made to the Town Trustees, and then space is assigned at various locations throughout the town. Fees vary. Call the *Town of East Hampton Harbormaster* (516-329-3078) for details.

The *Village of Sag Harbor* (516-725-2368) operates a marina at Marine Park on Bay Street in the village. There's moorage for yachts, cruisers, and sailboats, and some of the largest yachts in the world dock here in the summer. Rates are $1.90/foot, plus $6 for electric.

The *Shinnecock Canal County Marina* (516-852-8291) is run by Suffolk County Parks and Recreation Department. It offers approximately 50 berths during the season on a first-come, first-serve basis. There are electric hookups, sanitary facilities, and showers. Rates are $25/day on weekdays, $30/day on weekends for residents; $40/day on weekdays, $50/day on weekends for non-residents. The marina is located at the Shinnecock Canal, Hampton Bays.

The *Town of Southampton* (516-283-6000) offers town marina space in Eastport, East Quogue, Hampton Bays, Sag Harbor, and elsewhere, on a first-come, first-serve basis. A stay is generally limited to five to seven days, but there is no charge.

The *Village of Westhampton Beach* (516-288-1654) maintains Stevens Park Municipal Yacht Basin, on Library Avenue in the village, for public use. There are daily, weekly, monthly, and full-season rates and municipal launching ramps. The fees are $30 for up to 30 feet and $1 per foot beyond that, plus $4 for electric hookup. In addition, there are a limited number of boat parking spaces in the car parking lot behind Main Street. These are complimentary, but are limited to two hours during the day and three hours at night.

PRIVATE MARINAS

The Hamptons have a variety of private marinas where boats can be moored. The following are only a few of those available for public use.

East Hampton

East Hampton Point Marina (516-324-8400) 295 Three Mile Harbor. Rest rooms, showers, laundry, pool, tennis, ship store, great sunset views, complimentary continental breakfast, van service; fine restaurant on premises with deck for watching spectacular sunsets; other restaurants within walking distance; 45 slips.

The Harbor Marina of East Hampton (516-324-5666) 423 Three Mile Harbor Road. Restrooms, showers, beach, spectacular views, electric, repair shop, gas, fishing supplies, gift shop, full pumping service "no discharge" marina; fine restaurant and bar on premise; 100 slips.

Maidstone Harbor is located on Three Mile Harbor Road in East Hampton.

Tulla Booth

Maidstone Harbor Marina (516-324-2651) 313 Three Mile Harbor Road. Rest rooms, showers, pool; fine restaurant on premises; other restaurants within walking distance.

Hampton Bays

Hampton Watercraft & Marina (516-728-0922) 134 Springville Road. Restrooms, electric hookups; 30 slips.

Jackson's Marina (516-728-4220) 6 Tepee Street. Restrooms, showers, electric hookups, cable TV, fishing supplies, repairs, gas; 240 slips.

Montauk

Gone Fishing Marina (516-668-3232) East Lake Drive. Small shop on premises; 180 slips.

Montauk Marine Basin (516-668-5900) West Lake Drive. Rest rooms, showers, electric hookups, charter boats, fishing equipment; about 25 slips.

Montauk Yacht Club Resort Marina (516-668-3100) Star Island Road. Rest rooms, showers, laundry, three pools, tennis, fully-equipped health club, cable TV; two restaurants; 225 slips.

Star Island Yacht Club & Marina (516-668-5052) Star Island Road. Rest rooms, showers, laundry, pool, weekend entertainment, picnic area, fishing charters, fishing supplies; bar and grill; about 100 slips.

Uihlein's Marina (516-668-3799) West Lake Drive Extension. Showers; many restaurants and shops within walking distance; 10 slips.

West Lake Fishing Lodge (516-668-5600) West Lake Drive. Rest rooms, showers, charter boats, fishing supplies; bar and restaurant; 100 slips.

Sag Harbor

Baron's Cove Marina (516-725-3939) West Water Street. Rest rooms, showers, laundry, cable TV; access to pool; many restaurants and shops within walking distance; 84 slips.

Waterfront Marina (516-725-3886) Bay Street. Rest rooms, showers; many shops and restaurants within walking distance; 65 slips.

GROUP EXCURSIONS

HARBOR TOURS
516-287-4596.
Long Wharf, Sag Harbor.
Daily sightseeing tours and sunset cruises.
Rates: 90-minute sightseeing cruises: Adults, $16, or 2 adults for $27; children 5–12, $8; children under 5 free. Two-hour sunset cruises: Adults, $20; children 5–12, $12; children under 5 free.
Mailing address: P.O. Box 7, Sag Harbor, NY 11963.

The *American Beauty* is a 45-foot wooden power boat that docks at Sag Harbor's Long Wharf to take passengers on 90-minute sightseeing tours of Sag Harbor and Peconic Bays accompanied by a historical and nature guided narrative. There are three tours daily in summer. Evening sunset cruises are romantic and inspirational. There's nothing like a view of the setting sun from the water.

VIKING FLEET
516-668-5709.
West Lake Drive, Montauk.

The Viking Ferry in Montauk has several delightful options for boating excursions from

Summer excursions to Block Island, Martha's Vineyard, and New London; also casino cruises.

Rates: Block Island and New London: Adults, $17 one way/$34 round-trip; children ages 5–12, $17; children under 5 free; bicycles, $6; Martha's Vineyard: Adults, $80 round-trip; children ages 5–12, $40; children under 5 free; bicycles, $6; casino cruises, $15; packages, including overnight stays available.

Mailing Address: R.D. 1, Box 259, Montauk, NY 11954.

Montauk, including a daily trip to Block Island, Rhode Island, which leaves every morning at 9:00 a.m. and returns about 6:15 p.m. This trip takes about 1^3/$_4$ hours and allows almost 6 hours on the island (an excellent place for biking and hiking). A less frequent sunset trip to New London, Connecticut, leaves at 7:00 p.m. and returns about 11:00 p.m. They also sponsor special summer trips to Martha's Vineyard as well as a July fireworks cruise, a wine cruise, and a fall-foliage cruise. Casino cruises depart nightly at 7:00 p.m. and return at 12:30 a.m. These include opportunities to play slot machines, roulette, and table games. The $15 fare includes a $5 coupon to play and one cocktail.

BOAT CHARTER & RENTAL

Hampton Watercraft & Marine (516-288-2900) 99B Old Riverhead Road, Westhampton Beach. Rents boats, jet skis, and surfboards.

Uihlein's (516-668-3799) West Lake Drive Ext., Montauk. Rents cruisers, sailboats, and speedboats (for waterskiing). They also organize group excursions.

SAILING

Sailing is as popular in the bays and lakes of the Hamptons as it is in Narragansett or San Francisco Bay. Head winds make the bays ideal for racing, and the annual *Sag Harbor Cup Regatta* starts the season every June. Favorite local places to sail are Mecox Bay in Bridgehampton, Napeague Bay off Lazy Point, and Quantuck Bay in Quogue.

For sailboat rentals and instruction, there are few options available anymore. (It's the insurance, we're told.) Try *Uihlein's* (516-668-3799) in Montauk.

Deja Vu (516-668-6969) Montauk. Sailboat charters are available in the summer off Montauk. Contact Captain Bernard Shore.

Puff & Putt (516-668-4473) Main Street, Montauk. Rents sailboats by the hour that include Triumph, Sunfish, lasers, a catamaran, and a 15-foot Dayfish for use on Fort Pond. They also rent pedal boats, rowboats, and canoes. For landlubbers, there's a miniature golf course and a video room.

Windsurfing Hamptons (516-283-9463) 1686 North Highway (Route 27) in Southampton. Instruction and Sunfish rental. Also see the listing in the section "Surfing, Windsurfing, Waterskiing, Jetskiiing" in this chapter.

CANOEING & KAYAKING

You can explore quiet ponds, inlets, and bays in the Hamptons by canoe. Here a fisherman casts his line in Hook Pond — overseen by a tree-shrouded mansion.

Morgan McGivern

In a serene pond, shaded by overhanging trees, you sit quietly in your canoe as you watch a crane feeding. Suddenly, a graceful osprey swoops to the water, dives, and emerges with a fish in its talons, then departs. This image is the reason that canoeing and kayaking are so popular in the Hamptons, because there are dozens of these secluded, interconnecting ponds, streams, and bays.

Local groups often sponsor trips, guided by a naturalist, to visit bird and animal sanctuaries. The trips are educational, interesting, and fun. Watch the local newspapers for expeditions sponsored by the Group for the South Fork and The Nature Conservancy.

Amagansett Beach & Bicycle (516-267-6325) Montauk Highway at Cross Highway, Amagansett. Offers kayaks for rent.

Main Beach (516-537-2716) Highway 27, Wainscott. Rents canoes and kayaks either for individual use or for organized excursions. Main Beach is located across the street from the northern tip of Georgica Pond. The Pond provides a delightful paddle past The Creeks, one of the great estates of the Hamptons. The rich, marshy borders of the pond are feeding grounds for a variety of birds.

Puff & Putt (516-668-4473) Main Street, Montauk. Rents canoes, rowboats, and pedal boats for use on Fort Pond.

FAMILY FUN

Events and activities for children take place year-round in the Hamptons. In the spring, summer, and fall, hikes along the beaches and nature trails and bicycle rides along the back roads open a world of adventure and ideas to children's inquisitive minds. In addition, the following are just a few of the planned activities available to children.

East Hampton Historical Society Summer Camp (516-324-6850) Ages 5–11. Children dress in costume and experience life in the seventeenth, eighteenth, and nineteenth centuries in a unique hands-on atmosphere. At the East Hampton Town Marine Museum, they will create a fish print T-shirt, handle a lobster trap, and work a trawler rig. At the Boat Shop in East Hampton, they'll talk to practicing fishermen, help restore a wooden boat, and learn how to make and sail a boat. In East Hampton's Town House and the Clinton Academy, they'll experience school life in the nineteenth century. While at Mulford Farm, they'll churn butter, card wool, and work on a loom. Call for information.

Guild Hall (516-324-0806) 158 Main Street, East Hampton. May–Oct. Enjoyable workshops are conducted in drawing, sandpainting, mosaics, puppetry, soft sculpture, kite making, sculpting, and other artistic endeavors. Guild Hall also has theatrical productions and book events specifically for children.

Jodi's Gym (516-329-4907 or 212-772-7633) 24 Gingerbread Lane, East Hampton. Ages 6 months to 6 years. The children learn the fundamentals of gymnastics under expert tutelage.

Kid's Kapers (516-287-4300) 2 Pond Lane, Southampton. Kids Kapers is an entertainment series just for children that is held every Saturday morning in the summer and monthly the rest of the year at the Southampton Cultural Center.

Pathfinder Country Day Camp at Montauk (516-668-2080) Montauk. Ages 4–12. Swimming, boating, tennis, and crafts for children in the summer only.

Quogue Wildlife Refuge (516-653-4771) Old Main Road, Quogue. Guides lead children on well-marked trails, explaining along the way about the animals, birds, ponds, marshes, and plants. There are tame deer, hundreds of ducks, and several endangered bird species, including an American bald eagle. Call the refuge to arrange to see the nature center and the rescued animals being nursed back to health.

Riverhead Foundation for Marine Research and Preservation (516-369-9840) 431 East Main Street, Riverhead. Ages 6–10 and 11–14. Weeklong youth marine environmental programs acquaint children with the wonders and complexities of the marine environment. Children set up their own aquariums, go on field trips, collect plant specimens, select and care for tank inhabitants, and learn about beach and dune ecology. A whale watch cruise is included for older children.

Suffolk County Farm and Education Center (516-852-4600) Yaphank Avenue,

Yaphank. The farm and center offer a glimpse of life on a farm 100 years ago. Operated by the Cornell Cooperative Extension Service, this is a fully operational farm with pigs, sheep, goats, beef cattle, and other farm animals. An 1870 hay barn is a typical example of beam and peg construction and is often the starting point for hayrides. There's a grassy picnic area in the gardens.

FISHING & SHELLFISHING

The Hamptons, and particularly Montauk, which is considered the "Sportfishing Capital of the World," are noted for outstanding fishing. Over 30 of the world fishing records (registered in the International Game Fish Association Record Book) have been caught at Montauk. In 1993, for example, a 561-pound bluefin tuna, a 536-pound dusky shark, a 321-pound mako, and a 284-pound bluefish were only a few of the prizes. Seasonal tournaments attract anglers from all over the world. Cash prizes, trophies, and world records often reward the dedicated.

The rocky beach just below the Montauk Point Lighthouse is a popular place to fly-fish, especially for striped bass.

Morgan McGivern

Rules for fishing are distinctly different for saltwater fish, where no permit is required, and for freshwater fish, where one is required. For saltwater fishing, there's surf casting for the illusive, but remarkable, striped bass. Some enjoy the challenge of bagging a big game fish, while fishing offshore from a "party boat," with groups as large as 100 people, all vying for the catch of the day; or from a charter boat, generally with six or fewer people; or from their own yachts. The offshore lure is for tuna, marlin, mako, swordfish, and shark. Inshore fishing, closer to home base, will net such prizes as bluefish, striped bass, blackfish, cod, flounder, fluke, mackerel, pollock, porgy, sea bass, weakfish, and whiting.

Fishing for freshwater fish in the local ponds is a much more complicated proposition. New York State requires a fishing license, which can be obtained from any of the town offices, but you must be a resident to obtain one. With the license, you'll get a state booklet advising where fishing is permitted, if you live in East Hampton Town. If, on the other hand, you live in Southampton Town, there's one more step to take. Since the Town Trustees claim ownership over fish in local ponds, you are allowed to fish only if accompanied by a guide licensed by the Town Trustees. Call the Trustees for a list of their approved guides. For more information about the license, contact the *Town of East Hampton* (516-324-4143), *Shelter Island* (516-749-0291), or *Southampton* (516-283-6000). For a list of licensed guides, call the *Southampton Trustees* (516-283-6000 ext. 259). For excellent booklets and maps about freshwater fishing on Long Island, contact the *New York State Department of Environmental Conservation* (516-444-0273).

A shellfish license is required for harvesting shellfish from Hampton waters, and the times and quantities are strictly regulated. Contact the appropriate Town for a license (see telephone numbers above); you must be a resident to apply. *The New York State Department of Environmental Conservation* (516-444-0475) maintains a list of prohibited areas. It will also advise about pollution levels and water quality. The Department maintains a hot line (516-444-0480) that gives recorded information about any areas unsafe for harvesting due to storms or other temporary problems.

At the *Shellfish Hatchery* (516-668-4601), located off Edgemere Road in Montauk, clams, oysters, and scallops are cultivated and then seeded in nearby ponds and bays for harvesting. Group tours can be arranged with advance notice. The hatchery is operated by the Town of East Hampton.

PARTY BOATS

Lazybones in Montauk (516-668-5671) Johnny Marlin's Dock, 144 Jefferson Avenue, Montauk. Offers fishing trips twice daily, mid-Apr.–Nov., on a 50-foot cruiser. The boat can accommodate 35 people and concentrates on the gentle, inshore waters. Only soda and beer are sold on board. From Apr.-Jul., they look for flounder and blackfish; from Jul.–Sept., the catch is fluke; from Sept.–Nov., the quest is for striped bass. $25 adults/$12 children aged 12 and younger.

Marlin V (516-668-2818) Salivar's Dock, off Flamingo Road, Montauk. Marlin V is a 65-foot boat offering two half-day fishing trips daily, a full-day trip, and night fishing. It has enclosed lounges, a sundeck, modern fish-finding equipment, and a knowledgeable crew. $40 adults full-day/$25 adults half-day.

Viking Fishing Fleet (516-668-5700) West Lake Drive, Montauk. This is the largest party boat operator in Montauk. The trips range from a half-day for fluke fishing to all-night trips for night bluefish and striped bass. Half-day trips run from 8 a.m.–12 p.m. and from 1 p.m.–5 p.m. Viking boats have full restaurants on board, sundecks, and restrooms. Half-day fares include rod, reel, bait, tackle, and lessons. Night-fishing trips depart at 7 p.m. and return at 1 a.m. The $55 charge includes rod, reel, and bait. $25 adults half-day/$12 children ages 5–12/children under 5 free.

CHARTER BOATS

Charter fishing boats are very sophisticated these days. They take a maximum of six passengers and are equipped with fish finders, radar, and satellite navigation. The following charter boats are piloted by experienced captains who know exactly where to find fish. If you call *ProSport Charters* (516-668-2154), they will reserve a boat for you. Otherwise, you can call one of these fishing boats directly.

Abracadabra (516-668-5275) Captain Ray Ruddock will take anglers on excursions for shark, tuna, marlin, bass, bluefish, and fluke.

Blue Fin IV (516-668-9323) This custom-built Montauk sportfishing boat has sophisticated electronics, and a large cabin and is piloted by a second-generation captain, Michael Potts.

Breakaway (516-668-2914) Captain Richie Etzel will take up to six people on inshore fishing jaunts for tuna and shark.

Daybreaker (516-668-5070) Captain Mike Brumm pilots his 38-foot sportfisherman from Montauk to the Continental Shelf.

Fishhooker (516-668-3821) Offshore and inshore charters of half-day or full day, captained by Otto Haselman.

Florence B (516-324-6492) This new 35-foot sportfisherman will take you to the quiet bays or offshore with Captain Jeff Picken.

Oh, Brother Charter Boat (516-668-2707) Fishing offshore for shark, tuna, and marlin or inshore for bass and bluefish with Captain Robert Aaronson.

Star Island Yacht Club & Marina (516-668-5052) A number of fishing boats are chartered out of this marina. They'll be pleased to give you the telephone numbers of several captains.

Venture (516-668-5052) Captain Barry Kohlus operates a 41-foot Hatteras, built for sportfishing.

FITNESS FACILITIES & SPAS

EAST HAMPTON GYM
516-324-4499.
2 Fithian Lane, East
  Hampton.
Rates: $16 daily; call for
  membership
  information.

The East Hampton Gym offers a full range of fitness equipment from treadmills and stairmasters to a versiclimber. There's also a free-weight room and a full Cybex circuit.

**HAMPTON TENNIS
AND FITNESS CLUB**
516-653-6767.
Route 104 at the East
Quogue/Westhampton
border.
Rates: Vary according to
the activity.

The Hampton Tennis and Fitness Club offers a full-range, two-level facility with more than 40 aerobics classes, plus full Nautilus and Cybex circuits and cardiovascular exercise equipment; even the treadmills and stairmasters have heart monitors. It has 26 tennis courts, racquetball, basketball and volleyball courts, a pool, saunas, massage, a tanning salon, and two restaurants. For the youngsters, there's a nursery and playground, a pre-school and juniors summer camp, and a preschool that operates during the school year and even offers transportation. Daily, full-year, and summer memberships are available, as well as adult tennis camps with special rates that include tennis instruction.

**INTERNATIONAL
HEALTH AND
BEAUTY SPA AT
GURNEY'S INN**
516-668-2509.
290 Old Montauk
Highway, Montauk.
Rates: $20 daily; call for
membership information
and packages.

This spa uses a large, heated seawater pool for which Gurney's is noted and also has steam rooms, saunas, exercise rooms, 11 different types of massage, a full aerobics program, ballet, beach walks, hatha yoga, and weight training. Daily, monthly, and yearly memberships are available.

**OMNI HEALTH &
RACQUET CLUB**
516-283-4770.
County Road 39A,
Southampton.
Rates: $20 daily; call for
membership information.

This is a complete health and fitness facility, with over 60 classes weekly in aerobics, calisthenics, stretch and tone, yoga, and aquadynamics. There are treadmills, liferowers, two small pools, a steam sauna, a Jacuzzi, squash and racquetball courts, various types of massage, and more. Daily, monthly, and yearly memberships are available. In Southampton, the club is located next to the Hampton Jitney office.

RADU
516-329-0077.
24-26 Gingerbread Lane,
East Hampton.
Rates: Call for membership
information.

Radu is the guru of fit. He's had his body shop in East Hampton for a number of years as a satellite to his gym in Manhattan. He's noted for tough, disciplined, individualized fitness training.

WORLD GYM
516-723-3174.
Montauk Highway,
Hampton Bays.
Rates: $15 daily; call for
membership information.

This franchise in Hampton Bays opened in 1993 and includes aerobics classes, circuit training, free-weight training, and cardiovascular conditioning. Their Exerflex wood aerobics floor is the latest in safety and comfort. There's also a pro shop. Daily, monthly, and yearly memberships are available.

FLYING, GLIDING, BALLOONING, SKYDIVING

Except for the Wright Brothers' first flight, some of the most historic events in aviation history have taken place on Long Island. Glenn Curtiss experimented with his "pusher plane" in Garden City in 1909 and steadily expanded his company, building record-breaking racing planes during the 1920s. Charles Lindbergh launched his famous *Spirit of St. Louis* in 1927 from Long Island's Roosevelt Field, giving Long Island the title "the cradle of aviation." In the 1940s, Grumman Aircraft Engineering Corporation, headed by Leroy Grumman, who grew up in Huntington, watching the Curtiss aircraft spiraling through the skies, became a major military aircraft manufacturer. Today, although little aircraft manufacturing remains on Long Island, flying, gliding, ballooning, and skydiving are enjoyed as recreational activities.

FLYING

American Airman School (516-288-0210) Suffolk County Airport, Westhampton. Sight-seeing rides for one person, $40/35–40 minutes; instruction is available.

Hampton Air (516-288-5149) Bldg. 308, Suffolk County Airport, Westhampton Beach. Sight-seeing rides for up to 3 people, $109/hour; $60/half-hour; charter service and instruction are available; maintenance facility.

Sound Aircraft Flight Enterprises (516-537-2202) East Hampton Airport, Wainscott. Sight-seeing rides for up to 3 people, $95/hour; instruction is available.

GLIDING

Sky Sailors Gliders School (516-288-5858) Suffolk County Airport, Westhampton Beach. Introductory flight (with a licensed pilot at the controls, but student takes over the controls for a while) $70–$200, depending on length of flight and how high you want to fly; $60 children's flight.

BALLOONING

Although there are no hot air balloon rides available right in the Hamptons, *Adventures Aloft* (516-595-9213) 27 Claremont Street, Deer Park, often land in the Hamptons. If you choose to drift quietly in one of their balloons, bring a camera. This is a great way to see lakes, marshes, and areas of Long Island that you can't access by land.

SKYDIVING

For those who love to sky-dive or have a secret yearning to try, *Skydive Long Island* has the only student jump center on Long Island. They train in the morning for an afternoon jump. $200 for instruction and the first jump solo; $215 for instruction and the first jump tandem (beside an instructor); $70 for jumps thereafter. They're located at *Spadaro's Airport* (516-878-5867) on Montauk Highway in East Moriches.

GOLF

Much of golf's early history in the United States took place in the Hamptons. The first golf course (only six holes) was laid out on a lawn in Yonkers in 1888, but the Hamptons were not far behind. In 1891, the Shinnecock Hills Golf Club in Southampton became the first professionally designed course in the United States, complete with its own clubhouse. Designed by the renowned firm of McKim, Mead, and White, the 12-hole course was laid out by the Scottish golfer, Willie Dunn. In 1896, the Shinnecock Hills Golf Club hosted the second U.S. Open and also the U.S. Amateur Championship. The Open was held here again in 1986 and in 1995.

Other clubs were not far behind. The Maidstone Club in East Hampton was established in 1890 as a tennis club, but soon had its own 18-hole golf course. The National Golf Links of America, in Southampton, was established in 1908 along the lines of St. Andrew's in Scotland.

Most golf in the Hamptons continues to be played on private courses. If you're lucky enough to belong to one of the private clubs or have friends that do, have a great time! Otherwise, the following courses are available to the general public.

BARCELONA NECK
516-725-2503.
Barcelona Neck Preserve (off Route 114), between East Hampton and Sag Harbor.
Open: Year-round, dawn to dusk.
Size: 9 holes; par 35; 2,900 yards.
Rates: $10 weekdays; $15 weekends.
Mailing Address: Sag Harbor Golf Club, Golf Club Road, Sag Harbor, NY 11963.

This course, managed by the Sag Harbor Golf Club, has a small clubhouse that sells soft drinks, beer, snacks, hamburgers, and hot dogs. The land is owned by The Nature Conservancy and is also laced with hiking trails. Soft-spike shoes only, please.

MONTAUK DOWNS GOLF COURSE
516-668-5000.
Fairview Avenue, Montauk (in Montauk Downs State Park).
Open: Year-round 6:00 a.m.–7:00 p.m. on weekdays; 5:30 a.m.–6:00 p.m. on the weekends.
Size: 18 holes; par 72; 6,860/6,402 yards.
Rates: $25 weekdays; $30 weekends; $3 additional fee for a reservation.
Mailing Address: R.R. 2, Box 206A, Montauk, NY 11954.

The golf course within **Montauk Downs State Park** is a rare state treasure. Built in the 1920s by Carl Fisher as part of his grand scheme to turn Montauk into the "Miami of the North," the golf course was redesigned in the 1960s by Robert Trent Jones and Rees Jones. This has been rated one of the finest public courses in the United States. You'll find lockers, showers, a pro shop, a resident pro, and much more. Instruction is available. The restaurant in the clubhouse serves lunch and dinner with nightly entertainment and sometimes is used for theatrical productions. Six tennis courts and two swimming pools complete the facility.

POXABOGUE GOLF COURSE
516-537-0025.
Montauk Highway, Bridgehampton, NY.
Open: 7:00 a.m.–6:00 p.m. Apr.–Nov.
Size: 9 holes; par 30; 1,706 yards.
Rates: $15 Mon.–Thurs.; $20 Fri.–Sun.
Mailing Address: P.O. Box 890, Wainscott, NY 11975.
Directions: Located on Montauk Highway, 2 miles east of Bridgehampton.

Poxabogue Golf Course includes a pro shop, a driving range, and a restaurant for hungry and thirsty golfers; it is consistently rated as one of the favorite breakfast spots on the South Fork. The course is especially appreciated by those with limited time; it has six par-three and three par-four.

HIKING & RUNNING

Hiking trails are described in the section "Parks & Nature Preserves" in this chapter. For a book on hiking, try *Short Nature Walks on Long Island* (1993) by Rodney & Priscilla Albright. It lists 14 walks on the South Fork and includes maps and specific directions.

Jogging and running are also favorite pastimes in the Hamptons. Montauk Highway's broad shoulder attracts many joggers, as do the side roads. When school is not is session, local high schools also have running tracks that are available for public use.

HORSEBACK RIDING

The Hampton Classic Horse Show, held in Bridgehampton every year, draws the best riders in the East.

Jason Green

DEEP HOLLOW RANCH
516-668-2744.
Montauk Highway,
  Montauk, NY.
Open: Year-round.
Rates: $40 for 1 ¹/₂-hour
  beach and trail ride.
Mailing Address: P.O. Box
  835, Montauk, NY 11954.
Directions: Located on
  Montauk Highway, 3
  miles east of Montauk.

Established in Montauk in 1658, this is the oldest cattle ranch in the United States, and thus it claims to be the home of the first American cowboys. It is still in operation, although not as a cattle ranch; but there certainly are cowboys in residence. Deep Hollow Ranch offers trails on 4,000 acres of Suffolk County and New York State parklands that include picturesque beach rides along the Atlantic Ocean. Groups of six to seven people leave the ranch daily on the hour; western saddles are used. The owner, Rusty Leaver, first came to the ranch as a child in 1963 and became part owner of the ranch in 1971. Deep Hollow offers riding lessons, using both English and Western saddles. Pony rides and a petting farm entertain the small tikes, and a pony camp, where children aged 5–9 can learn to ride and care for horses, is offered in the summer. Also in the summer, there's a Texas-style family barbecue that includes BBQ beef, corn on the cob, grilled local fish, and homemade pies, eaten to the accompaniment of a singing cowboy. Other activities include roping lessons, horseshoes, and a hay-bale jungle gym for the kids. This is also the site of the annual *Back at the Ranch* concert.

RITA'S STABLE
516-668-5453.
West Lake Drive, Montauk.
Open: Year-round.

Rita's Stables has two locations: in Montauk and at Sears Bellows Park in Hampton Bays. In addition to trail rides, there are pony rides and a

Rates: $20 for $1/2$-hour trail ride; $30 for 1-hour trail ride.

Mailing Address: Benson Drive, Montauk, NY 11054.

Directions: Located 1 mile east of Montauk village. Turn left onto West Lake Drive at the Montauk Downs sign and take the first right after the little white house.

SEARS BELLOWS STABLES

516-723-3554.

Benson Drive, Montauk.

Open: Year-round 9:00 a.m.-6:00 p.m.

Rates: $20 for $1/2$-hour trail ride; $30 for 1-hour trail ride; $40 for $1 1/2$-hour lake ride.

Mailing Address: P.O. Box 14, Benson Drive, Montauk, NY 11954.

Directions: Located on Route 24, between Hampton Bays and Riverhead at Sears Bellows County Park; the entrance is beside the *Big Duck*.

petting farm for children. Inquire about group rates and their summer pony camp.

Sears Bellows Stables, in Sears Bellows County Park in Hampton Bays, offers approximately 20 miles of groomed trails that twist through the wild pine barrens region (recently recognized by New York State as worthy of preservation) and wind past ponds and streams. Organized rides vary in length; a maximum of six participants can choose either English or Western saddles.

The above stables are the only ones offering hourly trail rides. For those who want to take lessons, especially in dressage, hunting, and jumping, the following stables offer instruction.

Clearview Stables (516-283-0073) Long Springs Road, Southampton.

East End Stables (516-324-9568) Oak View Highway, East Hampton.

Quantuck Bay Farm (516-288-0303) 607 Main Street, Westhampton Beach.

Rosewood Farm (516-287-4775) 100 Majors Path, Southampton.

Sagpond Farm (516-537-2879) Narrow Lane, Sagaponack.

Stony Hill Stables (516-267-3203) Town Lane, Amagansett.

Swan Creek Farms (516-537-0662) Halsey Lane, Bridgehampton.

Topping Riding School (516-537-0948) Gibson's Lane, Sagaponack.

Two Trees Stables (516-537-3881) 849 Hayground Road, Bridgehampton.

HUNTING

The Hamptons offer some of the best hunting on the East Coast. Several large, private hunting preserves are located here. A license is required for all hunting, and advance permission from landowners is absolutely necessary before entering private property.

As the deer population has increased, so has the battle cry of home owners. Shelter Island has allowed two deer hunts each year for several years on the massive Mashomack Preserve, and North Haven has considered the same. Several state and county parks and town lands are open to deer hunting, but dates and locations are determined by a drawing. For information, contact the *New York State Department of Environmental Conservation, Bureau of Wildlife, Deer Info., Bldg. 40, SUNY, Stony Brook, NY 11790-2356.*

Duck and other bird hunters will find tens of thousands of duck, geese, and other waterfowl in the many tidal marshes, bays, and creeks in the Hamptons. Well-built duck blinds dot marshes and lake perimeters, and bird hunting is allowed in several state and county parks. For excellent maps and information about licenses and yearly seasons, contact the *New York State Department of Environmental Conservation* at the above address.

Riding to the hounds has proponents in this area as well. For information, see Chapter Nine, *North Fork.*

For skeet and trapshooting, the *Maidstone Gun Club* (516-537-7887) is located on Daniel's Hole Road in Wainscott.

PARKS & NATURE PRESERVES

The Hamptons are blessed with an enlightened and environmentally aware population, both among the permanent and the summer residents. The Nature Conservancy, a national environmental organization, owns many areas in the Hamptons and because of their perseverance, we can walk along trails that skirt marshes and dunes and that overlook bays and the ocean, realizing we would not have the privilege had they not persevered. The Nature Conservancy publishes a pamphlet, *The Nature Conservancy South Fork Shelter Island Preserve Guide,* (1990) (available at most bookstores and Chamber of Commerce offices) that describes each of its properties. The organization owns or manages 28 preserves on the South Fork and is responsible, along with Group for the South Fork and the Peconic Land Trust, for the preservation of 25,000 acres of open space and farmland. This figure represents 18 percent of the area's 255 square miles.

Many areas are not open to the public, except when accompanied by a guide, because of the sensitive nature of the land and its plant and animal

Suzi Forbes Chase

Through careful nurturing, the once rare osprey population is nesting in the Hamptons again.

inhabitants. Listed here are only a few of the areas where visitors are welcomed throughout the year. For more areas, please watch for announcements in local newspapers or call *The Nature Conservancy* (516-329-7689) or *Group for the South Fork* (516-537-1400).

It has long been a dream to create a hiking trail the length of Long Island that would be the region's version of the Appalachian Trail. Recently that dream has come closer to reality. The New York state legislature passed a bill, protecting the Pine Barrens region of central Long Island, that opens the way to the creation of the Paumanok Path, which is planned to stretch 60 miles from Rocky Point, near Wading River, to Montauk Point. For more information, contact the *Long Island Greenbelt Trail Conference* (516-360-0753) in Smithtown. In addition, the *Southampton Trails Preservation Society* and the *East Hampton Trails Preservation Society* are constructing trails. Those that already lie within the two townships are *The Red Creek Trail,* the *Long Pond Greenbelt,* and the 10-mile *Northwest Path.* Organized hikes and walks are sponsored by all organizations.

Suffolk County residents who wish to camp or to use the county parks should purchase a "Green Key Card." The price is $20 for three years and entitles residents to reduced fees for parking, camping, and other activities. The card can be purchased at the entrance to the parks, but be sure to bring proper identification, proving you are a full-time county resident. Call *Suffolk County* (516-854-4949) for details.

EAST HAMPTON TOWN

East Hampton Village

East Hampton Village Nature Trail No fee. The trail is a delightful area in the heart of East Hampton and is accessed from David's or Huntting Lane. Ducks and swans, often with their babies, happily paddle about in the tiny pond; birds and small animals hustle in and out of the underbrush along the wooded paths. It's a popular spot for parents and children.

Montauk

Hither Hills State Park (516-668-2554) Reservations required for campsites (516-668-7000) $16 per night, $7.50 reservation fee, $5 parking (day use only). This park has 168 tent and trailer campsites, hiking trails, rest rooms, a camp store, children's play area, and a picnic area. It is situated on 1,700 acres overlooking 2 miles of ocean beach in Montauk. Nightly entertainment includes movies, a children's summer theater, concerts, square dancing, games, and lots of fun. A variety of trails bisect this vast acreage, making available a wealth of scenic vistas, ponds, dunes (including the walking dunes), and marshes. The state park is adjacent to Hither Woods Preserve and the County Nature Preserve.

Montauk Point State Park (516-668-3781) $4 parking fee. With over 700 acres, hiking and nature trails, snack and gift shop, this park adjoins Theodore Roosevelt County Park and includes the Montauk Point Lighthouse (fee and under different management). Some trails near the lighthouse are currently closed, as efforts are made to stabilize the cliff from ongoing erosion. (See detailed information about the Montauk Point Lighthouse Museum in Chapter Six, *Culture.*) Many other hiking and nature trails are open, however, with some overlooking the ocean at the site of numerous shipwrecks. Surf fishing is a popular sport, especially for striped bass.

Theodore Roosevelt County Park (516-852-7878) $13 per night camping for county residents/$25 noncounty residents; $35 outer beach permits. On 1,185 acres, the park has picnic areas, campsites, a hostel for cyclists, and 3.5 miles of nature trails. The park headquarters are located in Third House, along with the Pharaoh Indian Museum; the rest of the park is off East Lake Drive in Montauk. There is camping space for about 400 families on the 3 miles of beach, but campers must use four-wheel drive, self-contained vehicles. A trailer park with access to the beach is also available. The 3-mile nature trail is a wooded, swampy area with wildflowers, ferns, and a variety of birds, turtles, and animals.

Northwest

Cedar Point County Park (516-852-7620) $13 per night camping for county
residents/$23 noncounty residents. $5 deposit for rowboat rental, $5 first
hour and $4 each hour after. This park has 190 tent and trailer campsites,
rest rooms, hot showers, a camp store, a playground, a basketball and volleyball court, a baseball diamond, nature trails, and free movies in the summer. It is located on a 608-acre point that juts into Northwest Harbor and
points toward Shelter Island and Sag Harbor. The old stone lighthouse on
its tip was built in 1868 to guide whaling ships to their home port of Sag
Harbor. When built, the light was actually on an island; the land masses
were joined together during the 1938 hurricane. One of the most interesting
trails is the beach walk to the lighthouse where, in early summer, a barrier
protects the nesting area of endangered birds, such as terns, plovers, and
giant ospreys.

Springs

Merrill Lake Sanctuary is a Nature Conservancy property of about 30 acres,
within the Accabonac Harbor Preserve (one of the primary spots on the East
End for bird-watching). You may see ospreys nesting as their young hatch in
late June and early July or graceful herons feeding in the marshy lagoons, as
well as a variety of other animal and plant life. The entrance is well marked,
off the Springs Fireplace Road.

SOUTHAMPTON TOWN

Bridgehampton

Long Pond Greenbelt in Bridgehampton is a 6.2-mile trail, threading past a
chain of ponds and wetlands. It is in the heart of the Atlantic flyway, making
it rich with bird life. Managed by The Nature Conservancy, trails lead into
the area from Sag Harbor's Mashashimuet Park.

Hampton Bays

Sears Bellows County Park (516-852-8290) $13 per night camping for county
residents/$23 noncounty residents. This Suffolk County park has 70 tent
and trailer campsites, a bicycle hostel, rest rooms, showers, nightly lectures
and movies, a picnic area, lake swimming, hiking trails, rowboat rentals,
freshwater pond fishing, and horseback riding. Access is from Bellows Pond
Road off Route 24 in Flanders.

Quogue

Quogue Wildlife Refuge (516-653-4771) Run by the New York State Department of Environmental Conservation, this is a marvelous place to acquaint children with various species of birds. They'll love all the ducks, the turkey that gobbles as they enter, and the tame deer. There's a nature center with exhibits and a sanctuary where staff take care of injured and orphaned animals. Guides lead exploratory walks. A resident population of Canadian geese make the refuge their permanent home, and children delight in seeing the baby geese march across the grass in the spring. The 7 miles of trails are well marked, and there are benches along the way. Access is off Old Main Road, across the Long Island Rail Road tracks in Quogue.

Sag Harbor

A monarch butterfly lights on seaside goldenrod at Morton National Wildlife Refuge in Noyack.

Jason Green

Morton National Wildlife Refuge (516-286-0485) Run by the U.S. Fish and Wildlife Service, this 187-acre preserve is a temporary home to migratory waterbirds. A self-guided nature trail explains what you are viewing; a map may be obtained from The Nature Conservancy (516-329-7689). The entrance is off Noyack Road, west of Sag Harbor.

ROLLERBLADING

Roller blading is currently as popular as bicycling. A favorite spot to practice the sport is Long Beach in Sag Harbor, especially in the evening when there's a blazing sunset. Watch the local newspapers for places to freestyle.

Quiet pathways and few cars make the Hamptons popular with rollerbladers.

Morgan McGivern

Amagansett Beach & Bicycle (516-267-6325) Montauk and Cross Highways, Amagansett. Rentals $25/day, including pads and helmet.

Espo's Surf & Sport (516-329-9100) The Old Barn, Main Street, East Hampton. Rates $8/hour, $25/day, including pads.

Main Beach (516-537-2716) Montauk Highway, Wainscott. Rentals $25/day. This shop has a terrific selection of in-line skates (and equipment for many other sports) both for sale and rent, and they also give lessons. They'll provide elbow and knee pads to soften the inevitable falls.

Rotations Bicycle Centers (516-283-2890) 32 Windmill Lane, Southampton. Rentals $25/day.

SCUBA DIVING & SKIN DIVING

For those who like to dive for sunken treasure or explore shipwrecks, many underwater opportunities quietly await them in the waters surrounding the Hamptons. Shipwrecks dot the ocean floor from Amagansett to the Montauk Lighthouse, but some of the finest diving is further offshore. About 40 miles off Montauk lies the wreck of the *Andrea Doria*, which sank in 1956 after a collision with the *Stockholm*. Because of its depth and poor visibility, however, this is considered a very dangerous dive. Wrecks of numerous other ships, though, are scattered along the coast.

There are less hazardous diving sites in Napeague Bay and off Block Island, as well as on the South Shore near the Shinnecock Inlet and the Ponquogue Bridge. Visibility is good along the South Shore, where divers can see tropical fish in the summer and other fish and shellfish year-round.

One must take a course and become certified in order to scuba dive; the course usually takes about four weeks. Also see **Peconic Scuba** in Chapter Nine, *North Fork*.

Weight-N-Sea Scuba School (516-329-9073) Run by certified PADI instructor Paul Casciotta, this school gives lessons in open-water and rescue diving, either in a group or individually. Lessons generally take place on Fort Pond Bay in Montauk from May-Nov. Paul is an experienced diver who knows the local waters. He'll take people in his small, two-person boat to nearby dive sites, such as the old World War II navy dock in Fort Pond Bay.

SURFING, WINDSURFING, WATERSKIING, JETSKIING

The waves are especially high in the Hamptons during hurricane season.

Morgan McGivern

SURFING

Surfing is a tremendously popular sport in the Hamptons. Witness the surfers out at 6:00 a.m. along Dune Road in Westhampton Beach or at Ditch Plains Beach in Montauk, but be aware that no surfing is allowed within 100 feet of public-bathing beaches. Although the waves may not equal that of Hawaii's beaches, they provide challenging and exhilarating rides, especially after storms. Hamptons' surfing has gained such acclaim that the U.S. Surfing

Association has considered holding the U.S. Amateur Surfing Championships at Ditch Plains. *The Eastern Surfing Association* (516-668-5040) in Montauk sponsors amateur surfing contests all year.

Espo's Surf & Sport (516-329-9100) The Old Barn, Main Street, East Hampton (summer only). Rents surfboards, boogie boards, and water skis.

Main Beach (516-537-2716) Montauk Highway, Wainscott. This store provides one-stop shopping for surfers, windsurfers, and all those who enjoy water-related sports. In addition to providing a daily surf report (516-537-SURF), Main Beach rents and sells surfboards, boogie boards, paddle skis, canoes, and kayaks. In the summer, it sets up a satellite mobile windsurfing shop with rental equipment at Lazy Point Beach on Napeague Harbor. No reservations are necessary.

Plaza Sporting Goods (516-668-9300) Main Street, Montauk Village. Rents surfboards, fins, and a variety of other sporting equipment. Surfboard rentals: $8/hour, $22/day.

WINDSURFING

The favorite windsurfing spots are Mecox Bay in Bridgehampton and Napeague Bay, off Lazy Point. (See **Main Beach** above).

Amagansett Beach & Bicycle (516-267-6325) Montauk Highway at Cross Highway, Amagansett. Rents windsurfing equipment.

Windsurfing Hamptons (516-283-9463) 1686 North Highway (Route 27), Southampton. Rents windsurfing equipment that you can put on your car and dip in the water wherever you choose, or they will deliver the equipment to Peconic Bay for you and give instructions to the uninitiated.

WATERSKIING

Waterskiing is permitted in Noyack Bay at Foster Memorial Beach. The Town of East Hampton also has designated a section of Three Mile Harbor, from Settlers Landing at the end of Hands Creek Road to Sammy's Beach, for waterskiing. Within Three Mile Harbor, the water is generally glassy smooth.

Uihlein's Marina & Boat Rental (516-668-3799) West Lake Drive Extension, Montauk. Ski boats and skis for up to four people can be rented for skiing on Lake Montauk. $110/hour.

JETSKIING

East End Jet Ski (516-728-8060) 9 Canoe Place Road, Hampton Bays. Just off the beaches of Shinnecock Bay in Hampton Bays at the Mariner's Cove

Marine, one- and two-person jet skis are available for rent. The rate is $50/half-hour and includes instruction and a fitted life preserver. Plenty of thrills are available at speeds of up to 40 miles per hour.

SWIMMING

East Hampton Town and Southampton Town conduct numerous swimming classes, ranging from beginners' classes to lifesaving courses, each summer at the town beaches. With many miles of bay and ocean, most swimming areas have been listed under the section "Beaches" in this chapter. There are few public swimming pools or places to swim in freshwater in the Hamptons.

Montauk Downs County Park (516-668-5000) This park has two pools. An excellent array of classes are taught every summer, and the pools are open long hours.

Emma Rose Elliston Park (516-283-6000) Big Fresh Pond, off Millstone Brook Road, North Sea. This park, for Southampton Town residents only, has a tiny beach on Big Fresh Pond with rest rooms, a lifeguard, and a picnic area. It's within a beautifully maintained park.

Trout Pond Noyack Road in Noyack. This pond is rated locally as the favorite freshwater swimming spot in the Hamptons, but beware! There are no lifeguards, and signs, posted by the Town of Southampton warning *No Swimming*, are placed there for a purpose. The depth of the pond is uneven and hard to predict, but, since there's not much beach, children generally paddle about on rafts or in inner tubes.

TENNIS & RACQUET SPORTS

The Meadow Club of Southampton, the first tennis club in the Hamptons, was established in 1887. The club now has more grass courts than any other on the East Coast, as well as smooth croquet lawns, all hidden away behind privet hedges. The Maidstone Club of East Hampton, not far behind, opened in 1891. Although a golf course was built at Maidstone, tennis continues to be the main interest of many members.

In the Hamptons, there are many more courts at private clubs than in public places, and most clubs, private and public, are open primarily in the summer. Several Hamptons villages, though, provide public tennis courts, but the fees and access vary from village to village. It's best to check first.

PUBLIC TENNIS COURTS

Amagansett

Abrahams Path Park (516-324-2417) Abrahams Path. 4 courts; $8 fee; rest rooms: attendant on duty; reservation required on day of play.

Bridgehampton

Bridgehampton High School (516-537-0271) Montauk Highway. 2 courts for public use; no fee weekdays, $10 Bridgehampton residents and $20 nonresidents on weekends; attendant on duty.

East Hampton

East Hampton High School (516-329-4143) 2 Long Lane. 6 courts; $10 fee; attendant on duty; sign up each morning.
Herrick Park (516-329-4143) Park Place. 3 courts; $10 fee; lights for night use; attendant on duty. Easily accessed from Park Place (the parking lot behind the shops on Main Street and Newtown Lane).
John Marshall Elementary School (516-329-4143) 30 Church Street. 2 courts for public use; $10 fee; attendant on duty; sign up each morning.

Montauk

Lions Park (516-324-2417) Essex Street. 3 courts for public use; $8 fee; attendant on duty; reservation required on day of play.
Montauk Downs State Park (516-668-5000) Fairview, off West Lake Drive. 6 Har-tru courts; $6 fee per hour; attendant on duty; rest rooms; showers; lockers; golf course; two swimming pools; restaurant.

Sag Harbor

Mashashimuet (516-725-4018) Main Street. 8 courts for public use (2 all-weather and 6 clay); hard courts $20 per hour; clay courts $25 fee per hour; attendant on duty. Although this is a membership organization, sometimes there are courts available on an hourly basis, and seasonal memberships are reasonable. Managed by the Hampton Tennis Company for the Parks and Recreation Association of Sag Harbor.

Springs

Springs Recreation Area (516-324-2417) Off Old Stone Highway. 3 courts for public use; $8 fee; attendant on duty; reservation required on day of play.

Southampton

Southampton High School (516-283-6000) Leland Lane. 5 courts for public use; no fee; first-come, first-serve basis.

Westhampton Beach

Westhampton Beach High School (516-288-3800) Oneck Lane. 8 courts for public use; no fee; sign up with attendant on duty. Preference given to district residents.

PRIVATE CLUBS

Although the following are membership clubs, they also offer short-term playing opportunities to nonmembers.

East Hampton

Buckskill Tennis Club (516-324-2243) Buckskill Road. 10 Har-tru courts; $36 hourly rate; pro shop; clubhouse.

East Quogue

Hampton Tennis and Fitness Club (516-653-6767) County Route 104 and Dune Road. 26 courts (4 indoor Har-tru, open year-round); rates range according to use; swimming pool; basketball and racquetball; fitness equipment. Offers adult tennis camps with special rates that include tennis instruction.

Montauk

Hither Hills Racquet Club (516-267-8525) Montauk Highway at Napeague, between Amagansett and Montauk. 5 Flex-pave courts; $30 fee per hour.

Quogue

Racquet Club of Quogue (516-653-9828) Montauk Highway and Lamb Street. 10 Har-tru courts; $30 fee per hour after 12:00 noon.

Southampton

Nort-sea Racquet Club (516-283-5444) 655 Majors Path. 10 Har-tru courts; $40 fee per hour when courts available. Offers instruction and will arrange games with varied-level players.

Triangle Tennis Club (516-287-3052) 411 Hampton Road. 3 all-weather courts; $35 fee per hour; reservations required a day in advance.

Westhampton Beach

East Side Tennis Club (516-288-1540) Montauk Highway. 12 Har-tru courts; game room; clubhouse; volleyball.

Westhampton Tennis & Sport Club (516-288-6060) 22 Depot Road. 24 Har-tru courts and 4 all-weather courts under a bubble. Membership only in the summer. In other seasons, hourly court rental ranges $25–$64.

WHALE WATCHING

The *Riverhead Foundation for Marine Research and Preservation* (516-369-9840) offers Whale Watch Cruises during the summer, departing from the Viking Dock in Montauk. A naturalist is always on board to explain what you are seeing. The best months for whale watching are from late Jul.–mid-Aug., when the whales are migrating. The trips are 4 $^1/_2$–7 hours, depending on how long it takes to sight the whales; there's often a bonus sighting of dolphins, seabirds, and other marine life. Prices for the trips are $36 for adults, $31 for senior citizens, $18 for children 5–12, children under 5 free, but the cruise is long and it is not recommended for children under 5. In the winter, the foundation also sponsors seal-viewing cruises.

Town Pond is a tranquil spot in East Hampton to have a picnic, read a book, or watch the swans.

Morgan McGivern

CHAPTER EIGHT
Practical Matters
INFORMATION

We promised a complete guide to the Hamptons, and it certainly wouldn't be complete without the following basic, though essential, information. We hope that whether you are a long-time resident or a tourist, you will turn first to this guide for accurate and complete information.

Insider's tip: In East Hampton, people with a 324 prefix often give their telephone number using the last four digits only.

Morgan McGivern

In the summer, flowers grow in abundant profusion in the Hamptons.

For local **time,** call **516-976-1616.**
For local **weather,** call **516-976-1212.**
For **extended weather** forecast, call **516-976-8888.**

AMBULANCE, FIRE, POLICE

Throughout Suffolk County the emergency number is **911,** but most small villages have their own fire and police departments that can be reached at the following local numbers.

Town	Fire	Ambulance	Police
Amagansett	516-267-3500		
Bridgehampton	516-324-4477		
East Hampton Town		516-324-0024	516-324-0024

East Hampton Village	516-324-0124		516-324-0777
Hampton Bays	516-924-5252		516-728-3400
Montauk	516-668-2464		516-668-3709
North Sea	516-924-5252		
Quogue			516-653-4175
Sag Harbor	516-324-6550	516-725-0058	516-725-0058
Southampton Town	516-283-0056	516-728-3400	516-728-3400
Southampton Village	516-283-0056		516-283-0056
Springs	516-324-1315		516-324-1315
Westhampton Beach	516-288-3444		516-288-3444

For other emergencies, please consult the following list or your telephone directory.

Emergency	**911**
AIDS Hot Line	516-853-3049 or 516-385-AIDS
Child Abuse Hot Line	800-342-3720
Coast Guard (South Shore)	516-878-0320 or 516-728-1171
Deaf Emergency	800-342-4357 or 516-924-8811
Domestic Violence Hot Line	516-666-8833 or 800-942-6906
General Fire, Rescue, and Emergency Number	516-924-5252
LILCO (light company) Emergency	516-755-6000
Poison Control	516-542-2323
Rape Hot Line	516-360-3606
Red Cross	516-924-6911
Runaway Hot Line	800-231-6946
Southampton Hospital	516-726-8200
State Police (in Hampton Bays)	516-728-3000 or 516-537-0237
Suicide and Crisis Counseling	516-751-7500

AREA CODES

The area code for all of Suffolk and Nassau County is **516**. Frequently called nearby areas are as follows:

Location	**Area Code**
New York:	
Manhattan	212
Brooklyn, Bronx, Queens, Staten Island	718

Westchester County   914

Connecticut:
Western Coastal Connecticut   203
Eastern Connecticut   860

TOWN HALLS

East Hampton's village hall is located in the former home of Lyman Beecher and his family, when he was minister of East Hampton. (Harriet Beecher Stowe had not yet been born, however.)

Morgan McGivern

On the East End, town government is the predominant local lawmaking and enforcement agency, but, within each town, individual incorporated villages and even smaller hamlets are self-governing. The incorporated villages generally have legal and law enforcement influence within their boundaries (and this includes maintaining their own police force), but the hamlets depend upon the town for these services. Most villages have a village hall where local business is conducted. Beach permits for village beaches, for example, are issued by the village, while permits for the town beaches are issued at the town office.

TOWN OFFICES

East Hampton Town Office (516-324-4143) 159 Pantigo Road, East Hampton, NY 11937.

East Hampton Town Satellite Office (516-668-5081) Main Street, Montauk, NY 11954.

Southampton Town Office (516-283-6000) 116 Hampton Road, Southampton, NY 11968.

VILLAGE OFFICES

East Hampton Village Office (516-324-4150) 86 Main Street, East Hampton, NY 11937.

North Haven Village Office (516-725-1378) 335 Ferry Road, Sag Harbor, NY 11963.

Quogue Village Office (516-653-4498) P.O. Box 926, Jessup Avenue, Quogue, NY 11959.

Sag Harbor Village Office (516-725-0222) P.O. Box 660, Main Street, Sag Harbor, NY 11963.

Southampton Village Office (516-283-0247) 23 Main Street, Southampton, NY 11968.

Westhampton Beach Village Office (516-288-1654) P.O. Box 991, Sunset Avenue, Westhampton Beach, NY 11978.

ZIP CODES

Town, Village, Hamlet	Zip Code
Amagansett	11930
Bridgehampton	11932
East Hampton	11937
East Quogue	11942
Eastport	11941
Hampton Bays	11946
Montauk	11954
North Haven	11963
Quogue	11959
Remsenburg	11960
Sagaponack	11962
Sag Harbor	11963
Southampton	11968
Speonk	11972
Wainscott	11975
Water Mill	11976
Westhampton	11977
Westhampton Beach	11978

CHAMBERS OF COMMERCE

East Hampton Chamber of Commerce (516-324-0362) 37A Main Street, East Hampton. Open May–Dec. 10:00 a.m.–4:00 p.m.; Jan.–Apr., 3–4 days a week, usually Wed.–Sat. 10:00 a.m.–4:00 p.m.

Hampton Bays Chamber of Commerce (516-728-2211) Montauk Highway, Box 64, Hampton Bays. Open 10:00 a.m.–5:00 p.m. Fri., Sat.

From the multitude of bays and harbors on the East End to the villages near the ocean, a welcome is extended to all.

Jason Green

Montauk Chamber of Commerce (516-668-2428) Main Street, Montauk. Open May–Oct. 10:00 a.m.–5:00 p.m. Mon.–Fri., 10:00 a.m.–3:00 p.m. Sat., 10:00 a.m.–2:00 p.m. Sun.; Oct.–Apr. 10:00 a.m.–4:00 p.m. Mon.–Fri.

Sag Harbor Chamber of Commerce (516-725-0011) 55 Main Street, Sag Harbor. (Mailing Address: P.O. Box 2810, Sag Harbor, NY 11963.) Open daily 9:00 a.m.–5:00 p.m. Jul.–Aug.; the rest of the year by telephone or mail.

Southampton Chamber of Commerce (516-283-0402) 76 Main Street, Southampton. Open 9:00 a.m.–5:00 p.m. Mon.–Fri.; 9:00 a.m.–4:00 p.m. Sat.

Greater Westhampton Chamber of Commerce (516-288-3337) 27A Old Riverhead Road, Westhampton Beach. Open in the summer 10:00 a.m.–4:00 p.m. Mon.–Sat.; in the winter 10:00 a.m.–2:00 p.m. Mon.–Fri.

BANKS, FOREIGN EXCHANGE, 24-HOUR ATMs

If you arrive in the Hamptons with currency from another country, be assured that you will not be stranded. Most banks will cash traveler's checks, and Cook Travel converts foreign money into American traveler's checks. In addition, Chase Bank in Southampton has a foreign money exchange and will be able to convert most currencies.

Chase Bank (516-283-7991) 60 Main Street, Southampton. Open 9:00 a.m.–3:00 p.m. Mon.–Thurs.; 9:00 a.m.–6:00 p.m. Fri.

Cook Travel Inc. (516-324-8430) 20 Main Street, East Hampton. Open 9:30 a.m.–5:30 p.m. Mon.–Fri.; 10:00 a.m.–5:00 p.m. Sat. Also (516-283-1740) 30 Nugent Street, Southampton. Same hours.

Why is it that we seem to run out of cash at the most inopportune times? In an effort to ease the panic, we are listing banks that serve the Hamptons and also Automatic Teller Machines (ATMs), with the cards that they accept. In this electronic age, we're never far from our money once we learn how and where to access it.

EAST HAMPTON TOWN

Amagansett

North Fork Bank and Trust (516-267-6000) 100 Montauk Highway.

Bridgehampton

Bridgehampton National Bank (516-537-1000) 2200 Montauk Highway. ATM: AE, Cirrus, D, Honor, MAC, MC, Plus, V.

East Hampton

Apple Savings Bank (516-324-6500) 50 Montauk Highway. ATM: Cirrus, NYCE.

The Bank of New York (516-324-0800) 66 Main Street. ATM: Cirrus, Honor, MC, NYCE, Plus, Pulse, V.

North Fork Bank and Trust (516-324-7230) 40 Newtown Lane. ATM: Cirrus, Honor, MC, NYCE, Pulse.

The Suffolk County National Bank (516-324-2000) 351 Pantigo Road and (516-324-3800) 100 Park Place. ATM: AE, Cirrus, D, Honor, MAC, MC, NYCE, Plus, Pulse, V.

Hampton Bays

The Bank of New York (516-728-0100) 47 West Montauk Highway. ATM: Cirrus, Honor, MC, NYCE, Plus, Pulse, V.

Marine Midland (516-728-6555) 248 West Montauk Highway. ATM: Cirrus, NYCE.

North Fork Bank and Trust (516-728-6500) 93 Montauk Highway. ATM: Cirrus, NYCE.

The Suffolk County National Bank (516-728-2700) Montauk Highway. ATM: Cirrus, Honor, MC, NYCE, Pulse, V.

Montauk

The Bank of New York (516-668-5771) Main Street. ATM: Cirrus, Honor, MC, NYCE, Plus, Pulse, V.

Bridgehampton National Bank (516-668-6400) The Plaza.

The Suffolk County National Bank (516-668-4333) Dock West Lake Drive and (516-668-5300) Montauk Highway. ATM: AE, Cirrus, Honor, MAC, MC, NYCE, Plus, Pulse, V.

Sag Harbor

Apple Bank for Savings (516-725-2200 or 800-525-1524; 516-472-4545 (customer service) 138 Main Street. ATM: Cirrus, MC, NYCE, V.

North Fork Bank and Trust (516-725-3500) Main Street. ATM: Cirrus, Honor, NYCE, Pulse.

The Suffolk County National Bank (516-725-3000) 17 Main Street. ATM: AE, Cirrus, Honor, MAC, MC, NYCE, Plus, Pulse, V.

SOUTHAMPTON TOWN

Southampton

Bridgehampton National Bank (516-283-1286) 425 County Road 39.

Chase Bank (516-283-7991) 60 Main Street. ATM: Cirrus, MAC, MC, NYCE, Plus, Pulse, V.

The Long Island Savings Bank (516-283-0100) 65 Nugent. ATM: Honor, NYCE, Plus, Pulse.

Marine Midland (516-283-2700) 25 Nugent Street. ATM: Cirrus, MC, NYCE, Plus, V.

North Fork Bank and Trust (516-283-8300) 46 Windmill Lane. ATM: AE, Cirrus, Honor, NYCE, Pulse, V.

The Suffolk County National Bank (516-283-3800) 295 North Sea Road, Southampton (Branch). ATM: AE, Cirrus, MC, NYCE, Plus, Pulse, V.

Water Mill

The Suffolk County National Bank (516-726-4500) Montauk Highway. ATM: Cirrus, MAC, MC, NYCE, Plus, Pulse, V.

Westhampton Beach

The Bank of New York (516-288-2220) 154 Main Street. ATM: Cirrus, Honor, MC, NYCE, Plus, Pulse, V.

Long Island Savings Bank (516-288-2200) 71 Sunset Avenue.

North Fork Bank & Trust (516-325-0500) Montauk Highway, Speonk. ATM only at 43 Main Street, Westhampton Beach. ATM: AE, Cirrus, Honor NYCE, Pulse, V.

The Suffolk County National Bank (516-288-4000) 144 Sunset Avenue. ATM: Cirrus, MC, NYCE, Plus.

ADDITIONAL ATMs

A t press time, the following cash machines (not located in banks) were in operation. Please remember, however, that they can and do change.

Bridgehampton

King Kullen Grocery Store (516-537-8103) Bridgehampton Shopping Plaza (only available during store hours). ATM: AE, Cirrus, D, MC, NYCE, Plus System, V.

Hampton Bays

King Kullen Grocery Store (516-728-9621), 268A West Montauk Highway (only available during store hours). ATM: AE, Cirrus, D, MC, NYCE, Plus System, V.

Southampton

A & P Supermarket (516-283-0045) Main Street. ATM: Cirrus, MAC, MC, NYCE, Plus, Pulse, V.

Southampton Hospital (516-726-8200) 240 Meeting House Lane. ATM: Cirrus, NYCE.

CLIMATE, WEATHER, TIDES

The climate in the Hamptons is generally moderate and mild, with cooling ocean breezes in the summer and brisk winds in the winter. For the daily weather report, call **516-976-1212;** for the extended local forecast,

Spring comes early in the Hamptons.

Morgan McGivern

call **516-976-8888**. The following temperature and precipitation figures are average.

Month	Average Temperature	Average Precipitation in Inches
January	29.9	4.18
February	31.1	3.85
March	38.2	4.11
April	46.5	3.97
May	56.2	3.82
June	65.5	3.59
July	71.5	3.00
August	71.0	3.45
September	64.1	3.46
October	54.0	3.39
November	45.0	4.53
December	35.2	4.31

* Based on the 1961-1990 daily averages collected by the National Oceanic and Atmospheric Administration in Bridgehampton.

Tidal information along the ocean and, to a lesser extent, in the bays is essential to a relaxed, enjoyable day. If you're sunning by the ocean, the beach generally is wide enough so that you can just move further back if the water starts to lap your toes. If, on the other hand, you are hiking or picnicking, you will not want to be stranded on a sandbar; and if you are boating, you will want to know the times of high and low tide in order to successfully navigate your way back to the dock. The Coast Guard can inform you of coastal weather conditions and give you tidal information; it's wise to call them before heading out to sea. Three Coast Guard stations serve the Hamptons and can give weather and tidal reports.

Coast Guard Group Moriches (516-395-4412) Remsenburg and Westhampton Beach.
Coast Guard Station Montauk (516-668-2716) Eastern tip of the South Fork.
Coast Guard Station Shinnecock (516-728-0078) Westhampton Beach to about 15 miles east of the Shinnecock Canal.

East Hampton's Dunemere Lane under a blanket of snow.

Morgan McGivern

COMPUTER, FAX, BUSINESS SERVICES

Someone calls from the office. Your expertise is needed. Instead of returning to the office, perhaps the work can be accomplished right here. The following businesses specialize in organizing and doing the routine jobs, so that you can concentrate on what you do best.

Charde Computer Service (516-324-2064) 15 Railroad Avenue, Suite 2, East Hampton. Owner John Charde and his staff are experts in advising about upgrades, removing bugs, and giving computer lessons; it also has a computer consulting service.
East Hampton Business Service (516-324-0405) 19 Railroad Avenue, East Hampton. This is a one-stop shop for all business needs, including typing, word processing, typesetting, mailing lists, printouts from floppy disks, copying (including color), blueprints, fulfillment and mailing house services, fax service, bookkeeping, accounting, and mailboxes. (This book was done with their invaluable help.)

Hamptons Online (516-287-6630, WWW: http://www.hamptons.com) This is a Hamptons on-line service, providing Internet and World Wide Web access, local information, educational seminars, and support services.

Peconic Online (516-329-5703, WWW: http://www.peconic.net) This is a Hamptons on-line service, providing Internet and World Wide Web access and local information.

Southampton Packaging & Shopping Service (516-283-5660) 22 Jaggar Lane, Southampton. This service provides packaging, mailing, messenger service, copying, fax, and mailboxes.

HANDICAPPED SERVICES

New York State Department of Environmental Conservation publishes an accessibility guide to all state recreational facilities. *Opening the Outdoors to People with Disabilities* can be obtained by calling 516-444-0345.

Suffolk County publishes a brochure describing accessibility to its county parks and golf courses. Also, a Suffolk County Green Key Card with a handicapped designation entitles its holder to free weekday admission to all county parks and reduced fees for activities. Contact the *Suffolk County Office of Handicapped Services* (516-853-3740 voice or 516-582-6616 TDD).

The *Town of East Hampton* provides various services in the *Disabilities Office* (516-267-2153), part of the *Department of Human Services.* For example, transportation in a handicapped accessible bus is provided for doctors' visits, shopping, etc. The office also provides wheelchairs with fat, rubber tires for beach use.

HOSPITALS & MEDICAL SERVICES

Southampton Hospital (516-726-8200) 240 Meeting House Lane, Southampton. 194 beds; 115 doctors on staff; 550 full-time employees; surgical, maternity, pediatrics, ambulatory, outpatient, and emergency departments; radiology; full laboratory services. Hampton Eye Physicians and Surgeons also use the hospital's operating facilities.

Prime Care (516-728-4500) 240 West Montauk Highway, Hampton Bays. Open 8:00 a.m.–6:00 p.m. Mon., Tues., Thurs., Fri.; 8:00 a.m.–4:30 p.m. Sat.; closed Wed., Sun. Walk-in medical office.

KENNELS

You've been invited to a country house for the party of the season, and you find that your host is allergic to pets. Yet, you never leave your pet behind. What to do? If a Hamptons' kennel is the answer for you, here are several suggestions. Remember, however, that advance reservations are a must.

Even dogs have chic outfits in the Hamptons.

Morgan McGivern

East Hampton Veterinary Group (516-324-0282 or 800-287-3484) Montauk Highway, East Hampton. Boarding and full veterinary services. Kennels are sized to the dog, and cats are kept in their own facility.

Olde Towne Animal Hospital (516-283-0611) County Road 39A, Southampton. Full-service veterinary hospital that also boards pets.

Westhampton Kennels (516-288-3535) 49 Tanners Neck Lane, Westhampton. Cat and dog boarding and full grooming services. Located on over four acres, private kennels are sized to the dog, each with an indoor and outdoor run. You can bring your own food and medication and be assured of 24-hour supervision. According to the owner, this is the pet resort of the Hamptons.

If these are not right for you, there is another kennel in Bridgehampton, run by Robin Foster. She takes pets only on referral from animal clinics and hospitals, however. In addition, for pet owners who would like to have someone come to their home *Florence Weinfurt* (516-726-2542) will give loving care in your absence to pets in homes from Amagansett to Southampton.

Not a kennel, but an animal rescue agency, the *Animal Rescue Fund* (516-537-0400) rescues and cares for injured and abandoned animals. Should you find a stray animal, ARF is located on Daniel's Hole Road in Wainscott. If you feel like taking a walk, stop by ARF. They will lend you a dog who would love the companionship, and you can both stroll along ARF's dog-walking trail.

LATE-NIGHT FOOD & SERVICES

GROCERIES

A & P (516-324-6215) Newtown Lane, East Hampton; (516-283-0045) Jagger Lane and Main Street, Southampton; (516-288-9443) Sunset Avenue, Westhampton Beach. Open 24 hours in the summer, except Sun.

King Kullen (516-537-8103) Bridgehampton Common, Montauk Highway; (516-723-3071) Montauk Highway and Terrace Road, Hampton Bays. Open 24 hours in the summer, except Sun.

7-Eleven (516-728-5130) 53 West Montauk Highway, Hampton Bays; (516-653-9889) Montauk Highway, East Quogue; (516-725-3931) Main and Water Streets, Sag Harbor; (516-283-8511) 20 County Road 39, Southampton; (516-288-9755) 61 Sunset Avenue, Westhampton Beach; (516-288-3446) Montauk Highway and Mill Road, Westhampton Beach. Open 24 hours year-round.

Brent's Amagansett General Store (516-267-3113) Montauk and Cross Highways, Amagansett. Open 24 hours on the weekends in the summer.

RESTAURANTS

East Hampton Bowl (516-324-1950) Montauk Highway, East Hampton. Open 10:00 a.m.–12:00 midnight on weekdays; 10:00 a.m.–3:00 a.m. on the weekends. Snack bar serves pizza, nachos, etc.

Hampton Bays Diner and Restaurant (516-728-0840) Montauk Highway and Flanders Road (Route 24). Open 24 hours in the summer; Oct.–Apr. 6:00 a.m.–12:00 midnight Sun.–Thurs., 24 hours Fri., Sat.

McDonald's (516-283-6777) 307 North Sea Road, Southampton. Open 24 hours.

Salivar's (516-668-2555) 470 West Lake Drive in Montauk. Open 24 hours. This diner has never changed, either in decor or in the food that it offers. Late-night party goers and early morning anglers want burgers, chili, or breakfast.

Southampton Princess Diner (516-283-4255) Montauk Highway at County Road 39, Southampton. Open 6:00 a.m.–11:00 p.m. Sun.–Thurs.; 24 hours Fri., Sat.

The Stephen Talkhouse (516-267-3117) Main Street, Amagansett. Open until 12:00 midnight on weeknights; until 3:00 a.m. Fri., Sat. in the summer; shorter hours the rest of the year. Serves hamburgers, seafood, and salads.

LATE-NIGHT FUEL & SERVICES

Should you find yourself stranded, either because of car trouble or lack of gas, the following numbers may help.

For *AAA members,* the emergency number is 516-746-3512 or 800-AAA-HELP day or night. For those who are not members of AAA, the following garages and gas stations are open late (and early in the morning) to provide fuel and road service.

CAR TOWING & REPAIR

B & B Auto Service (516-668-1195 days, 516-668-2217 nights) Edgemere Road, Montauk.

Bays Auto Repairs (516-728-0650) 192 West Montauk Highway, Hampton Bays.

Joe's Garage (516-283-2098) 1426 North Sea Road, Southampton.

North Main Street Citgo (516-324-8671) 150 North Main Street, East Hampton.

Village Auto Body (516-728-1500) 82 Old Riverhead Road, Hampton Bays.

EARLY-MORNING & LATE-NIGHT FUEL

Independent Gas Station (516-283-7670) 1630 North Highway, Southampton (next to B & M Automotive). Open 6:00 a.m.–10:00 p.m.

North Main Street Citgo (516-324-8671) 150 North Main Street, East Hampton. Open 6:00 a.m.–10:00 p.m. in the summer; 6:00 a.m.–8:00 p.m. off-season.

LAUNDROMATS

On vacation, washing machines and dryers are not always readily available. The following laundromats have been selected because they are clean, well maintained, and accessible.

Sag Harbor Launderette (516-725-5830) 20 Main Street, Sag Harbor. Large, very clean, well lit; attendant on duty.

Southampton Village Launderette (516-283-9708) 34 Nugent Street, Southampton. Very clean, well-lit; attendant on duty.

Tony's Tubs (516-728-1046) 218 West Montauk Highway, Hampton Bays. Very clean, new; attendant on duty; will help carry laundry to and from your car.

MEDIA

NEWSPAPERS

Country Magazine (516-287-5546) 2 North Main Street, Southampton. A very classy bi-weekly, full-color complimentary magazine with chic ads, articles about stylish celebrities, and commentary on the Hamptons' summer scene.

Dan's Papers (516-537-0500) Montauk Highway, Bridgehampton. An irreverent, tongue-in-cheek, tabloid-style paper, carrying current local news and unabashedly plump with the editorial opinions of its owner, Dan Rattiner. It just celebrated its 30th anniversary and claims to have the largest circulation in the Hamptons. Free and available throughout the area.

East Hampton Star (516-324-0002) 153 Main Street, East Hampton. A venerable newspaper in business since 1885, mostly in the able hands of the Rattray family who still steer the ship. It covers business and events in a no-nonsense, professional manner for the Town of East Hampton and beyond.

Grapezine (516-725-3387) Suffolk Street, Sag Harbor. Well-written, complimentary, monthly publication about the East End wine industry. It includes restaurant reviews and opinions of the editor and publisher, Michael Todd.

The Hampton Catalog (516-725-2351) P.O. Box 2668, East Hampton. A glossy, slick catalog with lush ads for clothing, gifts, cars, services, and more.

Hamptons Magazine (516-283-7125) 5 Main Street, Southampton. Free, glossy, up-scale, full-color magazine, published in the summer only. Fashion news, what's happening at the clubs, and gossip.

The Independent (516-324-2500) P.O. Box 5032, Montauk Highway at Cove Hollow Road (in the Red Horse Market), East Hampton. A tabloid-style paper that was launched in 1993, it reports local news and views.

Sag Harbor Express (516-725-1700) Main Street, Sag Harbor. The first newspaper on Long Island, the *Long Island Herald,* was established in Sag Harbor in 1791. Although the *Sag Harbor Express* is not a direct descendent, it's certainly close and is celebrating its 175th year. The *Corrector,* which began publishing in 1922, was incorporated into the *Sag Harbor Express.*

Southampton Press (516-283-4100) 135 Windmill Lane, Southampton. Established in 1897, this newspaper offers complete news, business, and events coverage in Southampton Town.

RADIO

BEACH-FM 104.7 (516-267-7800) P.O. Box 7162, Amagansett.

WBAB-FM and **WHFM-FM 95.3** (516-283-9500) 33 Flying Point Road, Southampton. Popular and rock music.

WBAZ-FM 101.7 (516-765-1017) 44210 County Route 48, Southold. Light, adult contemporary music.

WBLI-FM 106.1 (516-732-1061) 3090 Route 112 Medford. Popular music.

WEHM-FM 96.7 (516-267-7800) 249 Montauk Highway, Amagansett. Popular music.

WLNG-AM 1600 and **WLNG-FM 92.1** (516-725-2300) 1692 Redwood Causeway, Sag Harbor. Popular music, local news, and information.

WPBX-FM 91.3 (516-283-4000 ext. 290) Long Island University, Southampton Campus, Southampton. Classical, jazz, and progressive music.

WWHB-FM 107.1 (516-728-9229) 252 West Montauk Highway, Hampton Bays. Affiliated with WNEW, New York. Classic rock music.

TELEVISION

LTV, CH 27 (516-537-2777) 75 Industrial Road, Wainscott. Community access cable for the East End.

WVVH, CH 58, UHF CH 23 (516-537-0273) 75 Industrial Road, Wainscott. Commercial TV for the East End.

POST OFFICES

Amagansett (516-267-3344) Montauk Highway.

Bridgehampton (516-537-1090) Main Street.

East Hampton (516-324-0790) 7 Gay Lane.

East Quogue (516-653-5360) Bay Avenue.

Hampton Bays (516-728-0371) Ponquogue Road.

Montauk (516-668-2218) South Edison Street.

Quogue (516-653-4121) Midland Avenue.

Remsenburg (516-325-0550) 678 Main Street.

Sagaponack (516-537-1140) Main Street.

Sag Harbor (516-725-0108) Long Island Avenue.

Southampton (516-283-0268) 29 Nugent Street.

Speonk (516-325-0430) Montauk Highway.

Wainscott (516-537-3636) Montauk Highway at North West Road.

Water Mill (516-726-4811) Montauk Highway.

Westhampton (516-288-2828) Mill Road.

Westhampton Beach (516-288-1238) Main Street.

SCHOOLS

PUBLIC SCHOOLS

Amagansett School (516-267-3572) Main Street, Amagansett. Pre-kindergarten–6th grade.

Bridgehampton School (516-537-0271) Montauk Highway, Bridgehampton.

East Hampton Public Schools, District Office (516-329-4100) 76 Newtown Lane, East Hampton.

East Hampton High School (516-329-4130) 2 Long Lane.

East Hampton Middle School (516-329-4112) 76 Newtown Lane.

John M. Marshall Elementary School (516-329-4156) 30 Church St.

East Quogue School (516-653-5210) 6 Central Avenue, East Quogue. Kindergarten-6th grade.

Hampton Bays School (516-728-0420) 88 Argonne Road, Hampton Bays.

Montauk Public School (516-668-2474) South Dorset Road, Montauk. Kindergarten-8th grade.

Quogue School (516-653-4285) Edgewood Road, Quogue. Pre-kindergarten–6th grade.

Remsenburg-Speonk School (516-325-0203) Remsenburg. Kindergarten–6th grade.

Sagaponack School (516-537-0651) Main Street, Sagaponack. 1st–4th grade.

Sag Harbor Public Schools (516-725-5300) Division Street, Sag Harbor.

Elementary School (516-725-5301) Hampton Street.

Pierson High School (516-725-5302) Jermain Avenue.

Children admire pumpkins on the Montauk village green.

Morgan McGivern

Southampton Public Schools (516-283-6800) 70 Leland Lane, Southampton.
  Elementary School 30 Pine Street.
  Intermediate School 70 Leland Lane.
  High School 141 Narrow Lane.
Springs Public School (516-324-0144) School Street, East Hampton.
  Kindergarten–8th grade.
Tuckahoe School (516-283-3550) Magee Street, Southampton. Pre-kinder-
  garten–8th grade.
Wainscott Elementary School (516-537-1080) Main Street, Wainscott. 1st–4th
  grade.
Westhampton Beach Public Schools (516-288-3800) Mill Road, Westhampton
  Beach.
  Elementary School Mill Road.
  Junior High School Mill Road.
  Senior High School Lilac Road.

COLLEGES

Long Island University, Southampton College (516-283-4000) Montauk
  Highway, Southampton.

PRIVATE SCHOOLS

Hampton Day School (516-537-1240) Butter Lane, Bridgehampton.
Our Lady of the Hamptons Roman Catholic School (516-283-9140) North
  Main Street, Southampton.

Stella Maris Regional School (516-725-2525) Division Street, Sag Harbor.
Southampton Montessori School (516-283-2223) 135 St. Andrews Road, Southampton.
Tuller School of Maycroft (516-725-1181) North Haven, Sag Harbor.

BIBLIOGRAPHY

Two lists of books are included here, many used in research for this guide. **Books You Can Buy** are readily available in local bookstores. For a list of bookstores, see Chapter Five, *Shopping*.

Check local libraries for **Books You Can Borrow.** They contain a wealth of superb historical material, especially the ***Morton Pennypacker Long Island Collection*** of the ***East Hampton Library,*** the ***John Jermain Library*** in Sag Harbor, and the ***Rogers Memorial Library*** in Southampton.

BOOKS YOU CAN BUY

Art & Photography

Bookbinder, Bernie. *Long Island People & Places — Past & Present*. New York: Newsday, 1993.

Dunwell, Steve. *Long Island — A Scenic Discovery*. Dublin, New Hampshire: Foremost Publishers, Inc., 1985.

Harris, Bill. *Long Island — A Photographic Journey*. New York: Crescent Books, 1990.

Judd, Dianne and Don. *The Hamptons*. New York: Crescent Books, 1991.

Kanfer, Larry. *On This Island*. New York: Viking Penguin, 1990.

Miller, Ken. *The Hamptons, Long Island's East End*. New York: Rizzoli International Publications, Inc. 1993.

Pisano, Ronald G. *Long Island Landscape Painting, 1820-1920*. Boston: Little Brown & Company, 1985.

_____. *The Twentieth Century*. Boston: Little Brown & Company, 1990.

Robbins, Ken. *The Hamptons, "America's East End."* Wainscott, New York: Chips & Co., 1983.

Fiction & Literature

Brady, James. *Further Lane*. New York: St. Martin's Press, 1997.

_____. *Gin Lane*. New York: Thomas Dunne Books (imprint of St. Martin's Press), 1998.

The view from the cliffs in Montauk.

Morgan McGivern

Burnett, Frances Hodgson. *The Secret Garden*. Frances Hodgson Burnett, 1911.

Carson, Rachel L. *Under the Sea Wind*. New York: Truman Talley Books/ Dutton, 1941.

Cooper, James Fenimore. *The Sea Lions*. 1849. Reprint. University of Nebraska Press, 1965.

_____. *Precaution* (1820).

Elliston, William H. *Footprints in the Sand*.

Matthiessen, Peter. *Men's Lives*. New York: Vintage Books, 1988.

Melville, Herman. *Moby Dick*. 1851. Boston.

Payne, Robert. *The Island*. New York: Harcourt, Brace, and Company, 1958.

Thoreau, Henry David. *Journal*. 1906.

Whitman, Walt. *Letters from a Traveling Bachelor*. New York: Crowell, 1849.

History & Architecture

Esten, John, and Rose Bennett Gilbert. *Hampton Style: Houses, Gardens, Artists*. Boston: Little Brown & Co., 1993.

Fearon, Peter. *Hamptons Babylon: Life Among the Super-Rich on America's Riviera*. Secaucus, New Jersey: Birch Lane Press, 1998.

Gaines, Steven S. *Philistines at the Hedgerow: Passion and Property in the Hamptons*. New York: Little Brown & Company, 1998.

Goldberger, Paul. *The Houses of the Hamptons*. New York: Alfred A. Knopf, Inc., 1986.

Hefner, Robert J. *Windmills of Long Island*. Society for the Preservation of Long Island Antiquities and New York: W. W. Norton & Company, 1983.

Howell, George Rogers, *The Early History of Southampton, L.I. New York*. Albany, New York: Weed, Parsons and Company, 1887. Reprinted by Heritage Books, 1989.

Montauk's rocky promontory has been the site of numerous shipwrecks.

Morgan McGivern

Kelsey, Carlton. *Amagansett, A Pictorial History 1680-1940.* Amagansett, New York: Amagansett Historical Association, 1986.

Lee, Madeline. *Miss Amelia's Amagansett.* Amagansett, New York: Amagansett Historical Association, 1976.

Lightfoot, Frederick S., Linda B. Martin, and Bette S. Weidman. *Suffolk County, Long Island in Early Photographs 1867-1951.* New York: Dover Publications, Inc., 1984.

MacKay, Robert B., Geoffrey L. Rossano and Carol A. Traynor, eds. *Between Ocean & Empire — An Illustrated History of Long Island.* Windsor Publications, 1985.

MacKay, Robert B., Stanley Lindvall and Carol Traynor, eds. *AIA Architectural Guide to Nassau and Suffolk Counties, Long Island.* The American Institute of Architects, Long Island Chapter, The Society for the Preservation of Long Island Antiquities, and New York: Dover Publications, Inc., 1992.

Morris, Paul C. & William P. Quinn. *Shipwrecks in New York Waters.* Orleans, Massachusetts: Parnassus Imprints, 1989.

Rattray, Everett T. *The South Fork, The Land and the People of Eastern Long Island.* New York: Random House, 1979 (hardbound); Wainscott, New York: Pushcart Press, 1989 (paperback).

Zaykowski, Dorothy Ingersoll. *Sag Harbor, The Story of an American Beauty.* Sag Harbor, New York: Sag Harbor Historical Society, 1991.

Recreation, Food, Travel

Albright, Rodney and Priscilla. *Short Nature Walks on Long Island.* Old Saybrook, Connecticut: The Globe Pequot Press, 1993.

Angelillo, Phil. *Short Bike Rides on Long Island.* Old Saybrook, Connecticut: The Globe Pequot Press, 1989.

Epstein, Jason and Elizabeth Barlow. *East Hampton, A History & Guide.* New York: Random House, 1985.

Hamptons Handbook. New York: Gitter Guides, 1996.

Granny Poo's Restaurant Review. 9th ed. "East End Eating Epigrams." Sag Harbor, New York: Candico Productions Corp., 1996.

Griffith, William T. *The Nature Conservancy South Fork Shelter Island Preserve Guide.* Sag Harbor, New York, 1990.

The Ladies' Village Improvement Society Centennial Cookbook. East Hampton, New York: 1994.

Murphy, Robert Cushman. *Fish-Shape Paumanok, Nature, and Man on Long Island.* Great Falls, Virginia: Waterline Books, 1991.

Palmedo, Philip F. and Edward Beltrami. *The Wines of Long Island, Birth of a Region.* Great Falls, Virginia: Waterline Books, 1993.

Pump, Anna. *The Loaves and Fishes Cookbook.* New York: Macmillan Publishing Company, 1985.

SCOPE (Suffolk County Organization for the Promotion of Education). *Where To Go and What To Do on Long Island.* New York: Dover Publications, 1993.

Spinzia, Raymond, Judith, and Kathryn. *Long Island, A Guide to Suffolk & Nassau Counties.* New York: Hippocrene Books, 1988.

Thomas, Marguerite. *Wineries of the Eastern States.* Lee, Massachusetts: Berkshire House Publishers, 1997. An excellent guide to East Coast wineries, including those on Long Island's East End.

BOOKS YOU CAN BORROW

Adams, James Truslow. *History of the Town of Southampton.* Hamptons Press, 1918.
_____. *Memorials of Old Bridgehampton.* Hamptons Press, 1916.

Bailey, Paul, ed. *Long Island, A History of Two Great Counties, Nassau & Suffolk,* New York: Lewis Historical Publishing, 1949.

Barnes, Gean Finch. *Tales of the High Hills, Legends of the Montauk Indians.* Margaret H. Lamb, ed. East Hampton, New York: 1975. Prepared under the auspices of East Hampton Town Bicentennial Committee. Originally published in the *East Hampton Star* over 50 years ago.

Bayles, Richard M. *Historical and Descriptive Sketches of Suffolk County and Its Towns, Villages, Hamlets, Scenery, Institutions, and Important Enterprises.* Port Jefferson, New York, 1874.

Bryant, William Cullen. "Scenes in Eastern Long Island." *Picturesque America: or The Land We Live In.* Vol. 1. New York: D. Appleton and Company, 1872.

Craven, The Rev. Charles E. *A History of Mattituck, Long Island, N.Y.* Mattituck, New York, 1906.

Duvall, Ralph G. *The History of Shelter Island 1652-1932.* Shelter Island Heights,

New York: 1932. Supplement added in 1952 by Jean L. Schladermundt for 300th anniversary of Shelter Island.

Eberlein, Harold Donaldson. *Manor Houses and Historic Homes of Long Island and Staten Island*. Philadelphia and London: J.B. Lippincott, 1928.

Finckenor, Sr., George A. *A Capsule History of Early Sag Harbor*. Sag Harbor, New York: 1975.

Foster, Sherrill. "East Hampton on Long Island." Paper prepared for the Suffolk County Tercentenary in 1983.

Gardiner, Sarah Diodati. *Early Memories of Gardiner's Island*. East Hampton, New York: East Hampton Star, 1947.

Halsey, Abigail Fithian. *In Old Southampton*. New York: Columbia University Press, 1940.

Halsey, William D. *Sketches from Local History*. Southampton, New York: The Yankee Peddler Book company, 1966.

Hand, Alice E. Osborn. *Wainscott Dumplings*. 1954.

Hedges, H.P. *Early Sag-Harbor*. Address delivered before the Sag-Harbor Historical Society, February 4, 1896. Printed by J.H. Hunt, Sag Harbor, New York, 1902.

The History & Archaeology of the Montauk Indians. Suffolk County Archaeological Association, and Lexington, Massachusetts: Ginn Custom Publishing, 1979.

Hummel, Charles F. *With Hammer in Hand, The Dominy Craftsmen of East Hampton New York*. Charlottesville: University Press of Virginia, 1968.

Mannello, George. *Our Long Island*. Malabar, Florida: Robert E. Kreiger Publishing Company, Inc. 1964.

O'Sullivan, Ilse. *East Hampton & the American Revolution*. East Hampton, New York: East Hampton Town Bicentennial Committee, 1976.

Our Hampton Heritage. Vols. 1 and 2. Bridgehampton, New York: Dan's Papers, Ltd., 1983, 1984.

Overmeyer, Grace. *America's First Hamlet*. New York: New York University Press, 1957.

Pine, Robert H. "A Proposed Historic Preservation Program for the Village of Sag Harbor." *Sag Harbor, Past, Present, and Future*. Prepared for the Sag Harbor Historic Preservation Commission. Sag Harbor, New York, 1973.

Rattray, Jeannette Edwards. *East Hampton History*. East Hampton, New York, 1953.

_____. *Up and Down Main Street, an Informal History of East Hampton and Its Old Houses*. East Hampton, New York: East Hampton Star, 1968.

_____. *Resort with a History*. East Hampton, New York: East Hampton Chamber of Commerce, 1974.

_____. and Everett J. Rattray. *Whale Off.* New York: Frederick A. Stokes Company, 1932.

Robbins, Ken and Bill Strachan, eds. *Springs, A Celebration.* East Hampton, New York: Springs Improvement Society, 1984.

Rose, Barbara, ed. *Pollock Painting.* Photography by Hans Namuth. New York: Grinde, 1978.

Sleight, Harry D. *Sag Harbor in Early Days.* Hampton Press, 1930.

Stevens, William Oliver. *Discovering Long Island.* New York: Dodd, Mead & Company, 1939.

Stone, Gaynell, ed. *The Shinnecock Indians: A Culture History.* New York: Suffolk County Archaeological Association, 1983.

Vagts, Christopher R. *Suffolk, A Pictorial History.* Huntington Historical Society, 1983.

CHAPTER NINE
From Vines to Wines
NORTH FORK

Suzi Forbes Chase

Summer sheds light on North Fork grapes that are almost ready for harvest.

Although the North Fork of Long Island is not part of the Hamptons and is distinctly different in character, it has a fascinating history and numerous attractions of its own. Its burgeoning wine industry leads to comparisons with the early days of the Napa Valley. And as the wine industry grows, so do the tourist facilities. Old, established restaurants are thriving, and chefs in new restaurants are testing new ground. Interesting bed-and-breakfasts and inns are housed in gingerbread Victorian homes — remnants of the North Fork's days as a whaling port and transportation hub.

The North Fork is approximately 20 miles shorter than the South Fork, with the tip, Orient Point, approximately 120 miles from New York City. The trip can be made in 2 1/2 hours from New York and in less time from Connecticut. The North Fork has more of a permanent, year-round population than do the Hamptons; therefore, you're less likely to find shops and restaurants closed after Labor Day. In fact, a number of restaurants are open for lunch and dinner throughout the year. Visit the North Fork, and you'll be pleasantly surprised. It's a trip you'll undoubtedly want to repeat over and over again.

Although this chapter cannot identify all of the North Fork's many attractions, I have attempted to include the very best.

HISTORY

My manner of living is plain, and I do not mean to be put out of it. A glass of wine and bit of mutton are always ready.

George Washington

The early history of the North Fork is closely tied to that of the South Fork. Yet, although the South Fork has now acquired a cachet of social prominence, with large homes replacing potato fields and duck farms, the North Fork remains stubbornly rural, clinging to its water and land resources for sustenance. The winds, however, are shifting. As the local wine industry gains recognition, so does the region. Where scattered, homegrown restaurants once lured folks out for dinner after church on Sunday, a variety of fine, gourmet restaurants now beckon a sophisticated clientele.

Southold's history is almost as old as Southampton's. They were both settled in 1640 within only a few months of one another. Actually, a friendly rivalry exists over which was settled first. The truth lies buried in the records, or the absence of them. It is known that Southold's settlers immediately organized the first church, which is now the oldest church society in New York State.

It's also true that the intrepid traveler George Washington came through Greenport in 1757, bound for Boston to secure his commission as commander-in-chief of the Virginia troops from Governor Shirley of Massachusetts prior to the American Revolution. Already recognized as a fine seaport, Greenport offered the most desirable route to Boston from Virginia. Journeying to Greenport, Washington and his entourage stayed at a country house owned by Lieutenant Constant Booth and took the ferry the next day to New London, Connecticut. He thus avoided crossing 18 rivers on horseback in the freezing winter months. Fortunately, Governor Shirley fully concurred with his appointment and made his trip worthwhile. The house where Washington stayed was moved from Greenport some years ago to the nearby hamlet of Orient, where it is maintained today by the Oysterponds Historical Society.

Almost 100 years after George Washington's trip, there were still few bridges across the rivers that separated New York from Boston, the United States' two great northern cities, and travel by water was preferred to the bumpy, dusty stagecoaches. Greenport thus became an important transportation hub. In 1844, the Long Island Rail Road established its northern terminus in Greenport, thereby making the journey even shorter. Following along George Washington's path, travelers came to Greenport by railroad. They then boarded steamers for an overnight trip to Boston, complete with dinner, dancing, and gambling.

Because of its water orientation, the North Fork's commercial enterprises traditionally have been linked to the water — fishing, shipping, and boat-building. Jamesport had a thriving commercial fishing industry in the mid-1800s, and the first submarines purchased by the U.S. Navy in 1900 were built in New Suffolk.

The Horton Point Lighhouse was built in 1857 and continues to protect ships from the hazardous shoreline.

Suzi Forbes Chase

The whaling and shipbuilding industries flourished in Greenport, where many large sailing ships were built. By the late 1800s, 286 sailing vessels and 73 fishing boats made Greenport their home. As merchants and shipbuilders grew wealthy, they built grand Victorian homes, many of which still remain.

The advent of Prohibition didn't slow down the North Fork. It's said that the coastal villages of the East End prospered substantially during this time, not only from the moonshine itself, but also from servicing and repairing the boats of both bootleggers and revenuers. Often the vessels of bootleggers and revenue agents would be repaired side by side.

In the 1930s, Greenport gained distinction of another type. The sailing master for three successful America's Cup defenders lived in Greenport. Although the ships were headquartered in Newport, Rhode Island, Captain George Monsell brought all of the crews to Greenport to sign their contracts. One of the skippers and a first mate lived here, as well. Those were heady days when the *Enterprise* won the race in 1930, the *Rainbow* in 1934, and the *Ranger* in 1937.

What is most tempting about Greenport is the waterfront, that long, ragged fringe of wharves, boatbuilder's yards, and sail lofts from which one looks out across the harbor to the wooded bluffs of Shelter Island. Of course, the whalers in these waters have long since become completely extinct, and those square-rigged ships that sailed from here direct to the West Indies for molasses are also long since dead and gone.

William Oliver Stevens, *Discovering Long Island*, 1939

Greenport was still an important shipbuilding center, however, and other North Fork villages had developed thriving oyster and scallop industries. Peconic Bay scallops are still considered sweeter and more tender than those harvested elsewhere, making them prized by chefs around the world.

The beauty of the North Fork cannot be denied. Pure, unspoiled bays, inlets, and creeks to the south and majestic Long Island Sound to the north are linked together by miles of flat, rich farmland. Villages remain true to their New England roots with treasured old houses and buildings looking much as they did a century ago.

Fortunately for us, community-spirited citizens recognized the importance of preserving some of their oldest and most historic buildings. In Mattituck, Cutchogue, Southold, and Orient, buildings have been moved from locations where they were endangered and settled into clusters around a village green where they are open to the public. In Greenport, the Stirling Historical Society also maintains several buildings, and there's an interesting walking tour past historic, old homes. The majestic tall ship, *Regina Maris,* is currently in harbor awaiting restoration.

TRANSPORTATION

This chapter does not repeat the information contained in Chapter Two, *Transportation,* but it does, however, identify specific ways to reach the North Fork. For more complete information, please refer to Chapter Two.

BY CAR

From New York, the trip to the North Fork is infinitely easier than to the Hamptons. The Long Island Expressway (I-495) terminates in Riverhead, the gateway to the North Fork. It is from this point that the forks of this two-pronged piece of land diverge and grow wider. The first of the North Fork wineries is no more than a half-hour from the end of the Long Island Expressway.

BY FERRY

A pleasant way to travel from Connecticut is via the ***Bridgeport/Port Jefferson Ferry*** to the North Shore of Long Island, followed by a drive along Route 25A to the North Fork, less than an hour's trip along a meandering, rural road. For reservations and information, call 516-473-0286 on Long Island. Another route is via the ***Cross Sound Ferry*** from New London, Connecticut, to Orient Point on the eastern tip of the North Fork. For information and reservations, call 860-443-5281 in Connecticut. The third ferry route is from North Haven on the South Fork to Shelter Island and then by a second ferry from Shelter Island to

Greenport: *North Ferry* (516-749-0139) and *South Ferry* (516-749-1200). All of these routes are described in detail in Chapter Two, *Transportation.*

BY BUS

Suffolk County Transit (516-852-5200) Operates buses throughout Suffolk County to the North Fork, as far as the Orient Point Ferry.

Sunrise Express (516-477-1200 or 800-527-7709) $15 one-way; $29 round-trip. This company runs what they call a "super van/bus" service between the North Fork and Manhattan, with about three trips each way per day. Departures, depending on the day, are from 5:30 a.m.–7:00 p.m. and arrive in New York City at 8:00 a.m.–9:30 p.m. The latest bus from Manhattan is at 9:45 p.m., arriving at 11:45 p.m. There's also a stop in Queens, both ways.

BY TRAIN

Train travel to the North Fork from points on the North Shore of Long Island or from Manhattan is on the *Long Island Rail Road, North Shore branch* (718-217-5477 in New York, 516-231-5477 in Suffolk County, or 516-822-5477 in Nassau County), although it is rather infrequent. Three or four trains leave and arrive at Riverhead weekdays, but only two trains on weekends. If you can get off in Ronkonkoma, however, the options are increased to over twenty trains per day.

RENTAL CARS

Most national car rental companies have offices at *Long Island Islip/MacArthur Airport,* approximately 25 miles from Riverhead. In addition, the following companies are located on the North Fork.

Enterprise Rent-A-Car (516-369-6300) 1076 Route 58, Riverhead.

Pam Rent-A-Car (516-727-7020) Route 25, Riverhead.

Rent-A-Wreck (516-477-9602 or 516-477-9607) Main Road, Greenport; also 429 4th Street, Greenport.

TAXIS & LIMOUSINES

Classic Limousine Service of Eastern Long Island (516-727-5003) 56 Union Avenue, Riverhead.

Keri Taxi (800-727-5374 or 516-727-0707) 305 West Main Street, Riverhead. 24-hour service; all new cars; drivers are conscientious.

Southold Taxi (800-698-2944 or 516-765-2221) 24-hour service; limousines, vans, wagons, and cars; take both large and small groups; package delivery.

WINERIES

When men drink, then they are rich and successful and win lawsuits and are happy and help their friends.

Quickly, bring me a beaker of wine, so that I may wet my mind and say something clever.

Aristophanes

People in California, New York, and Europe are talking about Long Island's East End wines. There hasn't been this much excitement in the wine world since the Napa, Sonoma, and Alexander Valleys of California began serious production. In the 20 years of East End wine production, the number of wineries has grown to 18 on the North Fork and three on the South Fork. As the awards for the wines accumulate, the number of visitors to the tasting rooms increases, and so do the sales. That's good news for other businesses, too. New gourmet restaurants, caterers, motels, bed-and-breakfast establishments, gift shops, and wineshops are flourishing. Therefore, it seems natural to begin this chapter with a description of the wineries.

In the last ten years, the North Fork has gained a respected position in the wine industry. It all started when a local farmer, John Wickham, planted the first grapes on the North Fork in the 1950s; he sold them at his farm stand to home winemakers. Alex and Louisa Hargrave were the first commercial pioneers; they planted vinifera vines in 1973 and produced their first wines in 1977. Since then, others have followed. Modern, award-winning wineries that rival California's Napa Valley are now the sites of guided tours and tastings, along with a variety of courses and events. Wine production, however, is still so small at most North Fork wineries that a mobile bottling truck travels from winery to winery to handle that part of the operation. And, to put the production in perspective, there are still only 1,500 acres of land planted in grapes, while more than 6,000 acres are in potatoes, the North Fork's largest crop.

For anyone interested in wines, now is the time to visit. The enthusiasm and excitement are contagious. When you visit an East End winery, you're likely to meet the owner and the winemaker, who are often the same person. You'll find that most of today's wineries are family enterprises run by hardworking vintners who are absolutely serious about their wines. They will share their belief in the region, their dreams for their vineyards, and their growth objectives for their winery. In a few years, as demand and production grow, some of this personal contact inevitably will be lost.

An excellent book about North Fork wines, *The Wines of Long Island, Birth of a Region* (1993) by Philip F. Palmedo and Edward Beltrami, is recommended reading for anyone visiting the East End wineries. It is a comprehensive guide to the history of winemaking on the East End and includes profiles of the

Fund-raising wine tastings take place frequently. This one was at the Bridgehampton Racquet and Surf Club.

Morgan McGivern

wineries, the owners, and the winemakers. A comprehensive guide to East Coast wines, including an analysis of those on Long Island is *Wineries of the Eastern States* (1996) by Marguerite Thomas; this book highlights some of the regions wineries and includes interviews with winemakers and ratings for the wines. In addition, a tabloid-style newspaper, *The Grapezine* by Michael Todd is an excellent source of up-to-date information about the wineries; it is distributed free in most wineshops, wineries, and other outlets on the North and South Forks. You'll learn which wine won the latest awards, and what the winemakers are planning for the future; it even has restaurant reviews.

This section is neither a comprehensive guide to the wineries nor does it analyze the wines. We have identified each winery and hope to enhance your visit to this very special place by describing the settings and suggesting lodgings, restaurants, and cultural and recreational attractions. So, buy some cheese, a baguette of French bread, perhaps a sandwich, and plan a day. Actually, you should plan several days, with a leisurely stop for lunch at a winery, perhaps on a deck overlooking the vineyards.

Also, several excellent wineries are located on the South Fork. For information about South Fork wineries, see Chapter Four, *Restaurants & Food Purveyors.*

BEDELL CELLARS
516-734-7537.
Main Road (Route 25),
 Cutchogue.
Open: Daily 11:00 a.m.–5:00
 p.m.

Kip Bedell has been producing wines since 1985 and currently has 30 acres planted. Bedell bottles approximately 8,000 cases of wine per year. Consistently winning awards, especially for the Merlot, this winery is modern and efficient. Although no tours are given, the full range of wines is available for sampling on a complimentary basis in the showroom. If available, the Reserve Merlot is a prize that should be purchased. Group tours can be arranged.

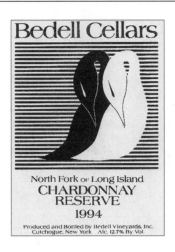

BIDWELL VINEYARDS
516-734-5200.
North Road (Route 48), Cutchogue.
Open: Daily 11:00 a.m.–5:00 p.m.

The tiny Bidwell tasting room and the small counter give little hint of the production of this East End winery. A new tasting room, however, is on the horizon. Bidwell has 33 acres of vines planted and bottled its first wines in 1986. It currently produces 8,000 cases annually. The winery is run by Robert, Kerry, and James Bidwell; the winemaker is Bob Bidwell. Group tours can be arranged by advance notice. There's a picnic area, and live music is offered on Saturdays in October.

COREY CREEK VINEYARDS
516-765-4168.
Main Road (Route 25), Southold.
Open: Daily 11:00 a.m.–5:00 p.m.
Mailing Address: P.O. Box 921, Southold, NY 11971.

The 30 acres in Southold that Joel and Peggy Lauber now call Corey Creek Vineyards was planted with vines in 1981, but the grapes were originally sold to local wineries. Now these mature vines are yielding grapes for estate-bottled wines, and the Laubers have a winning winery on their hands. Corey Creek produced its first bottles of Chardonnay in 1993, and it immediately earned rave reviews. If you see a bottle for sale in a wineshop, buy it. It's outstanding! Also available are a Reserve Chardonnay and a Merlot, and there are plans for a Pinot Noir and a Gewürztraminer. Production is now exceeding 3,000 cases annually and demand far outstrips the supply. A beautiful natural-sided wood building was completed in 1997 to house a handsome tasting and sales room. This is a great spot for a picnic as a huge deck overlooks the vineyards.

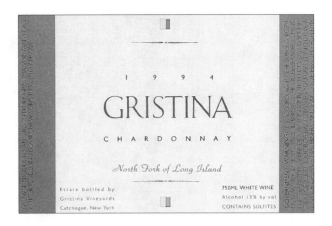

GRISTINA VINEYARDS
516-734-7089.
Main Road (Route 25),
Cutchogue.
Open: Daily 11:00 a.m.–5:00
p.m.

This classy winery offers classy wines in a classy setting. It is located in a gray-stained building, reminiscent of a New England farmhouse, with a huge fireplace inside and a broad deck with tables and chairs, surrounded by a white fence, outside — all made for lingering. The spacious, manicured lawns leading up the driveway set the tone. Gristina is owned by Jerry, Peter, and Mary Crail Gristina and managed by Peter; Adam Suprenant is the winemaker. The first Gristina wines were produced in 1988. Although no tours are offered, a selection of wines can be sampled. There are currently 30 acres planted, and the annual production is 6,000 cases.

**HARGRAVE
VINEYARDS**
516-734-5111.
North Road (Rte. 48) at
Alvah's Lane, Cutchogue.
Open: 10:00 a.m.–5:00 p.m.
Mon.–Fri.; 11:00
a.m.–5:00 p.m. Sat.;
1 p.m.– 5:00 p.m. Sun.

This is where it all began. Alex and Louisa Hargrave were the first to believe that Long Island's North Fork could produce great wines, and they were right. They currently have 80 acres of vines and produce 8,500 cases a year in a variety of wines. Mark Terry is the winemaker. They are particularly noted for their Pinot Noir, Merlot, and Chardonnay. No formal tours are conducted, but the Hargraves are generally in the winery and would be pleased to acquaint visitors with the process of winemaking. Excellent courses and seminars are also conducted (for a fee) and are generally taught by Louisa, who is a chemist. It's all part of their ongoing efforts to educate the public to the nuances of winemaking. The winery contains a conference room, with a magnificent, Tiffany stained glass window, that can be used for indoor picnics when not being used for classes or meetings; there is no outside deck.

The Hargrave winery in Cutchogue, where the first commercial vines on the North Fork were planted in 1973.

Suzi Forbes Chase

JAMESPORT VINEYARDS
516-722-5256.
Main Road (Route 25), Jamesport.
Open: Daily 10:00 a.m.–6:00 p.m.

This winery is partly new and partly old. Rising from the ashes of the defunct North Fork winery and with grapes from a Cutchogue vineyard planted by Ronald Goerler, Sr. and his son, Ron Jr. in 1982, the first Jamesport Vineyards wines were produced in 1987. Jamesport is the largest producer of Sauvignon Blanc, but makes a variety of other wines, including a champagne made with Pinot Noir and Chardonnay grapes. There are currently 60 acres planted, and the annual production is 5,000 cases. The winemaker is Sean Capiaux. The winery is located in a 200-year-old, cedar shake, potato and hay barn with soaring ceilings.

LAUREL LAKE VINEYARDS
516-298-1420.
Main Road (Route 25), Laurel.
Open: Daily 10:00 a.m.–6:00 p.m.

In 1993 Michael McGoldrick purchased 15 acres that had been planted in Chardonnay vines in 1980, and he bottled his first Laurel Lake Vineyards wines in 1994. But that was just the beginning. In 1997, he built a beautiful gray wooden winery with dormers and front and side porches that offer spots for quiet relaxation and picnics. Inside there's a soaring ceiling with a skylight, a glass-faced area for viewing the stainless steel tanks and barrels, and a hospitality area for tastings and sales. Gregory Gove is the winemaker, and Ed Cobelo is the vineyard manager. Expect expansion and award-winning wines in the future from this newcomer.

LENZ VINEYARDS
516-734-6010.
Main Road (Route 25), Peconic.
Open: Daily 10:00 a.m.–6:00 p.m. May–Oct.; 10:00 a.m.–5:00 p.m. Nov.–Apr.

Lenz, located in a rose-stained wood building, has an interesting entrance that is shaped somewhat like a hopper. The property is surrounded by a split rail fence, and grape vines cover the rustic, colonnaded porch. Although the first vines were planted here in

1980, the current winemaking team — owners Peter and Deborah Carroll, winemaker Eric Fry, vineyard manager Sam McCullough, and general manager Tom Morgan — was assembled in 1990. There are 60 acres of vines in production, and the average annual yield is 9,000 cases. There is no outside deck or scheduled tours. People come from miles around to buy the Gewürztraminer. The Pinot Noir, Cabernet Sauvignon, and Chardonnay are award winning, and the sparkling wines are refreshing and graceful.

MACARI VINEYARDS AND WINERY
516-298-0100.
150 Bergen Avenue (just off Route 48), Mattituck.
Open: Daily 11:00 a.m.–5:00 p.m.

One of the most exciting new ventures on the North Fork is taking place near the former Mattituck Hills Winery. In 1995, 105 acres of farmland were planted by the Macari family in a combination of Merlot, Chardonnay, Cabernet Franc, and Viognier. They then purchased the winery building and adjacent five acres of mature vines from Mattituck Hills. In 1998, they opened an impressive, natural-cedar-sided building with a stone foundation and a spacious covered deck with beautiful black wrought iron tables and chairs overlooking the vineyards. This would be a great place to hold an event. This thoroughly modern winery is fully computerized, yet the vines are tended with the utmost concern for the environment. The Macaris make their own fertilizer and use absolutely no herbicides or chemicals in caring for their vines. The first wines were offered in 1997, and winemaker Gilles Martin promises that although production may never reach the numbers of some of the neighboring properties, they are committed to producing the very highest quality wines. The Macaris have one of the largest farms on the North Fork — a total of almost 350 acres — and there are already plans to plant vines on an additional 80 acres. In addition, tours of the beautiful Macari farmstead may be offered soon, and winery visitors may be driven there by horse-drawn carriage.

OSPREY'S DOMINION WINERY
516-765-6188.
44075 Main Road, Peconic.
Open: 10:00 a.m.–6:00 p.m.
Mon.–Sat.; 12:00 noon–6:00 p.m. Sun.
Mailing Address: P.O. Box 275, Peconic, NY 11958.

Purchasing 70 acres that had been planted with grapes during the 1980s (and sold to other wineries), Osprey's Dominion owners Bud Koehler and Bill Tyree are now producing their own wines from these mature vines. The current annual production is 15,000 cases. A handsome, yellow stucco, retail and tasting outlet was built in 1996, where such classics as Chardonnay, Riesling, Merlot, and Cabernet Sauvignon may be tasted and purchased. Winemaker Bill Skolnik also makes a hot spiced wine, similar to a mulled wine and a light and crisp strawberry wine (they call this "strawberry shortcake in a glass") that was created for the annual Mattituck Strawberry Festival. It was so popular that they now sell this strawberry wine year-round. Osprey's Dominion also makes excellent grape jellies and vinegars, and you can buy sweatshirts, books, picnic backpacks (perfect for bicyclists), and gift baskets here. A pretty patio overlooks the vineyards. Additional weekend attractions include hayrides and art shows.

PALMER VINEYARDS
516-722-9463.
108 Sound Avenue (Route 48), Aquebogue.
Open: Daily 11:00 a.m.–6:00 p.m. Apr.–Nov.; 11:00 a.m.–5:00 p.m. Nov.– Apr.; self-guided tour.
Fee: Two complimentary tastings daily; up to $1.00 each additional one-ounce taste.

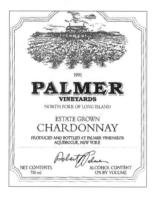

Owner Robert Palmer has a New York advertising agency, so promotion is his field. Not only are Palmer wines distributed in 16 states and six foreign countries, but they are also offered on American Airlines. Palmer Vineyards is one of the largest North Fork producers, bottling 20,000 cases annually; there are 100+ acres planted. Winemaker Dan Kleck produces outstanding wines. One of the finest is a barrel-fermented Chardonnay, but the Sauvignon Blanc, Gewürztraminer, and White Riesling are also excellent. Visitors (there can be as many as 500 a day) love the look and feel of this user-friendly winery. Clear, informative signs lead visitors on a self-guided tour past windows for viewing the tank, cask, and bottling rooms. This is one of the few North Fork wineries that has its own bottling operation. The tasting and sales room contains an oak bar and several oak and wrought iron Victorian booths that were once part of an authentic, eighteenth-century English pub. An inviting deck, overlooking the vineyards, is made for relaxing. There's even a small gift shop where T-shirts, caps, and more are sold. In the summer, food demonstrations are held on the deck, as well as concerts and special events.

PAUMANOK VINEYARDS
516-722-8800.
Main Road (Route 25), Aquebogue.
Open: 11:00 a.m.–6:00 p.m. Mon.–Sat., 12:00 noon– 6:00 p.m. Sun. May–Oct.; 11:00 a.m.–5:00 p.m. Mon.–Sat., 12:00 noon– 5:00 p.m. Sun. Oct.–May.

The vines for Paumanok Vineyards, owned by Charles and Ursula Massoud, were first planted in 1983. The first vintage was bottled in 1991, so the winery is relatively new. Nevertheless, there's great promise here. The winery produces 6,000 cases annually from their 52 acres of vines. The tasting room is spacious, with a glass viewing window overlooking the tank and barrel rooms below. Guided tours are offered when sufficient people have assembled. The large, outdoor deck is often the site of summer concerts. The Harvest Festival in the fall is a must, and a program of Christmas carols in December is enchanting.

PECONIC BAY VINEYARDS
516-734-7361.
Main Road (Route 25), Cutchogue.
Open: 11:00 a.m.–5:00 p.m. weekdays; 11:00 a.m.–6:00 p.m. weekends.

Ray Blum makes fine wines that deserve to be enjoyed with a gourmet meal. He planted his first grapes in 1979 and produced his first wines in 1984. He now has 76 acres in production and bottles about 6,000 cases a year. For absolutely stunning presentations, buy the beautiful bottles and glasses that are hand-painted by local artist, Jill Wanzer, and presented in beautiful boxes, which come in a variety of unique, floral patterns. Tours are not scheduled, but Mr. Blum will give personally escorted tours by appointment. His estate Chardonnay is excellent, but for an ambrosial dessert or after-dinner wine, the Vin de I'lle is smashing; it's more like a Barsac than a Sauterne.

PELLEGRINI
516-734-4111.
Main Road (Route 25), Cutchogue.
Open: Daily 11:00 a.m.–5:00 p.m.

It's always an advantage if you can purchase land that is planted with mature grapevines. In the case of Bob and Joyce Pellegrini, they bought 30 acres in 1988 that had been planted in 1982, enabling them to produce their first wines in 1991. Subsequently they bought another 16 acres and now manage 13 more. By 1997, production had increased to 10,000 cases annually. The winemaker is Russell Hearn. The Pellegrini winery opened in 1993 in a sensational new building; it's shaped like a cloister, with a grassy inner courtyard circled by a brick and flagstone walkway. Inside, vaulted ceilings and a multitude of windows create a light-filled space, with the tasting counter on one side and tables and chairs by the windows. There's also an outside deck for picnics or for lounging. A loft overlooking the room could be used for musicians as events unfold below. This is a winery built for visitors. Self-guided tours may be taken throughout the day, or visitors may watch the winery workers from a balcony above the tank and barrel rooms. Events sometimes take place in this wonderful space. A summer chef series called *The Kitchen at Pellegrini* has been especially popular.

PINDAR VINEYARDS
516-734-6200.
Main Road (Route 25), Peconic.
Open: Daily 11:00 a.m.–6:00 p.m.

Pindar Vineyards' white stucco building is somewhat out of character with the surrounding countryside, and its production of almost 20 different wines and some 80,000 cases annually is out of sync with its neighbors, but the wines are right on target. Dr. Herodotus Damianos is of

The gleaming white exterior of Pindar Vineyards' sales and tasting building in Peconic reflects owner Herodotus Damianos's Greek roots.

Suzi Forbes Chase

Greek decent (Pindar was an ancient Greek poet), and the distinctive labels on his bottles are derived from Greek mythology. Mark Friszolowski is the winemaker. Pindar's Mythology, a red wine blend, has received much praise and is a must for sampling, as are the Cabernet Sauvignon, the Chardonnay, and a refreshing Summer Blush that includes cranberry juice. Pindar's first vines on the 350-acre spread were planted in 1979, and the first release was bottled in 1983. This is the largest winery on the East End, and the tasting and sales room is built to accommodate visitors. There are scheduled tours of the winery, but in the summer and fall, there can be as many as 2,000 visitors a day and 70 people per tour, so the best time to go is in the winter or spring. On the other hand, the delightful outside pavilion is a terrific place for a picnic or just for summer sipping.

PUGLIESE VINEYARDS
516-734-4057.
Main Road (Route 25),
   Cutchogue.
Open: Daily 10:00 a.m.–
   5:00 p.m.

The Puglieses planted their first vines in 1980 and made their first wines in 1986. They now have 36 acres planted and produce almost 5,000 cases of wine annually, including Chardonnay and Merlot, as well as a sparkling wine. If packaging can sell a product, the Puglieses will sell a lot of wine. Lovely, hand-painted bottles are decorated by Patricia Pugliese, who is the winery owner with her husband Ralph. Their son, Peter, is the winemaker. Their Blanc de Blanc Champagne, made of 100 percent Chardonnay, is outstanding. Tastings are proudly offered at the winery. Rows of gift baskets with hand-painted bottles and glasses line a table in the tasting room, ready to be given as house gifts to lucky East End hosts. (Call in advance to order a personalized gift basket.) Picnic tables are set up under a grape arbor overlooking a pond and offer one of the most appealing places to sip and relax on the North Fork.

SCHNEIDER VINEYARDS
516-734-2699.
Website: www.schneider
vineyards.com.
Mailing address: P.O. Box
1152, Cutchogue, NY
11935.

Although they currently have no vineyards of their own and their state-of-the-art winery is still on the drawing board, Bruce and Christiane Baker Schneider produced their first wines in 1994. Selecting from the grapes grown on the finest vineyards on the North Fork, they hand-choose those they believe will produce the highest-quality wines. Bruce had apprenticed in Burgundy vineyards so he knows what he'd doing. They currently produce about 1,350 cases annually of Merlot and Cabernet Franc wines, and will offer their first Chardonnay in 1999 or 2000. Kip Bedell is overseeing production at present. The couple's 1994 Merlot was so popular, it quickly sold out, and the *Wine Spectator* had this to say of their 1994 Cabernet Franc, "Bright in flavor, serious and lush in texture." Wines may be ordered directly from the Schneiders, or they can be purchased at local and Manhattan wineshops. They also are offered at some of the finest restaurants in Manhattan.

TERNHAVEN CELLARS
516-477-8737.
331 Front Street, Greenport.
Open: 11:00 a.m.–6:00 p.m.
Thurs.–Sun.

This tiny boutique winery, which opened its doors in the summer of 1998, is located in the heart of Greenport. Specializing in hand-crafted Bordeaux-style wines (which they call clarets, a British term) the owners Carole Donlin and Harold Watts planted their five-acre parcel, Wesley Hall Vineyard, which is located in Cutchogue, in 1985 in a combination of Merlot, Cabernet Sauvignon and a small amount of Cabernet Franc. They produced their first wines in 1994, with the assistance of Russell Hearn, but Mr. Watts is now the winemaker. The partners currently produce about 500 cases a year and believe their top production will be about 1,000 cases a year. The tasting and sales room offers a view of the barrel room.

LODGING

THE BARTLETT HOUSE INN
Innkeepers: Bill and Diane May.
516-477-0371.
E-mail: greenport.com/ bartlett.
503 Front Street, Greenport, NY 11944.
Price: Moderate.
Credit Cards: MC, V.
Open: Year-round.

This big, old, shingled house was built in 1908 by New York State Assemblyman John Bartlett. It still has the original architectural details: ornate moldings, interior columns, and elaborate fireplace mantels. There's a grand front porch with magnificent fluted columns and wicker furniture. The house was restored in 1982 and was the first quality inn on the North Fork. All nine guest rooms have private baths. Room 2 has an antique iron and brass bed, an oak-manteled, wood-burning fire-

Special Features:
Nonsmoking inn; full breakfast; children over 12 welcome; no pets.
Directions: Located at the corner of Fifth and Front Streets (Route 25).

place, and Oriental rugs on polished, inlaid, oak floors. Room 3 has a brass headboard and a stained glass window in the private bathroom. The large rooms on the third floor have romantic, gabled ceilings. The full breakfast, which is served buffet-style, may include baked French toast or German-baked eggs (a combination of eggs and cottage and cheddar cheeses, homemade muffins and breads, and fresh fruit and juice.

FORDHAM HOUSE

Innkeeper: Jacqueline Smith.
516-477-8419.
817 Main Street, Greenport, NY 11944.
Price: Inexpensive–Moderate.
Credit Cards: MC, V.
Open: Year-round.
Special Features:
Nonsmoking house; broad front porch.
Directions: From the west, follow Route 25 through Greenport, turning left onto Main Street at the traffic light. The inn is $^1/_2$ mile farther on the left.

The pristine white exterior of this Victorian inn on upper Main Street offers little hint of the elaborately carved woodwork and stained glass windows within. Built by shipbuilder H. Fletcher Fordham, the house is a showcase of turn-of-the-century construction. Victorian fretwork embellishes doorways, a wooden mantel graces the drawing room fireplace, and a bay window floods the living room with light. Each of the four roomy guest rooms has been furnished with fine antiques, including some four-poster beds. Two rooms have private baths; the other two rooms share one bath. All baths ingeniously combine modern comfort with an old-world charm that includes pedestal sinks, pull-chain toilets, stained glass windows, and wainscoted walls. A full breakfast that may include French toast with sausage or blueberry pancakes with Canadian bacon, fresh fruit, juice, and coffee is served.

THE HEDGES

Innkeepers: Albert and Rita Costello Cohen.
516-765-5022.
56655 Main Road, Southold, NY 11971.
Price: Moderate.
Credit Cards: None.
Open: Year-round.
Special Features:
Nonsmoking inn; children over 12 welcome; no pets.
Directions: On Main Road, just east of town.

When a sea captain built this charming, weathered shingled house in 1730, it was embellished with all of the interior archways and elaborate woodworking details that he could afford. For example, there are rosettes and fluted columns on each door frame. In keeping with this display of prosperity, the Cohens have furnished the three guest rooms with antique brass and four-poster beds, as well as such accessories as a Bombay dresser and a Thonet rocker, and there are quilts on the extremely comfortable beds. In the back, there's an extensive vegetable, herb, and flower garden where guests can pick their own raspberries and blueberries or just sit on a bench and enjoy the bounty. It's a short walk to a private beach.

HOME PORT BED & BREAKFAST

Innkeepers: Pat and Jack Combs.
516-765-1435.
2500 Peconic Lane, Peconic.
Price: Moderate.
Credit Cards: None.
Open: Year-round.
Mailing Address: P.O. Box 333, Peconic, NY 11958.
Special Features: Continental-plus breakfast; children accepted; no pets.
Directions: From Main Road traveling east, turn left onto Peconic Lane. The inn is on the right.

The Combs, who hark from a family of baymen who settled the North Fork in 1640, have taken their gracious 1876 Victorian farmhouse, with its many lovely fireplaces, and have converted it into a comfortable bed-and-breakfast. It's filled with interesting antiques, such as the Victorian headboard and marble-topped Victorian dresser in the Gold Room and the four-poster bed in the Peach Room. All three guest rooms have semiprivate baths and are decorated with Waverly fabrics. A magnificent 1840s mahogany breakfront in the South Room, one of the common rooms, is stunning. There's a cozy fireplace in the dining room to take the chill off cool winter mornings (there are five fireplaces in all). The Teddy Roosevelt Room, filled with fishing and hunting gear and books by and about Teddy Roosevelt, shouldn't be missed. Examples of Mr. Combs' exquisite duck decoys and those of his son, Michael, might be on view (carving has been a family pastime for six generations), if they haven't all been sold.

SOUND VIEW INN

Manager: Ellen Levin.
516-477-1910;
fax: 516-477-9436;
restaurant 516-477-0666.
Route 48, Greenport.
Price: Inexpensive–Very Expensive.
Credit Cards: AE, CB, D, DC, MC, V.
Open: Year-round.
Mailing Address: P.O. Box 68, Greenport, NY 11944.
Special Features: Pool; view; tennis court; private beach; restaurant and cocktail lounge; telephones; nightly entertainment; daily maid service; air-conditioning; cable TV; children accepted; no pets.
Directions: From Southold traveling east, turn left at Youngs Avenue to Route 48. Turn right (east) onto Route 48. The inn is on the left in 3 miles.

Although this is a motel, the rooms are attractive, clean, and well maintained. It's located on Long Island Sound, with a wide stretch of private beach, and each of the 49 rooms has a balcony with a spectacular view. Several of the units have kitchenettes, and they all have coffeemakers. The restaurant feels as if it's suspended over the water; there are wraparound windows for incredible sunset views. It's a very romantic setting. There's often a live band for dancing on the weekends, and the lounge has a piano bar.

TOP O' THE MORNIN

Innkeepers: Patty and
Tommy Monahan.
516-734-5143.
26350 Main Road,
Cutchogue, NY 11935.
Price: Inexpensive–
Moderate.
Credit Cards: None.
Open: April–mid-Jan.
Special Features: On $1/4$
acre adjacent to golf
course; continental
breakfast; children
accepted; air
conditioned; non-
smoking B&B; Irish
hospitality.
Directions: From the west,
follow Main Road (Route
25) to Cutchogue. The
B&B will be on the right.

This unique and thoroughly charming B&B opened in 1997, and guests who stay here have a terrific time. Tommy will crank up the old victrola, or put some rolls into the player piano, and folks can participate in impromptu sing-alongs into the night. Patty was a professional singer and she'll set a lively and entertaining pace. The pretty Victorian farmhouse was built in 1910, and its clapboard is now painted a mellow yellow, while the elaborate gingerbread stands out in white. Antique wicker tables and chairs sit on the broad front porch, sharing space with pots of flowers. In addition to the music room, there's a living room with a sofa upholstered in red and white, and a Victorian hall tree. The guest rooms are bright and inviting. One has a verdigris iron bed, wide-plank pine floors, and very pretty rose wallpaper. Another has a brass bed and features violet colors. These two share a wonderful bath with a green tile floor, white tile walls, a pedestal sink, and a platform tub with brass fixtures. The remaining room has its own private bath. It also includes a carved four-poster bed, an antique armoire, and teal carpeting. The beautiful bath has a pedestal sink, a white tile floor, and a shower. Patty fixes a hearty Irish breakfast that on Sundays often includes Irish soda bread.

TREASURE ISLAND BED & BREAKFAST

Innkeepers: Norman and
Marjorie Whitehead.
516-477-2788.
14909 Main Road, East
Marion.
Price: Expensive.
Credit Cards: AE, MC, V.
Mailing Address: P.O. Box
337, East Marion, NY
11939.
Open: Year-round.
Special Features: On six
acres; waterfront; bird
watching; air
conditioned; continental
breakfast; beach passes
and towels provided; not
appropriate for children;
no pets; smoking on
outdoor terraces only.

This unique waterfront estate is located on the causeway to Orient Point, where it is almost surrounded by Dam Pond. To the north is Long Island Sound and Truman Beach, while on the south there's Orient Harbor and Gardiner's Bay. Situated on a slight hill, the bed-and-breakfast offers glorious sunset views, opportunities for abundant bird watching, and romantic vistas of the starry skies from the columned porch and the terrace. Norm Whitehead summered here at his grandparents' estate while he was growing up, and he remembers they named it Treasure Island, either because his grandmother found some lovely antique pieces of furniture in the attic, or because they found some money buried in the yard. Today this lovely "island" is a spot we can all treasure. The Whiteheads made extensive renovations before converting the home to a bed-and-breakfast. There are three spacious bedrooms. A suite on the main floor has a bedroom with a soundside view and a sitting room overlooking the bay. This room is furnished with a matching antique Eastlake Victorian bedroom suite, and it has its own private bath, beautifully finished with antique slate-like tiles and Corian counter tops. The other two rooms are on the second floor. Both are furnished with Victorian antiques (one has a beautiful wicker chaise), and they share one full and one half hall bath. A continental breakfast is served in a corner of the spacious living room, and guests often sit on the terrace or the glass-enclosed porch to watch the fascinating assortment of birds and animals that parade by.

RESTAURANTS & FOOD PURVEYORS

RESTAURANTS

ALDO'S RESTAURANT
516-477-1699.
105 Front Street, Greenport.
Cuisine: Bistro fare.
Serving: B, L, D.
Open: Year-round.
Owner/Chef: Aldo
  Maiorana.
Price: Inexpensive–
  Moderate.
Credit Cards: AE.
Special Features: BYOB;
  outside patio.

Aldo began his enterprise as a baker, and he still continues to bake great bread. For breakfast, you can eat whatever is hot out of the oven, along with freshly brewed coffee. For lunch and dinner, the restaurant becomes an authentic French bistro; the food is more substantial, and the atmosphere is homey and comforting. This is a bring-your-own-wine spot, which provides an excellent opportunity to buy and sample the local wine varieties. The sophisticated food might include osso buco, duck à l'orange, or grilled chicken in champagne. You'll find very friendly service, a charming old building with a pressed tin ceiling, and walls filled with elegant old-world Italian frescoes that you can purchase and take home with you.

CLAUDIO'S RESTAURANT
516-477-0627.
111 Main Street, Greenport.
Cuisine: Seafood.
Serving: L, D.
Open: Mid-Apr.–Jan. 1.
Price: Moderate–Expensive.
Credit Cards: MC, V.

In 1870, Manuel Claudio opened Claudio's Tavern. The restaurant has been in the same family ever since, making it the oldest restaurant in America to be owned continuously by the same family. The incredible, 10-foot-high Victorian bar was salvaged from an old hotel in New York in 1885 and brought to the tavern by barge. The decor is a riot of beveled mirrors, stained glass, and carved wood. Claudio's history includes interesting interludes with bootleggers, trapdoors, and dumbwaiters. The food is as fresh as seafood can be and includes lobster, shrimp, scallops, and other fish and shellfish.

COEUR DES VIGNES
516-765-2656.
57225 Main Road,
Southold.
Cuisine: French.
Serving: L, D.
Open: Daily except Tues.
Owners: The Pavlou
family.
Chef: Aristodemos Pavlou.
Price: Moderate–Very
Expensive.
Credit Cards: AE, MC, V.

For almost 20 years, La Gazelle, a fine French restaurant that was consistently rated the North Fork's most romantic, occupied this pretty columned building on the outskirts of Southold. Alas, after the death of chef/owner Robert Hascoat, it closed. In 1998, however, a charming new French restaurant opened in its place. With this restaurant — brightened by fresh white paint and a handsome new black and green carpet — the Pavlou family have filled the void. Chef Pavlou is a graduate of the Cordon Bleu in Paris. There are three small dining rooms — one with beamed ceilings — and all with lacy curtains on the windows. The menu includes some lovely items, although they are pricey. There are braised sweetbreads, a rack of lamb with pine-kernel herb butter crust, and a sautéed Dover sole in a sauce meunière. For dessert, you must try the Saragilee, a dessert that the Chef's grandmother used to make in Cyprus. It consists of a thin homemade pastry that is wrapped around an almond and cinnamon filling, baked in the oven, and then finished with a citrus/honey syrup. The wine list includes a lovely selection of French, California, Italian, and Long Island wines.

DALY'S OLD MILL INN
516-298-8080.
West Mill Road, Mattituck.
Cuisine: American.
Serving: L, D.
Open: May–Dec.
Owner: Jeremiah Daly.
Price: Inexpensive–
Expensive.
Credit Cards: AE, MC, V.
Special Features: Outdoor
waterfront dining;
fireplace; entertainment;
boat dock.
Directions: From Route 48,
travel north on Cox Neck
Road to West Mill Road.
Follow West Mill Road
to the end.

Down by the Mattituck Creek, a little inlet that feeds into Long Island Sound, stands an historic old mill, built on pilings that suspend it over the creek. With its red-shingled exterior and attractive little deck, with tables overlooking the tiny local fishing fleet, there is little hint of its bawdy Prohibition days when rumrunners stealthily paddled underneath by night to hoist their bounty through trapdoors into the kitchen. The old beams, posts, barnwood walls, and bare wood floors look much as they did originally, and the huge brick fireplace in the taproom continues to warm its inhabitants. The dining room, however, is much more refined and offers watery views from its large windows. This is serious food — a mix of fish of the day, which is purchased from local fishermen and meat that includes a rack of lamb and a boneless duck à l'orange, as well as chicken and pastas. There's a good selection of Long Island wines, plus wines from California and Europe. On weekend evenings, there's also live entertainment.

GREENPORT TEA COMPANY
516-477-8744.
119A Main Street, Greenport.
Cuisine: American Continental.
Serving: L, HT; B weekends only.
Open: Mar.-Dec.
Owner: Adrienne Noonan.
Price: Inexpensive.
Credit Cards: AE, D, MC, V.
Special Features: Wheelchair accessible.

There's nothing like the Greenport Tea Company, either in the Hamptons or in Manhattan. The Victorian building with its high ceilings is an enchanting spot. Shelves on one wall hold teacups and saucers, teapots, and gourmet food products available for purchase. Tea is served in china cups and from old teapots, each one different. The food is also unique: clam pie, shepherd's pie, soups, salads, corn bread, and Irish brown bread. You can also get a glass of local wine or a beer to wash it down with. Best of all, however, is high tea, served from tiered serving trays, laden with the best fresh scones that you'll ever eat; an old, Irish recipe is responsible for these moist and tender morsels. A variety of finger sandwiches changes with the season; there may be salmon, tomato, or cucumber, but they're always made-to-order and finished with freshly chopped parsley. The bottom tier is reserved for luscious fresh lemon tarts, mini-pastries, and fresh fruit. It's the sort of place where our grandmothers took our mothers after a day of shopping. Do ask Adrienne's husband Bill to play the old Victrola for you.

JAMESPORT COUNTRY KITCHEN
516-722-3537.
Main Road (Route 25), Jamesport.
Cuisine: American.
Serving: L, D.
Open: Year-round, closed Tues.
Owner/Manager: Matthew Kar.
Chefs: Matthew Kar and Jean-Paul Hascoat.
Price: Moderate.
Credit Cards: AE, MC, V.

Matthew Kar prides himself on featuring the wines and produce of the North Fork in his cuisine. The wine list contains 65 varieties, primarily from Long Island, and the prices range from $14–$32. This is an excellent place to sample local wines with food prepared from local ingredients. The menu is well priced and changes every week to reflect the freshest local produce. It relies on simple, straightforward dishes, but with interesting, fresh twists. A Caesar salad can be ordered either plain, with grilled shrimp, or with thinly sliced, grilled filet mignon; the sautéed chicken comes with feta cheese, fresh spinach, grilled eggplant, tomatoes, and black olives. Even the hamburgers have an interesting twist; the meat is mixed with herbs, grilled, topped with Boursin cheese, and served on focàccia. We found the salmon cakes, served with a jalapeño tartar sauce, to be perfection. An entrée that included a wedge of salmon had an herbed crust, with a light herb-caper butter drizzled over the top. Reservations are absolutely necessary at this popular restaurant; you should ask for the far room, which is quieter and away from the door. Even though the setting of plain tables and lack of decor doesn't match the sophistication of the food and the wines or the knowledgeable service, this restaurant is a particular favorite of full-time residents.

LEGENDS
516-734-5123.
835 First Street, New
  Suffolk.
Cuisine: American.
Serving: L, D, LN.
Open: Year-round.
Owners: Dennis and Diane
  Harkoff.
Chefs: Alberto Marinato
  and Kevin Bolinski.
Price: Inexpensive.
Credit Cards: AE, D, MC, V.
Special Features: Best sports
  bar on the East End.
Directions: From Route 25
  in Cutchogue, turn south
  at the light and drive 1.5
  miles to the blinking
  light. Turn left onto New
  Suffolk Avenue and then
  left onto First Street.

Divided into two sections, Legends has a sophisticated, upscale restaurant on one side with fresh flowers, candles gracing the linen tablecloths, and soft music playing. Pictures of sports figures line the walls, and a polished racing scull hangs from the ceiling. On the other side, the café has tables along the windows and a raised sports bar that includes 22 television monitors. You can actually watch both figure skating and football at the same time without so much as craning your head. The menu includes an extensive seafood selection, pork chops, steak, and chicken. All except a very few of the wines are from the North Fork and are available both by the glass and by the bottle; also there's a vast selection of more than 200 beers from 26 countries. Desserts include a chocolate-peanut butter pie and a walnut roll. This lively place has a happy hour on weekdays from 4:00 p.m.-7:00 p.m., karaoke every Thursday night, and nightly dinner specials, such as Monday night prime rib for $9.95.

PORTO BELLO
516-477-1717.
1410 Manhanset Avenue (at
  Sterling Harbor Marina),
  Greenport.
Cuisine: Italian.
Serving: D.
Open: Mid-Apr.–Oct.
Owner: Francesca Di Vello.
Chef: Rob Howie.
Price: Moderate–Expensive.
Credit Cards: AE, MC, V.
Special Features: Waterfront
  dining; fireplace; outdoor
  deck; boat dock; pianist on
  weekends.
Directions: From Main Street
  of Greenport (Route 25),
  turn right onto Champlin
  Place. At its end, turn right
  onto Manhanset Avenue.
  The Stirling Harbor Marina
  is on the right in 1/4 mile.
  Drive past scores of boats
  in drydock to the
  restaurant, which is on the
  water at the end.

Porto Bello's setting can't be topped. It sits at water's edge, surrounded by manicured lawns with views of the harbor filled with classy yachts and the village of Greenport beyond. This Italian ristorante has been welcoming North Fork residents and visitors since 1991. There's a giant stone fireplace for cool evening dining and an outside deck for the summer. One evening, we started with a delicious funghi Porto Bello, a luscious combination of grilled mushrooms and roasted red peppers, tossed with olive oil and balsamic vinegar. Our pasta was rigatoni salmone, a combination of rigatoni, smoked salmon, tomatoes, basil, and cream. For entreés, we enjoyed the pollo alla grìglia, a marinated grilled breast of chicken and vitello di scaloppine Marsala, a veal scaloppini topped with mushrooms.

Laurin Copen

John Ross's restaurant in Southold offers elegant cuisine and an exceptional selection of current and vintage, local wines. Here, John decants a bottle.

ROSS' NORTH FORK RESTAURANT
516-765-2111.
Route 48, Southold.
Cuisine: North Fork Regional.
Serving: L, D.
Open: Daily mid-Feb.–Dec., except Mon.
Owner/Chef: John Ross.
Price: Inexpensive–Expensive.
Credit Cards: AE, CB, DC, MC, V.
Special Features: Wheelchair accessible.
Directions: On Route 48, between Youngs Avenue and Horton Lane in Southold.

Almost 30 years young, John Ross' Restaurant is considered by many to be the finest restaurant on the North Fork. It has a very attractive interior with soft peach and mauve colors, romantic lighting, and fresh flowers. The service is friendly and knowledgeable. The emphasis on local wines is evidenced by the floor-to-ceiling display at the entrance, and you'll find some excellent, older vintages; wine list selections include a history of the industry on the North Fork and descriptions of the local wineries. This is a serious, very professional restaurant. The food is prepared by John Ross with a deft hand. Local ingredients are used whenever possible. For dinner, the grilled salmon, served with a smoked salmon cake and dill sauce, is flaky and tender. Desserts also feature what's fresh in season. One night, there might be an apple-cranberry-raisin pie, served with rum-raisin ice cream, or there will be a white and dark chocolate mousse, served with black raspberry ice cream.

THE SALAMANDER CAFE
516-477-8839.
Manhanset Avenue (in Brewer Yacht Yard), Greenport.
Cuisine: North Fork Regional.
Serving: Jul. 4-Labor Day only, L, D.
Open: Apr.-mid-Nov.

Claudia and Steve Helinski opened the Salamander Cafe in 1994 and filled an immediate need. The decor is unpretentious and simple with ebony tables on bare floors and local art on the walls, but the food is utterly sophisticated. The menu changes every week. A recent sampling included appetizers of roasted asparagus with capers and orange vinaigrette, and local smoked

Owner/Chef: Claudia Helinski.
Price: Moderate.
Credit Cards: None.
Special Features: Wheelchair accessible; deck dining.
Directions: From Main Street of Greenport (Route 25), turn right onto Champlin Place. At its end, turn right onto Manhanset Avenue. Brewer Yacht Yard is just beyond Sterling Harbor Marina.

salmon with mint and cilantro crème fraîche. Entrées might feature lime grilled halibut with cumin vinaigrette, or grilled breast of North Fork duck in a port wine glaze, or soft shell crabs in an almond crust with balsamic vinaigrette. A nice selection of American wines and beers is available, including 14 wines by the glass. All of the desserts are prepared on the premises, and include a luscious date-nut bread pudding, served with strawberry sauce.

THE SEAFOOD BARGE
516-765-3010.
62938 Main Road (Route 25) at Port of Egypt Marina, Southold.
Cuisine: Seafood.
Serving: L, D.
Open: Lunch & dinner daily May–Oct.; weekends only Nov.–Apr.
Owner: Richard Ehrlicht.
Chef: Scott Jaffe.
Price: Inexpensive–Very Expensive.
Credit Cards: AE, DC, MC, V.
Special Features: Nonsmoking restaurant; wheelchair accessible; waterfront dining.

Since being dubbed "the best restaurant on the North Fork" by the *New York Times*, The Seafood Barge has been packed; and it deserves to be. As one might expect, the entrées include a variety of fresh seafood that ranges from lobsters to grilled salmon, served with corn salsa, cilantro-lime vinaigrette, and sweet potato chips. One of my favorites, however, is the grilled swordfish, served with fresh cranberry beans and sautéed baby vegetables. The setting is crisp and bright with royal blue tablecloths topped by butcher paper, white plates, and a bottle of wine on every table to serve as a reminder of the excellence of East End wines; the wine list includes over 80 wines, and 90 percent are from Long Island. Don't miss dessert! The apple tarte tatin and chocolate mousse cake are great. The restaurant overlooks green lawns that slope to the boats in the marina beyond.

CAFES

The Cheese Emporium and Cafe (516-477-0023) 208 Main Street, Greenport. Open daily in the summer 8:00 a.m.–6:00 p.m.; 8:00 a.m.–11:00 p.m. Fri., Sat.; closed several days in the winter. Owner: Bruce Bollman. Choose from over 60 varieties of coffee and a gourmet array of cheeses and pâtés, as well as candy from the Greenport Fudge Factory, which has its own counter where you can buy fudge in a variety of flavors. This little cafe with its tin ceiling, tile floor, Victorian fretwork, and marble-topped tables is a popular local spot. For breakfast, you can have freshly baked pear-raisin or orange-almond muffins; in the afternoon, there are salads, sandwiches on homemade bread, and ice-cream concoctions that can be eaten at tables outside under the awning. Naturally, cappuccino and espresso are available, and this is the ideal place to put together a winery tour picnic.

FOOD PURVEYORS

A trip to the North Fork in June yields U-pick farm fresh strawberries — in the fall, apples. Throughout the summer, farm stands are filled with fresh fruit, flowers, and vegetables. The following are only a few of the excellent resources on the North Fork that frequently lure restaurateurs and food shop owners from Manhattan.

Briermere Farms (516-722-3931) 4414 Sound Avenue, Riverhead. Open daily in the summer 8:00 a.m.–6:00 p.m.; shorter hours in the winter. The fresh vegetables and fruits from the farm are displayed on a covered porch at this roadside stand, but those in the know never stop here without also going inside to the bakery. This is where you can buy the same fabulous pies that are served in several fine local restaurants. All of the cream pies are "to die for," but I can never resist the raspberry cream pie or the blueberry-peach cream pie. I usually call to reserve one in advance if I know I'm driving by because they quickly sell out.

Crescent Duck Farm (516-722-8700) Edgar Avenue, Aquebogue. No retail outlet, call for availability. At one time in the 1960s, there were 60 duck farms in the South Fork village of Quogue alone, and Long Island duckling gained a nationwide reputation. Now Crescent Duck Farm is the only one remaining on either the North or the South Fork. This farm has been in the Corwin family since the 1600s, and they have been raising ducks used by the finest East Coast restaurants since 1908.

George Braun Oyster Co. (516-734-6700) Main Road, Cutchogue. Open daily 8:00 a.m.–6:00 p.m. George Braun is often rated the best fish market on the East End by local residents. Founded in 1928, the company is the Cadillac of seafood markets, offering homemade clam or lobster pies and a wide selection of fresh fish and shellfish. Most local restaurants and many restaurants in Manhattan are supplied by George Braun. For the freshest Peconic Bay scallops, striped bass, flounder, oysters, and clams, this is the place to come.

Orient Country Store (516-323-2580) 930 Village Lane, Orient. Open 7:30 a.m.–5:30 p.m. Mon.–Sat.; 8:30 a.m.–5:00 p.m. Sun. This quaint store is a throwback to another era. It has its original wooden floors and a three-stool counter in the back for coffee or a sandwich. The prices are old-fashioned, too. A huge Reuben sandwich, for example, is still $2.50. It's next door to the old post office, where wooden floors, old-fashioned, brass stamp windows, and brass mailboxes with combination locks continue to prevail.

Wickham's Fruit Farm (516-734-6441) Main Road (Route 25) Cutchogue. Open

Apr.–Dec. 9:00 a.m.–5:00 p.m. Mon.–Sat. It was John Wickham who first experimented with grape growing in the 1950s, providing the start of the North Fork's prized industry. Today the family grows a variety of fruit that includes apples, peaches, nectarines, pears, apricots, cherries, grapes, raspberries, strawberries, and melons. Call the farm to find out about U-pick days. You also can buy delicious fruit pies, fruit breads, jams and jellies, and apple cider at the farm stand in season.

Will Miloski's Poultry Farm (516-727-0239) Main Road, Calverton. Open: 8:30 a.m.–5:30 p.m. Wed.–Mon.; closed Tues. Raises free-range chicken and turkeys and supplies many of the local restaurants.

WINESHOPS

Claudio's Wines and Liquor (516-477-1035) 219 Main Street, Greenport. Open in the summer 10:00 a.m.–7:30 p.m. Mon.–Thurs., 10:00 a.m.–9:30 Fri., Sat.; in the winter 9:00 a.m.–6:30 p.m. Mon.–Thurs., 9:00 a.m.–8:00 p.m. Fri., Sat. Owner: Harvey Katz. An excellent selection of Long Island wines, as well as other wines.

Peconic Liquors (516-734-5859) Main Road (in the King Kullen Shopping Plaza), Cutchogue. Open daily 9:00 a.m.–8:00 p.m. Owners: Beverly Cierach and Cindy Richards. This shop features an outstanding selection of local wines. Drop by for a friendly chat and guidance in making your selections from the knowledgeable owners.

Showcase Wine & Liquor (516-765-2222) 46455 Route 48, Southold. Open 9:00 a.m.–7:00 p.m. Mon.–Thurs.; 9:00 a.m.–8:00 p.m. Fri., Sat. Owner: Corinne Ferdenzi; Manager: Mike Ricciardi. This very attractive and well-organized shop offers the largest selection of Long Island wines on the North Fork.

SHOPPING

L ike an explosion, the *Tanger Factory Outlet Center* (516-369-2724 or 800-4-TANGER) on Route 25 at the end of I-495 (the Long Island Expressway) in Riverhead has hit the shopping scene. Open 10:00 a.m.–9:00 p.m. Mon.–Sat.; 10:00 a.m.–7:00 p.m. Sun. Opened in 1994, by 1996 there were almost 70 outlet stores, and by 1997 another 40–50 were added, bringing the total to 125–150. The shops currently range from The Gap and Reebok to Geoffrey Beene to Lenox.

ANTIQUES

Antiques and Old Lace (516-734-6462) 31935 Main Road, Cutchogue. Open daily 11:00 a.m.–5:00 p.m. Owners: Gene and Pat Mott. You'll find 5,000 square feet of space in this shop filled with interesting furniture that ranges from armoires to curved glass china cabinets to oak rolltop desks, as well as Oriental rugs, clocks, baskets, art glass, and more.

Interesting antique shops like The Furniture Store Antiques can be found on Greenport streets.

Suzi Forbes Chase

The Furniture Store Antiques (516-477-2980) 214 Front Street, Greenport. Open daily 12:00 noon–5:00 p.m. Owners: Jay and Miz Johnson. Vintage clothing and linen, china and glassware, jewelry, and furniture are all sold here. Don't miss the hallway with all of the old tools or the back room that may have an old woodstove.

Jan Davis Antiques/L.I. Doll Hospital (516-765-2379) 45395 Main Road, Southold. Open daily in the summer 12:00 noon.–5:00 p.m., except Tues., Wed.; shorter hours in the winter. Mailing Address: P.O. Box 1604, Southold, NY 11971. Owner: Jan Davis. This quality roadside shop was built as a country store in 1856. Today you'll find Victorian furniture, light fixtures, sterling silver candlesticks, glassware, and dolls that range from bisque to Mme. Alexander. Jan expertly repairs dolls, so you'll find several in the back room being elegantly coiffed or gowned.

Kapell Antiques (516-477-0100) 400 Front Street (Route 25), Greenport. Open daily 9:00 a.m.–5:00 p.m. Owner: David Kapell. This shop is located in a great old building that also houses a real estate agency run by Mr. Kapell, who is furthermore the mayor of Greenport. The antiques are of the highest quality and include massive desks, dining room tables, a giant old scale, ship models, paintings, folk art, early tools, and an impressive selection of vintage Steinway pianos. Don't miss his monthly flea markets!

The Pickwick Shop (516-765-3158) 45475 Main Road (Route 25), Southold. Open year-round, except Tues., Wed. 11:30 a.m.–5:30 p.m. Owner: Roberta Hering. This little shop has a mix of all sorts of things from furniture to Wedgewood china.

BOOKS

Burton's Bookstore (516-477-1161) 43 Front Street, Greenport. Open year-round 10:00 a.m.–5:00 p.m. Mon.–Sat.; 12:30 p.m.-4:30 p.m. Sun. Owner: George Maaiki. This complete bookstore carries a wide selection of hardbound and paperback books, greeting cards, and calendars.

GALLERIES & GIFTS

Doofpot (516-477-0344) 308 Main Street (in Stirling Square), Greenport. Open daily 10:00 a.m.–5:00 p.m. May–Dec.; shorter hours the rest of the year. Owner: Maryanna Zovko. This unique shop carries a marvelous array of brilliant, hand-painted ceramic vases, cachepots, urns, and tables, selected by the owner and imported from Italy and Spain. You'll also find luminous Venetian glass and chandeliers. Romantic old-world frescoes that are too large to fit into this tiny shop are displayed and sold at Aldo's Restaurant.

The Down Home Store (516-734-6565) 37070 Main Road (Route 25 at Skunk Lane), Cutchogue. Open Mar.–Dec. 10:00 a.m.–5:00 p.m. Mon.–Sat. (except closed Tues.); 11:00 a.m.–5:00 p.m. Sun. Owner: Terry Hofer. Once you see the marvelous array of handcrafted items in this shop, you will come back again and again. You will find elegantly painted furniture in faux finishes and also furniture hand-painted with flowers and wildlife. There are small rugs, dried herb wreathes, hammocks, teddy bears, birdhouses, china, splatterware.

Island Artists Gallery (516-477-3070) 429 Main Street, Greenport. Open daily 12:00 noon–5:30 p.m. This co-op artists' gallery sells works made by local artists. You will find watercolors, oils, stained and etched glass, and art in a variety of other mediums.

Jamesport Country Store (516-722-8048) Main Road (Route 25), Jamesport. Open daily 10:00 a.m.–5:30 p.m. Owner: Howard Woldman. This great old brick building with wooden floors houses a terrific little country store that carries such items as beach plum jam and honey, wicker, baskets, candles, and most other things that you think a country store should carry, except groceries, of course.

Old Town Arts & Crafts Guild (516-734-6382) Main Road, Cutchogue. Open: 10:00 a.m.–5:00 p.m. Mon.–Sat.; 12 noon–5:00 p.m. Sun. in Jul.–Aug.; weekends the rest of the year except closed mid-Dec.–mid-May. This is a marvelous place to buy gifts or personal treasures. The co-op of North Fork artists was founded in 1948 and displays and sells members' high-quality art that includes knit work, patchwork quilts, jewelry, oil and watercolor paintings, toys, carved wooden items, ceramics, and pottery.

Preston's Outfitters and Preston's Ship and Sea Gallery (516-477-1990) 102 Main Street Wharf, Greenport. Open daily 9:00 a.m.–6:00 p.m. Owner: George Rowsom. Preston's Ships Chandlery has been outfitting ships and their sailing

crews since 1883. Today nautical needs are still supplied, as well as clothing. In addition, a marvelous shop full of nautical gifts brings shoppers from miles around. There are ship models, hundreds of paintings and prints, scrimshaw, Nantucket baskets, shells, and so much more. If it's a nautical object, it's likely Preston's will have it. If you can't get here in person, call to receive the catalog.
Southold Historical Society Gift Shop (516-765-5500) 54325 Main Road, Southold. Open 10:00 a.m.–4:00 p.m. Tues.–Sat., Mem. Day–Christmas. You'll find interesting items here that you won't find elsewhere. Pretty white lace parasols, lovely lined baskets, T-shirts, books, quilts, pottery, and antiques, such as a roll-armed wicker rocker. Many of the items are new, but the antiques are in excellent condition. The Treasure Exchange (516-765-1550), a consignment shop across the street, sells items such as antique furniture, silver, and china.

HOUSEWARES

Cookery Dock (516-477-0059) 132 Main Street, Greenport. Open daily in the summer 10:00 a.m.–5:00 p.m. Owner: Arlene Marvin. This fine cooking shop has all of the things that we need to be great cooks, including pots and pans, pot holders, cookbooks, and much more.

PHOTOGRAPHY SHOPS

Camera Concepts (516-727-3283) 21 East Main Street, Riverhead. Open 10:00 a.m.–5:30 p.m. Mon.–Sat. This full-service camera shop carries video cameras and supplies as well as still cameras. They also process film and carry one of the largest selections of telescopes on Long Island.
Mike Richter Photography (516-477-0479) 207 Main Street, Greenport. Open in the summer 9:00 a.m.–6:00 p.m. Mon.–Sat.; 11:00 a.m.–4:00 p.m. Sun.; shorter hours the rest of the year. From cameras to film, this shop has it all. Mike is also available for special photography assignments.

CULTURE

CALENDAR OF EVENTS

Especially during the summer and fall, the wineries hold events that range from dinners to concerts, from theatrical productions to poetry readings and murder mystery events. Check the local newspapers or call the wineries for a schedule.

March

Easter Egg Hunt (516-298-8567) Every year on the Saturday before Easter, the Mattituck Historical Society holds its popular Easter Egg Hunt.

May

Antique and Classic Boat Show (516-477-0004) For 16 years, Greenport has featured more than 40 wooden boats of all styles in its Classic Boat Show.

Memorial Day Parade (516-765-2276) Southold holds a parade every year to commemorate Memorial Day. Sponsored by the local American Legion.

June

Festival of Arts and Earth (516-477-2139) This annual event is held at Brecknock Hall, a massive stone mansion between Greenport and East Marion. Outdoor theatrical and musical performances are included.

The Mattituck Strawberry Festival (516-298-5333) Eagerly awaited each year, the festival is sponsored by the Mattituck Lions Club. There are over 250 booths, featuring arts and crafts, as well as strawberry shortcake for everyone.

July

Croquet Tournament (516-323-2480) Held in late July or early August, this annual event is sponsored by the Oysterponds Historical Society in Orient.

Gem, Mineral, and Jewelry Show This annual event, now in its sixteenth year, is held at Mattituck High School on the last weekend in July.

Greenport Carnival This carnival ends with a fireworks display on both Saturday and Sunday of Independence Day weekend.

July 4th Music Festival (516-727-0900) This all-day, annual event in Riverhead has featured such national artists as the Benny Goodman Orchestra and Richie Havens. Sponsored by the East End Arts Council.

Mattituck Street Fair (516-298-5474) The village of Mattituck has a street fair on historic Love Lane, the second Saturday in July every year.

Outdoor Art Shows (516-323-2400 or 516-477-1319 Greenport; 516-298-8567 Mattituck) Greenport and Mattituck hold annual outdoor art shows in July, generally on the same day.

August

Outdoor Arts & Crafts Show (516-323-2655) Now in its forty-fifth year, this event, held on the first weekend in August, takes place on the village green in Cutchogue and is eagerly awaited each year.

Polish Festival Riverhead has been noted for this two-day festival for a number of years. Booths serve kielbasa and funnel cakes. Polish crafts abound, and the Polka Festival attracts hundreds of avid dancers.

September

Harvest Festival The Mattituck Chamber of Commerce holds an annual Harvest Festival and Clam Chowder Contest each year in September.

Historic Seaport Regatta (516-477-0004) An annual sailing event in early September between Greenport and Sag Harbor.

Maritime Festival and Fishing Tournament (516-477-0004) This festival is held annually in Greenport Harbor and includes a wooden boat parade and regatta, wine and seafood tasting, and much more. Sponsored by the East End Seaport and Marine Foundation of Greenport.

October

Apple Pie Fest The Cutchogue Methodist Church is famous for this annual event on the second weekend in October.

Historic House Tour This tour is held annually in Southold in October.

November

Christmas Open House (516-323-2655) In late November, the Old Town Arts and Crafts Guild in Cutchogue holds this annual event.

December

Christmas House Tour (516-323-2480) Sponsored yearly by The Oysterponds Historical Society in Orient.

MOVIES

Mattituck Theatre (516-298-4400) Main Road (Route 25) in the Mattituck Plaza near the A & P. Open every night year-round. This is an eight-plex theater, showing first-run movies.

Village Cinema Greenport (516-477-8600) 211 Front Street, Greenport. Open every night Apr.–Dec. with matinees on the weekends; Dec.–Apr. may be open only on the weekends. This is a four-plex theater, showing first-run movies.

MUSEUMS

Cutchogue

CUTCHOGUE-NEW SUFFOLK HISTORICAL COUNCIL
516-734-7122.
Main Road, Cutchogue.
Open: 1:00 p.m.–4:00 p.m.
Sat.–Mon. Jul.–Aug.;
shorter hours the rest of the year.
Fee: Adults $1.50; children $.50.

This interesting collection of historic buildings was assembled through a community effort that began in 1959 with a query from the Smithsonian Institution about North Fork Indians. One of the finest historic preservation efforts on the East End, community-spirited citizens moved and restored the buildings now included in the complex. The oldest building is the Old House, which was built in 1649 and is one of the oldest houses in New York State. It is furnished with handcrafted furniture and accessories of the period, creating a unique example of how early East End settlers lived. The Wickham Farmhouse, which dates to 1704, served as a Wickham family home for more than 250 years. It is a double Cape Cod-style farmhouse, furnished with a variety of eighteenth- and twentieth-century antiques. The Old Schoolhouse was built in 1840 and served as a one-room school until 1903. The Carriage House dates to the early nineteenth century and now contains an old carriage and the council's information center.

Greenport

STIRLING HISTORICAL SOCIETY AND MUSEUM
516-477-0099.
Main Street, Greenport.
Open: 1:00 p.m.–4:00 p.m.
Sat., Sun. Jul.–Sept.
Mailing Address: P.O. Box 590, Greenport, NY 11944.
Fee: None.

The historical society museum of Greenport, which was originally called Stirling after the Earl of Stirling, who received the original land grant for this area from the British crown in the 1600s, contains many interesting historical documents, objects, books, and artifacts that tell Greenport's history, including a wooden washing machine and a barometer stopped by the 1938 hurricane.

Mattituck

AMERICAN ARMORED FOUNDATION, INC. (THE TANK MUSEUM)
516-588-0033.
Love Lane, Mattituck.
Open: Year-round 11:00 a.m.–4:00 p.m. Sun.; 11:00

This museum, one of the largest of its kind in the United States, displays restored tanks and artillery. It is dedicated to "honor every man and woman who gave his or her services to this country in times of peace and defended this country in times of peril." There are currently more than 65

a.m.–4:00 p.m.
Wed.–Sun. Mem.
Day–Labor Day.
Mailing Address: 2385 5th
Avenue, Ronkonkoma,
NY 11779.
Fee: Adults $5; children
under 12 and seniors $4;
children under 4 free.

tanks and artillery pieces dating from the Civil War through Operation Desert Storm on display, plus uniforms, optics, helmets, and rifles.

**MATTITUCK
HISTORICAL SOCIETY**
516-298-5248.
Main Road (Route 25),
Mattituck.
Open: 2:00 p.m.–4:00 p.m.
Sat., Sun. Jul.–Aug. or by
appointment.
Fee: None.

This house, used as the headquarters for the Mattituck Historical Society, was built in 1800 as a home for the Tuthill family. The museum contains a toy and children's clothing exhibit, wedding and ball gowns, and rare musical instruments, including a square rosewood piano. Other buildings on the property include a one-room 1846 schoolhouse, a barn, and a milk house.

Orient

**OYSTERPONDS
HISTORICAL SOCIETY**
516-323-2480.
Village Lane, Orient.
Open: Call for hours.
Fee: Adults $3; children
$.50.

This collection of buildings in the delightful hamlet of Orient, which is a designated National Historic District, includes a variety of nineteenth-century buildings. In the former village inn, the parlors, dining room, and kitchen are furnished in a style that reflects a range of periods from 1790–1940; there is also a marvelous toy and train collection. The Old Point Schoolhouse was built in 1873 and contains a library of historical documents. The Amanda Brown Schoolhouse serves as the Beach Plum Museum Shop, where society members sell craft items. One of the most interesting buildings in the collection, the Webb House, is an authentic "George Washington Slept Here" structure, since he stayed in the house in 1757 when traveling to Boston to receive his commission to lead the Virginia troops into battle prior to the American Revolution. The house was then owned by Lt. Constant Booth and was located in Greenport. This beautiful building was later moved to this site and expertly restored. The society sponsors frequent walking tours of the village, a holiday house tour, an annual croquet tournament, and numerous cultural events, such as Gilbert and Sullivan musicals and plays.

Riverhead

**AQUARIUM PREVIEW
CENTER**
516-369-9840.

Operated by the Riverhead Foundation for Marine Research and Preservation, the

431 East Main Street, Riverhead.
Open: 10:00 a.m.–5:00 p.m. Sat. & Sun.; 12 noon–5:00 p.m. Mon.–Fri.
Mailing Address: P.O. Box 1361, Riverhead, NY 11901.
Fee: Adults $4; students and seniors $3.50; children 12 and younger $2.

Aquarium Preview Center includes 12 saltwater and freshwater aquariums and a 22-foot touch-tank, as well as a jelly fish tank and a variety of rehabilitating sea turtles. The aquarium provides insight into the important work of the foundation, which offers refuge to injured seals, dolphins, whales, porpoises, and sea turtles that are brought to the facility for protection, rehabilitation, and recovery before they are released back into the ocean. This is a wonderful place for children to become acquainted with the fragility of the sea and sea creatures and the environmental concerns associated with the ocean. In the summer, during the whale migration season, the Riverhead Foundation for Marine Research and Preservation also sponsors ocean excursions to view the world's largest mammals, and in the winter, it sponsors trips to watch seals.

HALLOCKVILLE MUSEUM FARM AND FOLKLIFE CENTER
516-298-5292.
6038 Sound Avenue (Route 48), Riverhead.
Open: 12:00 noon–4:00 p.m. Wed.–Sun. Apr.–mid-Dec.; by appointment the rest of the year.
Fee: Adults $3; children and seniors $2.

Peter Hallock was one of the first settlers on the North Fork, and this was his family homestead. The farm, which is on the National Register of Historic Places, was in the Hallock family for almost 200 years, and it's remained virtually intact. Children and adults will see how a turn-of-the-century farm operated. Included are the 1765 Hallock Homestead, furnished as it would have been from 1880–1910, a shoemaker's shop, a smokehouse, workshops, a large English-style barn, and an outhouse. The Hallockville Museum Farm is also the home of the Suffolk County Folklife Center. Craft demonstrations, festivals, school programs, and special summer camps take place year-round. They might include decoy carving, whittling, quill pen making, fishnet mending, or horseshoeing. The Hallock family still gathers at the family farm once a year for the annual picnic.

SUFFOLK COUNTY HISTORICAL SOCIETY
516-727-2881.
300 West Main Street, Riverhead.
Open: 12:30 p.m.–4:30 p.m. Tues.–Sat.; research library open Wed., Thurs. & Sun.
Fee: None.

The Suffolk County Historical Society is the second-oldest historical society on Long Island. The museum, research library, archives, and education program offer a glimpse into the rich life of Suffolk County. In addition, the Weathervane gift shop has unusual gift items that include historical books and maps, as well as genealogical supplies.

Southold

CUSTER INSTITUTE
516-765-2626.
Bayview Road, Southold.
Open: Every Sat. night at
dusk, or call Barbara
Latuna (516-722-3850) for
an appointment and a
schedule of events.
Fee: Donation.

The Custer Institute is an astronomical observatory with an auditorium, library, and small museum. It is open to the public every Saturday night to observe stars, planets, and meteors. Concerts, classic films, art exhibits, lectures, and other cultural events are held year-round, and an astronomy jamboree that includes lectures, solar viewing, and stargazing is held every fall.

**HORTON POINT
LIGHTHOUSE AND
NAUTICAL MUSEUM**
516-765-2101.
Lighthouse Road at Long
Island Sound, Southold.
Open: 11:30 a.m.–4:00 p.m.
Sat., Sun. Mem.
Day–Columbus Day.
Mailing Address: P.O. Box
1, Southold, NY 11971.
Fee: Suggested donation,
adults $2.

Although construction was not completed until 1857, the Horton Point Lighthouse was commissioned by President George Washington in 1790. It served as one of the links in the chain of lighthouses that guided ships through the treacherous inlets and rocky points of Long Island Sound. The light was removed from the lighthouse in 1933 and installed on a tower nearby, but it was reinstalled in 1990 as part of the renovation of the lighthouse. Although the light continues to serve its original function and is maintained by the U.S. Coast Guard, the museum in the base is operated by the Southold Historical Society. The Nautical Museum contains sea chests, paintings, maps, ships' logs, and other remnants of the active North Fork shipping trade. A climb up the stairs to the tower to see the light will be rewarded by a fine view of Long Island Sound. Events such as garden tours and ice cream socials are held on occasion.

**SOUTHOLD
HISTORICAL SOCIETY**
516-765-5500.
Main Road at Maple Lane,
Southold.
Open: 1:00 p.m.–4:00 p.m.
Wed., Sat., Sun. in the
summer only. A gift shop
is located in the Prince
Building on Main Street
which is open 10:00
a.m.–4:00 p.m. Thurs.–
Sat. May– Christmas. The
Treasure Exchange, a
consignment shop, is
open 10:00 a.m.–4:00 p.m.

The Southold Historical Society maintains and operates a collection of buildings in the center of Southold that includes the 1900 Ann Currie Bell Hallock House & Buttery; the 1750 Thomas Moore House; the 1842 Cleveland Grover Gagen Blacksmith Shop; the Downs Carriage House that dates from 1840; the Pine Neck Barn of eighteenth-century origin; and the Bay View School that dates from 1822. There's a wonderful millinery display of nineteenth- and twentieth-century hats and fabrics, and you'll learn about spinning and weaving, scrimshaw, old ovens and fireplaces, and so much more. The society main-

Thurs.– Sat. May–Nov.
Mailing Address: P.O. Box
1, Southold, NY 11971.
Fee: Free, but donations
welcomed.

tains its headquarters in the ornate Prince Building on Main Street, where its delightful gift shop is located. The Treasure Exchange, a consignment shop, is located on the museum grounds and sells antique furniture, silverware, and china. Events such as garden tours and ice cream socials are held on occasion.

SOUTHOLD INDIAN MUSEUM
516-765-5577.
Bayview Road, Southold.
Open: 1:30 p.m.–4:30 p.m.
Sat. & Sun. only in July & Aug.
Mailing Address: P.O. Box
268, Southold, NY 11971.
Fee: Donation.

The Southold Indian Museum was organized in 1925 and is now incorporated by the Long Island Chapter of the New York State Archaeological Association. The museum is noted for its extensive collection of local Algonquin Indian artifacts, many of which were found on the North Fork of Long Island. There are several items that date from 10,000 years ago. The collection includes not only arrowheads and spears, but also displays many pieces of pottery unearthed nearby. In a dramatic illustration of how advanced this agrarian society was when the first English settlers arrived in 1640, an exhibit of various corn types illustrates the farming techniques used.

MUSIC, THEATER, CULTURAL EVENTS

The North Fork made musical history with the Greenport Brass Band, which was formed initially in 1851 as part of the New York State Militia. Their popularity was so great in the early 1900s that folks would come to Greenport on a steamer from New York City just to listen to the concerts. The concerts are still held every Friday at 8:00 p.m. in the summer and continue to draw crowds.

The wineries sponsor a number of interesting cultural activities during the summer. Palmer Vineyard, for instance, sometimes has a Victorian Murder Mystery, which is performed by the Wild Thyme Players; a winery tour is included. At other times, a popular poetry series called **Voices on the Vine** is held. *Summer Showcase Outdoor Concerts* take place weekly throughout the summer at the Silversmiths Corner on Town Green in Southold. Past events have included performances by The Bay Chamber Players, North Fork Fiddler and Friends, Barber Shop Harmony, and Clinton Church Gospel Choir.

The *North Fork Community Theatre* presents summer theatrical productions in a church in Mattituck.

Glenn Horowitz-Bookseller

The Greenport Brass Band was formed in 1851 as part of the New York State Militia. They were so popular in the early 1900s that folks came out on steamers from New York City to hear the concerts.

RECREATION

BEACHES, PARKS, NATURE PRESERVES

Just as on the South Fork, car parking permit stickers are required at all town and village beaches. In Riverhead Town, which includes Aquebogue and Jamesport, the daily fee is $10; an annual parking permit sticker is $5 for residents, $75 for nonresidents. In Southold Town, the parking fee is $8.66 daily/$32.48 season. A nonresident season pass can be obtained for $108.25. The following beaches and many more are open to the public.

Indian Island County Park (516-852-3232) Riverside Drive (Route 105), Riverhead. This is a 274-acre Suffolk County Park at the mouth of the Peconic River and is rich with birds and wildlife, among the trees and marshes. The park contains 150 campsites, which cost $13 per night for county residents who have a Suffolk County Green Key Card (costs $20, good for three years), and $23 for nonresidents. There are also group camping areas, picnic areas, hiking trails, a long stretch of sandy beach (but no lifeguard), and a playground for children. In addition, canoeing, fishing, and bird-watching are encouraged.

Orient Beach State Park (516-323-2440) $5 parking from Mem. Day–Labor Day. Consistently rated as the best local beach, this is far more than just a beach. There's a concession stand that serves local seafood and holds barbecues on the weekends, a bathhouse with showers and rest rooms, a playground, and a picnic area with grills. This long spit of land, jutting 4 miles out into Gardiner's Bay, is packed with swimmers and picnickers in the summer. For those who like to walk, a hike from the parking lot along Long Beach to the point will pass ponds, marshes, and numerous birds and will end at a new lighthouse.

BICYCLING

Bicycling on the North Fork is a pleasure. The land is flat and the road shoulders are wide. There are relatively few cars and lots of sites to see. The following shops rent bicycles and provide parts and repairs.

Bike Stop (516-477-2432) 200 Front Street, Greenport. Open daily 10:00 a.m.–5:00 p.m. Rents new Schwinn mountain bicycles for $18/half-day, $22/full day.
Country Bike Time Shoppe (516-298-8700) 6995 Main Road (Route 25), Mattituck. Owner: Greg Williams. Rents mountain bicycles for $22/day, $65/week. Expanded into a spacious new building in 1997, this is one of the largest bicycle shops in Suffolk County.

BOATING, CANOEING, FISHING

Eagle's Neck Paddling (516-765-3502) 49295 Main Road, Southold. This company offers kayak sales, rentals, and paddling instructions. They also conduct guided kayak tours with instructional lectures about the surrounding wildlife, geology, or star-gazing. In addition, they conduct a 2 ¹/₂ hour sunset tour every Fri. and Sat. Rental fees are $37/full day, $25/half-day for a single kayak, and $60/full day, $40/half-day for a double kayak. Guided tours range from $45 to $50.
Hyde's Inn (516-727-9856) 1111 West Main Street, Riverhead. Open daily Mem. Day–Labor Day. $35/day per canoe. This funky riverside pub rents canoes in the summer for lazy rides along a tranquil and beautiful section of the Peconic River where you'll see birds and flowers and will be sheltered by overhanging trees. Then come back to Hyde's for a waterfront picnic or a burger from the restaurant or at the full bar. There are also outdoor grills and a volleyball court.
Peconic Paddler (516-727-9895) 89 Peconic Avenue, Riverhead. Open daily, except Tues. 8:00 a.m.–5:00 p.m. $43 per canoe/4–5-hour trip. Peconic Paddler sells a wide variety of kayaks (over 400 in stock) and canoes, and also has an extensive fleet available for rent. They will provide instructions,

and they also make several trips a day to a spot 8 miles up the Peconic River, where they will put the canoe or kayak in the water and then let you can drift back down at your own pace. Many people take along a picnic lunch and make a day of it.

Peconic River Cruises (516-369-3700) Riverhead Village Dock, Riverhead. Open Apr.–Dec. A variety of sightseeing cruises on the Peconic Bay and Long Island Sound are offered by this company which operates a 111-foot authentically reproduced paddle wheeler. The tours include a sunset cruise, a luncheon cruise, and a cruise to Sag Harbor. Rates range from $24.95–$57.

MARINAS

Brewer Yacht Yard (516-477-9594) 500 Beach Avenue (off Manhanset Avenue) Greenport. Part of the Brewer Yacht Marina network, a series of fine marinas located throughout New England and Long Island, Greenport has 200 slips and provides electric hookup, a laundry, a swimming pool, showers, rest rooms, and an acclaimed sailing school. The Greenport Sailing School employs an instructor certified by the American Sailing School who teaches classes to beginning and advanced sailors on a variety of sailboats. The marina sponsors races, regattas, and trips to other member marinas. This is also the home of The Salamander Café (see Chapter Four, *Restaurants & Food Purveyors*), which is open Apr.–mid-Nov.

Sterling Harbor Marina (516-477-0828) 1410 Manhanset Avenue, Greenport. This is an exceptional marina and includes a full gym, aerobics classes, a manicurist, a masseuse, a pedicurist, delivery of the *New York Times*, full laundry facilities (will do the laundry for you and deliver it to your boat), rest rooms, electric and cable hookup, and full repair services. There's also a fine Italian restaurant, Porto Bello (see Chapter Four, *Restaurants & Food Purveyors*), which is open from mid-Apr.–Oct.

CHILDREN'S ACTIVITIES

Frank Field's Miniature Railroad (call the Greenport Chamber of Commerce for location). On a wooded piece of land on Middleton Road in Greenport, Frank Field gives complimentary rides to children on his marvelous miniature railroad every Sunday in the summer.

Greenport Carousel (516-447-3000) Front Street, Greenport (temporary location until Greenport Waterfront Park completed). When Grumman Aerospace Corporation employed thousands of people on Long Island, they maintained a lovely park on the North Shore where summer picnics, baseball games, and other recreation took place. The centerpiece of the park was a handsomely carved carousel. After the park closed, the ornate carousel sat idle for many years; its future sometimes debated, but often forgotten until the village of Greenport obtained it. Today's children can now ride the carousel in the summer, but tomorrow's children will ride the carousel in a new pavilion, soon to be built in a new Greenport waterfront park. A competition to design the waterfront park with a boardwalk, promenades, a pavilion for the celebrated carousel, and much more has attracted submissions from more than 300 recognized architects from around the world. Work is scheduled to begin in late 1998.

Long Island Game Farm (516-878-6644) Chapman Boulevard, Manorville. Open 10:00 a.m.–6:00 p.m. Mem. Day–Columbus Day and briefly for a Fall Harvest Festival and during the Christmas holidays. Adults $11.95; children age 2–11 $9.95; children under 2 free; seniors 60+ $6.95. There are train rides on a restored 1860s train, a carousel, pony rides, in-the-wild animal show, and a petting bambiland. Call for special events.

Splish Splash Water Park (516-727-3600) 2549 Middle Country Road, Riverhead. Open Mem. Day–Labor Day; daily 9:30 a.m.–7:00 p.m. Jul.–Aug.; weekends only the rest of the season. Adults $20.95; children under four-feet-tall and seniors $16.95; parking $5. There are lockers, showers, food facilities, a 40-acre water park, a wave pool, three kiddy pools, a cliff-diver ride, a river ride, water slides, and special water shows.

GOLF

Indian Island Country Club and Golf Course (516-727-7776) restaurant (516-727-0788) Riverside Drive (Route 105), Riverhead. The manicured greens and gated entrance look more like an exclusive private club than a public golf course. Beautifully maintained by the Suffolk County Department of Parks, Recreations, and Conservation, it's an 18-hole/par 72, 6,508/6,055-yard course with a pro shop, a clubhouse, lockers, showers, rental clubs and carts, and a very good restaurant serving breakfast, lunch, and dinner. $19/weekdays, $20/weekends for Suffolk County residents with a three-year pass; $28/weekdays, $30/weekends for nonresidents. The club and the course are all part of the Indian Island County Park.

Island's End Golf & Country Club (516-477-0777) Main Road, Greenport. This golf course is actually part of a private club, but nonmembers are able to play for a fee. It's an 18-hole/par 72 course with a driving range, a pro shop, a clubhouse, a snack bar, a restaurant, and rental clubs and carts. $29/weekdays, $33/weekends for nonmembers.

HORSEBACK RIDING, HUNTING, POLO

Hedgewood Farm (516-298-9181) Main Road, Laurel. This farm has a 12-acre riding facility where hunt seat equitation and western pleasure riding is taught. They have a lighted indoor arena that permits year-round lessons; they conduct escorted trail rides, if given advance notice; and they also offer pony rides.

Hidden Lake Farms Riding School (516-765-9896) North Road, Southold. On this 95-acre spread, riders can learn to ride English-style and to fox hunt ("riding to the hounds"). Three large outdoor rings, a cross-country course, trails to the beach, and a lighted indoor arena make this a very versatile school. Group and individual lessons can be arranged, as well as escorted trail rides.

Southampton Hunt & Polo Club, Inc. (516-537-1110) 171 Sound Avenue (Route 48 at the Big E Farm), Jamesport. This private polo club has exhibition games four times a week from mid-May–Oct. The games, which are generally played on Wed. and Fri. nights at 5:00 p.m. and on Sat. and Sun. at 10:00 a.m., are open to the public on a complimentary basis. This is a terrific place to spread a blanket on the lawn and enjoy a gourmet picnic with a bottle of North Fork wine, while watching the "Sport of Kings." For those who want to learn the game, lessons can be arranged.

WATERSPORTS

Hampton Dive Center (516-727-7578) 369 Flanders Road (Route 24), Riverhead. Hampton Dive Center is a scuba diving school that offers courses leading to scuba diving certification; courses are taught twice a week for four weeks and cost $149. Once certification is earned, they regularly take members on dives. Generally, the dives are nearby, either off the jetties on the South Fork or off boats nearby in the ocean, but they also sponsor diving trips to the Caribbean and other spots. You can rent scuba equipment, and they allow nonmembers to accompany them on local dives, which generally cost $60–$85 per trip.

Sound View Scuba Center (516-765-9515) North Road (Route 48), Southold. This full-service, year-round company offers sales of scuba diving equipment as well as instructions leading to certification. They also organize kayak dive tours, as well as the sale and rental of kayaks, water skis, and wake boards.

INFORMATION

EMERGENCY TELEPHONE NUMBERS

In both Riverhead and Southold Towns, the *Police and Fire Emergency Number* is **911**.

AREA CODES

The area code for all of Suffolk and Nassau County is **516.** Frequently called nearby areas are as follows:

Location	Area Code
New York:	
Manhattan	212
Brooklyn, Bronx, Queens, Staten Island	718
Westchester County	914
Connecticut:	
Western Coastal Connecticut	203
Eastern Connecticut	860

TOWN & VILLAGE OFFICES

Greenport Village Office (516-477-0248) 236 Third Street, Greenport, NY 11944.

Riverhead Town Office (516-727-3200) 210 Howell Avenue, Riverhead, NY 11901.

Southold Town Office (516-765-1801) Main Road, Southold, NY 11971.

ZIP CODES

Town, Village, Hamlet	Zip Code
Aquebogue	11931
Cutchogue	11935
East Marion	11939
Greenport	11944
Jamesport	11947
Laurel	11948
Mattituck	11952
New Suffolk	11956
Orient	11957
Peconic	11958
Riverhead	11901
South Jamesport	11970
Southold	11971

CHAMBERS OF COMMERCE

North Fork Tourist Information Center (516-477-1383) Main Road, Greenport. Open May–Columbus Day weekend 10:00 a.m.–4 p.m.

Riverhead Chamber of Commerce (516-727-7600) 540 East Main Road, Riverhead. Open year-round 8:30 a.m.–4:30 p.m. Mon.–Fri.; Mem. Day–Labor Day open 8:30 a.m.–12:00 noon Sat.

BANKS WITH ATM MACHINES

Only the banks that have ATM machines have been listed below. Other banks are also located on the North Fork.

Greenport

North Fork Bank and Trust Co. (516-477-0036) 230 Main Street. ATM: Cirrus, Honor, MC, NYCE, Pulse.

Mattituck

Bridgehampton National Bank (516-298-0190) Main Road. ATM: AE, Cirrus, D, Honor, MAC, MC, Plus, V.

North Fork Bank & Trust Co. (516-298-5000) Headquarters: Route 25, Mattituck; Branches: (516-298-8884) 245 Love Lane and (516-298-8882) Main Road. ATMs at both branches: Cirrus, Honor, MC, NYCE, Pulse.

Suffolk County National Bank (516-298-9400) 10900 Main Road. ATM: AE, Cirrus, D, Honor, MAC, MC, NYCE, Plus, Pulse, V.

Southold

Fleet Bank (800-841-4000) 51300 Main Road. ATM: Cirrus, NYCE, MC, V.

HOSPITALS & MEDICAL SERVICES

Central Suffolk Hospital (516-548-6000) 1300 Roanoke Avenue, Riverhead. Full-service hospital.

Eastern Long Island Hospital (516-477-1000) Manor Place, Greenport. Small hospital with full services.

MEDIA

Radio

WBAZ-FM 101.7 (516-765-1017) 44210 County Road 48, Southold. "The music of the beach" plays light, popular music.

WRIV-AM 1390 (516-727-1390) 40 West Main Street, Riverhead. Adult contemporary music.

Newspapers

Newsday (516-727-7335) 209 West Main Street, Riverhead. This is the East End news bureau for Long Island's newspaper.
Suffolk Life Newspapers (516-369-0800) 1461 Route 48, Riverhead. *Suffolk Life* is the primary weekly newspaper of Riverhead and the North Fork. It is published in 34 different editions and has a circulation of 488,000. It has been published continuously for 34 years.
Times/Review Newspapers (516-298-3200) 7785 Main Road, Mattituck. This local company is publisher of *The Suffolk Times* (covering Southold Township) and *The News-Review* (covering Riverhead Township), as well as a *North Fork Vacation Guide*, a *Shelter Island Vacation Guide*, *The Wine Press*, and *Tanger Times*.
Traveler Watchman Newspapers (516-765-3425) Main Office: Traveler Street, Southold; Satellite Office: (516-727-1992) 436 East Main Street, Riverhead. General coverage weekly.

POST OFFICES

Aquebogue (516-699-1318) Main Road (Route 25).
Cutchogue (516-734-5222) Griffin Street.
East Marion (516-477-1570) Main Street.
Greenport (516-477-0038) 131 Front Street.
Jamesport (516-722-3778) Main Street.
Laurel (516-298-4511) Main Road (Route 25).
Mattituck (516-298-4230) 140 Love Lane.
New Suffolk (516-734-7343) 375 First Street.
Orient (516-323-2515) 980 Village Lane.
Peconic (516-765-3772) Peconic Lane.
Riverhead (516-727-2335) Second Street.
South Jamesport (516-722-4452) Second Street.
Southold (516-765-2677) 720 Travelers Street.

CHAPTER TEN
A Charming Green-Clad Island
SHELTER ISLAND

Shelter Island is really a local secret. Merely one half-mile from the South Fork and one mile from the North Fork of the eastern end of Long Island, it is nevertheless remote and secluded — an ideal haven. In fact, most people who regularly come here hope that the rest of the world will never hear about Shelter Island's charms. Covering an area of approximately 8 thousand square acres, Shelter Island is six miles long and four miles wide. It boasts of famous artists, writers, and performers who seek isolation in a beautiful setting.

Suzi Forbes Chase

Shelter Island was settled in 1652.

HISTORY

As Long Island stretches out her arms to the Atlantic, she gathers within her embrace a little group of islands. Largest and fairest among them, fertile and beautifully wooded, is Shelter Island, lying in the waters of Gardner's (sic) and Peconic Bays, separated from Greenport and the northern arm of Long Island Sound by about a mile of sunny water, and on its southern side looking across Sag Harbor, and the long, low line which stretches away to Montauk.

From an 1889 brochure for Prospect House,
reprinted by The Grapevine of Shelter Island Heights, 1987

Shelter Island's history includes a mixture of entrepreneurial enterprise, independence, and tolerance. This island was chosen by James Farrett, the personal representative of the Earl of Stirling, as his own land grant. It appears that he inspected it as early as 1638, but he never actually occupied the island. In 1641, he sold Shelter Island to a merchant, Stephen Goodyear, who subsequently sold it in 1651 to four businessmen with interests in the Barbados sugar industry.

Nathaniel Sylvester was one of those businessmen. After returning to England and marrying, he sailed with his bride in 1652 to their new home. Although they suffered shipwreck and lost many of their possessions, the manor house that they built on Shelter Island, along with its surrounding gardens, must have been as fine as many in England. The Sylvester Manor House, although changed over the years, is still owned by members of the Sylvester family.

Prior to the Sylvester's arrival, the Manhanset tribe, led by their *sachem*, Pogatticut (brother to the sachems of the Montauks of East Hampton, the Shinnecocks of Southampton, and the Corchaugs of the North Fork) ruled Shelter Island. Pogatticut and his people voluntarily left the island shortly after the Sylvesters arrived.

It was apparent from the beginning that the Sylvesters were peaceable people with open minds. For about five years in the mid-1600s, persecution of members of The Society of Friends (Quakers) was particularly severe in Massachusetts. Many were imprisoned, whipped, tortured, branded with hot irons, and banished from their homes. Those fortunate few who found their way to Shelter Island were treated by the Sylvesters with sympathy and understanding. They were given food, protection, clothing, and permission to practice their religion.

From 1660 to 1673 a tug-of-war took place between the British and the Dutch over Long Island. Eventually Shelter Island, not immune to the conflict, was confiscated by the Dutch. It was regained later by Nathaniel Sylvester, at a cost of 500 pounds, but only after the Dutch landed on the island with 500 men, surrounded his house, and demanded payment, merely days before they again surrendered the territory to the British.

The Havens' homestead was built in 1742 and now serves as a museum.

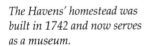

Jason Green

Other families of importance soon joined the Sylvesters. William Nicoll became the first Supervisor of Shelter Island in 1726 and occupied the estate left to him by his father. The Havens family came shortly thereafter in 1742 and purchased an estate of 1,000 acres from Nathaniel Sylvester. By 1769, the house that James Havens' father, William, had built was used as a school by day and a tavern by night, as well as a home, serving such concoctions as a mug of flip, a brandy sling, and a nip of grog to wayfarers. In 1795, Jonathan Havens was elected to serve in the new Congress of the United States, representing the district that contained Shelter Island.

The Dering name emerges in 1760 when Mary Sylvester, who had married Thomas Dering in 1756, inherited Sylvester Manor from her father and consequently moved her family into the manor house. The Sylvester, Nicoll, Havens, and Dering families were cultured people who cherished family life on the island. In 1743, the first church was built, and by 1791, a school had been established.

Around 1800, Timothy Dwight, President of Yale College, journeyed the length of Long Island and included Shelter Island in his travels. He observed that, "To the credit of the inhabitants, especially of the principal proprietors, it ought to be observed that they have customarily made considerable exertions to support schools and obtain the preaching of the gospel."

Shelter Island (along with Gardiner's Island) had one of the finest stands of white oak found on the East Coast. These trees were especially prized after the magnificent forests of Connecticut and Massachusetts were exhausted. In the mid-1800s, a shipyard was established on Shelter Island; the massive trunks necessary for keels and masts were cut from the area known as the "Great Woods."

One of the legacies of The Shelter Island Grove and Camp Meeting Association is the wealth of charming, Queen Anne Victorian houses.

Suzi Forbes Chase

Throughout Shelter Island's history, religion has played an important role. In 1871, the highest point of land on the Island became the home of The Shelter Island Grove and Camp Meeting Association of the Methodist Episcopal

Church. They called the area Prospect, and summer visitors began arriving in numbers. The handsome Prospect House, a colonnaded Victorian hotel with a piazza encircling the building, overlooked the harbor toward Greenport and accommodated up to 300 guests. The restaurant, where communal meals were held, is the nucleus of the present Chequit Inn. Some of the charming Victorian cottages and the fine houses built by the prominent citizens of the day now form the delightful village of Shelter Island Heights.

Shelter Island remains a quiet, peaceful retreat, secluded and hidden, and yet accessible to both the North and South Forks by a ten-minute ferry ride. Although the grand Victorian hotels are no longer here, newer, smaller hotels and inns now provide lodging. You'll find excellent restaurants, interesting shops, and an abundance of recreational options.

TRANSPORTATION

This hand-stenciled sign welcomes turtles to cross the road.

Suzi Forbes Chase

Part of the delight of Shelter Island is its island status and the necessity of reaching it by boat. The ferries that putt back and forth are efficient throwbacks to an earlier age. There are no amenities here, just a drive- or walk-on, open-decked ferry that shuttles between the island and the North or South Forks. Both ferries operate year-round, but trips are much more frequent in the summer.

North Ferry (516-749-0139) From Shelter Island 5:40 a.m.–11:45 p.m. From Greenport 6:00 a.m.–12:00 midnight. $7 one-way for car and driver; $8 for same day, round-trip; $1 for each additional passenger; bicycles $2 each way, $1 each rider.

South Ferry (516-749-1200) From North Haven 6:05 a.m.–1:50 a.m. From Shelter Island 6:00 a.m.–1:45 a.m. $7 one-way for car and driver; $8 round-trip, $1 each for passengers, bicycles $2 one-way, $3 round-trip, $1 each rider.

For those traveling to Shelter Island from Manhattan, the North Shore branch of the *Long Island Rail Road* may be an option, although its schedule is limited. There are generally three or four trains during the week and two trains on the weekends. The Greenport station, however, is merely steps from the Shelter Island ferry dock, and after a short water ride, you'll be in Shelter Island Heights.

For taxi service, contact *Shelter Island Go'Fors Taxi* (516-749-4252) 1 Thomas Avenue, Shelter Island.

LODGING

In addition to the following listings, the *Pridwin Hotel* (516-749-0476) on eight acres overlooking Crescent Beach on Shore Road offers lodging in its 50 rooms. The *Peconic Lodge* (516-749-0170) next door on Shore Road is open for guests year-round, although the restaurant and other facilities are closed.

BEACH HOUSE
Owner/Manager: Jan Carlson.
516-749-0264.
Price: Inexpensive–Expensive.
Credit Cards: None.
Open: Year-round.
Mailing Address: P.O. Box 648, Shelter Island Heights, NY 11965.
Special Features: Limited wheelchair access; continental breakfast; on a private beach; no children under 14; pets maybe.
Directions: Given when reservations are confirmed.

This lovely, contemporary home is located on the beach in a quiet, secluded area, far from the shops and action of Shelter Island's business areas. There are four rooms and all have spectacular sunset views of the bay. One of the rooms has an antique cannonball, tiger maple bed, a balcony overlooking the beach, and a spacious, private bath with a skylight. Another room is decorated with Victorian antiques and has a window seat overlooking the bay. The grounds are nicely landscaped, and there are benches on the lawn overlooking the bay and the small private beach. Breakfast includes homemade breads and muffins, fresh fruit, juice, and cereal.

CHEQUIT INN
Innkeepers: Linda and James Eklund.
516-749-0018;
fax: 516-749-0135.
23 Grand Avenue, Shelter Island Heights.

This large, white, 1870 Victorian inn sits proudly on the only commercial street in Shelter Island Heights. In 1994, Linda and James Eklund, also owners of the Ram's Head Inn, purchased this venerable old inn. Every winter since, they have worked to

Laurin Copen

In the summer, dinner is served on the porch of the Chequit Inn, which has a view of Dering Harbor.

Price: Moderate–Very Expensive.
Credit Cards: AE, MC, V.
Open: Year-round.
Mailing Address: P.O. Box 292, Shelter Island Heights, NY 11965.
Special Features: Nonsmoking inn; continental buffet breakfast; a restaurant on the premises.
Directions: From South Ferry, travel north on Route 114, following the signs to North Ferry. After crossing the bridge to Shelter Island Heights, take Chase Avenue up the hill. The inn is straight ahead. From North Ferry, it is on the right, approximately 4 blocks after exiting the ferry.

upgrade the inn's facilities, such as installing all new operating systems. The lobby is filled with old wicker, a huge oak library table, a woodburning fireplace, and a spacious porch that overlooks the village. There are 35 rooms (all with private bath). Those on the third floor of the main building are bright and cheerful and have carpeted floors, painted furniture, and such whimsical touches as old sleds used for coffee tables. Rooms in the weathered gray Summer Cottage behind the main building have endearing little quirks. Suite 7–8, for example, has an interesting little room with a sink and a wicker chair (sort of a sitting room/bath), and the rest of the bathroom is located between this room and the bedroom. The furniture in the bedroom is painted white (some has stenciling), and there are antique beds. There are more rooms in Cedar House across the street. When weather permits, lunch is served on an outside terrace under the trees; otherwise, you can eat lunch in the small dining area near the bar. At night, the bar is a lively place with pool tables, a dartboard, and rock bands on Saturday night. Although lunch is limited to salads and sandwiches, dinner is outstanding. The dining room, on the second floor of the hotel, overlooks the village and has a broad porch used for dining in the summer. It's a romantic restaurant with exceptional food.

DERING HARBOR INN
Manager: John M. King III.
516-749-0900;

The Dering Harbor Inn is high on the bluff overlooking Dering Harbor and the boats in the marinas. It's a 1960s-style building, with a massive,

fax: 516-288-6001; restaurant 516-749-3460. 13 Winthrop Road, Shelter Island.
Price: Moderate–Very Expensive
Credit Cards: AE, MC, V.
Open: May–Oct.
Mailing Address: P.O. Box 3028, Shelter Island Heights, NY 11965.
Special Features: Limited wheelchair access; saltwater pool; fireplaces in some rooms; tennis, volleyball, basketball, and badminton; air-conditioning; nonsmoking rooms; cable TV; kitchenettes in most rooms; a restaurant on the premises; children welcome; no pets.
Directions: To reach it from Route 114, travel east on Winthrop Road. The inn is on the left.

OLDE COUNTRY INN
Innkeepers: Jeanne and Franz Fenkl.
516-749-1633.
11 Stearns Point Road, Shelter Island Heights.
Price: Moderate–Expensive.
Credit Cards: MC, V.
Open: Year-round.
Mailing Address: P.O. Box 590, Shelter Island Heights, NY 11965.
Special Features: Wheelchair accessible; nonsmoking inn; full breakfast; large, private deck; fireplace; piano; intimate bar; not recommended for children under 12; no pets.
Directions: From Shelter Island Heights, take New York Avenue to West Neck Road, turning right toward Crescent Beach.

double-sided, stone fireplace separating the cavernous lobby from the dining room. Rooms are located in one- and two-story, gray-stained buildings with decks overlooking Dering Harbor. This is a co-op, so all of the suites and villas have kitchens. Decor will vary, but most rooms are spacious and well appointed in a Caribbean-meets-the-Hamptons style. Room 7, for example, is a single-level unit with a fireplace, screened-in porch, full kitchen, and a lovely view; steps from the deck lead to a private stretch of lawn. In all, there are 25 rooms with private baths. The grounds are lovely, with two tennis courts and a saltwater pool that appears to be suspended over the bay. Michael Anthony's Restaurant opened in 1997 and has received excellent reviews. It is open for lunch and dinner daily and for Sunday brunch.

The historic Shelter Island House, built as a hotel in 1886, and perched high on the cliff above Crescent Beach was renovated and opened as a bed-and-breakfast inn by innkeepers Jeanne and Franz Fenkl in 1994. Polished oak floors are a crisp backdrop for lovely Victorian furniture. There's a living room with a fireplace, a piano, and a tiny Victorian bar with another fireplace. The guest rooms include iron and brass beds, an exquisite old Victorian coatrack, marble-topped dressers, and upholstered Victorian chairs. Each of the 13 guest rooms has a private bath with a pedestal sink, built-in shelves, and a tiled tub surround. Two of the rooms have Jacuzzis and one has a soaking tub. There's also a separate cottage. Breakfast, either eaten in the pretty breakfast room or on one of the decks, might include crêpes with orange liqueur, omelettes, or waffles with sour cream and fresh berries. In 1996 the Fenkls teamed up with Chef Marcel Iattoni to serve winter dinners at tables set up in the living room. The restaurant proved to be

In .2 mile continue straight ahead onto Shore Road when West Neck Road turns left. Turn left onto Stearns Point Road at the next intersection. The inn will be on the left.

RAM'S HEAD INN

Owners: James and Linda Eklund.
516-749-0811; fax: 516-749-0059.
108 Ram Island Drive, Shelter Island.
Price: Inexpensive–Very Expensive.
Credit Cards: AE, MC, V.
Open: Year-round.
Mailing Address: P.O. Box 638, Shelter Island Heights, NY 11965.
Special Features: Nonsmoking inn; overlooks the water; tennis; boating; sauna; exercise room; continental buffet breakfast; children welcome; no pets; a fine restaurant on the premises.
Directions: From South Ferry, travel north on Route 114 for 1 1/3 miles to Cartwright Road (Route 114 will make a sharp left turn here, but Cartwright Road continues straight ahead). In 1 1/2 miles, you will come to a stop sign. Turn right onto Ram Island Road. In .7 mile, turn right onto Ram Island Drive and continue for almost 2 miles to Ram's Head Inn, which is on the right.

so popular that they built a romantic dining room with a fireplace, and also a spacious covered outdoor pavilion. Now the restaurant is open year-round, and the food is so good that reservations are an absolute must. Only dinner is served, but it's served with panache and style. Don't miss it.

For the ultimate getaway, nothing compares to the Ram's Head Inn, which stands on an isolated bluff overlooking Coecles Harbor. The fireplace in the lobby offers a warm welcome in the winter, and the pretty sunporch, with its woodstove, green wicker furniture with floral cushions, brick floor, and games at the ready, make this a year-round retreat. The broad, outside terrace overlooks four and one-half acres of manicured lawns that slope to the tennis court and beyond to 800 feet of private beach. There are Adirondack lawn chairs, small boats for guests to use, and hammocks strategically placed in shady groves. The exercise room is equipped with bicycle and step equipment and a sauna. The 17 rooms are fresh and bright, with wicker and white-painted furniture interspersed with antiques; colorful fabrics are used for bedspreads and curtains. Although at present only nine rooms have private baths, more baths are being added every year, so that eventually they will all have private baths. The buffet breakfast includes muffins, sweet rolls, cereal, juice, fruit, and beverages. Special holiday weekends sometimes include a dramatic production, with the guests playing some of the roles.

STEARNS POINT HOUSE
Owner: Jan Carlson.
516-749-4162.
7 Stearns Point Road,
Shelter Island Heights.
Price: Moderate–Expensive.
Credit Cards: None.
Open: Year-round.
Mailing Address: P.O. Box
648, Shelter Island
Heights, NY 11965.
Special Features:
Nonsmoking house;
continental breakfast;
children and pets maybe.
Directions: From Route 114,
travel west on West Neck
Road toward Crescent
Beach. After West Neck
Road turns into Shore
Road, turn left onto
Stearns Point Road,
which is the first left.

Located on three-quarters of an acre, this charming, old farmhouse has polished wooden floors and beautiful wicker furniture with flowered chintz cushions. The house is within an easy walk of Crescent Beach. All four bedrooms have private baths and either king- or queen-sized tester, canopied beds. Breakfast includes home-baked muffins, fruit breads, cereal, fresh fruit, and juices. Stearns Point Road is a quiet country lane, away from street traffic and the village of Shelter Island Heights — pure peace and quiet.

SUNSET BEACH
Owner: Andre Balazs.
Manager: Kim Ngugen.
516-749-2001.
35 Shore Road, Shelter Island.
Price: Expensive–Very
Expensive.
Credit Cards: AE, MC, V.
Open: Mid-may–Sept.
Mailing Address: P.O. Box
278, Shelter Island
Heights, NY 11965.
Special Features: Overlooks
the water; beach across the
street; pond; sundecks;
TV; telephones; bicycles;
paddleboats; a restaurant
with a water view on the
premises; children and
pets welcome.
Directions: From Route 114,
travel west on West Neck
Road toward Crescent
Beach. West Neck Road
will become Shore Road,
which you should follow
to the beach. The resort is
on the left.

This neat little motel has occupied its prestigious spot across from Shelter Island's premier beach for many years, but it used to be furnished with old-fashioned vinyl chairs and formica-topped tables. All that changed in 1997 when Andre Balazs added this outpost to his collection of boutique hotels. (He is also the owner of Chateau Marmont in Hollywood and The Mercer in Manhattan.) Following a thorough makeover, the outside has been transformed from dull brown to a lively combination of white, marine blue, and yellow. Best of all, the rooms are bright and inviting—decorated in a beachy/casual minimalist style with white walls, carpeted floors, and private baths. You'll find a TV & VCR, robes, air conditioning, a telephone, and a minibar stocked with drinks, in every room. But what you'll love most are the enormous private decks with beautiful water views (the beach is about 200 feet away). There are pretty gardens on the property with a little pond as a centerpiece, and there are paddle boats and mountain bikes for the use of the guests, as well as the sandy beach across the street. The waterfront bistro and bar has wonderful food. As might be imagined, Sunset Beach is attracting a star-studded cast.

RESTAURANTS & FOOD PURVEYORS

RESTAURANTS

COGAN'S COUNTRY RESTAURANT
516-749-2129.
23 North Ferry Road (Route 114), Shelter Island.
Cuisine: American/Italian.
Serving: D, BR, L (summer only).
Open: Daily in the summer; weekends only in the winter.
Owners: James and Kathleen Cogana.
Chefs: James Cogan.
Price: Inexpensive–Expensive.
Credit Cards: AE, MC, V.
Special Features: Broad porch and small patio for outside dining.

The location is the same, and the restaurants have the same decor, but they are most assuredly different. During the winter, James Cogan has for years created homey American dishes at Cogan's Country Restaurant, but in the summer, the restaurant metamorphoses into Duvall's Corner, an American/Italian restaurant that is operated by Frank Sadocha. This building once served both as Shelter Island's first general store and a post office, and the funky decor still includes the old meat cases and counters that have settled into the wooden floors, plus stained glass windows and antique furniture, that create a comfortable, rural atmosphere. The porch in front is a pleasant place to eat in the summer. James is a graduate of the Culinary Institute of America, and it shows. He's been creating his homey American cuisine at Cogan's Country Restaurant for 16 years. You'll receive his very special corn fritters and spiced applesauce as soon as you're seated. The soups are excellent, especially the rich French onion. For entrées, there's a wide selection of meat and fish, with daily blackboard specials. In addition to the restaurant, the couple owns **All Seasons Catering,** which has mobile kitchens and refrigerated cabinets, allowing them to cater almost anywhere — at the beach or in a garden. During the summer, Frank will serve you pastas and fresh fish, accompanied by warm focàccia.

RAM'S HEAD INN
516-749-0811;
fax: 516-749-0059.
108 Ram Island Drive, Shelter Island.
Cuisine: American.
Serving: D.
Open: Year-round.
Owners: Linda and James Eklund.
Chef: Tom Ritzler
Price: Moderate–Very Expensive.
Credit Cards: AE, MC, V.

The Ram's Head Inn has the most romantic restaurant on the East End. It's elegant and gracious, with a view of Coecles Harbor by day. By night, the high ceilings, polished oak floors topped with Oriental rugs, and handsome oil paintings are illuminated by a glowing fireplace and candlelight. It's magical. In the summer, French doors open to a terrace for outside dining. Chef Tom Ritzler is outstanding. One night, we started with a Gorgonzola cheesecake and as an entrée was served chicken breast with caramelized onions and sun-dried tomatoes. Another night, we enjoyed the fresh

The lovely lawns and gardens of the Ram's Head Inn and the view of Coecles Inlet beyond provide a lovely backdrop for summer dining on the porch.

Laurin Copen

Special Features: Outdoor dining in season; fireplace.
Directions: From South Ferry, travel north on Route 114 for 1 ¹/₃ miles to Cartwright Road (Route 114 makes a sharp left turn here, but Cartwright Road continues straight ahead). In 1 ¹/₂ miles, there will be a stop sign. Turn right onto Ram Island Road. In .7 mile, turn right onto Ram Island Drive and continue for almost 2 miles to Ram's Head Inn, which is on the right.

SUNSET BEACH
516-749-3000.
35 Shore Road, Shelter Island.
Cuisine: Mediterranean.
Serving: L, D.
Open: Mid-May–Sept.
Chef: Pascal DeSeach.
Price: Moderate–Expensive.
Credit Cards: AE, DC, MC, V.
Special Features: Bi-level outside deck; water and sunset view.

swordfish. The Sunday night jazz evenings (in the summer) are marvelous, as are the frequent wine tastings. On Sundays in the winter, fireside dinners are served 1:00 p.m.–8:00 p.m.

When seen from the parking lot, you may not expect a lot from this little beachside restaurant. But expectation mounts as you climb the stairs and hear the happy buzz of the crowd. When you're seated on one of the three outside decks (two are covered and one is not), with their spectacular sunset and harbor view, you know that you'll have a great evening. The decor includes rattan chairs, strings of little lights, and bright red-and yellow-patterned oilcloth tablecloths. The spirited background music perfectly suits the young, energetic crowd. The food is excellent. You might start with a shrimp summer roll with peanut sauce or risotto with zucchini and pignoli nuts. Entrées feature local seafood and include a Shelter Island bouillabaisse, steamed mussels with crisp French fries, grilled swordfish with a baby spinach salad, and grilled salmon with ratatouille.

FOOD PURVEYORS

Baggio's Pizza & Cafe (516-749-0595) 53 North Ferry Road (Route 114) at Jaspa Road, Shelter Island. Open 11:00 a.m.–9:00 p.m. Sun.–Thurs.; 11:00 a.m.–10:00 p.m. Fri., Sat. in the summer; shorter hours the rest of the year. Owner: Mike DeMarsico. Here you'll find gourmet pizzas made with very thin crusts; the specialty is Sicilian pizza with meatballs. Our favorite is a white pizza with ricotta and mozzarella cheeses, delicately touched with spices and garlic. For nonpizza lovers, there are charcoal-broiled hamburgers, calzone, and best of all — nacho fries (fries that are smothered in a tangy cheese sauce).

Stars, The Market/Coffee Cellar (516-749-3484) 17 Grand Avenue, Shelter Island Heights. The Market is open daily in the summer 9:00 a.m.–9:00 p.m.; the Coffee Cellar is open daily in the summer 6:30 a.m.–10:00 p.m.; both open shorter days and hours the rest of the year. Owner: Cheryl Hannabury. Upstairs, The Market has a terrific gourmet grocery, with cheeses, vinegars, oils, and pastas, as well as a deli with sandwiches, salads, quiches, and bakery goods; there are tables inside and along the sidewalk. Downstairs, the Coffee Cellar has a selection of café lattés, mochas, cappuccinos, etc. (both hot and iced), plus bakery and dessert goods. After a play or a concert, this is the place for breakfast or for dessert.

SHOPPING

Books & Video (516-749-8925) 17 Grand Avenue, Shelter Island Heights. Open daily 10:00 a.m.–8:00 p.m. Owner: Paul Olinkiewicz. This is the only bookstore on Shelter Island and has old and new books, hardbound and paperback. There's a small selection of used, local history books. They also rent videos.

Fallen Angel Antiques (516-749-0243, or 749-7801, messages only) Washington Street (in the Chequit Annex, known as Cedar House), Shelter Island Heights. Open Mem. Day–Columbus Day. Owner: Joan Markell. This shop has a delightful, little treasure trove of quilts, silver, prints, wearable art, and other specialty items.

The Island Gallery (516-749-0733) 8 Grand Avenue, Shelter Island Heights. Open long weekends 10:00 a.m.–5:00 p.m. June–Aug.; Sat. & Sun. in the spring and fall; closed the rest of the year. This artists' cooperative has been in business for over 25 years, attesting to the commitment and expertise of its members. It exhibits lovely art, from watercolor to sculpture, that includes local landscapes, flower gardens, houses, animals, and more.

Showtime *by acclaimed sculptor Peggy Mach, who lives and works on Shelter Island.*

Peggy Mach

Peggy Mach Gallery (516-749-0247 or 749-2215) Corner West Neck Road and North Menantic Road, Shelter Island. Open 11:00 a.m.–5:00 p.m. on the weekends. Once you see one of Peggy Mach's sculptures, you won't be satisfied until you own one. Her subjects are so lyrical and so poignant that you almost feel as if you can talk to them, and they certainly "talk to you." Her subjects include dancers, clowns, lovers, and executives, sculpted in clay and stone and cast in bronze. Ms. Mach's work is included in important private and museum collections throughout the world, and she lives and works on Shelter Island.

The Whale's Folly (516-749-1110) Bridge Street, Shelter Island. Open 10:00 a.m.–5:00 p.m. Fri.–Mon. Mem. Day–Columbus Day only. The handcrafted items in this store are very special. Vivid watercolor paintings by Island artist, Olive Reich, are for sale, as well as wicker furniture, pretty china platters, and painted wicker baskets.

CULTURE

CALENDAR OF EVENTS

April

Easter Egg Hunt (516-749-0107) Sponsored by the Shelter Island Heights Fire Department Auxiliary.

Easter Sunrise Service Sponsored by all Shelter Island churches.

May

Memorial Day Parade Sponsored by the Shelter Island American Legion Post.

June

Shelter Island 10K Run (516-749-RUNN) Annual event begins at 5:30 p.m., but activities lead up to the event all afternoon.

July

Fireworks Show (516-749-0399) Sponsored by the Shelter Island Chamber of Commerce.

August

Annual Arts and Crafts Show (516-749-0399) Sponsored by Shelter Island Chamber of Commerce, as well as the Fire Department Country Fair, Shelter Island.
Annual Shelter Island Heights Firemen's Chicken Barbecue (516-749-0107).

September

Historical Society Fair, Shelter Island (516-749-0025) Sponsored by the Shelter Island Historical Society.

October

5K Co-ed Run (516-749-0399) Sponsored by the Shelter Island Chamber of Commerce.
Halloween Party and Parade (516-749-0184) Sponsored annually by the Shelter Island Fire Department.

December

Christmas Tree Lighting (516-749-0399) At the Town Hall, Shelter Island.

RECREATION

BICYCLING

Shelter Island is an especially popular destination for cyclists. The minimal amount of traffic makes the roads relatively safe, even though there are no shoulders. The roads are fairly level, except for several significant exceptions, such as Shelter Island Heights. Many people ferry their bicycles over by car to the island, but if you prefer to rent a bicycle on the island, the following firm has bicycles for rent.

Piccozzi's Bike Shop (516-749-0045) Bridge Road, Shelter Island Heights. Mountain bicycles, English varieties, and tandem bicycles. $18/full day, $14/half day for 3-speed bicycles; $22/full day, $18/half day for mountain bicycles.

BOATING

Marinas

Coecles Harbor Marina & Boatyard (516-749-0700) End of Harbor Avenue on Coecles Harbor, Shelter Island. This full-service marina and repair shop has 40 slips, a ship's store, a snack bar, a swimming pool, and offers sailboat and bicycle rentals.

Piccozzi's Dering Harbor Marina (516-749-0045) Bridge Street, Shelter Island Heights. Docking is provided here in 35 slips for boats up to 160 feet in length. There are rest rooms, hot showers, electric hookups, barbecues, a laundromat, a game room, and bicycles for rent.

BOAT RENTALS

Shelter Island Kayak Tours (516-749-1990) Route 114 at Duvall's Road. This company provides kayak rentals and guided tours of the abundant waters surrounding Shelter Island, including nature areas that contain a wealth of bird and fish life. They offer two 2-hour tours a day leaving at 9:30 a.m. and at 5:30 p.m. at $45 per person. You can also rent a kayak for your own tour. The prices are $10/hour for a single kayak and $15 for a double.

GOLF

Shelter Island Country Club (516-749-0416) Goat Hill, Shelter Island Heights. 9 holes; par 35; 2,900 yards; clubhouse open to the public; small pro shop; resident pro; full-service restaurant. This is one of the most challenging courses on the East End; it meanders over steep hillsides near the lovely community of Shelter Island Heights. The classy clubhouse, with its broad porches, was built in 1898 and is set high on a hill with a commanding view of the bays. The course opened in 1902, making this the sixth oldest, continuously operating golf course in the United States. It was a private club until 1940.

HORSEBACK RIDING

Hampshire Farms & Equestrian Center (516-749-0156) Bowditch Road, Shelter Island. This 85-acre center offers riding instruction on an individual or group basis in hunting, jumping, and dressage, as well as summer youth programs; a large, indoor, lighted arena permits lessons year-round. The four outside rings and cross-country course provide experience for hunters and riders. They also offer escorted trail rides if notified in advance.

PARKS & NATURE PRESERVES

Mashomack Preserve, on over 2,000 acres of land, is owned by The Nature Conservancy and is open to the public. This is the information center.

Suzi Forbes Chase

Mashomack Preserve (516-749-1001) Entrance about 1 mile from the South Ferry. Over 2,000 acres; woods; marshes; freshwater ponds; tidal creeks; occupies almost one-third of Shelter Island. In the late 1970s, The Nature Conservancy successfully launched the largest fund-raising effort in its history. They took title to this land in January, 1980. Referred to as "The Jewel of the Peconic," this preserve contains one of the largest concentrations of nesting osprey, which, until recently, were almost extinct, as well as a wide variety of other birds, animals, and plants. Excellent maps and brochures are available at the visitor's center for the nature trails and hikes, which range from 1 1/2 miles to an 11-mile loop. Educational and recreational activities are provided, from canoe trips to bird-watching expeditions, and there's a children's program. The old Nicoll Manor House, a ten-bedroom Victorian mansion with four fireplaces, is used primarily by staff for preserve programs, fund-raising events, and environmental meetings.

INFORMATION

EMERGENCY NUMBERS

In case of emergency, call **911.**

Police   516-749-0600
Fire
Shelter Island   516-749-0184   Shelter Island Heights   516-749-0107

TOWNS & VILLAGES

Shelter Island Chamber of Commerce (516-749-0399) Box 598, 47 West Neck Road, Shelter Island, NY 11964.
Shelter Island Town (516-749-0291) 44 North Ferry Road, Shelter Island, NY 11964.
Village of Dering Harbor (516-749-0020) Shore Road, Dering Harbor, NY 11965.
Village of Shelter Island Heights (no town office).

POST OFFICES

Shelter Island Heights Post Office (516-749-1115) 6 Grand Avenue, Shelter Island Heights, NY 11965. Open 8:00 a.m.–5:00 p.m. weekdays; 9:00 a.m.–1:00 p.m. Sat.
Shelter Island Post Office (516-749-0250) State Road, Shelter Island, NY 11964. Open 8:00 a.m.–5:00 p.m. weekdays; 9:00 a.m.–1:00 p.m. Sat.

BANKS

The Bank of New York (516-749-0440) 48 North Ferry Road, Shelter Island.
North Fork Bank and Trust (516-749-1300) 20 West Neck Road, Shelter Island. ATM: Cirrus, Honor, MC, NYCE, Pulse.

CHURCHES

Our Lady of the Isle Roman Catholic Church (516-749-0001) 5 Prospect Avenue, Shelter Island.
St. Mary's Episcopal Church (516-749-0770) St. Mary's Road, Shelter Island.
Shelter Island Friends Meeting (516-749-0555 or 324-8557) Route 114, Shelter Island. In the woods at Quaker Martyr's Monument, Sylvester Manor, Shelter Island.

Union Chapel was the centerpiece of the Shelter Island Grove and Camp Meeting Association of the Methodist Episcopal Church in the 1870s. Services are still held here in the summer.

Suzi Forbes Chase

Shelter Island Presbyterian Church (516-749-0805) 32 North Ferry Road, Shelter Island.

Union Chapel in the Grove (516-749-1164) Shelter Island Heights. Interdenominational services, Sunday 10:00 a.m. (summer only).

FAX & BUSINESS SERVICES

The Executive Option (516-749-3101; fax: 516-749-3102) 71 North Menantic Road, Shelter Island. Typing, word processing, copying, fax services, and other office services.

LATE-NIGHT CAR REPAIR

Piccozzi's Service Station & Garage (516-749-0045) Shelter Island.

NEWSPAPERS

Shelter Island Reporter (516-749-1000) P.O. Drawer 3020, 9 Grand Avenue, Shelter Island Heights. Weekly newspaper, reporting the news of Shelter Island.

IF TIME IS SHORT

In my opinion, every trip to New York City, especially if it's in the summer, should include a visit to the Hamptons. I love the energy of the city — the "can do" attitude — the feeling that anything is possible. But I also appreciate the slower pace, the tranquility, and the beauty of the Hamptons. I admit to a certain prejudice, however, about both places, and I know it's difficult for many who live beyond New Jersey to believe that such a profound contrast to Manhattan's hurried pace and masses of people is so close at hand. So, come and see for yourself. A day in the Hamptons will convince you to come again and to stay longer.

HISTORY

If you're a history buff, a walk through most of the Hamptons' villages will include seeing buildings that date to the early seventeenth century. The **Southampton Historical Museum,** just off Main Street in *Southampton,* is composed of a collection of 12 buildings and 35 individual exhibits that range from an authentic village store to Revolutionary War artifacts. In *East Hampton,* **Mulford Farm** provides a glimpse of life on a working farm in the seventeenth century. Throughout the villages, picturesque windmills offer poignant reminders of the area's agricultural origins.

RECREATION

Traveling through the Hamptons by bicycle is an excellent way to see the countryside. The roads are relatively flat and major highways have wide shoulders. In addition, opportunities for nature lovers abound. The **Long Pond Greenbelt** (a 6.2-mile trail) in *Bridgehampton* threads its way along a chain of ponds and wetlands in the heart of the Atlantic flyway, making it a rich resource for bird-watching. In *Montauk,* **Hither Hills State Park,** a 1,700-acre preserve, includes two miles of ocean beach. There are campgrounds, picnic sites, nightly entertainment, movies, and a vast network of hiking trails.

BEACHES

The beaches of the Hamptons are glorious — broad, wide strips of fine, clean, white sand that stretch for miles, bordered on one side by the relentlessly steady surge of the ocean and on the other side, bordered either by sandy dunes covered with sea grass or by magnificent mansions. If you can only go to one beach, I suggest **Main Beach** in *East Hampton.* It's within walking and bicycling distance of the town, and if you have a car, there's a parking lot where you can park for a fee. (However, be sure to call 324-4150 to find out if parking is permitted the day you want to go.) In addition, there are bathrooms, changing facilities, and a fine snack bar.

NORTH FORK WINERIES

Most of the East End wineries are on the North Fork, an easy two-hour drive from Manhattan. If there is only time for a day trip, my suggestion would be to leave early enough to have time to visit two wineries, have lunch, and then visit two more wineries before heading back to the city. Start the tour at **Palmer Vineyards** in *Aquebogue.* The self-guided tour is interesting, and the tasting room includes the remnants of an authentic British pub. Musical events often take place on the weekends. Next, stop at **Pellegrini** in *Cutchogue,* which has a winery building that is reminiscent of a cloister. Have lunch either at **Ross' North Fork Restaurant** in *Southold,* where the excellent regional food can be accompanied by a vintage bottle of North Fork wine from the owner's outstanding cellar or at **The Seafood Barge,** also in *Southold,* which offers fresh-from-the-sea fish dishes and a superb harbor view. As an alternative, you may wish to eat a picnic lunch and enjoy a local vintage on the deck of one of the wineries. Before leaving the North Fork, stop at the spectacular **Pindar Vineyards** winery in *Peconic* and at **Peconic Bay Vineyards** in *Cutchogue.* At the latter, sample the ambrosial dessert wine, Vin de I'lle, and you'll be in a mellow mood for your return journey.

LODGING

If there's time for just one night in the Hamptons, I would suggest one of the following inns, although selecting only three was difficult. Please note that I have included only inns that are open year-round; there are many wonderful places to stay that are closed during the winter months.

EAST HAMPTON TOWN

East Hampton Point (516-324-9191) 295 Three Mile Harbor Road, East Hampton. For those who seek total privacy, these charming cottages are the solution. Each is an individual suite, often on two levels, that includes a kitchen and a private deck. Baths are spacious and most have skylights and Jacuzzis. The cottages are connected by brick pathways and are bordered by abundant flower beds. There's a pool, a marina, a restaurant with a spectacular harbor view, a tennis court, and an exercise facility located in a former chapel.

The J. Harper Poor Cottage (516-324-4081) 181 Main Street, East Hampton. This transformation of an East Hampton Main Street mansion into a very elegant bed-and-breakfast took place in 1996. The architecture and decor feature William Morris designs, and the fabrics and wallpapers were imported from England. Each of the five guest rooms is generously proportioned and has elegant tiled baths (several with Jacuzzis) and fireplaces. There's a lovely courtyard in back that overlooks an expansive formal garden.

SOUTHAMPTON TOWN

1708 House (516-287-1708) 126 Main Street, Southampton. This was another newcomer to the Hamptons' inn scene in 1996 — a restoration of an old boardinghouse that had fallen on sad days. Each of the nine guest rooms and three cottages is spacious and luxurious. They are furnished with antiques from the owner's antique shop and decorated with Ralph Lauren fabrics. In the brick-floored wine cellar, wine and cheese are served in the evening.

RESTAURANTS

To select a few restaurants from the many excellent choices was almost as difficult as choosing a few places to stay. I have selected the following partly to offer choices in location, cuisine, and setting.

EAST HAMPTON TOWN

Dave's Grill (516-668-9190) 468 Flamingo Road, Montauk. For fresh-from-the-boat seafood, Dave's can't be beat. Ditto for Thursday night dinners with live jazz. This is a casual and engaging restaurant with an enclosed patio for summer dockside dining. Don't miss the desserts. The chocolate bag is an outrageous combination of chocolate and caramel sauces, ice cream, and bananas, enclosed in a chocolate crust shaped like a bag.

The Laundry (516-324-3199) 31 Race Lane, East Hampton. The setting is relaxed, attractive, and cosmopolitan; the food is consistently good. The menu includes a wide variety of options, allowing diners to choose an appetizer, a salad, or a three- or four-course dinner. This restaurant is a local favorite.

Nick & Toni's (516-324-3550) 136 North Main Street, East Hampton. Lights! Camera! Action! It's always a "scene" at Nick & Toni's. Sophisticated but charming, this outstanding restaurant is so popular that summer reservations should be made weeks in advance. A star-studded, svelte clientele likes to nosh on chewy Tuscan bread, juicy, flavorful meats from the wood-burning oven, and luscious desserts. It's worth every penny.

Turtle Crossing (516-324-7166) 221 Pantigo Road, East Hampton. Here you'll get great BBQ in an unpretentious little café. You can order an overflowing platter of spit-roasted chicken or smoked ribs doused in delicious sauces that the *New York Times* has acclaimed as the best BBQ on Long Island. Don't leave without having a fat square of warm bread pudding with Jack Daniel's sauce.

SOUTHAMPTON TOWN

American Hotel (516-725-3535) Main Street, Sag Harbor. This is the Hamptons' most celebrated French restaurant. Fine French/American cuisine is served in an elegant setting that includes a fireplace in one room and a glass ceiling in another. An exceptional wine list has won the highest awards year after year, and the selection of cigars was renowned long before cigar smoking became chic.

Karen Lee's Restaurant and Wine Bar (516-537-7878) Main Street, Bridgehampton. My all-time favorite, romantic Hamptons' restaurant is Karen Lee's. Soft candlelight plays across starched linen and illuminates the massive bouquets of flowers. We love everything on the menu from the moist, crisp-skinned chicken to the Tuscan-style pot roast to the outstanding desserts. This is a great place to sample local wines.

Savanna's (516-283-0202) 268 Elm Street, Southampton. As soon as it opened in 1995, Savanna's became the Nick & Toni's of Southampton. A sophisticated setting with a terrific, outdoor dining pavilion, interesting food prepared and presented with flair, a fine wine list, and a popular bar — all add up to a splendid new restaurant.

Southampton Publick House (516-283-2800) 40 Bowden Square, Southampton. Part microbrewery, part restaurant, this casual, affordable place jumps on summer weekends when live entertainment and dancing are featured. There are eight microbrews on tap, and the wine selection includes local favorites. The menu ranges from salads and burgers to steaks. The most expensive entrée, a 20-ounce, Cajun-spiced rib eye, is priced at $20.

Index

LODGING BY PRICE CODE

RESTAURANTS BY PRICE CODE

Price Codes

Inexpensive	Up to $25
Moderate	$25–$35
Expensive	$35 to $50
Very Expensive	$50 or more

RESTAURANTS BY CUISINE

SHOPPING

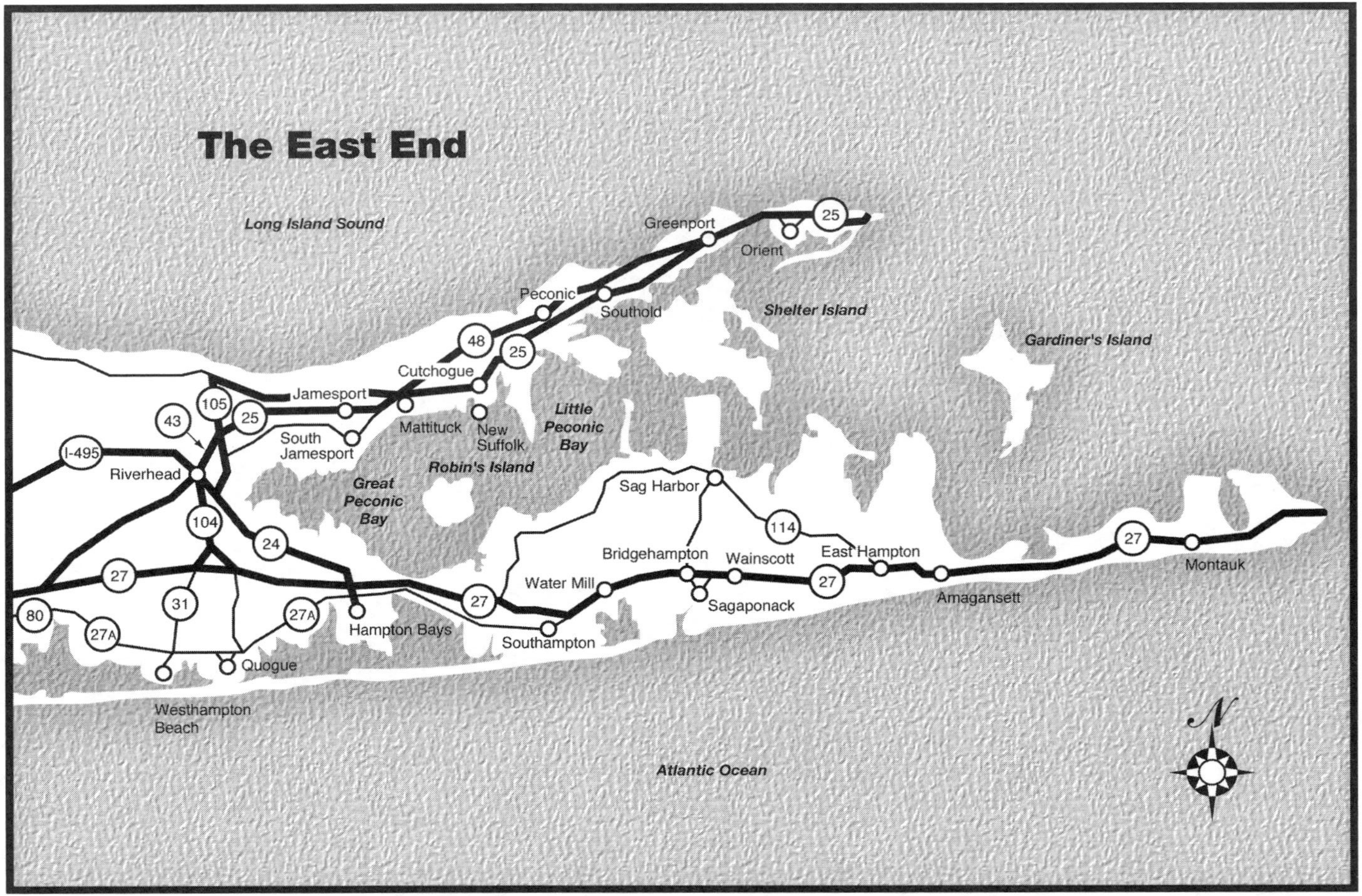

The East End

Long Island Sound

Gardiner's Island

Shelter Island

Atlantic Ocean

Little Peconic Bay

Great Peconic Bay

Robin's Island

Montauk
27
Amagansett
East Hampton
27
Wainscott
114
Sagaponack
Bridgehampton
Sag Harbor
Water Mill
Southampton
27
Hampton Bays
27A
Quogue
Westhampton Beach
31
104
24
27
27A
80
Riverhead
43
105
25
I-495
Jamesport
South Jamesport
Cutchogue
48
25
Mattituck
New Suffolk
Peconic
Southold
Greenport
Orient
25

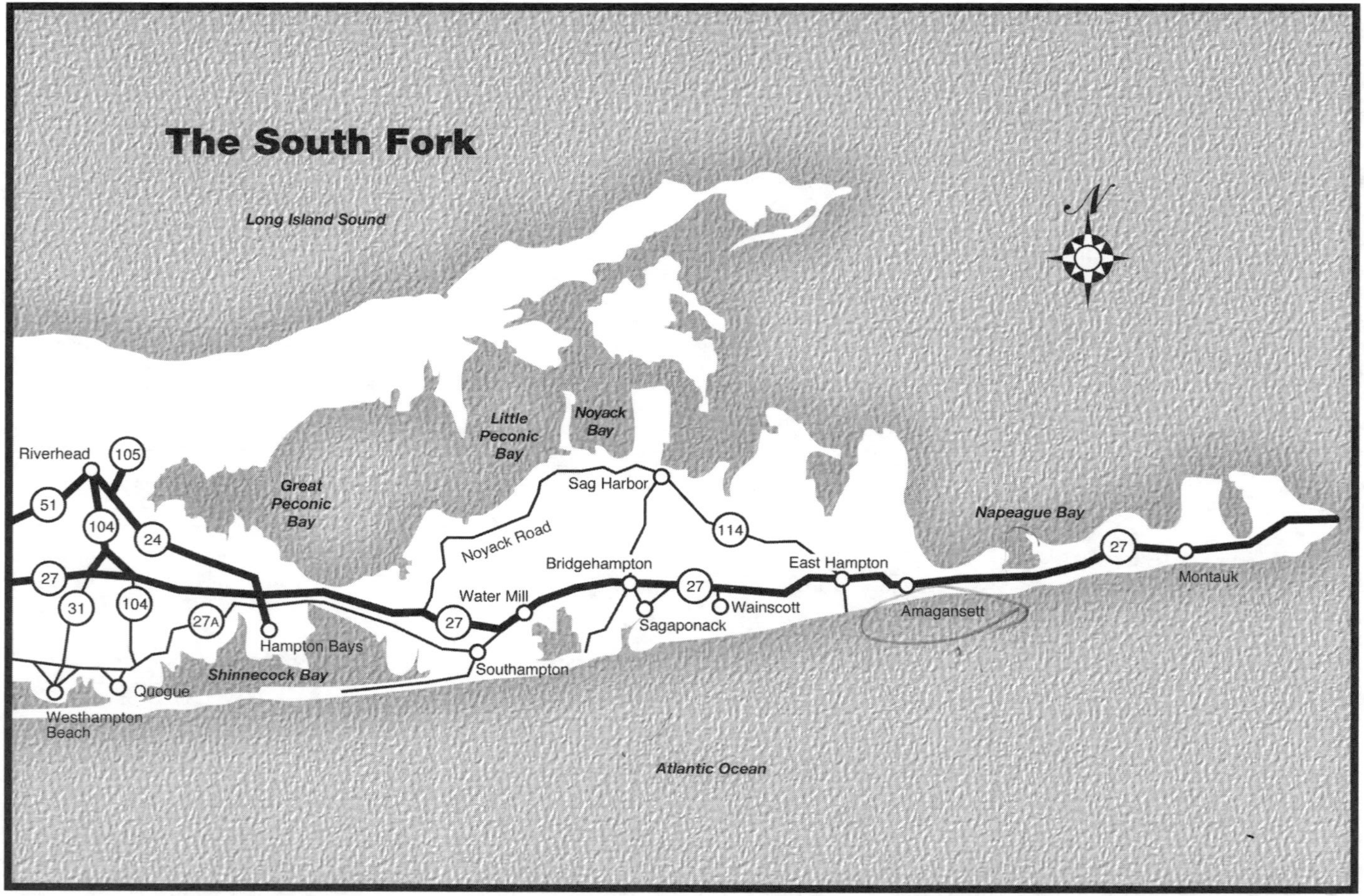

The South Fork

Long Island Sound

Riverhead

Great
Peconic
Bay

Little
Peconic
Bay

Noyack
Bay

Napeague Bay

Sag Harbor

Noyack Road

Bridgehampton

Water Mill

Southampton

Hampton Bays

Shinnecock Bay

Quogue

Westhampton
Beach

Wainscott

Sagaponack

East Hampton

Amagansett

Montauk

Atlantic Ocean

105
24
104
51
27
31
104
27A
27
114
27
27

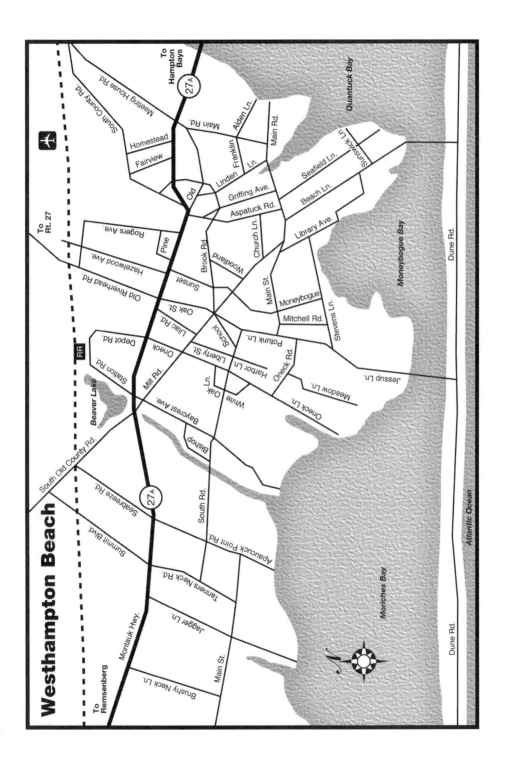

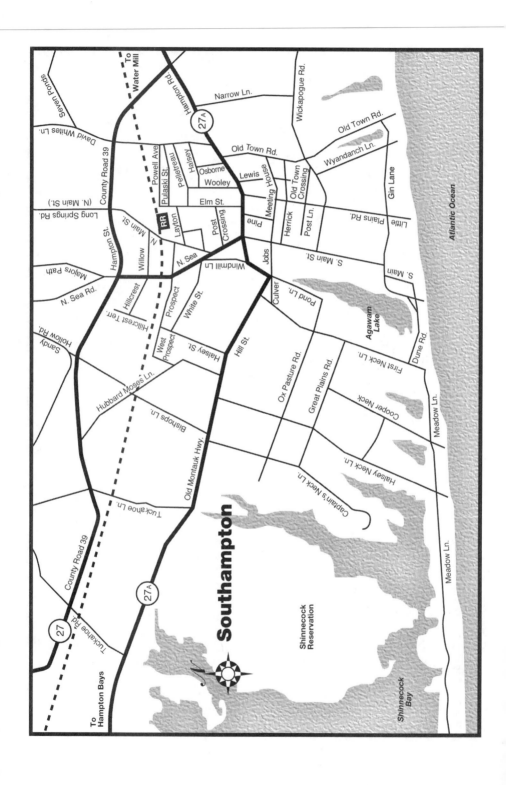

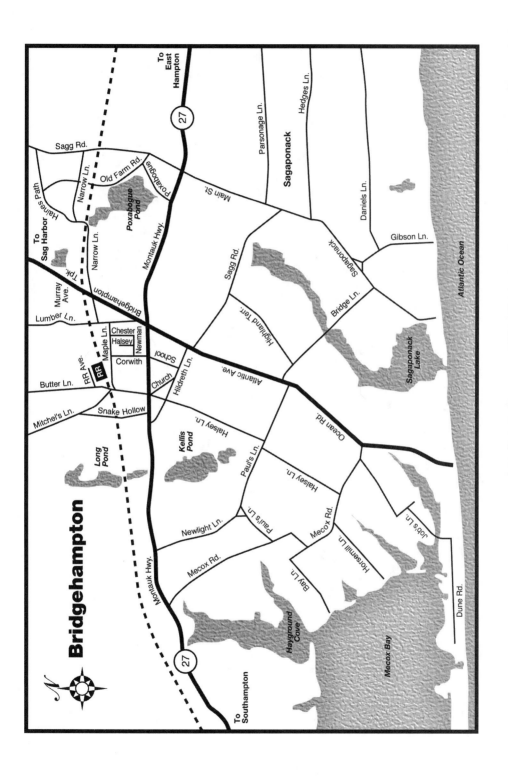

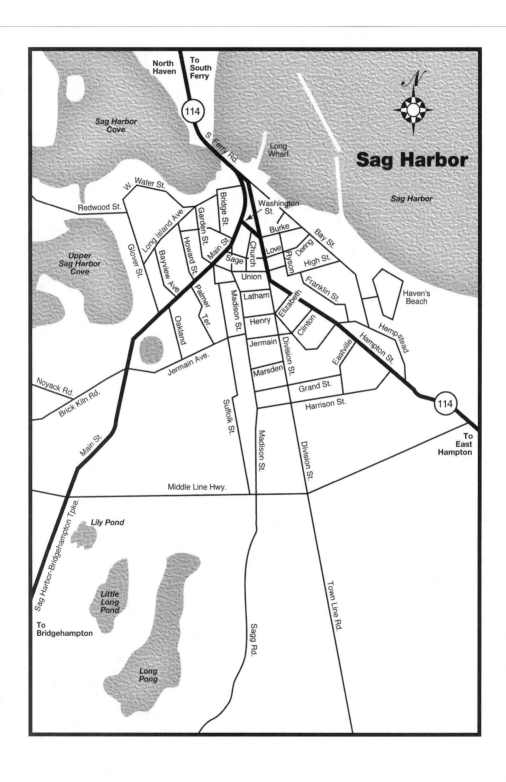

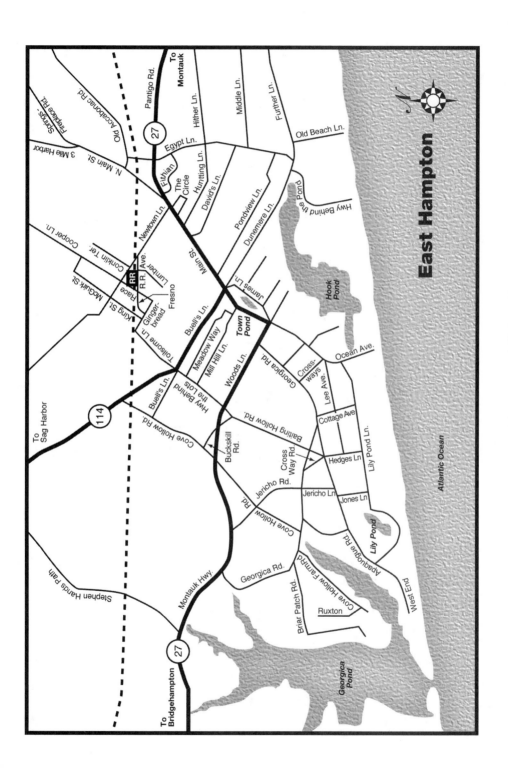

East Hampton

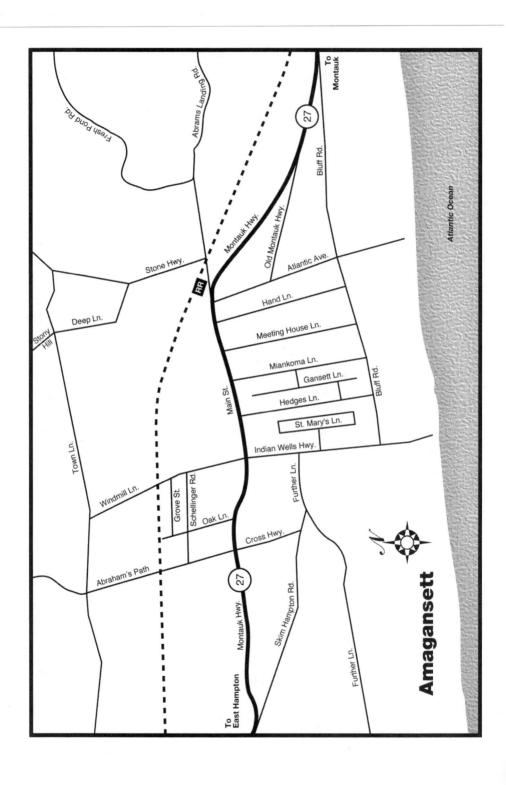

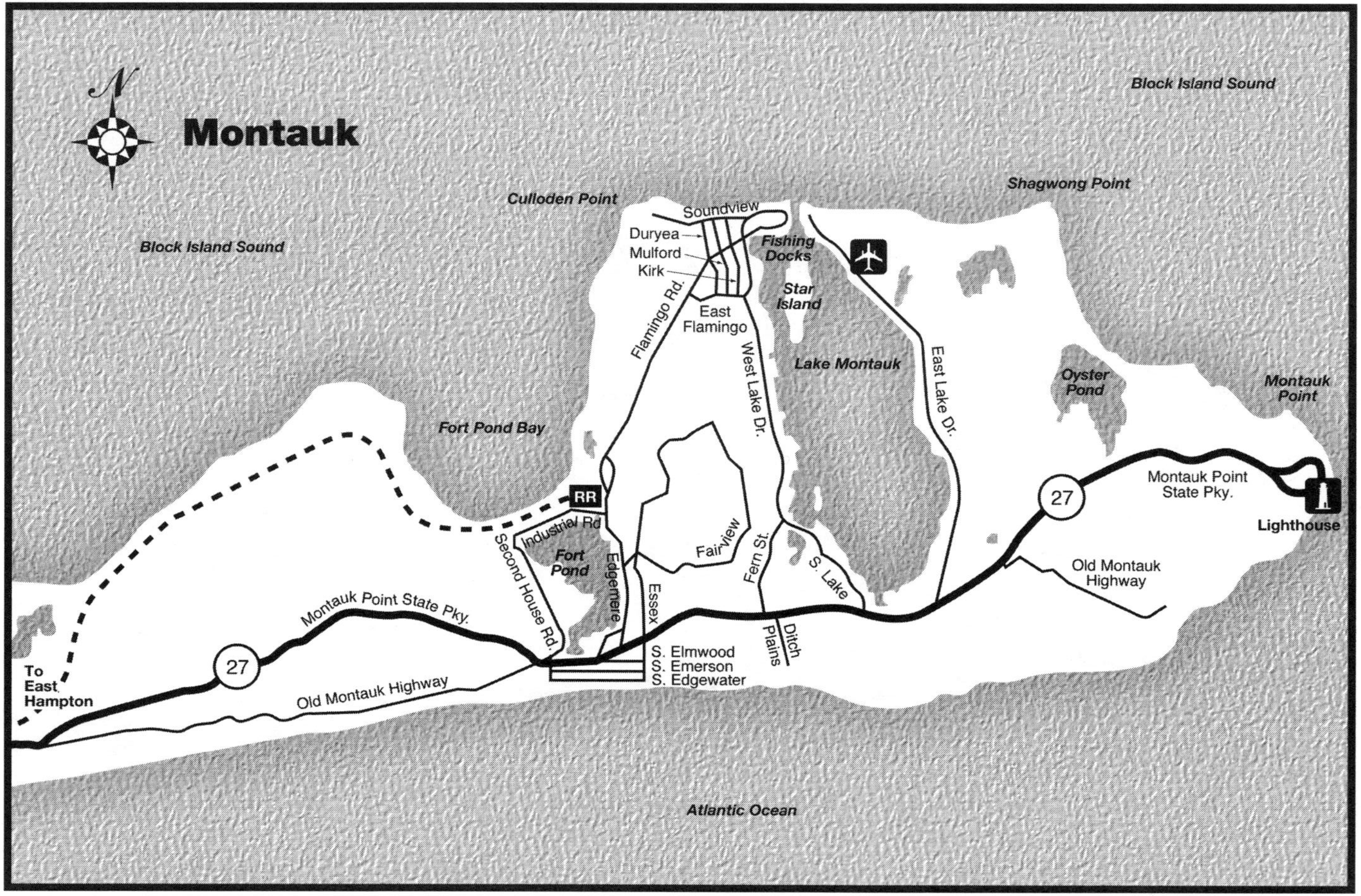

N
Montauk
Block Island Sound
Culloden Point
Shagwong Point
Block Island Sound
Soundview
Duryea
Mulford
Kirk
Fishing Docks
Star Island
Flamingo Rd.
East Flamingo
West Lake Dr.
Lake Montauk
East Lake Dr.
Oyster Pond
Montauk Point
Fort Pond Bay
RR
Industrial Rd
Fort Pond
Second House Rd.
Edgemere
Essex
Fairview
Fern St.
S. Lake
Ditch Plains
S. Elmwood
S. Emerson
S. Edgewater
27
Montauk Point State Pky.
Old Montauk Highway
Montauk Point State Pky.
Old Montauk Highway
Lighthouse
To East Hampton
Atlantic Ocean

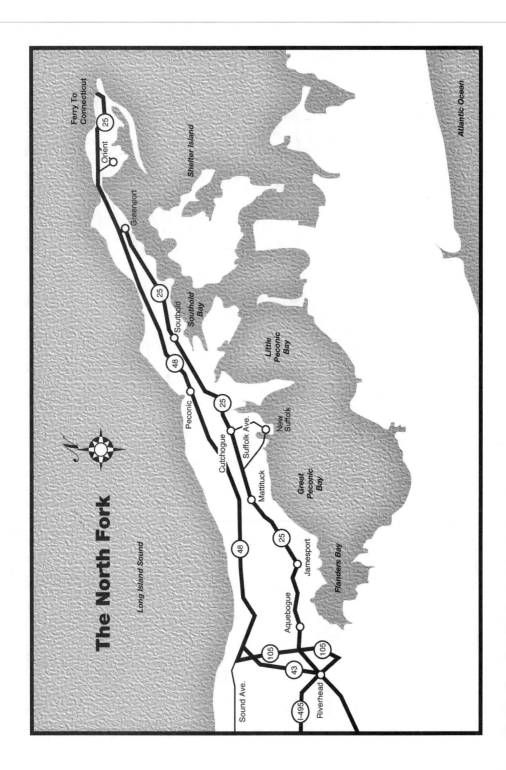

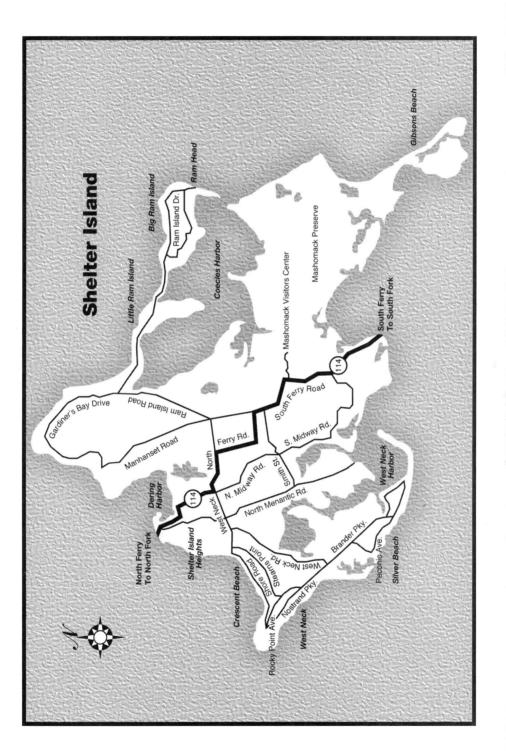

Shelter Island

About the Author

Suzi Forbes Chase was raised in Seattle but calls the East Coast home now. After obtaining a BA and a JD degree from the University of Washington, she moved to Manhattan in 1979, where she worked in public relations while also pursuing her writing career. After frequently traveling to the Hamptons in all seasons and spending summers there, she is now living in the Hamptons and writing full-time. A member of the American Society of Journalists and Authors, she has written 14 travel books, a cookbook (*The Red Lion Inn Cookbook*, published by Berkshire House), and numerous magazine and newspaper articles.